the great perpetual learning machine

the great perpetual learning machine

being a stupendous collection of ideas, games, experiments, activities, and recommendations for further exploration

by jim blake and barbara ernst

with tons of illustrations

 little, brown and company

boston-toronto

First Edition

т 11/76

All photographs, unless otherwise noted, were taken by Barbara Ernst.

Published simultaneously in Canada by Little, Brown & Company (Canada) Limited

Printed in the United States of America

Library of Congress Cataloging in Publication Data

Blake, Jim, 1938-
  The great perpetual learning machine.

  Includes bibliographies and index.
  1. Creative activities and seat work —
Handbooks, manuals, etc. 2. Text-books —
Bibliography. 3. Children's literature —
Bibliography. I. Ernst, Barbara, 1945-   joint author. II. Title.
LB1537.B59   372.5   76-24124
ISBN 0-316-09938-4
ISBN 0-316-09937-6 pbk.

Acknowledgments

Anyone who helps children learn knows that the best sources of ideas are all the other people who help children learn. These sources, taken together, represent a kind of folklore kept alive by the spirit of sharing. To write this book we simply tapped what we knew of that lore through our own experience as teachers and through association with a long list of people who have done good things with kids. We couldn't name them all, or even identify all of them, but we offer a general thank you to all those who recognize in these pages some pet idea or special resource that they helped to pass along.
  There's a shorter list of people who helped in some more immediate way with their time, skills, ideas, and support. In particular: Bruce (help in launching the project), Chris and Bunny (typing assistance), Rick (photographic advice), Colleen (many last-minute illustrations), Diane (music ideas), Michael (advice on math and games resources), Lisa (science library research), and the Brookline Teacher Center, including all our friends and colleagues (lots of ideas and encouragement). Special thanks go to Jan for sorting us out, keeping us happy, and putting up with our bursts of frustration. From initial enthusiasm to final patient editing of the manuscript, thanks to Dick and Melissa at Little, Brown and Company.

We have included prices to give you a general idea of costs — all prices are from 1974–1975 catalogs and subject to change (of course!). Also, many suppliers have minimum order requirements and/or postage and handling charges — we recommend that you write for current, complete information before ordering.

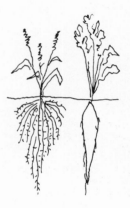

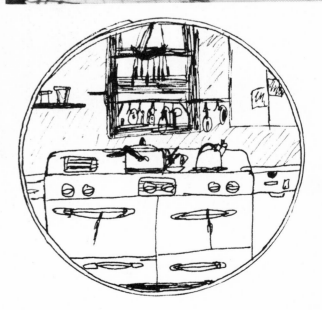

If you have ever taken some kids to a place they've never been before — a pond, a museum, a city park — you've watched the explosion of curiosity and discovery that follows. Whether or not you designed it that way, it was a rich learning experience. Perhaps, afterward, it led you and the kids to investigate other things, read books, ask questions, or share the experience by writing or telling about it. As far as we're concerned, that's what education is all about — whether it occurs at home or at school, in backyards or neighborhoods.

In our society, most people are not used to thinking of themselves as teachers — but teaching is primarily helping people learn things, and all of us, including other kids, can do that. It involves sharing knowledge about how to make something useful and/or beautiful, helping a child look up a word in a dictionary, wondering together about the way a spider spins its web, providing an environment in which kids are free to make mistakes and encouraged to explore new ideas.

Our book is an attempt to share some of the resources, materials, books, and ideas that have helped us enrich our kids' exploration of the world around them. It is for anyone who is excited by a child's natural curiosity and unafraid of saying, "I don't know, but let's find out together."

introduction

contents

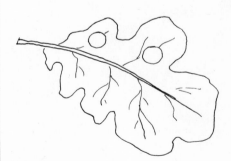

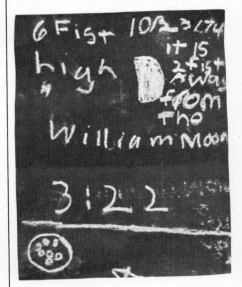

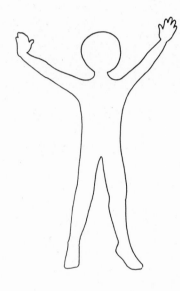

Personal Writing Idea

1. Make a guinea pig journal by stapling paper together. Decorate it if you want.

2. Take the guinea pig to a table. Draw a picture of it on a separate page of your guinea pig journal.

3. Take the guinea pig out of its pen and let it move around on a table top. Look at it VERY CLOSELY and write down EVERYTHING you notice about how it looks. Make a list of all the words you can think of to describe how your guinea pig looks. Write them in journal.

setting up

setting up

organizing space

Rick Sullo

There are lots of ways to organize classroom space and space in the home — and the arrangements of furniture, shelves, and so on, vary throughout the year with changing needs. The diagramed floor plan at right shows one way of setting up a classroom that utilizes learning centers. It's always nice to have pillows or a couch or other comfy furniture around if fire regulations permit — kids spend a good part of every day in their classroom and it should feel comfortable and inviting. Depending on space and facilities, you might want to have a dress-up or cooking corner and more individual work spaces. One teacher in our school has her kids create private "forts" — enclosing desks with curtains and movable "walls" — each uniquely reflecting the individual child's interests and personality. The organization of classroom space should include your children's own preferences; although I've never tried it, I'm intrigued by the idea of kids' designing and creating their own space, given an empty room.

The following books will give you lots of interesting ideas for ways to create learning spaces in home or classroom, as well as suggestions for making and/or using commercially made furniture in arranging an informal classroom.

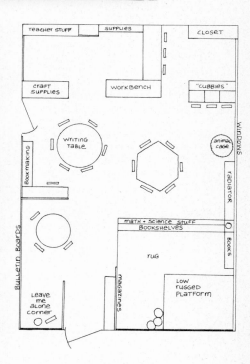

Nomadic Furniture
James Hennessey and Victor Papenek

Pantheon Books
Random House
201 East 50th Street
New York, New York 10022
$3.95

This has quickly become a favorite (and probably even a classic) among seekers after alternative designs for do-it-yourself furniture and living space. In the authors' unique subtitle description, it's about "how to build and where to buy lightweight furniture that folds, inflates, knocks down, stacks, or is disposable and can be recycled. Being both a book of instruction and a catalog of access for easy moving, with many easy-to-follow diagrams, photographs and drawings by the authors." Its usefulness to parents and teachers comes from the many designs for things like desks, storage units, private play spaces, and other things appropriate to kids. There is something fundamentally nomadic about childhood itself, after all.

Making Children's Furniture and Play Structures
Bruce Palmer

Workman Publishing Company
231 East 51st Street
New York, New York 10022
$3.95

If you've been waiting for a solid book with a whole gamut of ideas for making inexpensive kids' furniture from cardboard and other cheap materials, this may be it. A set of specific plans for neat little play structures, chairs, storage units, desks, and toys, it's *Nomadic Furniture* limited to kids' stuff. Some you might want to build just for the fun of doing it, though all the designs are useful alternatives to conventional children's furnishings that deserve to find their way into homes and classrooms. Besides cardboard of varying thicknesses, designs utilize plywood, cardboard drums, dowels, and very little else.

Triangle house

Materials
fifteen pieces single-wall corrugated, 30″ × 30″ or 40″ × 40″
sixty 3/16″ bolts, 1″ long
sixty wing-nuts to fit bolts
120 washers, flat, to fit bolts
ruler or other straightedge
marking pen or pencil
masking tape
acrylic enamel and brush
mat knife
mudge-tool

If you're making the house for very young children (up to five years of age), you can cut corrugated panels 24″ square. For older children, make 36″ panels.

Make panel template using ruler and protractor to measure the 60° angle. Score with mudge-tool and punch holes in flaps. Lay out template on other corrugated sheets and cut out remaining panels. Punch holes for bolts and score flaps.

Flex scored flaps. Trim off excess on flaps so that panels can be joined easily. Assemble house, starting with the roof and working down. Arrange panels 1 through 5 with flaps facing *up*. Bolt together. Add other panels, working from center out. (*Note:* There is no panel between 6 and 7. This is the crawl-door.)

When house has been assembled, turn it over, tape edges, and paint. Bottom flaps not connected to other panels can be taped or cut off.

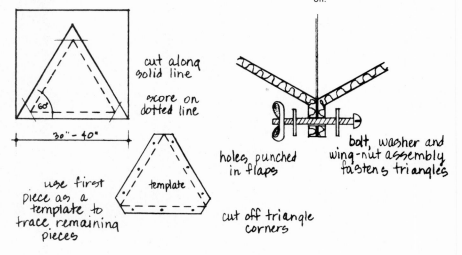

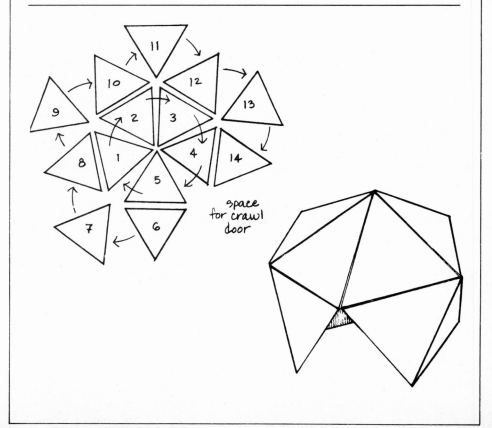

A trolley which can be pushed away under a work top makes a good storage place for paint.

It can be pulled out when it is needed and children can get round it. It is also easier to clean than a cupboard.

A trolley is also valuable for work with sand and water.

Room to Learn
Joan Dean

Citation Press
Library and Trade Division
Scholastic Magazines
50 West 44th Street
New York, New York 10036
$4.35

More and more these days, teachers are arranging their classrooms to meet the individual needs of kids within a flexibly organized space. Trying to modify classrooms and furnishings originally intended for whole-class teaching poses some big problems. Joan Dean draws on her experience in British primary schools to bring together a helpful collection of specific solutions to problems like these. The book is a series of annotated sketches showing specific rearrangements, adaptations of furniture for new uses, and wholly new furnishings or equipment that fulfill needs for informal classes. Ideas are presented in three sections: working space, language areas, and a place to paint.

a home learning center

Have you got a piece of cellar, garage, hallway, playroom, big kitchen, attic, child's room or some other handy nook available? Any of these might do nicely as a place to put together an all-around, hands-on learning center for your kids (and maybe you, too).

The center you design is one that will fit your family's interests, the kind of space you have, and the equipment or materials you're willing to collect.

Here are some suggestions:

woodworking and fix-it place

This is best for the cellar or garage, but be sure to have a space that's dry and has plenty of light. Besides carpentry, here's the place for taking apart old appliances and machines. (See pages 218–219 for tool suggestions.)

dress-up closet or corner

If there's a flair for the dramatic around, a big box, bunch of hooks, or closet can store old clothes or other fun things to wear, and may inspire some homemade plays. Put up a long mirror, and how about some theater posters?

craft space

Ideally, this should be near a sink, but most important is a large work surface and plenty of leeway for mess. (See pages 193–216 for arts and crafts ideas.) The surface can double as a place to do games and puzzles. It would also be nice to have this in the same place as your big storage area for creative stuff.

scrap resources area

The organizing element in this area is a set of roomy shelves to house your likely-to-be-voluminous collection of scrap materials and other things to make things with. (See pages 8–12.) Melon crates or sturdy liquor cartons serve well, and they make a good way to sort things into appropriate categories. (A little sorting and classification work for the younger folks, huh?) You probably don't want this in your front hall, so maybe the basement or garage.

nature center

Bring the outdoors inside (well, a reasonable amount of it). It can be oriented toward animals, insects, or plants, and can include prints, maps, and specimen displays. Think of it as a museum, or make it a working area with table and storage for collecting tools and recording materials. (See Nature and Ecology, pages 23–85.)

art display

Nearly every parent has some kids' artwork stuck to the refrigerator. If you go to some trouble to set up a special display area you can do wonders for encouraging top-quality creations. A movable screen is one way, a hallway another. Have a table and art materials accessible for home efforts, too. (See Arts and Crafts, pages 193–228.)

experiments laboratory

A place for inventing, mixing chemicals, and doing all manner of scientific investigations has a very strong appeal for many kids and gives them a valuable opportunity to experiment in a way they may not be able to in a classroom. The space does not need to be large but certainly requires a table or counter and some shelves. (See Science, pages 87–128.)

quiet book corner

A soft rug and maybe some comfy chairs in a nook where kids can keep their favorite books is all you need for reading activities (and maybe writing activities, too). If your kitchen is big enough, kids usually feel that that is a happy place to be. Keep the TV somewhere else! (See pages 295–298 for reading books.)

some helpful books

Here are some other books you should know about before setting up a classroom or home learning center. They are chock-full of general resources and information — lists of books and materials, ways to set up an individualized classroom program, specific activities for learning centers, and even suggestions on using your community as a "classroom"!

The Integrated Day in an American School
Betsye Sargent

National Association of Independent Schools
4 Liberty Square
Boston, Massachusetts 02109
$2.50

Multiple Choice
Esther Kattef and Jane Manselli

New England School Development Council
55 Chapel Street
Newton, Massachusetts 02160
$5

The best way to get an overall view for running a good classroom is to read a teacher's explanation of how it's done. These two booklets, one descriptive of a primary room and the other of an intermediate program, complement each other well even though they were written from different perspectives. *The Integrated Day* lays out a complete program in diagrammatic form, giving clear details about individual activities for small children. *Multiple Choice* is an expository account of how to organize a classroom to make it sensitive to individual needs among older children, with numerous activities to excite their interest.

Materials for the Open Classroom
Skip Ascheim

Dell Publishing Company
1 Dag Hammarskjold Plaza
New York, New York 10017
$3

A survey, in roomy format, of some of the most appealing materials that have been generated by the informal, hands-on approach to children's learning. The editor uses his space to give extensive critiques on many items as well as personal essays about current education.

Learning: The Magazine for Creative Teaching

Learning Magazine, Subscription Department
1255 Portland Place
Boulder, Colorado 80302
$1.50 per issue, $10.00 per subscription (9 issues yearly)

Learning Handbooks

Learning Handbooks, Department 1004
P.O. Box 818
Maple Plain, Minnesota 55559
$2.50 each

The most helpful professional publications currently available, *Learning* magazine and handbooks together offer a rich mine of creative, workable, and often exciting ideas. They speak clearly to teachers who are working in environments that meet the individual needs of children. Handbook titles are:

> *Motivating Today's Students*
> *Building Independent Learning Skills*
> *Resolving Classroom Conflict*
> *Developing Individual Values in the Classroom* (see p. 264)
> *Creating and Using Learning Games* (see p. 18)
> *Dealing with Questions about Sex*
> *Developing Skills in Critical Reading*
> *Opening Your Class with Learning Stations*

The Whole Kids Catalog
Peter Cardozo and Ted Menten

Bantam Books
666 Fifth Avenue
New York, New York 10019
$5.95

As the title suggests, this is a *Whole Earth*–style collection of reviews and excerpts of books, sources, and materials to help extend the many different interests kids have. The jam-packed selection includes things like hobbies, magic, moviemaking, puzzles, and games.

Change for Children
Sandra Nina Kaplan et al.

Goodyear Publishing Company
15115 Sunset Boulevard
Pacific Palisades, California 92072
$6.95

This excellent guide for teachers includes everything from setting up an open classroom "environment" to very specific learning center activities, complete with worksheets for reproduction! Games, mapping activities, graphing, writing ideas, a "nym" center (synonyms, homonyms, and antonyms — of course!), and much more, are included — along with excellent ideas for informal record keeping. This is one of the most generally useful "setting up" books we've seen!

Yellow Pages of Learning Resources
Group for Environmental Education

The M.I.T. Press
28 Carleton Street
Cambridge, Massachusetts 02142
$1.95

"Resources" in this usage is applied to people and places (airports, electricians, courtrooms) in the working community at large. The authors have used the "directory" motif as a way of listing the possibilities, explaining how to go about making contact, and giving examples of the kinds of information one might get from asking good questions during field trips or interviews.

general supplies

Lots of people have worked up lists of basic supplies: things you can scrounge or buy as raw materials for a full scope of learning activities. We've reprinted one such list here, but you can get more extensive lists from the following sources:

National Association of Independent Schools
4 Liberty Square, Boston, Massachusetts 02109
List of Equipment and Materials for Workshops on the Integrated Day, $1.00

Education Development Center, Distribution Center
39 Chapel Street, Newton, Massachusetts 02160
Materials List: A Useful List of Classroom Items to Be Scrounged or Purchased, $1.00
Instructional Aids, Materials, and Supplies, $1.50

Children's Museum
The Jamaicaway, Boston, Massachusetts 02130
Recycle Notes, $1.30 (Not so much a list as a set of single-sheet ideas for ways to use scrounged materials.)

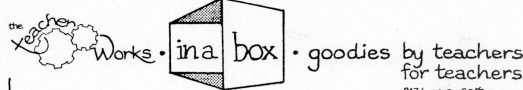

the teacher
Works • in a box • goodies by teachers for teachers

2136 n.e. 20th ave. • portland • oregon • 97212

SCROUNGE LIST

The Teacher Resource Service, New Orleans, Louisiana, suggests the following as a beginning list of materials for classroom use which you can rescue from your garbage can or scrounge from local businesses. Add your own ideas and share the wealth (and the work of collecting) with other teachers. Start a central resource area for scrounged stuff.

1. Household items you might be throwing away every day (well, maybe not _every_ day...)

egg cartons
cardboard tubes
plastic containers (margarine tubs, bleach
    bottles, squeeze bottles, etc.)
juice cans (from small frozen type to large
    readymade type)
meat and produce trays
strawberry boxes and baskets
bottle caps
corks
aluminum pie tins
styrofoam packing material
coat hangers
magazines
sturdy boxes
corrugated paper and cardboard
buttons
spools
ribbon
yarn, string, rope
old clothes (dresses, socks, costumes)
old stockings
hats
jewelry
eyeglasses

Mardi Gras beads and trinkets
fabric and fabric scraps
old greeting cards
wrapping paper
broken appliances with moving parts
    (e.g., clocks, radios, fans, etc.)
electronic equipment scraps
plumbing pipe
popsicle sticks
old toothbrushes
rug and carpet pieces
egg-shaped containers from "L'eggs" pantyhose
wood scraps and pieces
any useable paper, poster, or cardboard
candles and wax
rubber bands
nails and screws
paper bags and plastic bags
maps
durable containers
foam rubber
envelopes
brown envelopes and manilla folders
    (new or used)

2. Things you may no longer need or which you might want to donate out of the goodness of your heart.

large appliance boxes or crates
boards
bricks and concrete blocks
old furniture (especially desks, lamps and
    shelves)
wallpaper (leftovers and wallpaper books)
rugs
pillows and cushions
fabric and felt
wire screen and chicken wire
baskets
rulers, yardsticks and tape measures
leftover paint

sewing patterns
books (especially childrens' books)
records
musical instruments
tiles and linoleum squares
straws
games and puzzles
clay
natural and found objects (e.g., flat stones
    pine cones, feathers, driftwood, rice,
    beans, etc.)
carbon paper
ditto stencils and paper

the teacher Works · in a box · goodies by teachers for teachers

2136 n.e. 20th ave. · portland · oregon · 97212

SCROUNGE LIST   page 2

Things you may no longer need, con't.

kitchen utensils   crayons
all sorts of paper products (crepe paper, used   pencils and pens
    or new paper cups and plates, tissue   tools (hammers, saws, screwdrivers, etc.)
    paper, "Contact" paper, etc.)   sewing machines
paste and glue   record players
tape   typewriters
staplers, staples and paper clips   orange crates
scissors and paper cutters   toys (old or new)

3. Items to be scrounged from businesses and institutions.

Airlines--plastic cups (used OK), packing boxes
Art supply stores and stationery stores--leftover or damaged paper; any leftover or damaged
    stock (e.g., paint, pencils, paper clips, staplers, staples, markers, etc.)
Architects--blueprints and blueprint paper; slide rules and other tools
Billboard companies--pieces of billboards to use as posters, wall coverings, etc.
Building supply companies--wood and lumber, tiles, wallpaper books, color samples, leftover
    formica
Bottling firms--bottle caps, large cardboard tubes
Churches--old candles
Container companies--large cardboard sheets, damaged containers--sturdy and of uniform size
Contractors--lumber, pipes and wire, wallpaper, linoleum, tiles, molding wood, wood curls, etc.
Department stores--stocking boxes, lingerie boxes, fabric swatches, rug pieces, corrugated
    packing cardboard, packing boxes from appliances and pianos, styrofoam packing material,
    decorative displays, old posters and business forms (blank on one side), shoe boxes,
    envelopes, etc.
Dime stores--boxes, leftovers or damaged packs of crayons, leftover toys, school supplies, etc.
Drug stores--small plastic bottles, crayons and other school supplies
Electric power companies--wire, large spools, assorted packing materials
Furniture stores and factories--large packing boxes, packing material, fabric scraps and
    swatches
Garment factories, clothing firms--buttons, decorative tape, ribbon, yarn, trim, spools,
    fasteners, fabric scraps, etc.
Gift shops and boutiques--candles, packing boxes, styrofoam packing material, wrapping
    paper, ribbon, etc.
Grocery stores, supermarkets, outdoor markets--cartons, packing materials, fruit crates,
    large cardboards and materials from displays, discarded display racks, styrofoam fruit
    trays, baskets of any sort
Hardware stores--sample hardware books, sample tile charts, linoleum samples, rope, chain,
    wood, molding strips, etc.
Ice cream stores--3-gallon ice cream containers
Leather craft companies, pocketbook, belt and shoe manufacturers--scrap pieces of leather
    and lacings
Lumber companies--scrap wood, damaged bricks, concrete blocks, doweling, wood curls, etc.
Offices of any sort--discontinued business forms and posters (anything blank on one
    side), pencils and erasers, office furniture, file cabinets, lamps, typewriters,
    envelopes, manilla folders, large brown envelopes (used OK), etc.

tw.

the teacher Works • in a box • goodies by teachers for teachers

2136 n.e. 20th ave. • portland • oregon • 97212

SCROUGE LIST   page 3

Items to be scrounged from businesses, con't.

Paint stores--any leftover paint, samples, sample books, wallpaper books, end rolls of
    wallpaper, tiles, linoleum, etc.
Paper companies and printing companies--endcuts and damaged paper and posters (blank on one
    side): any size, weight or color
Phone company--colored wires, old telephones, large spools
Plastics companies--trimmings, cuttings, tubing, scrap plastic and plexiglass
Plumbers and plumbing supply companies--wires, pipes, tile scraps, linoleum
Repair shops--unclaimed appliances (preferably working, but non-working OK too): record
    players, typewriters, sewing machines, radios, TV's, clocks, fans
Restaurants--ice cream containers, corks, boxes and cartons, bottle caps
Rug companies--any leftovers or scraps, sample swatches, end pieces from carpets
Textile companies--color samples, any scraps or pieces
Tile and ceramic companies--leftover or damaged tile, etc.
Toy stores--leftovers, damaged products, packing materials, boxes
Upholsterers and tailors--buttons, scrap material, spools, cord, string, etc.

tw

storage systems

Finding a way to store all the stuff you scrounge, buy, or otherwise collect to supply the many kinds of learning activities suggested in this book demands a good storage system. The next worst thing to having no materials is having a whole lot of materials scattered all over the place. In that condition they not only are hard to locate when they're needed most, but they also tend to get used up too quickly, misused, or not used at all. Most likely you will have to create your own system, but it is one of the most valuable ways you can spend your time if you plan to set up a rich learning environment.

What you basically need is some clear way of sorting out things by kind on shelving located as close as possible to the area where the materials will be used. You have the choice of establishing one single resource center that will serve all needs (science stuff, art supplies, math materials, games, all-purpose supplies) or setting up separate centers to supply any one kind of activity by itself.

Whichever choice you make, here are some ways to put it together.

shelving

Something that can be compartmentalized is most handy, and so one answer is a set of large containers that will stack up in a sturdy way, such as:

    melon crates
    heavy-duty cardboard cartons (liquor
        boxes, for instance)
    cardboard tubes from International
        Paper Company
    large tin boxes from tea shipments

These can be bolted together, attached to a plywood backing, or mounted inside a wooden framework.

Regular wooden shelving can be made from stock lumber or sawed-up strips of plywood, composition flooring (cheapest), or heavy Masonite.

You can construct a single, freestanding, solid unit from such materials, or you can build up shelves with stacked bricks, or you can mount them directly on a wall with metal brackets.

Triple-walled cardboard creates other possibilities, since it is cheap and can be easily cut for slotted constructions; you can make compartments and shelves all at once.

Primary source:
Tri-Wall Containers
100 Crossways Park West
Woodbury, New York 11797

containers

Some of the things people have found useful are:

  shoe boxes
  wooden mushroom boxes
    plastic sweater boxes
  store-goods boxes of every size
  corrugated cardboard cartons, cut down
    if necessary
  cardboard storage trays with sloping
    sides (commercially available)
  large tin cans
  plastic dishes

labeling

Even the neatest arrangement is not very useful unless things are clearly marked. Depending on the type of container, use felt-tip markers, a label maker, or rubber-stamp letters.

general activities

Now that you've got some ideas for organizing the learning space in your home or classroom, we'd like to share with you some general resources for making that space come alive! A lot of the ideas presented in this section, however, don't even require a particular, defined "place." Learning occurs wherever and whenever children discover something new — whether alone, with peers, or with a caring adult. The ideas, resource books, and games recommended here cross all "subject" boundaries — and reflect our belief in the interdependence of all kinds of learning skills, social as well as academic.

What can you do with a MARSHMALLOW?

Take a marshmallow. Do what you want with it — taste it, smell it, look at it, shake it, squish it. What does a marshmallow remind you of?

As white as _____.
As fluffy as _____.
As soft as _____.
As _____ as _____.

write a story —

1. Write a description of a marshmallow.
2. Write some sentences using words that all start with the same letter about a marshmallow.
3. Describe what it would be like if your bed was made from marshmallow.
4. Describe what it would be like if you were a mountain climber and you were climbing the highest mountain in the world — one that was made of MARSHMALLOW.
5. Think of your own idea.

books

The Brown Paper School

Little, Brown and Company
34 Beacon Street
Boston, Massachusetts 02106
$3.95 each

This short series of books has thoroughly delighted us and all the friends we've been able to show it to so far. Each title is a shining example of what we most like to recommend: imaginative, fun-filled

idea books for people inside or outside school who want to learn things. The group of people who wrote them give this general description:

The Brown Paper School is a series of small books about big ideas, written and designed for kids and grown-ups together. The series comes from a group of California teachers, writers and artists who get together every now and then to work on stuff for kids and to have a good time. They believe learning only happens when it is wanted; that it can happen anywhere and doesn't require fancy tools. [These books] are dedicated to anyone who thinks so too.

My Backyard History Book is organized around the idea that learning about the past (like a lot of other things) begins best at home. Activities include photography, archaeology in your attic, family trees, and building models and exploring cemeteries. It's a way of coming at history without memorizing names of presidents and war dates or having to ignore your own personal time and space. Your own family's history may be only a tiny fragment of the whole span of passing time, but it's an exciting place to start.

See reviews of the other Brown Paper School books — *The I Hate Mathematics! Book,* page 132, and *The Reasons for Seasons,* page 174.

Zephyros Education Exchange

1201 Stanyan Street
San Francisco, California 94117

The Zephyros Education Exchange is a way for teachers and parents to share the ideas that they create and use with their children. Zephyros is a collaborative of teachers, parents, and artists in the San Francisco area who publish a series of "Deschool Primers" that contain a lot of these ideas. Despite a somewhat cumbersome, oversize newspaper format, most of them are well worth having around. The activities are often unique, always exciting, and their presentation will encourage you to view learning from new perspectives.

Listed on the next page are Zephyros's descriptions of the entire series of Deschool Primers to date. *Your City Has Been Kidnapped,* also available from Addison-Wesley Publishing Company, is one of our favorites. It's about the mystery and magic that is city life — a collection of activities, games, photos, and questions that can serve as a textbook, sensory guide, or source book for locating city treasures! See pages 18 and 263 for reviews of other titles we've found especially appealing.

DESCHOOL PRIMER No. 1
A box of Tapes, Films and Documents on "PROTEST" is no longer available for sale. If you want to see a set of this material stop by 1201 Stanyan. You are welcome to copy any of this material.

DESCHOOL PRIMER No. 2
FINDING COMMUNITY is a guide to community research and action. This text is designed for use at the high school or university level. It's expensive, so you might want to get a copy from a local library. 217 pp $3.45.

DESCHOOL PRIMER No. 3
YOUR CITY HAS BEEN KIDNAPPED is a collection of teaching strategies that utilize the city as a classroom. These ideas have been used in various grade levels from pre-school to graduate school to no school. 64 pp $1.50.

DESCHOOL PRIMER No. 4
is a "NEWSBOOK" collection of inventive lesson plans, games, learning experiences. Contents include soft sculpture, fantasy, a capitalistic lunch, matrix games, and at least one mystery.   24 pp $1.50.

DESCHOOL PRIMER No. 5
A WHALE FOR SALE consists of ideas for the home learner. Things in this primer explore building a ferro concrete whale, mask making, a beastiary & trash use. 40 pp $1.50.

DESCHOOL PRIMER No. 6
is a scrapbook on how to solve problems, womens theater, a visit to China, ideas for a child care, center, and a learning faire.
128pp $3.50.

DESCHOOL PRIMER No. 7
is a "NEWSBOOK" collection of ideas ranging from how to build igloos to space frames, imperialism, cooperation games and poetry kit 2B.   24pp $1.50.

DESCHOOL PRIMER No. 8
is about imagination. Robert and Lorene Shields (San Francisco Mime Artists) provide the imagery you provide the magic.
40pp $2.50.

DESCHOOL PRIMER No. 9
is a wrestling manual. Lesson plans in this guide include How to Program An Inchworm, Being A Sentence, The Family Game, Sun Printing and lots more strange holds for learning.   128pp $1.50.

DESCHOOL PRIMER No. 10
is a TIME MACHINE. Times & places you can visit include: People of the Sun, Californians of 1849, The Puritans, China at the turn of the century, and lots more.   224pp
It's a great history workbook! $4.50

DESCHOOL PRIMER No. 11
is the 30 MINUTE SEX Book. Each page of this book is a definition. Distribute the pages to your students or place them on walls where they can be read & you've got the 30 MINUTE SEX course.   48pp $3.00

DESCHOOL PRIMER No. 12
is a collection of games on government, inflation, talking pictures, love, bubbles, and the seven deadly whims. This newspaper is a favorite of Zealous Zelda. 24pp of activities.
$2.00

DESCHOOL PRIMER No. 13
is a Bill Board. That's right. It's a collapsible portable learning center about space ship Earth. This primer is 25 feet long by 9 feet wide and is just perfect for a lonely wall and imaginative classroom of kids. $24.00
(for adventurers and art lovers only)

DESCHOOL PRIMER No. 14
is about new games. If you can imagine the NY Times Sunday Paper full of new games, tournament suggestions, computer puzzles, and plans for glorifying a chain link fence, you have some idea what this newspaper primer looks like.   72pp $2.50

DESCHOOL PRIMER No. 15
is about food. Games and classroom activities focus on nutrition, making a sun machine, ash can gardening, and how to attack local vending machines. It's yummy.
64pp $2.50.

Reprinted by permisson of Zephyros Education Exchange.

Happy Birthday to U.S.
Murray and Roberta Suid

Addison-Wesley Publishing Company
2725 Sand Hill Road
Menlo Park, California 94025

Although written to help kids "celebrate and understand the Bicentennial," this activity book will be valuable for years! It includes a wonderful assortment of do-it-yourself activities to involve children in learning about our country — its land, people, values, culture, and more. Make an almanac, write a song, photograph the changes in your neighborhood, write down a family folktale, imagine a day without electricity, stage a debate . . . the ideas are varied and intriguing!

65 **TOYS**
Among the Bushmen of Africa, little boys pretend that tiny sticks are spears like those their fathers use to hunt animals. If you saw one of these African children playing with his toy spear, you could guess something about how his tribe makes a living.

Is it the same for our tribe? Make a list of the toys and games you and your friends play with. (You might ask a toy store the names of their most popular toys for kids your age.) Next to each toy or game, write down what, if anything, it shows about how people live in our culture.

From *Happy Birthday to U.S.* by Murray Suid and Roberta Suid. Copyright © 1975 by Addison-Wesley Publishing Company, Inc. All rights reserved. Pp. 31, 58, 67.

36 **DREAMING A BETTER PLACE**
Poets, politicians, and architects dream about an ideal environment. (The word for such a perfect place is "*Utopia*.") And sometimes they try to make their dream come true. In recent years, entire new towns have been built from scratch in Virginia and Maryland.

Pretend you are a planner and can start all over with the land where you live. Ask your friends and family what kind of place they would like. Here are some things to think about:

How big will it be?

Where will people live?

What will the buildings look like?

Where will people play?

Where will people work and sell their goods?

Where will they meet to talk and make decisions, and make music?

What laws will be necessary?

How will people get from one place to another?

How many people or families will live together? Will people live in family groupings?

In the space below, try to describe your dream place in words.

When you've got everything in writing, turn the page and make a picture of your dream. Use cut-outs from magazines with your own drawings and photos. Remember, you don't have to be an artist to dream.

60 **HOW MUCH ARE YOU WORTH?**
For nearly a hundred years, slavery was a legal part of the U.S. Constitution. Only with the Thirteenth Amendment in 1865 was it banished from the land. (Lincoln's Emancipation Proclamation of 1863 freed the slaves only in certain states.)

To get an idea of what it must have felt like to be treated as something for sale, paste a picture of yourself in the space below. Then have a friend write an advertisement selling you. It should include your good points, your work skills, and your cost.

Workjobs

Workjobs for Parents
Mary Baratta-Lorton

Addison-Wesley Publishing Company
2725 Sand Hill Road
Menlo Park, California 94025

Workjobs is a collection of 101 original activity-centered learning projects for young children, aged four to seven. These are concrete, imaginative activities that kids will enjoy and learn from. They require no sophisticated equipment and, although they can easily be done independently, they encourage conversation and play with an adult. *Workjobs for Parents* is a selection of forty or so of these "workjobs" that are most appropriate for parents to make and use with their children at home.

Activities included are putting lids on different-size jars, sorting groceries by initial sound, sorting buttons, testing household items for "floatability," making a "feely board" or "sock boxes" to develop tactile perception, and much more!

Survival Kit for Substitutes
Vita Pavlich and Eleanor Rosenast

Citation Press
Scholastic Magazines
50 West 44th Street
New York, New York 10036
$3.65

A Sourcebook for Substitutes and Other Teachers
Miriam Freedman and Teri Perl

Addison-Wesley Publishing Company
2725 Sand Hill Road
Menlo Park, California 94025
$4.92

These books are both valuable sources of ideas and activities for substitute teachers. As the authors clearly state, substitutes have a unique position in any classroom and can contribute a great deal to children's learning. The activities in *A Sourcebook for Substitutes* are geared primarily to older children, but both books contain a wealth of exciting and worthwhile games, projects, and ideas that would be adaptable to almost any age.

Whether they involve studying fingerprints, learning Morse code, doing some "instant theater," mapping the room, or making geometric pictures, the activities will not only enhance any classroom program, but will also provide many hours of enjoyable learning at home.

Workman Publishing Company

231 East 51st Street
New York, New York 10022

Workman Publishing Company has one of the nicest collections of general activity books for kids that we've seen. Their game and craft book format is especially pleasing, and sure to catch your eye in local bookstores. Here are some of our favorite titles; see pages noted for reviews.

Frisbee, Stancil E. D. Johnson
The Great American Marble Book, Fred Ferretti
Growing Up Green, Alice Skelsey and Gloria Huckaby (see p. 67)
Jump Rope!, Peter L. Skolnik (see p. 246)
The Kids' Kitchen Takeover, Sara Bonnett Stein (see p. 102)
Making Children's Furniture and Play Structures, Bruce Palmer (see p. 4)
Pin It, Tack It, Hang It, Phyllis and Noel Fiarotta
Play Book, Steven Caney (see p. 196)
Snips & Snails & Walnut Whales, Phyllis Fiarotta
Sticks & Stones & Ice Cream Cones, Phyllis Fiarotta
Toy Book, Steven Caney (see p. 196)

Good Cents
The Amazing Life Games Company

Houghton Mifflin Company
1 Beacon Street
Boston, Massachusetts 02107
$3.95

Good Cents is "every kid's guide to making money" — and how to have fun at the same time! It's organized by the times kids might have available (weekends, holidays, etc.) and written in a clear, exciting style for kids themselves. The cartoon drawings, photos, and general graphics make it particularly appealing. With a fanciful title, each job idea is entertaining and very doable by kids with a minimum of adult assistance — here are a few examples:

The Saturday & Sunday Stuff & Junk Company
The Used Music Company and Record Exchange
America Needs Clean Dogs
Old Toys Fixit Factory
The Anytime-It-Snows Shovelers Company
The Wax and Wick Works

games

Games are a naturally fun way of learning all kinds of stuff, and thus earn an important place in our section on "setting up." Whether played for fun or profit (i.e., to reinforce a particular academic skill), games are a worldwide means of socializing and testing oneself in a nonthreatening atmosphere. They lend themselves to enjoyable adult-child interaction, and are best when rules are flexible — allowing children (together with adults) to explore different ways of creating and solving their own problems.

Card games, board games, dice games, paper-and-pencil games, social games — even puzzles and mazes — all have a wonderful capacity to intrigue and delight children of all ages. Play them with your kids and share the fun!

game resources

Here are two play resources you really ought to know about if you're interested in games. They are both involved in sharing the pleasures of playing and creating all kinds of games. The following descriptions of the Games Preserve and the New Games Foundation come from information they each sent us, in their own words.

RD 1 · FLEETWOOD, PA. 19522

Our profession is games. We bring our play/work wherever we find the need and share skills with people all over the country. We built the Games Preserve — 25 acres of lovely grounds — to help people find new games and more satisfying ways to play them.

There are more games here than you could play in a year. If you tire of them, we have a whole library of more games. If you have a special kind of game you want to learn about, we can help you find it. If you are interested in designing a new game or modifying an old one, we can do it for you or show you how.

Playshops at The Games Preserve are training sessions in the ways of creating and changing the rules that allow people to find and share delight. The first rule is that nobody has to play. You play only because you want to. We offer sessions like:

FINDING OUT WHEN TO QUIT
DISCOVERING WHAT YOU ENJOY
CHANGING A GAME TO MAKE IT MORE
   SATISFYING
APPRECIATING THE GAME / APPRECIATING
   THE PLAYERS
CONSTRUCTIVE CHEATING

NEW

GAMES
FOUNDATION ™

P.O. Box 7901,
San Francisco, California 94120

Our staff have many skills and many games to share with you. This is our professional goal, and we deeply enjoy its pursuit.

New Games is an attitude toward play. Our games are structured so there are no winners: we center on the joy of playing, everyone becoming a part of the process. We emphasize that everyone can play, bringing together diverse racial and economic groups and different ages, getting families to play together, involving those

left out of traditional sports. We use inexpensive equipment, and play games that do not require great strength. New Games means permission to run and jump for no good reason. . . .

New Games Foundation is attempting to disseminate the New Games concept as widely as possible. We teach others how to make new games, passing the idea along rather than selling a service. One of our primary activities involves the staging of New Games Tournaments throughout the country. It can take place in a high school gym or a wildlife preserve, accommodate 20 to 4,000 people at a time, last a few hours to several days. Tournaments are something like fairs: the area becomes a kaleidoscope of movement and color. There are frisbees, stilts, hula-hoops, food stands, musicians, board games, and sometimes cloud-watching. Everyone can have the satisfaction of participating, and come away happily exhausted. The New Games Book will be published in late Spring of 1976; it will contain many New Games, information about setting up tournaments, and much more!

Interplay Games Catalog
Bernard DeKoven
Intensive Learning Center

Curriculum Publications Division
School District of Philadelphia
219 North Broad Street
Philadelphia, Pennsylvania 19103
$15

"Interplay is a games system, the content of which is social interaction" (manual, page 3). It consists primarily of four volumes — well over five hundred game descriptions — with a manual for teachers. The *Interplay Games Catalog* is an outgrowth of a curriculum development project of the Intensive Learning Center of the Philadelphia school system.

The games themselves are structured to encourage social awareness and growth, and involve children in supporting one another in a cooperatively playful atmosphere. This unique collection, though somewhat overwhelming to the casual reader, is a rich and very special resource.

New Games and Tournaments for Classroom Earth

Zephyros Educational Exchange
1201 Stanyan Street
San Francisco, California 94117
$2.50

This is Deschool Primer No. 14 from Zephyros — a community of people who "print and circulate ideas developed by teachers in and out of the classroom" (see page 14). In their usual, zany newsprint format, it is a presentation of some of the most exciting, playful game ideas we've seen in any publication — with a clear emphasis on "people-games."

Articles and ideas by Pat Farrington (New Games Foundation) and Bernie DeKoven (Games Preserve) highlight this collection. Have a tug-of-war with toilet paper (if it breaks, both sides lose!), create a "Magic Fantasy Fence," play "Snake-in-the-Grass" (invented by a ten-year-old), learn how to cheat creatively . . . and have a wonderful time!

Creating and Using Learning Games
Craig Pearson and Joseph Marfuggi

Learning Handbooks
530 University Avenue
Palo Alto, California 94301
$2.50

This is a somewhat technical handbook for teachers, with the emphasis on skill-reinforcement games for the classroom. It contains valuable guidelines for creating and using appropriate games, suggestions for over fifty game formats, and some ideas for simulation–value clarification activities. (See page 8 for reviews of other Learning Handbooks.)

Math, Writing, and Games
Herbert R. Kohl

Vintage Books
Random House
201 East 50th Street
New York, New York 10022
$2.45

This is a superb book, and more than half of it presents ways of learning with games. Herb Kohl not only recognizes the value of playing games, but also respects children's active contributions to their own learning. He describes mostly board games — simple and complex — and the unique variations his kids have invented: "I have seen dozens of versions of chess, checkers, Monopoly created by children. . . . Watching children play, I decided if one presents young children with the components of games, they will generate games themselves" (page 97).

With clear, practical suggestions for setting up a classroom or home games center, a list of materials needed, and ways of measuring what a child has learned by playing games, *Math, Writing, and Games* is an excellent resource for parents and teachers alike.

Playing cards have a fascinating appeal for children of all ages — and are packed with possibilities for learning on a variety of levels. These two books are the best we've seen for children's card games.

Fifty Card Games for Children
Vernon Quinn

U.S. Playing Card Company
P.O. Box 12126
Cincinnati, Ohio 45212
$1

Here is a handy, inexpensive paperback book of card games that children enjoy — some old favorites and several newer ones. Also included is "an easy lesson in contract bridge" — a clear, simply stated description of the language, bidding, and play.

Deal Me In!
Margie Golick

Jeffrey Norton Publishers
145 East 49th Street
New York, New York 10017

"More than any other 'educational toy' I know of, a deck of cards has the potential to exploit the child's readiness, through play, to take an active role in the learning process" (page 6).

In addition to descriptions of more than fifty popular games and a dozen card tricks, Margie Golick has included guidelines and strategies that will maximize their educational value. Among the skills developed through card games are the concept of sequence, coordination and dexterity, number concepts, visual discrimination, and social skills. *Deal Me In!* is a valuable resource for parents and teachers, and we recommend it highly.

making your own games

Making your own games is an exciting, fun activity — and homemade games are often more useful for skill reinforcement. Before making a game for or with your kids, have a variety of stimulating materials around, be aware of the kinds of commercial games your children enjoy and any favorite interests they might have (dinosaurs, cars, sports, etc.) for possible game "themes," and be clear about the purpose for which you're designing the game.

Children will also enjoy creating games and/or adapting old favorites to meet their own needs. Try giving your kids games *without* specific directions — let them make up their own rules, varying them as they go along!

Game Materials

felt-tip markers
wooden disks
wooden cubes (for making dice)
dice
checkerboards
old game boards
cardboard/oaktag
file folders (for making game boards)
toy money
paper fasteners (for making spinners)
magazines/comics (for cutout
  illustrations)
playing pieces (miniature cars, animals,
  old game pieces)
index cards
plain playing cards
egg cartons
pegboard and pegs
counters (marbles, pebbles, seeds)

Check local printers for plain "tickets."
They come in a wide variety of bright
colors, and cost between fifty and
seventy-five cents per hundred. They
are ideal for card games, made of
sturdy oaktag with rounded corners —
size as shown by this outline.

Creative Publications
P.O. Box 10328
Palo Alto, California 94302

**Selective Education Equipment
(SEE)**
3 Bridge Street
Newton, Massachusetts 02195

Both Creative Publications and SEE
have an assortment of game materials —
blank game boards, dice, spinners, playing
pieces, and blank playing cards. Write for
their catalogs if you can't find these materials through local sources.

Packaging

The packaging of a game is as important as the game itself. Design games that can be stored in one container and also stored conveniently in your home or classroom — always cover cans or boxes with colorful, attractive paper. Have interesting materials around to stimulate your own creativity. It's hard to overemphasize the importance of exciting packaging — it can make the difference between a game that's never used and one that cannot be put down, regardless of how much fun it is to play! Here are a few packaging materials you should have around:

coffee cans (with lids)
plastic containers
stick-on labels
cigar boxes
shoe boxes
contact paper
Ziplock bags
envelopes — all sizes
yarn
scrap paper, fabric, wallpaper
material scrounged from factories
felt-tip markers

Look for a source of scrap wooden pieces in your Yellow Pages. These came from Blotner's in Lawrence, Massachusetts, and are sold by weight.

Helpful Game Tips

1. Games should have short, easy-to-follow directions (which could be introduced to kids as one way to play the game, after they've had a chance to create their own rules).
2. List materials/contents of game somewhere on the container.
3. For card games — make sure cards are manageable and easily read.
4. Make your games self-correcting whenever possible — either include an answer sheet or put answers directly on playing materials.
5. All game boards should be laminated or covered with clear contact paper for durability — especially for classroom use.
6. Make an identification symbol on all game pieces for a particular game to keep track of stray pieces and make it easier to keep game parts together.
7. Have a sense of humor when making games — kids love absurdities! Make your games personal by including your children's names, places in your neighborhood, and other personally relevant information.

Old Standbys

The following games are particularly good for adapting to skill-reinforcement games.

Any matching game will lend itself to a wide variety of adaptations; ask your children for their favorites!

Crazy Eights
War
Go Fish
Rummy
Checkers
Old Maid (rename to avoid stereotyping!)
Concentration
Dominoes
Bingo
Tic-Tac-Toe
dice games
puzzles
Chutes and Ladders
Monopoly

nature and ecology

nature and ecology

general resources

There are almost unlimited opportunities to observe and enjoy and learn from our natural environment. The exploration of nature outdoors holds a special fascination for kids — whether they are wondering why the sky is blue, or speculating on the inhabitant of a mysterious hole dug under a tree root. The flow chart on this page is designed to give you some specific ideas for investigations that could arise during or following a visit to a nearby pond. Whether you go outside to answer a particular question (how many leaves are on that tree?) or to just watch and wonder, any outdoor walk with your children will engender a similar wealth and variety of questions, observations, and activities.

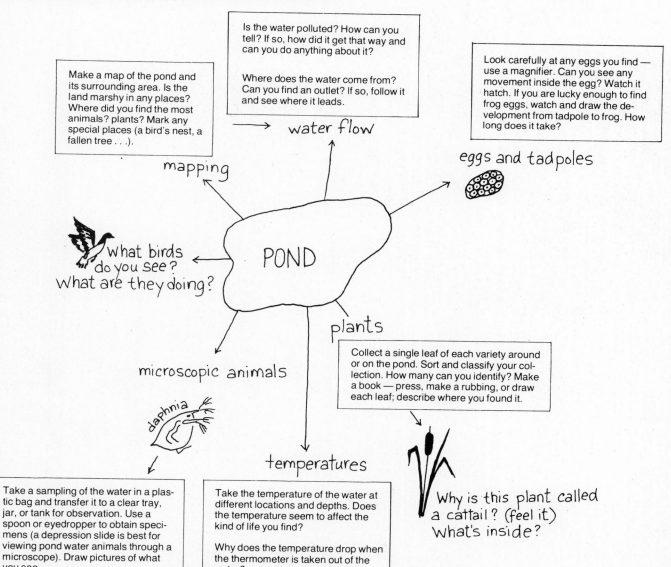

Is the water polluted? How can you tell? If so, how did it get that way and can you do anything about it?

Where does the water come from? Can you find an outlet? If so, follow it and see where it leads.

water flow

Make a map of the pond and its surrounding area. Is the land marshy in any places? Where did you find the most animals? plants? Mark any special places (a bird's nest, a fallen tree . . .).

mapping

Look carefully at any eggs you find — use a magnifier. Can you see any movement inside the egg? Watch it hatch. If you are lucky enough to find frog eggs, watch and draw the development from tadpole to frog. How long does it take?

eggs and tadpoles

what birds do you see? What are they doing?

POND

plants

Collect a single leaf of each variety around or on the pond. Sort and classify your collection. How many can you identify? Make a book — press, make a rubbing, or draw each leaf; describe where you found it.

microscopic animals

daphnia

temperatures

Take a sampling of the water in a plastic bag and transfer it to a clear tray, jar, or tank for observation. Use a spoon or eyedropper to obtain specimens (a depression slide is best for viewing pond water animals through a microscope). Draw pictures of what you see.

Take the temperature of the water at different locations and depths. Does the temperature seem to affect the kind of life you find?

Why does the temperature drop when the thermometer is taken out of the water?

Why is this plant called a cattail? (feel it) What's inside?

Here are some investigations that arose from a trip to our local pond, and the notes children made.

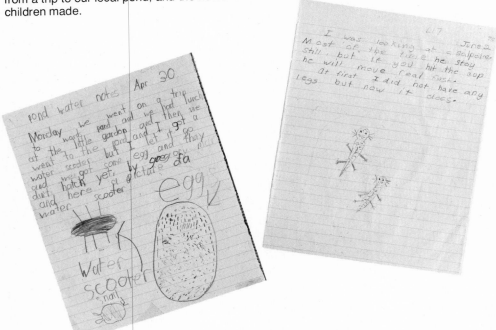

books

Here are some excellent general reference books for all kinds of nature study.

Living Things in Field and Classroom

Minnemast
University of Minnesota
720 Washington Avenue, SE
Minneapolis, Minnesota 55455
$3.25

So many things that can initiate learning out-of-doors are sometimes overlooked — buds on twigs, a bird with something in its beak, an ant dragging a caterpillar along the ground, the direction in which dandelion fluff is blowing. . . .

Any single observation can be the beginning of exciting exploration and lead to the joy of further discovery. . . . What is inside buds? Why doesn't the bird swallow the worm . . . ? Where is the ant dragging the caterpillar? What happens to the dandelion seeds after they blow away?

The most interesting questions often do not have neat, precise answers, but this should not prevent your investigating them anyway. The out-of-doors is so full of interacting things, that answers are always new and interesting and different, depending on when, where and what you are observing (page 99).

This very useful book explores the many possibilities for a class or family studying living things that are observed in or collected from their natural habitats. It is an excellent source of general information as well as of specific, clearly explained activity ideas for a wide variety of plants and animals likely to interest children.

Living Things in Field and Classroom is generously illustrated with clear drawings and handy reference charts, and includes understandable directions for keeping specimens or creating indoor environments. It contains several composite drawings of common local environments with suggested questions that arouse curiosity and lead to further exploration, such as "In a Vacant Lot" below (from page 105).

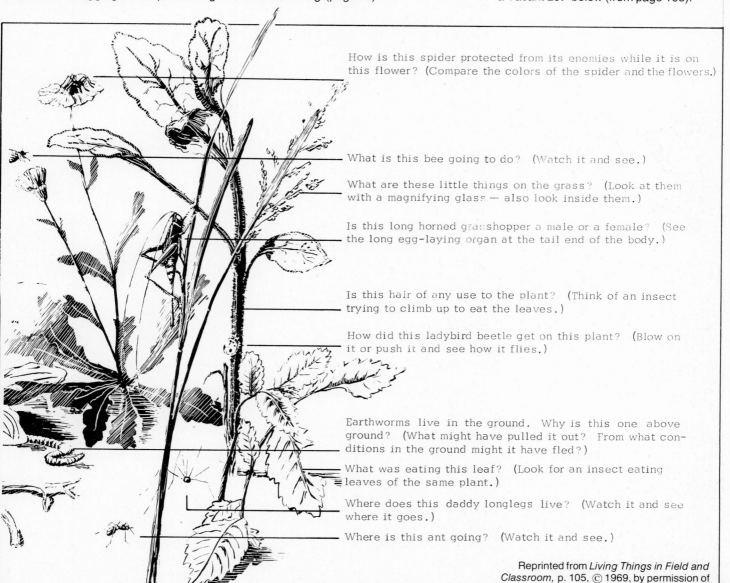

How is this spider protected from its enemies while it is on this flower? (Compare the colors of the spider and the flowers.)

What is this bee going to do? (Watch it and see.)

What are these little things on the grass? (Look at them with a magnifying glass — also look inside them.)

Is this long horned grasshopper a male or a female? (See the long egg-laying organ at the tail end of the body.)

Is this hair of any use to the plant? (Think of an insect trying to climb up to eat the leaves.)

How did this ladybird beetle get on this plant? (Blow on it or push it and see how it flies.)

Earthworms live in the ground. Why is this one above ground? (What might have pulled it out? From what conditions in the ground might it have fled?)

What was eating this leaf? (Look for an insect eating leaves of the same plant.)

Where does this daddy longlegs live? (Watch it and see where it goes.)

Where is this ant going? (Watch it and see.)

Reprinted from *Living Things in Field and Classroom*, p. 105, © 1969, by permission of the University of Minnesota.

Discovering the Outdoors
Laurence Pringle, editor

The Natural History Press
Doubleday and Company
501 Franklin Avenue
Garden City, New York 11530
$4.95

Made up of articles originally published by *Nature and Science* magazine, this book nicely blends information, questions, and activities that will intrigue all nature-loving upper elementary age children. It is a guide to investigations of plant and animal life found "almost anywhere outdoors — from a city park or weedy lot to a small suburban swamp or a great forest."

Ten-Minute Field Trips
Helen Ross Russell

J. G. Ferguson Publishing Company
6 North Michigan Avenue
Chicago, Illinois 60602
$4.85

This book is a "teacher's guide to using the school grounds for environmental studies," but it would be equally valuable to any adult with a desire to share nature experiences with kids and with little knowledge of "where to begin." There's even a short chapter on the value of saying "I don't know," which creates a good reason for children to find answers for themselves. *Ten-Minute Field Trips* suggests innumerable ways and places for children and adults to explore the natural world around them together. It contains lots of background information, clear sketches of animals and plants, and stimulating questions to encourage closer examination of nature.

Learning about Nature through Games
Virginia W. Musselman

Stackpole Books
Cameron and Kelker Streets
Harrisburg, Pennsylvania 17105
$3.95

This handy book describes more than three hundred simple, fun ways to identify and become familiar with the sights and sounds of nature — on trips or in your own backyard. Whether taking a "bug's-eye view" of the world, going on a nature scavenger hunt, or making a "flower puzzle," your children are sure to enjoy the wide variety of activities suggested.

Examining Your Environment

Winston Press
25 Groveland Terrace
Minneapolis, Minnesota 55403
$3 each

In addition to being profusely illustrated with a wide variety of visually stimulating photographs, drawings, cartoons, and charts, this series of books is fascinating reading! Examining Your Environment is aimed at upper elementary children, but is one of the most exciting new series we've seen for adults as well.

The series of twelve books deals with subjects as broad in scope as *Pollution* and as specific as *The Dandelion* with an equal richness of detail. Each book contains interesting background information, loads of questions to inspire any child's natural curiosity, and a smorgasbord of tempting activities that encourage children to truly examine their environment.

Astronomy, see p. 81 for review
Birds
The Dandelion, see p. 66
Ecology
Mapping Small Places
Mini-climates, see p. 72
Pollution, see p. 30
Running Water, see p. 98
Small Creatures
Snow and Ice
Trees, see p. 64
Your Senses, see p. 258

Catalogue of Curriculum Resources
Science Teachers' Association of Ontario

Donco Quality Printers
212 Division Street
Kingston, Ontario K7K 3Z1, CANADA

This catalog describes more than a hundred inexpensive guides compiled by the Science Teachers' Association of Ontario. The majority of subjects dealt with relate to environmental sciences and all are geared to classroom use.

Each guide uses a specific item, locale, or phenomenon as a focal point for a variety of concrete, interdisciplinary activities.

Most of the guides are from ten to sixty stapled pages, including equipment lists and sources of information as well as specific ideas. Although they are aimed at teachers, the guides are useful for any adults who need a "starting point" for stimulating children's investigations of the world around them.

Some of the titles most intriguing to us are: *The Bicycle, Orienteering, The Cemetery, Populations, Maple Syrup Time, Study of a Lawn, Thermometers,* and *Snow Study.* Several of the STAO guides are reviewed in more detail in our Science section, pages 108, 109, 122, and 123.

materials

The following materials would be extremely handy for studying nature indoors and/or outdoors — for observation, capturing and keeping specimens, creating environments, and so on. With the exception of specialized equipment, such as microscopes or aquariums, most of these items can be scrounged or purchased fairly inexpensively from hardware stores or pet shops.

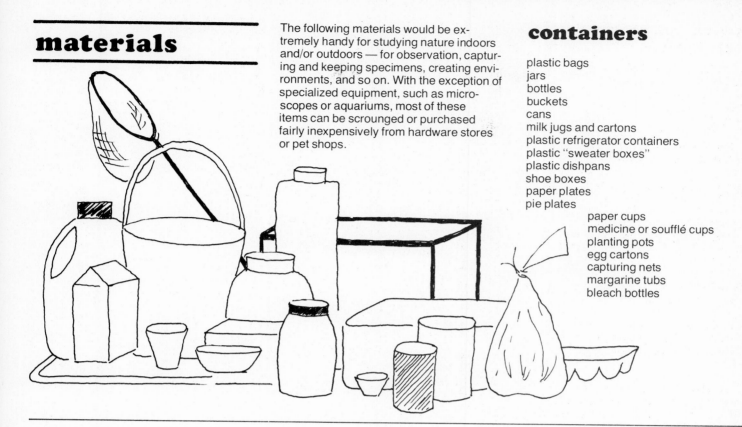

containers

plastic bags
jars
bottles
buckets
cans
milk jugs and cartons
plastic refrigerator containers
plastic "sweater boxes"
plastic dishpans
shoe boxes
paper plates
pie plates

paper cups
medicine or soufflé cups
planting pots
egg cartons
capturing nets
margarine tubs
bleach bottles

general equipment

plastic and cardboard trays
old newspaper
sawdust, wood chips, shavings
sponges
food coloring
plaster of Paris
potting soil, sand, gravel
water bottles
untippable water dishes
masking tape
wire hangers
Popsicle sticks, tongue depressors
cardboard tubes
small notebooks

¼" hardware cloth
mosquito netting
cheesecloth
wire-mesh screening
chicken wire
wire
string

aluminum foil
waxed paper
clear plastic wrap

thermometers
magnifiers

microscope
standard glass slides
depression slides
aquariums
measuring tapes and rulers
tweezers

eyedroppers
balances and weights
stopwatch
stethoscope
T-pins
light source

more publications

Save the Earth! An Ecology Handbook for Kids
Betty Miles

*Alfred A. Knopf
457 Halm Road
Westminster, Maryland 21157
$2.50*

This delightful book is one of the few action-oriented ecology books we've seen that's written for children. It is visually in keeping with its subject — clean and uncluttered, with simple line drawings. It contains easy-to-read, understandable information, poems, projects, and suggested ways to make a child's efforts count (including how to write an environmental complaint letter!).

*No Bag, Please
Try this project when you are going shopping. Take a big shopping bag with you to put things in. When you pay for something watch carefully. Does the person at the counter start to put it in a bag for you? If this happens, say "I don't need a bag, thanks." Then see how the store person acts. Surprised? Pleased? A little bit angry? Confused? Then see how you feel. Ordinary? Embarrassed? Good?*

— from *Save the Earth!*, page 26

*Water Count
As soon as you get up in the morning, put a little notebook and a pencil in your pocket.
All day long, make a note every time you use some water.
Don't forget.
At the end of the day, see how long your list is. Are you surprised at how many different ways you have used water? How many gallons do you think you used? (Do you know that every flush of a toilet takes eight gallons of water?)*

— from *Save the Earth!*, page 70

Pollution
Examining Your Environment

*Winston Press
25 Groveland Terrace
Minneapolis, Minnesota 55403
$3*

One of the excellent Examining Your Environment series (see page 28), *Pollution* suggests some very specific activities — primarily geared to creating an aware-

ness of pollution and an understanding of its causes and effects in our lives. Children and adults using this book will discover "Who are the litterbugs? How much garbage is collected from your block in a week? Why do cars and trucks add to air pollution? Which type of detergent produces the most foam? How can noise be reduced?" — all through experiments and activities that encourage discovery of the answers.

lowering string marked at 6" intervals

screw eye

cork

bottle

A Water Sampler
from <u>Pollution</u> (page 53)

Outdoor Education Equipment
Russel E. Bachert, Jr., and Emerson L. Snooks

*Interstate Printers and Publishers
19–27 North Jackson Street
Danville, Illinois 61832
$8.50*

This very handy book contains more than a hundred ideas for building field equipment for outdoor study. The directions are easy to read and each is accompanied by a clear drawing. Whether constructing a safe trap for capturing animals, a clinometer for measuring ground slope, or a rain gauge, children are not only encouraged to create their own investigative devices but are also given a clearer understanding of how they work than can be obtained from using commercially made equipment. Each item includes questions to stimulate observation as well as directions for construction and use.

The Curious Naturalist

*Massachusetts Audubon Society
5 Great Neck Road
Lincoln, Massachusetts 01773
subscription: $3.50/year*

This monthly magazine for beginning naturalists deals with a different central topic in each issue, such as "Life in the Mountains," "Solar Energy," and "Slowing Down" (on hibernation and preparation for winter). Each issue contains general background information readable at upper elementary ages and useful to all adults, as well as suggested projects related to the topic being discussed.
The Curious Naturalist is well illustrated with photographs and sketches. Its ecological orientation is especially refreshing in that it deals with the human animal as an integral part of nature.

enough large nails taped to bottle for weights to make it sink

Eco-News

*The Environmental Action Coalition
235 East 49th Street
New York, New York 10017
$2 / 10-month subscription*

This is an excellent, practical newsletter about ecology for city children. Each issue includes lots of interesting information and suggested activities. The *Eco-News* people also encourage kids' contributions and responses to pollution problems published in the newsletter.

ECO-NEWS

© The Environmental Action Coalition, Inc. 1974

A Young People's Environmental Newsletter

235 East 49th Street, New York, N. Y. 10017 · 486-9550

VOL. 5, NO. 5   JANUARY 1975

Where Does All the Garbage Go?

Garbage cans overflowing with paper, plastic, soda cans, orange peels, and coffee grounds...trucks in the early morning, groaning and clanking as the garbage is crushed inside... garbage men calling to each other as they toss rattling cans back onto the sidewalks. These are sights and sounds that are very familiar to city kids.

But what happens to the garbage after it is thrown onto the trucks? People today throw away lots and lots of garbage. But no one seems to know or care what happens to it.

Garbage is a problem. People who try to solve this problem call garbage by a special name -- solid waste. Solid waste won't go away by itself. It can't disappear into water or air. Picking it up and taking it away is one of the most important jobs for city workers.

Getting rid of solid waste is called disposal. Sometimes disposal means that solid waste is just piled up in open dumps and left to sit there. Sometimes it is buried under several feet of dirt in sanitary landfills. And sometimes it is burned in incinerators.

This issue of Eco-News will explain some of the problems in getting rid of solid waste. Next time you see a garbage truck on your block, you will know where all the garbage goes!

The following authors have contributed several valuable and interesting general nature books. These may often be found in libraries and/or local bookstores.

Margaret Waring Buck

Along the Seashore
In Ponds and Streams
In Woods and Fields
In Yards and Gardens
Pets from the Pond
Small Pets from Woods and Fields
Where They Go in Winter

Abingdon Press
201 Eighth Avenue South
Nashville, Tennessee 37202

All of these books are amply illustrated with clear drawings of plants and animals found in the particular environment treated. They contain a wealth of detailed information about a wide variety of plants and small wild animals: where to find them, how to catch and keep and care for them properly. The emphasis is on observation, appreciation, and enjoyment of nature everywhere.

David Webster

Brain Boosters
Snow Stumpers

The Natural History Press
501 Franklin Avenue
Garden City, New York 11530

Can you make an "ice cube keeper"?
What is the biggest shadow you've ever seen?
Can you build a 3' high paper tower with one sheet?
How much do you weigh in a moving elevator?
Why does a pond freeze and melt from the edge out?
Does snow melt in your tracks because your boots are hot?

David Webster has a unique talent for creating intriguing brainteasers and experiments for kids. Both these books are full of puzzles and "mystery photos" that encourage children (and adults!) to look carefully at their surroundings and try to discover the "why" of common, often overlooked but fascinating natural phenomena.

Elizabeth K. Cooper

Science in Your Own Backyard
Science on the Shores and Banks
Insects and Plants: The Amazing
   Partnership
And Everything Nice: The Story of Sugar,
   Spice, and Flavoring
Silkworms and Science

Harcourt Brace Jovanovich
757 Third Avenue
New York, New York 10017

Every one of these books is full of fascinating and often unusual information. Whether exploring the yard on your stomach, learning how to be a "fish watcher," or discovering the "mystery of vanilla," you and your child are bound to be captivated by subject and treatment alike! There are lots of related experiments that encourage discovery, such as finding out what makes mustard "hot" or how a dragonfly nymph jet-propels itself through the water.

The following comprehensive series cover almost all aspects of the natural environment and natural history. They are expensive if you desire the entire series, are beautifully and profusely illustrated, and definitely can enrich any home or school library. The only limitation to Our Living World of Nature is that it deals exclusively with plants and animals and their relationship to their environments. The Life Nature Library has a "Young Readers Edition" for several titles, but these lack the wealth of superb photographs for which Time-Life publications are renowned.

Our Living World of Nature

McGraw-Hill Book Company
Webster Division
1220 Avenue of the Americas
New York, New York 10020
$4.40 each

The Life of the African Plains
The Life of the Cave
The Life of the Desert
The Life of the Far North
The Life of the Forest
The Life of the Jungle
The Life of the Marsh
The Life of the Mountains
The Life of the Ocean
The Life of the Pond
The Life of Prairies and Plains
The Life of Rivers and Streams
The Life of Sea Islands
The Life of the Seashore

Life Nature Library

Silver-Burdett Company
Morristown, New Jersey 07960
$6.99 each

Animal Behavior*	The Mammals*
The Birds	The Mountains
The Desert	The Plants
Early Man*	The Poles
The Earth*	The Primates*
Ecology	The Reptiles*
The Fishes	The Sea*
The Forest	The Universe
The Insects	

The Land and Wildlife of Africa
The Land and Wildlife of Australia
The Land and Wildlife of North America
The Land and Wildlife of South America
The Land and Wildlife of Tropical Asia

*Young Readers Edition available for these titles at $4.20 each.

Golden Guides

Western Publishing Company
1220 Mound Avenue
Racine, Wisconsin 53404
$1.50 or $1.95

These small, pocket identification guides to practically everything you might find outdoors — on a hike, at the seashore, or in your own backyard — are invaluable! They are available in almost any local bookstore, relatively inexpensive, and easy to carry around.

Each book contains considerable background information on the general subject being treated, as well as such details as would be helpful in identifying or locating the particular object — whether it's a rock, constellation, bird, tree, or insect. The color illustrations are excellent.

There are almost fifty different titles; those listed below are just some of our favorites.

Pond Life	*Trees*
Spiders	*Seashores*
Weather	*Rocks and Minerals*
Game Birds	*Fossils*
Birds	*Weeds*
Stars	*Insects*

organizations

The following places are excellent sources of information about nature for teachers, parents, and children. Many of them would be ideal places to visit and all of them have brochures, catalogs, or packets of information. If you write for information, be sure to mention that you want materials for use with children.

National Audubon Society

950 Third Avenue
New York, New York 10022

This organization publishes several aids to the study of animals and plants native to North America. It also sponsors wildlife preserves throughout the country that are open to the public.

Massachusetts Audubon Society

5 Great Neck Road
Lincoln, Massachusetts 01773

This is an independent organization with chapters and wildlife sanctuaries throughout Massachusetts. The central office in Lincoln maintains a very complete nature library and is an excellent source of information, pamphlets, recommended books and places to visit. They also publish some excellent, inexpensive aids to environmental education in the form of "teaching sheets" and excerpts from *The Curious Naturalist* (see page 30), which can be ordered from anywhere in the country.

Smithsonian Institution

1000 Jefferson Drive, SW
Washington, D.C. 20560

This is a unique source of information in all areas of natural and applied science. The Smithsonian is one of the world's foremost research organizations and, as such, can and will respond to almost any question from children as well as adults. Have you ever wondered, for example, how many elephants there are in the world? Or what causes an earthquake? Or what a trilobite looks like?

The National Museum of Natural History and the National Zoological Park are both parts of the Smithsonian. They are fascinating experiences for children, with exhibits that often encourage a hands-on approach. Both have special tours for children.

U.S. Department of the Interior

National Park Service / Bureau of Outdoor Recreation

Washington, D.C. 20240

These are the two departments of the U.S. government that have a wide variety of information and resources related to environmental education. The national parks and wildlife refuges are excellent, and are located throughout the country.

Zero Population Growth, Inc.

1346 Connecticut Avenue, NW
Washington, D.C. 20036

This organization has a complete packet of information, resources, and activity ideas related to the problems of pollution and overpopulation. This packet has been specifically written and put together for people working with children; their fact sheets make these problems very real! Did you know, for example, that one American baby (throughout its life) will require 26 million gallons of water, 28 tons of iron and steel, 1,200 barrels of petroleum, 13,000 pounds of paper, and 50 tons of food? He or she will also throw out 10,000 no-return bottles, 2.3 automobiles, 126 tons of garbage, and 9.8 tons of air pollution! Imagine!

Check to see if there is a *science museum* or *natural history museum* in your area. Most of these have a wealth of information and special displays relating to the environment, and they are fascinating places to visit with kids!

developed units (ESS)

The Elementary Science Study (ESS) is a government-sponsored curriculum group that has produced a wealth of excellent units of study for children. Although they are geared to classroom use, the materials are often available separately and the guides are chock-full of exciting ideas.

These units are child-centered in the best sense of the phrase. The emphasis is always on learning by discovery and the belief that children learn best from doing, coming to their own conclusions as they explore a wide range of materials.

The ESS units are available from three sources that we know about:

McGraw-Hill Book Company (M-H)
Webster Division
1221 Avenue of the Americas
New York, New York 10020

Selective Educational Equipment (SEE)
3 Bridge Street
Newton, Massachusetts 02195

American Science and Engineering
  (AS&E)
20 Overland Street
Boston, Massachusetts 02115

Since prices are subject to change and vary considerably, we suggest that you write for free catalogs from these suppliers. McGraw-Hill publishes all the guides and distributes kits, but those units available from SEE invariably have lower prices and all SEE's items are available separately. AS&E is relatively new to the ESS market and we cannot guarantee their quality or compatibility with ESS specifications, but their prices are considerably lower than those of the other two suppliers.

"T.G." is our abbreviation for Teacher's Guide. These are excellent handbooks for anyone working with children in the particular area covered, and contain materials lists, background information, suggested specific activities, and stimulating questions for starting or following up activities.

unit title	suggested grade level	printed material	basic equipment	film loops	source	related pages
Animal Activity	4–6	T.G. *Experiments on Animal Activity*	activity wheel		M-H	49–51
Animals in the Classroom	all ages	T.G. *The Curious Gerbils*			M-H	49
Attribute Games and Problems	K–8	T.G. problem cards	A Blocks, People Pieces, Color Cubes, Creature Cards		M-H SEE* AS&E	184–187
Balloons and Gases	5–8	T.G.	balloons, containers, dropper bottles, glass tubing, medicine cups, balance		M-H AS&E*	

*equipment available separately
**indicates review and more detailed description

unit title	suggested grade level	printed material	basic equipment	film loops	source	related pages
Batteries and Bulbs	4–6	T.G. prediction sheets, test cards, project sheets	bulbs, bulb holders, wire assortment, wire clippers, rubberized magnets, compasses, nails, Fahnestock clips		M-H SEE* AS&E*	115–117
Behavior of Mealworms	4–8	T.G. *How Barn Owls Hunt* *How a Moth Escapes Its Cocoon* set of 6 illustrations	bran, live mealworms, hand magnifiers, plastic containers		M-H SEE* AS&E*	
Bones	4–6	T.G. *Picture Book* picture packet *How to Make a Chicken Skeleton*	disarticulated cat, rabbit, and mink skeletons; trays; set of Mystery Bones	5 (X-ray)	M-H SEE AS&E	255–257
Brine Shrimp	1–4	T.G.	brine shrimp eggs, containers, hand lenses, medicine droppers, measuring cups and spoons	2	M-H SEE* AS&E*	
Budding Twigs	4–6	T.G.			M-H	64–65
Butterflies	K–5	T.G.		6	M-H	
Changes	1–4	T.G.			M-H	
Clay Boats	2–8	T.G.	balance, uniform weights, trays, plastic boxes, oil-base paints, pails, medicine cups		M-H SEE* AS&E*	96–97
Colored Solutions	3–8	T.G.	food coloring, salt, vinegar, droppers, pails, balance, trays, containers, beaker		M-H SEE* AS&E*	
Crayfish	4–6	T.G.			M-H	
Daytime Astronomy	5–8	T.G.			M-H	81–82
Drops, Streams, and Containers	3–4	T.G.	flexible tubing, containers, droppers, assorted papers and liquids, food coloring		M-H AS&E*	94

*equipment available separately
**indicates review and more detailed description

Developed Units — Continued

unit title	suggested grade level	printed material	basic equipment	film loops	source	related pages
Earthworms	4–6	T.G.	containers, trays, ice chest, hand lenses		M-H AS&E*	
Eggs and Tadpoles	K–6	T.G.	frog eggs (SEE only), containers, fishnet, thermometers, droppers, magnifiers	8	M-H SEE* AS&E*	26
Gases and "Airs"	5–8	T.G. worksheets	tubes, jars, racks, syringe pumps, rulers, flexible tubing, chemicals, clay	4	M-H SEE* AS&E	
Geo Blocks	K–6	T.G. problem cards	set of 330 blocks		M-H SEE* AS&E*	
Growing Seeds	K–3	T.G.	assorted seeds, vermiculite, containers	2	M-H SEE* AS&E*	58–59
Heating and Cooling	5–7	T.G. problem cards	assorted wire, metal sheets, metal screens, metal and glass rods, tubes, candles, foil		M-H AS&E*	107–112
Ice Cubes	3–5	T.G.	ice chest, trays, molds, containers, cubes, thermometers, washers, medicine cups		M-H SEE* AS&E*	111–112
Kitchen Physics	6–9	T.G. worksheets	balances, buckets, tension plates, capillary block, assorted liquids, T-pins, droppers	3	M-H SEE* AS&E*	93–99
Life of Beans and Peas	K–4	T.G.			M-H	57–68
Light and Shadows	K–3	T.G.			M-H	81–82, 251
Mapping	5–7	T.G. *Making Maps* mapping games	geoboards, measuring wheel, thermometer, string, compasses, index cards, graph paper, tubes		M-H AS&E*	157

*equipment available separately
**indicates review and more detailed description

unit title	suggested grade level	printed material	basic equipment	film loops	source	related pages
Match and Measure	K–3	T.G.	containers, tubes with caps, egg timer, tape measure, tongue depressors, caliper		M-H AS&E*	
Microgardening	4–7	T.G. *Illustrated Handbook of Some Common Molds*	culture dishes, syringes, set of 8 cultures, potato dextrose agar, growth and culture tubes	7	M-H SEE* AS&E*	
Mirror Cards	1–6	T.G.	mirrors, set of cards		M-H	188
Mobiles	K–4	T.G.	round reeds (assorted sizes), T-pins, yarn, twine, clips, mobile cards		M-H SEE* AS&E*	
Mosquitoes	3–9	T.G.			M-H	
Mystery Powders	3–4	T.G.	soufflé or medicine cups, stir sticks, plastic bags, dropper bottles, pails, hand lenses		M-H SEE* AS&E*	105
Optics	4–6	T.G.	light-source housing, dowels, black masks, mirror stands and mirrors, filters, containers		M-H AS&E*	
Pattern Blocks	K–6	T.G.	250 blocks (6 color-coded shapes), mirrors		M-H SEE* AS&E	182
Peas and Particles	3–8	T.G. picture packet (9 illustrations, 2 charts)	paper cups, medicine cups, containers, trays, marbles, Styrofoam balls, measuring spoons		M-H SEE* AS&E*	189–190
Pendulums	4–6	T.G.	pendulum supports, bobs, 1″ glass, wooden and steel balls, doweling, fish line, hangers	5	M-H AS&E	122–123
Pond Water	1–7	T.G. Pond Water cards			M-H	26

*equipment available separately
**indicates review and more detailed description

Developed Units — Continued

unit title	suggested grade level	printed material	basic equipment	film loops	source	related pages
Primary Balancing	K–4	*The Balance Book* (T.G.)	balances, boards and fulcrums, sorting bin, assorted weights (blocks, balls, sponges, foam)		M-H AS&E*	170
Printing Press	1–6		type box, type, inking plate, brayer, spacers, ink, press		M-H AS&E*	
Rocks and Charts	3–6	T.G.	assorted rocks (21 kinds), balance, rubberized magnets, streak plates, hand lenses		M-H SEE* AS&E*	70–71
Sand	2–3	T.G.	balance, sieves, assorted grades of natural and colored sand	5	M-H*	
Senior Balancing	4–8	T.G. problem cards	assorted pegboard beams for making a variety of balances, fulcrums, washers, nuts and screws		M-H AS&E*	170
Sink or Float	2–7	T.G.	trays, salt, oil-base clay, medicine cups, cylinders, cubes and spheres of different materials (plastic, wood, aluminum, glass)		M-H SEE* AS&E*	96–97
Small Things	4–6	T.G. worksheet package set of 20 illustrations *The Faithful Eye of Robert Hooke*	student microscopes, assorted stains, glass slides, depression slides, tweezers	11	M-H SEE* AS&E*	
Spinning Tables	1–2	T.G.	2 spinning tables, drive belts, extra disks, cubes, spheres (assorted), chalk, food coloring		M-H AS&E*	
Starting from Seeds	3–7	T.G.			M-H	58–59
Stream Tables	4–9	T.G. and cards (10)	pail, recirculating pump, cloth tape, tubing, hose clamp, T-connector		M-H AS&E*	
Structures	2–6	T.G.	clay, straws, pins, copper wire, washers		M-H (T.G. only) AS&E*	181

*equipment available separately
**indicates review and more detailed description

unit title	suggested grade level	printed material	basic equipment	film loops	source	related pages
Tangrams	K–8	T.G. Tangram cards	Tangram puzzles (4″ × 4″)		M-H SEE* AS&E*	179
Tracks	4–6	T.G. *Track Picture Book* Track cards Mystery Track cards		1	M-H	
Water Flow	5–6	T.G. idea cards (30)	window box, support frame, plugs, vinyl tubing, plastic straws, hose clamps, T-connector		M-H AS&E*	97–98
Where Is the Moon?	3–7	T.G. *Where Was the Moon?*			M-H	83
Whistles and Strings	3–6	T.G.	tubes and caps, straws, flexible tubing, buckets, funnels, assorted strings, screw eyes		M-H AS&E*	232

*equipment available separately
**indicates review and more detailed description

animals

Whether the animal is a classroom or household pet, a one-day visitor, or a creature discovered outdoors, its presence in home or classroom can form the basis of a tremendous variety and depth of learning. Taking care of an animal not only develops a sense of responsibility but also stimulates a barrage of questions and observations as a result of children's natural curiosity. This section presents some recommended resources and ideas for animal selection and care, and investigations and activities that capitalize on and encourage this natural curiosity.

It's helpful to have the following materials handy: ▶

magnifiers
microscopes
containers — plastic bags, jars, buckets
cardboard and cardboard tubes
hardware cloth, screening
water bottles
newspaper
sawdust, wood chips or shavings
untippable water dishes
measuring devices — tapes,
   rulers, balances, stopwatch,
   thermometer

selection and care

books on animal care

Common Native Animals
M. F. Vessel and E. J. Harrington

*Thomas Y. Crowell Company
666 Fifth Avenue
New York, New York 10019*

This book is a classic in its field, and the most thorough, easy-to-use general resource we've seen on animals most commonly found in the United States. It is basically organized by major groups of animals (mammals, birds, reptiles, amphibians, fish, and invertebrates). Within each category are maps indicating areas where a particular animal is most likely to be found, information on finding and caring for a wide variety of animals, excellent drawings of common animals, and much more. *Common Native Animals* is a highly useful general resource book for anyone whose kids are forever discovering new "pets"!

Shelf Pets: How to Take Care of Small Wild Animals
Edward R. Ricciuti

*Harper and Row Publishers
10 East 53rd Street
New York, New York 10022
$4.50*

The wild pets described in this book are animals that can be kept easily on a shelf or in a corner of any room. It is written in a style that captures the wonders of nature in the flowing grace of a garter snake, the chirp of a cricket, or the delicate design of a spiderweb. *Shelf Pets* also gives specific care and feeding information, directions for constructing appropriate cages, and descriptions of dangerous species as well as of those that make acceptable pets.

T.F.H. Publications

*211 West Sylvania Avenue
Neptune, New Jersey 07753*

T.F.H. has a paperback book on the selection and care of almost any animal you could think of! The books are generally accurate, well written, complete, and fully illustrated. Write for the T.F.H. catalog or check your local pet store for a full range of their titles.

Look What I Found!
Marshal T. Case

*The Chatham Press
15 Wilmot Lane
Riverside, Connecticut 06878
$4.95*

This delightful book is an easy-to-read, visually exciting guide to the care and feeding of small wildlife. It contains basic information on a wide variety of animals likely to be found by children exploring the natural world around them. Among many other fascinating suggested activities, *Look What I Found!* tells you how to set up a marine aquarium, how to study birds in your neighborhood, and how to hatch reptile eggs! It encourages ecologically responsible attitudes throughout.

1. Know what plants and animals are protected by law in your state. Ask your local fish and game warden, nature center or humane society about these laws, and never violate them.

2. Do not touch the nests of birds or burrows of animals. The parents may abandon the young if their homes are disturbed by people.

3. If you roll logs over or look under rocks, place them back as you found them. Many animals depend on these for shelter. If their homes are exposed to open air and sunlight, they will be destroyed.

4. Dead trees are homes for many animals — leave them standing.

5. Do not pick wildflowers or snap limbs from bushes or trees — leave them for other people to enjoy.

6. Never collect more wild animals than you can care for at home. When you are ready to release them, take them back to the place where you found them.

7. Carry an extra collecting bag with you and pick up litter. Leave the open areas cleaner than you found them (page 9).

special notes

Almost all animals react poorly to fluctuations in temperature; some may even die if left in a cold room at night. An ordinary desk lamp usually provides sufficient heat.

Reptiles need a regular source of calcium. If not being fed whole animals, they should be given the supplement "ostioform," which is available from pet shops.

Salmonella is a disease commonly carried by many animals, especially in populated areas, which can be transmitted to humans. It is a good idea to wash your hands after handling animals, but a must after handling turtles and other aquatic reptiles.

$\frac{1}{4}''$ **fold hardware cloth** — **bedding material** — **block**

Toilet training a rabbit can make a *big* difference in ease and frequency of cage cleaning, and will allow the animal to roam more freely in home or classroom. This method takes advantage of a rabbit's natural inclination to use the same spot over and over again.

Note: This will probably work only with young rabbits!

Make a "toilet" from a dishpan and line the bottom with newspaper or other absorbent bedding material. Place a piece of ¼" hardware cloth on top, folded over or supported by wood strips so that it leaves space underneath even with the rabbit sitting on it.

Put the "toilet" in your rabbit's favorite spot of the cage and/or room. (We let our rabbit run free during the day, when he used a corner behind the piano. When he was caged at night, the "toilet" was placed in a corner of his cage.)

After about two weeks, our rabbit consistently returned to the "toilet" when it was left in his cage. When the rabbit has become accustomed to using the "toilet," it can be placed in any convenient corner and left there. It should be washed out daily.

popular small pets

animal	housing	bedding	food and water	light and heat	advantages	objections
mice	metal or glass cage 18″ × 12″ × 6″	wood shavings or torn paper	lab chow, cereals, seed, fruit, vegetables, bread; water bottle (clean water at all times)	normal, not extreme 72° F	become tame, easy to handle, good for breeding experiments; easy to house	very smelly — cage needs daily cleaning; young difficult to keep
white lab rats	metal or glass cage, bigger when full grown 24″ × 20″ × 10″	wood shavings, torn paper	as for mice, pellets; water bottle (clean water at all times)	normal, not extreme 75° F	as for mice, except young survive better — suitable for many experiments	smelly, gnaw — less easy to handle as adults
hamsters	preferably wire or metal cage 24″ × 24″ × 10″	wood shavings, torn paper	as for rats and mice; water bottle (clean water at all times)	normal, not extreme 70° F	easy to house and care for, become tame and easy to handle, usually friendly and relatively clean	gnaw, nocturnal, fight each other; father needs to be removed when babies are born; especially prone to injury
gerbils	wood, metal, or glass cage; fish tank for burrowing — 20″ × 20″ × 10″ NOTE: "Habitrail" cages are dangerous as gerbils ingest plastic.	preferably soil for burrowing, wood shavings or torn paper possible (plain white paper — dye from colored paper may be harmful)	as for other small rodents — love sunflower seeds but will overeat them; water bottle — if fresh vegetables are provided daily, no other water is necessary	room temperature 75° F, higher temperature possible	become very tame, cage needs rare cleaning (monthly), very curious; mated pairs care for young jointly	tend to get dropped easily, destructive to cages, not allowed in some states
guinea pigs	wire, wooden, glass, or metal cage 30″ × 24″ × 12″	wood shavings, torn paper	pellets, fruit, vegetables, old bread, vitamin C in some form; large water bottle	not full sun; 70° F — can die of cold — a desk light will keep them warm	big and easy to hold, become tame, generally clean	gnaw, not very active
rabbits	large wood or metal cage with removable pan or outdoor location; bottom- and topless wire-screen cage for easy cleaning (see top photo on page 48)	paper or screening with pan beneath	pellets, vegetables; large water bottle or untippable water dish (plenty of water — they stay cleaner)	normal — 70° F, cooler temperature possible	big and easy to handle, become very tame; can be "toilet trained" (see page 43)	need space, cage cleaning is usually a big job

	Cage	Bedding	Food	Conditions	Care	Notes
water turtles (wood, box)	glass or plastic tank, at least 5 times as long as the turtle	water (deep enough to swim in) with rocks or floating log to climb on and feed from	mostly carnivorous — raw meat, insects, pieces of fish, dog food — some vegetables	warm, light; room temperature 75° F+	hardy, need little care, interesting	need warmth (light over tank), may get eye infections, danger of salmonella (see page 43) more frequent in pet-store turtles than those found in wild
land tortoises (wood, box)	wooden box or yard — at least 5 times length of animal	sawdust, shavings — keep entire bedding damp; water source	mostly vegetarian, fruits and vegetables, some raw meat	warm, light; room temperature 68°–70° F	very hardy, need little care, long-lived, can be held with little danger	hibernate and may not eat in winter
anoles (chameleons)	20 gal. glass or plastic tank	gravel, sand, rocks with plants and branches — keep moist	live insects, need some calcium source; water dish	warm, light; 75°–80° F	need little care	should be kept in twos or threes
garter snakes	20 gal. glass or plastic tank for 18"–20" snake (at least 1/3 length of snake), cover critical — very fine screen or cheesecloth — snake will damage nose on coarser screen	gravel or soil with plants, branch — must be dry	earthworms, flies, raw fish	warm, light; 70°–75° F	need little care, eat only once a week or so	cannot be kept long in captivity, won't always eat
frogs and toads	glass or plastic tank, room to move	frogs — half dry, half water (enough to hang legs), spray dry area with water occasionally toads — moss, pine needles, hollow log or sand to bury in — small pool or water source	insects, worms, grubs, pill bugs, snails, slugs, mealworms, ants, etc.	moist, cool — no heat source, out of direct sun; 65°–70° F	varied diet, easy to cage, take up little space, can't scratch or hurt kids, have few needs	need live food, may not eat in cold weather — pickerel and gray tree frogs have harmful secretions, wash hands after handling!
goldfish and guppies	small glass or plastic tank (10 gal. / 10 fish), thermometer, bubbler and filter advisable	nothing necessary — gravel, pebbles	standard fish food (check pet store for special care of tropical fish)	no direct sun; room temperature, avoid sudden changes	need little attention, interesting to watch, guppies breed fast	chlorine and dissolved copper salts from tap may contaminate water — run water 1 hour before filling tank
birds*	metal bird cage, some Plexiglas or glass sides to protect from drafts	gravel on paper	bird seed — obtain care booklet at purchase of bird	warm, light — avoid drafts	need little care, become tame	many birds are unable to accept classroom environments

*(We recommend bird-watching outdoors rather than caging this unique creature!)

cages and containers

rolled screen cages—for insects

Most people we know who do much with insects or animals like to build their own cages. If you have more than one or two creatures it gets expensive to buy a lot of cages, and since the urge to make homes for creatures has a way of descending on you *right now,* you're not likely to have the money available so urgently. Also, kids can and should build these if they are going to be responsible for the animals' care.

Any size is possible, as determined by diameters of either tops or bottoms. An eight- or nine-inch pie plate diameter and approximately ten inches of screen height makes a handy size for most insects and creatures up to one inch in length.

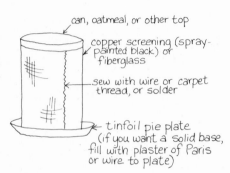

can, oatmeal, or other top

copper screening (spray-painted black) or fiberglass

sew with wire or carpet thread, or solder

← tinfoil pie plate
(if you want a solid base, fill with plaster of Paris or wire to plate)

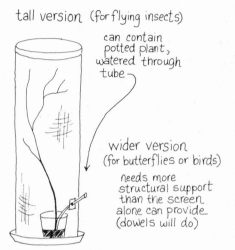

tall version (for flying insects)

can contain potted plant, watered through tube

wider version
(for butterflies or birds)

needs more structural support than the screen alone can provide
(dowels will do)

rolled screen cages—for larger animals

This is probably the fastest cage to build, if not the cheapest for its (possible) size. We estimate that, with materials on hand, the whole thing could be built within a half hour; cutting the screening to size and sewing its ends together are the only tasks involved. It also has the virtue of being quickly dismantled for cleaning or storage.

These cages can be made as tall as you want, and allow space for developing maze-ways and climbing apparatus that delight rodents and children equally.

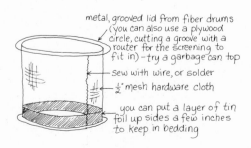

metal, grooved lid from fiber drums (you can also use a plywood circle, cutting a groove with a router for the screening to fit in) —try a garbage can top

Sew with wire, or solder

½" mesh hardware cloth

you can put a layer of tin foil up sides a few inches to keep in bedding

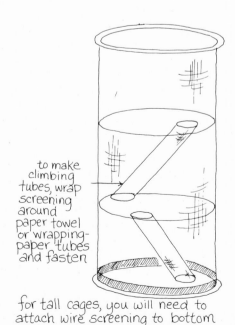

to make climbing tubes, wrap screening around paper towel or wrapping-paper tubes and fasten

for tall cages, you will need to attach wire screening to bottom

the ubiquitous aquarium

Clumsy, breakable, and expensive, fish tanks are nevertheless the most widely adaptable container for all manner of small animals (not to mention fish).

Since they come in a wide variety of sizes, you can find one suitable for almost any type of creature or environment described on these pages. Slightly broken ones (there always seems to be one not too far away) are still highly useful for anything but aquariums, and not so hard to fix if most of the glass is still in place (see repair information at right).

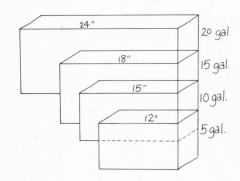

To make a transparent container of any other size, you can glue together quarter-inch Plexiglas sheets with clear cement or model airplane glue. A less secure box can be simply taped together. Moisture-seal it with melted pitch (tar), beeswax (not paraffin), or epoxy glue. Completed box should be able to hold up to an inch of water.

A clear cement (Weldit or epoxy glue) applied on both sides seals cracks

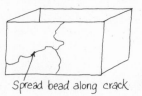

Spread bead along crack

For holes, cut a piece of glass or Plexiglas that covers within 1″ of hole's edges. Spread clear cement under surface of patch.

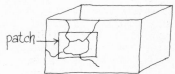

patch

Replacing one side with Plexiglas, screening, or even wood is satisfactory for cages that don't need a high bed of dirt or shavings

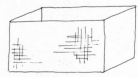

eight other varieties . . .

Hand-Built Types

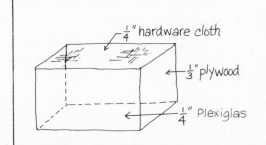

any flat top
screening
plastic dishpan

can hold
mice and other small rodents temporarily

materials
plastic dishpan, 12″ × 10″ × 8″
window screening or hardware cloth
Plexiglas or other flat material, 14″ × 12″

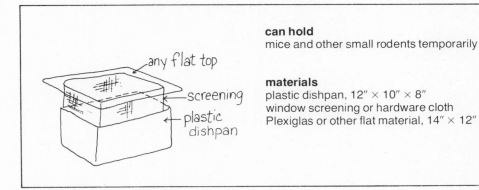

$\frac{1}{4}$″ hardware cloth
$\frac{1}{3}$″ plywood
$\frac{1}{4}$″ Plexiglas

can hold
small rodents, snakes, other reptiles

materials
1/3″ plywood
1/4″ or 1/8″ Plexiglas
1/4″ hardware cloth

can hold
rabbits, guinea pigs

materials
1/4" hardware cloth
dowels or sticks, height of cage
newspaper

can hold
insects, snakes, spiders

materials
1- or 2-gal. glass jar (hard to find as they're
    being replaced by plastic — try hotels or
    caterers)
netting for cover

can hold
small rodents, guinea pigs

materials
child's plastic swimming pool
1/4" hardware cloth
newspaper

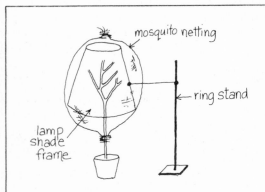

mosquito netting

ring stand

lamp shade frame

can hold
flying insects, spiders

materials
large lamp-shade frame
mosquito netting, 3 yds.
ring stand
pot with plant or branch

Commercial Types

2 oz. bottle
removable cover

can hold
gerbils, other small rodents, fish

description
plastic cage (14½" × 10½" × 6½") with
    metal grill that snaps in; includes
    squeezable plastic water bottle — ver-
    satile and inexpensive

source
Selective Educational Equipment (SEE)
3 Bridge Street, Newton, MA 02195
$7.50

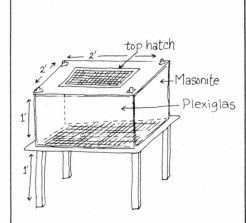

top hatch
Masonite
Plexiglas

can hold
small animals in "wild" environment

description
½" birch ply with 2 sides Masonite, 2 sides
    Plexiglas; screened top hatch; available
    with or without legs, also 2' × 4' size

source
Workshop for Learning Things
5 Bridge Street, Watertown, MA 02172
$42.50 (with legs)

activities

The following ideas for animal study have been included to give you an idea of the tremendous range of activities and exploration possible. Your children may think of many more.

gerbils, for example

The following is a projected series of topics and activities related to gerbils that might develop as a result of keeping a gerbil in home or classroom. Similar charts could be made for any animal or experience with animals.

Habitat (Desert)

Gerbils come from the Mongolian desert — can your child find it on a map or globe? Make a desert environment in an old aquarium. Put in small desert plants such as cacti. Use dirt and watch your gerbil make tunnels — at least six inches of dirt will be necessary.

Have your child watch and look at the gerbil carefully. How many toes does it have? Are front and back legs or feet different? How? How are they used? Make paw prints of the gerbil using a stamp pad, then compare them to prints or tracks found outdoors. Does the gerbil leave tracks of all its paws? How can you tell whether it was hopping or jumping from its track? Measure the distance between prints; can you find any patterns?

Activity and Growth

Measure the gerbil each day or once a week for a month or two. Make a bar graph showing the results. How fast is your gerbil growing? Is its growth regular or erratic? Does growth seem to stop at any particular age? Compare the growth of two or more gerbils. Try measuring both length and girth; can you find a relationship? Does a more active gerbil stay "slimmer"?

If They Have Babies

Have your child keep a journal of the babies' growth, behavior, and learning patterns. Each entry should be dated and supplemented with pictures drawn by the child. When were they born? How did they look? What day did they start exploring the cage?

Learn the differences between male and female. Have your child watch gerbils mating. How long before you can notice pregnancy? Did the mother gerbil's behavior change? How? How long before babies are born? Take notes on all observations.

What are parental roles?
How quickly do they learn?
Which types of behavior are instinctual?
Can you make a graph of growth?

The Curious Gerbils
Elementary Science Study

McGraw-Hill Book Company
1221 Avenue of the Americas
New York, New York 10020
75¢

This is a delightful little book for children. It contains some basic information, but mostly questions and ideas to stimulate a child's curiosity and encourage inquiry-oriented activity.

Feeding

Compare amount eaten with weight of the gerbil; weigh before and after feeding.

Discuss possible different foods gerbils like or might like. Have your child predict the gerbil's preferences, then put a bit of each kind on a table or in the cage and watch what it does. Which food did the gerbil pick first? Were any foods totally ignored?

Does a gerbil find food by sight or smell? Can you devise an experiment to find out? Try putting the food in a see-through plastic bag and a smell-through paper bag.

more animal activities

Try creating imaginary animals (or combinations of animals) — with drawings, written descriptions, adventures, and so forth.

Listen to and make up animal songs, such as "Three Blind Mice" or "I went to the animal fair . . ." or "Old Mac-Donald."

Read *Aesop's Fables* or Kipling's *Just So Stories;* have your kids make up their own animal fables and legends.

You can obtain ant farms from biological supply houses — make sure you get a queen. Ants may be inactive or die in winter.

Personal Writing Idea

1. Make a guinea pig journal by stapling paper together. Decorate it if you want.

2. Take the guinea pig to a table. Draw a picture of it on a separate page of your guinea pig journal.

3. Take the guinea pig out of its pen and let it move around on a table top. Look at it VERY CLOSELY and write down EVERYTHING you notice about how it looks. Make a list of all the words you can think of to describe how your guinea pig looks. Write them in journal.

Here are some language activities that can apply to any animal

birds

Bird-watching can be a fascinating hobby for young and old alike. The Audubon Society (see page 33) has a wealth of information on birds — pictures, books, study prints, and so on — and keeps track of local organizations and bird-watching activities. The Examining Your Environment series (see page 28) has the best general information on studying birds with kids that we've seen in book form.

Making a bird feeder and putting it up in your backyard will attract several local varieties, and it can be particularly interesting to watch seasonal changes of bird populations in your area. Most bird-watchers keep track of the birds they see, and often you'll even get to "know" individual birds!

Simple Feeders You Can Make

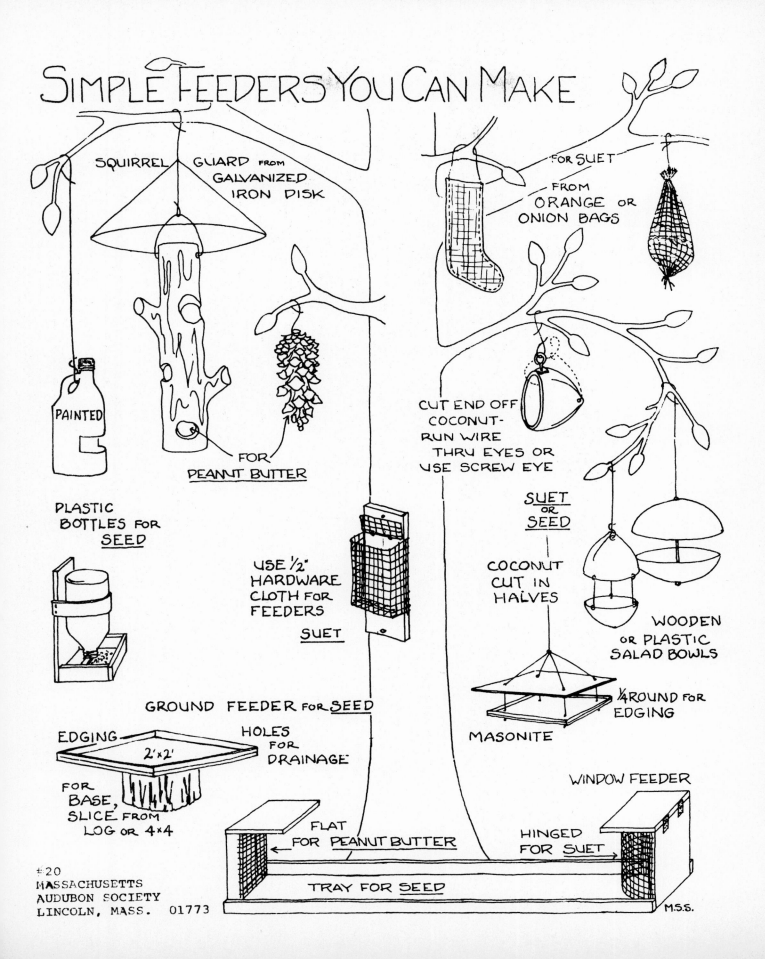

SQUIRREL GUARD FROM GALVANIZED IRON DISK

FOR SUET FROM ORANGE OR ONION BAGS

PAINTED

FOR PEANUT BUTTER

CUT END OFF COCONUT— RUN WIRE THRU EYES OR USE SCREW EYE

PLASTIC BOTTLES FOR SEED

USE ½" HARDWARE CLOTH FOR FEEDERS

SUET

SUET OR SEED

COCONUT CUT IN HALVES

WOODEN OR PLASTIC SALAD BOWLS

¼ ROUND FOR EDGING

MASONITE

GROUND FEEDER FOR SEED

EDGING

2'×2'

HOLES FOR DRAINAGE

FOR BASE, SLICE FROM LOG OR 4×4

WINDOW FEEDER

FLAT FOR PEANUT BUTTER

HINGED FOR SUET

TRAY FOR SEED

#20
MASSACHUSETTS AUDUBON SOCIETY
LINCOLN, MASS. 01773

M.S.S.

activity books

Animals Are Like This
Irving Leskowitz and A. Harris Stone

Prentice-Hall
Educational Book Division
Englewood Cliffs, New Jersey 07632
$3.95

This is a book of experiments on small animals, primarily insects. It asks such questions as, "What happens to an earthworm's rate of breathing when the temperature of its surroundings changes? How would you find out which foods and flavors flies are attracted to? How do ants find their way from place to place?" — and gives suggestions of experiments to answer them, as well as background information.

This is one of a series of inquiry-oriented science books written by A. Harris Stone (see page 91 for other titles). It is a great source of ideas for teachers and students interested in challenging investigations of animal behavior.

Discovering Nature Indoors: A Nature and Science Guide to Investigations with Small Animals
Laurence Pringle, editor

The Natural History Press
501 Franklin Avenue
Garden City, New York 11530
$4.95

This collection of "Science Workshop" articles from *Nature and Science* magazine contains a rich supply of project ideas and general information on a variety of common but rarely studied animals. Among other things, it tells how to set up a saltwater aquarium, how to catch and study houseflies and cockroaches, and how to start a "school" for mice. It also has a handy listing of biological supply houses for those interested in obtaining unusual animals, cocoons, and so on.

The following authors have contributed several good animal-study books for children. They may be found in most school and/or public libraries.

George F. Mason

Animal Baggage	*Animal Tails*
Animal Clothing	*Animal Teeth*
Animal Habits	*Animal Tools*
Animal Homes	*Animal Tracks*
Animal Sounds	*Animal Weapons*

Richly illustrated with sketches of animals in their natural habitats, this series of books is a treasure trove of detailed information about almost any aspect of animal behavior or physical characteristics. Each book is written in a concise, easy-to-read style for upper elementary age children.

Millicent E. Selsam

Egg to Chick
All Kinds of Babies
Questions and Answers about Ants
Is This a Baby Dinosaur?
Hidden Animals

These are just a few titles that we are familiar with and especially like; Ms. Selsam has written more than forty-five science books for young children (see page 63 for suggested titles on plants). Most of the books we've seen are profusely illustrated and written for beginning readers.

Seymour Simon

Discovering What Earthworms Do
Discovering What Frogs Do
Discovering What Gerbils Do
Discovering What Goldfish Do

Each of these books contains suggestions and ideas for independent activity or study, as well as general information on care. The books are readable from about age seven and are inquiry oriented:

Listen for noises that gerbils make. Do they make any noise when they gnaw at food or other things in the cage? Do they make any noise when they dig or scratch? Do they squeak at all? In what position do your gerbils rest or sleep? Do they sleep and rest in the same spot every day? Do they ever sleep in the center of the cage?

Dorothy E. Shuttlesworth

All Kinds of Bees
Animal Camouflage
Dodos and Dinosaurs
Gerbils and Other Small Pets

Dorothy Shuttlesworth is the author of several nature books for children. They are primarily information oriented, well illustrated, and written for upper elementary ages.

developed units [ESS]

These units, developed by the Elementary Science Study (ESS), are an excellent starting point for the investigation of animal behavior. Children are encouraged to make discoveries based upon observation and experiments created to answer their own questions.

A teacher's guide is available for each unit. These guides give background information and suggest several open-ended activities; they are a valuable resource for any adult interested in sharing a child's exploration of a particular animal.

A complete list of ESS units, including information on sources and accompanying materials, can be found on pages 34–39.

unit title	notes
Animal Activity	using activity wheels with rodents
Animals in the Classroom	a teacher's journal of activities with gerbils and desert lizards
Behavior of Mealworms	
Bones	Mystery Bones and *Bone Picture Book* are especially good for young children
Brine Shrimp	life cycle from hatching
Butterflies	metamorphosis of the monarch
Crayfish	a fascinating creature, very common in freshwater ponds
Earthworms	
Eggs and Tadpoles	excellent film loops available
Mosquitoes	
Pond Water	kids love this!
Small Things	investigations with a microscope
Tracks	outdoor sleuthing

magazines

Ranger Rick

National Wildlife

International Wildlife

*National Wildlife Federation
1412 Sixteenth Street, NW
Washington, D.C. 20036*

The best argument for using magazines with kids who are studying animals is that they provide a source of good pictures that can be cut out, pasted, or posted for display. Decorating their rooms with lovable seals and fierce wildcats comes naturally to the kids we know, as does gluing rabbits into the illustration pages of a story notebook, and there are innumerable ways to use animal photos in a classroom.

The best-quality glossies we've seen are in these National Wildlife Federation publications, which are recommendable for a lot of other reasons too.

Ranger Rick is the edition for kids. It rates fairly high just as a magazine, regardless of animal interests. The prose is appropriate and devoid of that syrupy condescending tone that infects many publications for kids, especially animal copy. There is dramatized animal fiction that you don't mind reading yourself, and superb illustrations, nonphoto as well as photo. It is low (gratefully) on busywork as well.

organizations and places to go

A visit to a *zoo* will give your children an exciting experience with animals of much greater variety than is possible in home or classroom. It is sure to stimulate drawing and writing activities, and comparisons with familiar pets — for instance, a domesticated cat compared with lions and tigers. Are there differences other than size? How does zoo life compare with life in the wild? This kind of question might prompt a discussion of the humane care of animals and inquiry into zoo facilities. If possible, call ahead and find out when the animals are fed and if you can talk with a zookeeper that likes kids!

A trip to an *animal hospital* or a *veterinarian* will give children an understanding of specialized animal care. Try to find a vet who will talk with children, answer their questions, and perhaps show them how he or she gives a shot.

What Can She Be? A Veterinarian
Gloria and Esther Goldreich

*Lothrop, Lee and Shepard
105 Madison Avenue
New York, New York 10016
$3.95*

We have chosen this book to review primarily because it helps to counteract the stereotype of male doctors that children are exposed to. In this well-illustrated book, written in easy-to-read language, the reader finds out about "Dr. Penny": how she decided to become a veterinarian, what she does during a day, and how she enjoys her work.

Science and *natural history museums* often have permanent and/or rotating displays of animals. Some, such as the Museum of Science in Boston, have live animal exhibits and talks for children. See page 33 for other organizations that are good sources of information about animals.

Several other sources for information or possible places to visit are listed in your trusty *Yellow Pages*. The kinds of places will vary from one part of the country to another, but the following will give you an idea of the possibilities:

aquariums, hatcheries, fish stores, wholesale fish and seafood suppliers or packers, docks
cattle farms, pig farms, poultry farms and breeders, slaughterhouses
university laboratories (where in-depth experimental activities on live animals might be taking place)
pet stores and dealers, ASPCA and local chapters

Chris Guttmacher

plants

Discovering the green world is a fascinating experience for adults and children alike — whether it comes from opening up a seed to find out "what's inside," admiring the shape and color and texture of an eggplant at the supermarket, or watching a fern frond unfurl in the woods. Although sharing a tidbit of information or learning to identify plants adds a special thrill to your discoveries, it is more important to encourage an attitude of awareness, appreciation, wonder, and curiosity in yourself and your children.

activities

**Make a
Collection
of Seeds**

Compare size, shape, texture, color
Make rattles, mosaics, jewelry

Play seed games
  Jacks
  Kalah

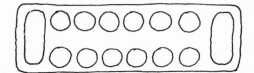

How many?
  Sort, weigh, measure, and count them

What kinds of seeds do we eat?
  How many seeds are in one fruit?
  Are they all the same size?

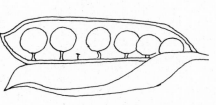

What is a seed?
  Open one up — can you find the tiny embryo inside?
  Will the embryo grow without the seed coating?

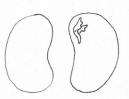

Growing Seeds

Have kids design their own experiments

  Will it grow in the dark?
  How much water is necessary? Optimum? How much water is too much?

Do small seeds grow into small plants?

Keep a record of the plant's growth

  Dig up the seed after a day or two — are there any changes?
  Measure the plant daily; make a graph with strips of paper

Have a "seed race"

  Which "breaks ground" first?
  Which grows fastest? Tallest?
  Which has the most leaves?

Adapted from *Living Things in Field and Classroom* (pages 74–80, see page 27 for review), this chart suggests questions to stimulate kids' observations of plants found outdoors.

flowers
Is it a single flower? A cluster of flowers?
What color is it?
What does it smell like?
Can you find any pollen? Seeds?

fungi
Where is it growing? What is it growing on?
What color(s) is it? What's inside?

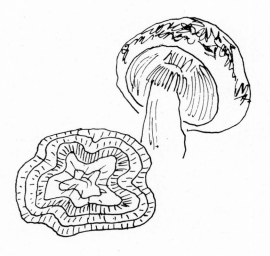

fruits
What is it? What's inside?
How is it attached to the plant?

galls
What is it attached to? Is there anything inside? Is there a hole in it?

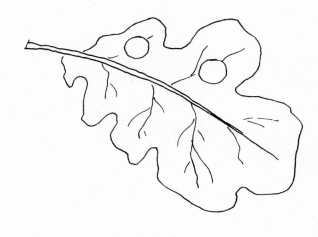

leaves
What shape is it? Are the edges smooth, wavy, or jagged? Does it have lobes or points? Are there hairs on it? Are there holes or marks on it? What do you think made them?

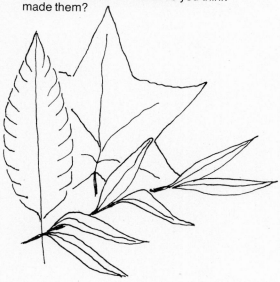

roots
Where do they grow? How long are they? Compare their length to the height of the plant. What shape are they?

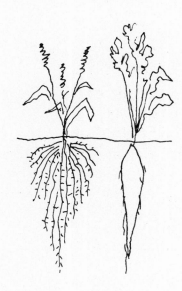

seed pods
What shape is it? How does it open? Can you find one already open? How does it look different? What is its color, texture, and hardness? What's inside?

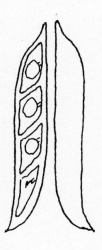

twigs
Are there any buds or leaves? How are they arranged? Can you find any scars? What do you think caused them? What's inside the bark? How many layers?

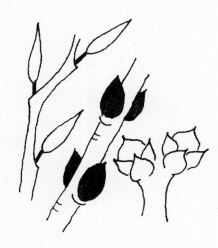

Terrarium making is an ever-popular project with children of all ages. *Living Things in Field and Classroom* (see page 27 for review) has an excellent description of terrariums, how to keep plants healthy, and a lot of general information on indoor gardening with kids; the following is a reprint of pages 12–14.

THE TERRARIUM

A terrarium is a covered transparent container planted with a miniature community of plants. It needs little attention and is quite easy to make. Several small ones may be more useful than one large one. Children enjoy making their own terraria in plastic boxes or peanut butter jars. Three types of terraria are described here.

In order to make any terrarium you will need:

I. A glass or plastic container. (Anything from a peanut butter jar to a large aquarium will do. A plastic shoe box is especially handy.) Your container should be deep enough to allow some headroom for the plants to grow in.

2. A removable transparent cover. (Glass or plastic wrap will do.)

3. Drainage material, such as sand or gravel.

4. Soil.

5. Plants and seeds.

MOIST WOODLAND TERRARIUM

This is probably the most useful kind for keeping small plants such as ferns, mosses and fungi, and for rooting cuttings.

Put a half-inch layer of sand or gravel or a mixture of both in the bottom of your container for drainage. Add one inch of moist soil. This should preferably be in the proportions of one-third soil, one-third sand and one-third peat moss or humus, but ordinary garden or potting soil will do. (The soil should be moist enough to cling together in balls when pressed in the hand.)

Make holes in the soil, gently insert the roots of the plants, and press the soil around them. A carpet of moss around the plant keeps the soil from spattering. Sprinkle carefully with water and cover almost all the way with glass or plastic.

Adjust the lid so that a little but not much moisture collects on it. Water only when the soil appears dry, once a week or less. Unless the lid is open, keep the terrarium out of direct sunlight because it will overheat.

Appropriate plants for a woodland terrarium are mosses and shelf fungi, ferns, small house plants or cuttings of ivy, begonia, coleus, or tradescantia, or seeds of different kinds. As plants get too large, prune them or replace them. If you can get woodland soil and moss in your terrarium, watch for surprises as old woodland plants die and new ones appear.

In early spring plant a terrarium with any young plants that are just beginning to appear. Their rapid growth in the warm room will be spectacular. Young violet plants, wild ginger, emerging scillas, small weeds or moss and young seedlings can be used. It is also interesting to place a piece of old log or a spadeful of garden soil in a terrarium and water it. In a few days you will have an interesting assortment of young plants and small animals. Encourage the children to study them with magnifiers.

DESERT TERRARIUM

This kind is easier to keep than a woodland terrarium, but not as much happens in it. Use moist soil mixed with an equal part of sand over the drainage layer. Small cacti and some succulents such as jade plants, hens and chicks, and aloe will grow under these conditions. (Handle the cacti with tweezers or gloves.) After the plants are in place the soil should be kept evenly moist until the roots are established, but never add so much water that you can see any standing in little pools. From then on water sparingly, perhaps once a week, so that the surface of the soil remains fairly dry. Keep in a sunny spot and do not add a lid. A wire screen can be put over the top if an animal (such as a horned toad) is to be housed in the desert terrarium.

BOG TERRARIUM

The bog terrarium is especially interesting because insect-eating plants can be grown in it. Put in the drainage layer, then a layer of sphagnum moss. No soil is necessary. Order materials and plants for a bog terrarium from a biological supply house, unless you are near a natural bog. Keep it cool, covered almost all the way, and well lighted. Keep the gravel layer under water all the time.

There are many modifications of terraria. Large woodland ones can be made with a sloped drainage layer and a bog or shallow pool at one end. They present many opportunities for artistic creativity in addition to their biological uses.

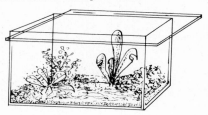

resource books

The Elementary Science Study (ESS) has several units that deal with plants and seed growth — Growing Seeds, Life of Beans and Peas, and Starting from Seeds. (See pages 34–39 for sources and related materials.) Each teacher's guide contains a wealth of involving activity ideas, suggested experiments, and background information.

Seeing What Plants Do
Joan Elma Rahn

Atheneum Press
122 East 42nd Street
New York, New York 10017
$4.95

This delightful children's book is chockfull of simple experiments on growing plants that need only basic household materials. It also contains valuable information on plant parts and is well illustrated with clear line drawings.

Plants Are Like That
A. Harris Stone and Irving Leskowitz

Prentice-Hall
Educational Book Division
Englewood Cliffs, New Jersey 07632
$4.25

One of a series of books by A. Harris Stone (see page 91 for review), this title suggests a variety of experiments for older kids to discover some of the chemical and physical processes that take place in plants. Using simple, household materials for the experiments, kids will find out ways plants obtain and use food and energy, how they grow, what they do with water, and how they use light. *Plants Are Like That* is full of intriguing information, clearly written, and well illustrated with line drawings.

Millicent E. Selsam

Plants That Heal
Plants That Move
Play with Plants
Play with Seeds
The Plants We Eat

William Morrow and Company
Lothrop, Lee and Shepard
105 Madison Avenue
New York, New York 10016

There are lots of good books for kids on plants — check your local library for those that appeal to you and your children. Of these, Ms. Selsam's books are some of the best we've seen. They are full of fascinating information and easily understandable, well-illustrated activity ideas and experiments.

Green Fun
Maryanne Gjersvik

The Chatham Press
15 Wilmot Lane
Riverside, Connecticut 06878
$1.95

Snapdragon puppets, a grass whistle, the peanut elf, and a daisy wreath are only a few of the engaging "toys, tricks and amusements" in this little book. Simply written with lovely photographs, *Green Fun* is a treasure that will be enjoyed by children and adults alike!

trees

The Tree Identification Book
George W. D. Symonds

William Morrow and Company
105 Madison Avenue
New York, New York 10016
$5.95

With this incredible volume, you can identify almost any tree in the country during any season of the year, from its thorns, leaves, flowers, fruit, twigs and buds, bark or needles. It actually has detailed, life-size photographs of nine different kinds of acorn!

This book and its companion volume, *The Shrub Identification Book,* are the most comprehensive, uniquely useful, and downright essential books on the subjects that we've come across.

City Leaves, City Trees
Edward Gallob

Charles Scribner's Sons
597 Fifth Avenue
New York, New York 10017
$6.50

This beautiful photographic identification book is a handy guide to trees commonly found in the city. Written and illustrated by the author of *City Rocks, City Blocks and the Moon* (see page 70 for review), this book shows the same superb sense of appreciation for the beauty of nature in a typical concrete environment!

Trees
Science 5/13 Project Team

Purnell Educational
850 Seventh Avenue
New York, New York 10019
(in sets of 6)

Children's Museum
The Jamaicaway
Boston, Massachusetts 02130
(single copies)

Full of literally hundreds of excellent activity ideas, this book is an unusually comprehensive "unit for teachers." It is classroom oriented and includes, with typical British thoroughness, notes on getting started, objectives, materials recommended, and so on.

Nevertheless, it is a marvelous resource! With activities organized by season, it suggests exploring leaf litter, making surveys, measuring and even planting

Nina

trees, investigating pollution, discovering animal communities dependent on trees, and much more. (See page 91 for review of the complete Science 5/13 series.)

Trees
Examining Your Environment

Winston Press
25 Groveland Terrace
Minneapolis, Minnesota 55403
$3

"Measuring Green Giants," "Be a Branch Manager," "Out on a Limb," and "Using Old Christmas Trees" are just a few of the intriguing chapter titles in this excellent book. It is directed at upper elementary children and therefore uses very readable, straightforward language to give background information as well as to suggest activities. Visually exciting, it is profusely illustrated with dramatic photographs and clear drawings, cartoons, and diagrams.

Suggested activities include investigations with bark, measuring the height and circumference of trees (with directions for making your own instruments), dissecting twigs, discovering patterns in leaves, and lots more. Its fourteen-page "key to common trees" is a handy "extra." (See page 28 for review of the Examining Your Environment series.)

Oct 2
all my rubbing
went up and down
Gordon

Oct. 2, 1974
Joanne
the tree is about
it's wide 6 fists
in high to the leaf part.
I took a leaf from two
parts of the tree and
they don't look exactly
the same at all.

Oct 3. 1974
The slanted trees
leafe is much biger than
the apple trees is. Gordon
Oct. 4, 1974
I made rubbings
of the apple tree
and the slanted tree
you can tell that
the apple tree
bark is much
moor apart then
the slanted.

9/25/74
The orange things on the branch get a little sticky after
exposed to sun light. We found
them 9/24/74.
we fand a branch of. Red dots
and orange dots. When I put water on
Red dots they shrunk and
when I put water on the orange dot
thay grow Greg

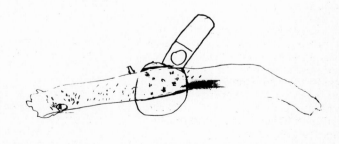

dandelions

Lions in the Grass
Phyllis S. Busch

World Publishing Company
2231 West 110th Street
Cleveland, Ohio 44102
$4.50

Clearly and simply, with superb photographs, this delightful book tells "all about" dandelions in language easy to read and understand. It encourages young children to explore and discover the fascinating world of nature for themselves through an appreciation of this common, hardy plant. We recently discovered that this lovely book is out of print, so check your libraries for it!

Did you know . . .

that the dandelion seeds can germinate (sprout) even after soaking in a salty ocean for twenty-eight days?

that the Russian dandelion yields sufficient latex (milky juice) for it to be used as a source of rubber?

that the dandelion was once the official remedy for illness that came on in winter?

that the dandelion has a vitamin A content twenty-five times that of tomato juice and fifty times that of asparagus?

that the dandelion plant does not have a stem?

that the dandelion has a milky juice that is given out when it is wounded and that, like blood, congeals to form a protective scab?

— adapted from *The Dandelion,* page 20

Dandelion, Pokeweed, and Goosefoot
Elizabeth Schaeffer

Young Scott Books
Addison-Wesley Publishing Company
Reading, Massachusetts 01867

Do you know where to look for a plant to cure a cough, to ease a stomachache, or to polish a pot? This interesting, attractively illustrated book describes the uses and origins of many plants on which the early settlers depended for their food and medicine.

The writing style is clear and easily understandable. Directions on starting an herb garden, collecting and drying plants, making teas and salads, and dyeing cloth complete the book — making it a resource for activity ideas as well as for choice tidbits of historical information.

The Dandelion
Examining Your Environment

Winston Press
25 Groveland Terrace
Minneapolis, Minnesota 55403

The dandelion plant is often called a weed, but in some parts of the world it is a cultivated crop and the early colonists brought it to America as an essential food and medicine. Personally, I have always welcomed its cheery yellow appearance along with robins and pussy willows as a sure sign of spring!

This book, one of the excellent Examining Your Environment series (see page 28), is full of fascinating information and hundreds of stimulating activity ideas. Included are close observations of the plant's structure (its flower stem is hollow!) and ways to study "dandelion populations." A selection of myths and poems, directions for making coffee or dye from the dandelion's root, and dandelion curls or whistles from the flower stems, make this book a real favorite!

gardening with kids

CHILDREN & PARENTS GARDENING TOGETHER
By Alice Skelsey & Gloria Huckaby

INDOORS   OUTDOORS

Growing Up Green
Alice Skelsey and Gloria Huckaby

Workman Publishing Company
231 East 51st Street
New York, New York 10022
$4.95

Gardening is caught — not taught. Enjoy!

— *Growing Up Green*, page 19

information and guidelines on exploring the green world of growing things with kids. To keep interest up and weeds down, it even suggests keeping a log of the kinds of weeds found!

One of the most attractive qualities of *Growing Up Green* is its emphasis on kids and adults working, discovering, and sharing the experience of gardening together. It contains a delightful blend of detailed information (like how to fertilize your garden with scraps from the kitchen) with ways to enjoy the pure sensory pleasures of nature. The book's writing style flows beautifully, its drawings and photographs are appealing, and it is chock-full of fascinating garden activities.

The surest way for a child to grow up green is to be exposed to parents [and teachers!] who are still growing green. . . . What you hope your child [ren] will gain along with you is an enthusiastic, easy awareness that comes from day-to-day encounters with nature.

— *Growing Up Green*, pages 9–13

Start with a beautiful day and discover what to do until the seeds come up! This lovely, marvelously warm book is almost surprisingly full of practical, down-to-earth

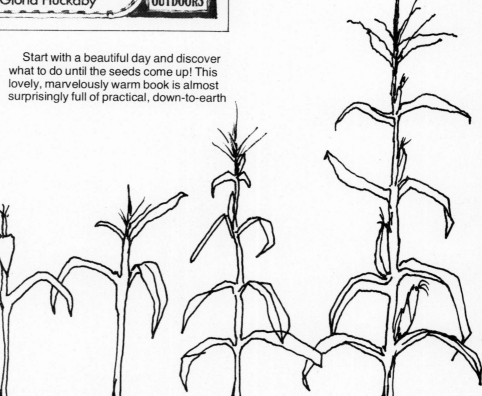

The Organic Living Book
Bernice Kohn

The Viking Press
625 Madison Avenue
New York, New York 10022
$1.25

Written in a clear, straightforward style and addressed to children as well as to adults, this is a lovely introduction to the hows and whys of organic foods and gardening. It contains recipes as well as basic gardening information, and is nicely illustrated with simple line drawings.

"Learn to Be a Label-Looker" and "You Just Might Learn to Love Yoghurt" are two of my favorite chapters — mostly because you don't even have to be a gardener to enjoy and learn from the activities!

First, scrub the carrots well, but leave the skins on.
Grate them into a big bowl.
Mix in a couple of handfuls of raisins.
Squeeze the juice from a lemon over the mixture. (Use only half a lemon if you don't have many carrots.)
Pour some honey or corn syrup over the salad until it tastes just right.

— *Kids Are Natural Cooks,* page 13

See pages 102–104 for more good recipes for kids.

carrot salad

our planet earth

The earth is always changing. Rocks are being formed, islands are appearing and disappearing, land is eroding, and the continents themselves are drifting apart. There are so many factors involved in these changes, ongoing for billions of years, that it is difficult to grasp the immensity of the process.

The books and activities recommended in this section attempt to give children a feel for this natural, continuing process of change. Through an increasing awareness of the natural phenomena surrounding them — the pattern in a rock, climate changes reflected in the rings of a tree, living fossils like the horseshoe crab — children will learn to appreciate and value the uniqueness of our small planet and the interdependence of all nature throughout its history.

It is only a little planet
But how beautiful it is . . .
— *Robinson Jeffers*

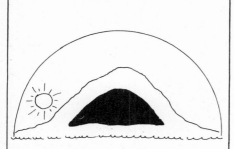

Babylonians, who lived around 3000 B.C., thought the earth was a hollow mountain supported and surrounded by the sea. Inside the mountain was the dark world of the dead. The sun, moon, and stars moved across the solid curve of the sky.

Egyptians believed that the earth was a resting god and the sky was a goddess bending over it. Between them sat the god of the air, supporting the sky. The sun god sailed in his boat each day across the sky.

rocks

City Rocks, City Blocks and the Moon
Edward Gallob

Charles Scribner's Sons
597 Fifth Avenue
New York, New York 10017
$5.95

Geology is people, plants and animals living together on this earth. Geology is mountains and tall buildings, muddy city rivers, and rain water running down a city street; dust storms, and the wind blowing sand and leaves across a city park. Geology is looking for fossils in old rocks as a record of ancient life, or your dog's footprints in today's wet-cement sidewalk (pages 6–7).

This beautiful book makes geology a living study. Its simple text and superb photographs will inspire adults and children alike to take a closer look at city rocks — a tree breaking through the pavement, mica crystals in the walls of a school building, rain and frost eroding words from a gravestone, marble statues. . . . It tells you where to look for and how to identify all kinds of rock, whether granite curbstones or fossil-rich limestone; and gives basic, easy-to-understand information on its formation.

Rocks and Rills: A Look at Geology
A. Harris Stone and Dale Ingmanson

Prentice-Hall
Educational Book Division
Englewood Cliffs, New Jersey 07632
$3.95

"What makes a rock fracture? Perhaps frying a marble will help you find out." *Rocks and Rills* suggests a wide variety of experiments that can be done with simple household materials to understand the forces behind the process of geological change. It is one of a series of science books by A. Harris Stone (see page 91).

Secrets in Stones
Rose Wyler and Gerald Ames

Scholastic Book Services
906 Sylvan Avenue
Englewood Cliffs, New Jersey 07632
60¢

This small paperback is the nicest rock book we've seen for young kids. The photos are excellent, and the text is informative as well as easy to read and understand. It contains lots of basic information on rock formation and suggests several simple activities related to observation and collection of stones.

The Young Experimenters' Workbook: Treasures of the Earth
Harry and Laura Sootin

W. W. Norton and Company
55 Fifth Avenue
New York, New York 10003
$3.54

This delightful children's book is chockfull of suggested experiments and activities, plus easy-to-read descriptions of a wide variety of rocks. (See page 114 for other titles by Harry Sootin.)

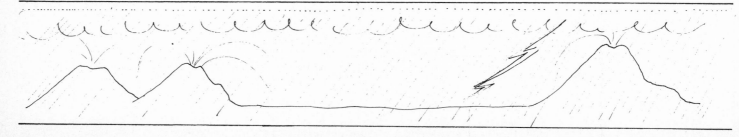

Rocks are scaled in hardness from 1 (very soft) to 10 (very hard). To test the hardness of a stone, try scratching your fingernail (which is 2.5 on the scale), a steel knife blade (5.5), or glass (6.0). A rock will scratch anything not as hard as it is.

how hard is it ?

How many different ways can you sort your collection of rocks and stones?

what size, color, or shape is it ?

Put a small stone in a bag, or wrap it in a cloth. Set it on a rock and hit it with a hammer or a hard, heavy stone. Is the stone all one color inside?

what's inside?

Write or tell a story about one of your stones. What kind is it? How was it formed? How did it get to where you found it? How old is it? Stretch your imagination — be the stone and tell about your feelings!

make a collection of rocks

leaf fossils

Some of your rocks might contain fossils, which are simply pieces or prints of plants and animals imbedded in the stone when it was formed. Look in sandstone, limestone, and shale.

fossils

make a crystal

If a rock is made of crystals, it was once a liquid! Dissolve some salt in warm water, then pour it into a jar (about half full). Tie a string on a stick and let the string hang in the water. Watch what happens in a few days, as the water evaporates. What shape are the crystals? Does changing the amount of salt change the size or shape of the crystals?

tumbling

No matter where you find them, all round stones were once in flowing water that tumbled them and made them smooth. Could you do what the water does? Take a handful of sharp-edged stones; put them in a box and tumble them around. Shake the box for an hour — or a week if you can! How long do you think it would take to make a stone smooth?

make your own

Cover a leaf or shell with Vaseline and place it on a smooth surface. Place a circular strip of cardboard around it, securing it with clay. Mix and pour plaster of Paris over the object; when it hardens, lift it and remove the leaf or shell.

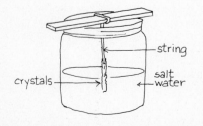
string
crystals
salt water

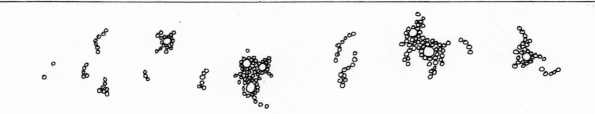

dirt

It is not every day that a volcano is born or an island disappears or an earthquake destroys a city. While the earth is constantly rearranging its features, most of its changes are through the slow and steady action of erosion. In a single year, over 600 million tons of clay, mud, mineral fragments, and tiny lumps of rock are carried down the Mississippi River and deposited in the Gulf of Mexico. Even the splash of a single raindrop on the soil counts for something in the remolding of the earth.

"Plant" a piece of string in a pot with rich, black dirt. After about a month, take the string out of the soil. What's happened to it?

Make some rocks very hot in a fire, and then pour cold water on them. What happens? How does this experiment help you to understand the formation of soil?

Obtain samples of soil from as many places as possible — swamps, hillsides, woods, meadows, dunes, river flats. Keep each sample separate. How do they differ? Compare color, particle sizes, density.

The Dirt Book
Eva Knox Evans

Little, Brown and Company
34 Beacon Street
Boston, Massachusetts 02106

A Handful of Soil
Seymour Simon

Hawthorn Books
260 Madison Avenue
New York, New York 10016

These two children's books explore one of the commonest, yet most vital, substances on earth. *The Dirt Book* tells the story of where it came from, how it was made, and why it's important to us; *A Handful of Soil* contains a wide variety of simple experiments and activities to find out what's in it. Both encourage children to investigate, observe carefully, and understand the interdependence of all living things with the earth under our feet.

weather

Mini-climates
Examining Your Environment

Winston Press
25 Groveland Terrace
Minneapolis, Minnesota 55403
$3.60

Mini-climates deals with the interrelationships of temperature, light, moisture, wind, and soil in a relatively small plot of earth, and their effect on plant and animal life. One of this book's nicest features is that it helps children to understand the tremendous complexity and variety of natural forces in a very "down-to-earth," immediate fashion in their own neighborhoods.

A few of the suggested activities are measuring air temperature at various heights above a lawn, recording the changing hours of daylight and darkness throughout the year, taking relative humidity readings with handmade instruments, making a feather wind vane, and studying the porosity of different soils. It is one of the excellent, visually exciting, and activity-rich books in the Examining Your Environment series (see page 28).

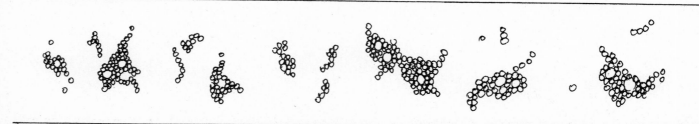

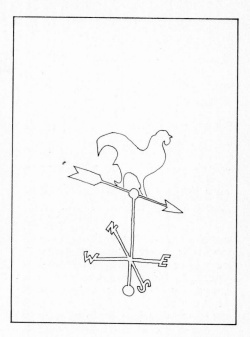

The Winds of Weather
A. Harris Stone and Herbert Spiegel

Prentice-Hall
Educational Book Division
Englewood Cliffs, New Jersey 07632
$3.95

"What is wind? How do you measure its speed? How does wind affect weather?" These are some of the questions that can be answered by reading and doing the experiments in this book. Simple household materials and scientific enthusiasm are all that is required for original research on how wind affects clouds, water, heat, land, and air pollution. One of a series of books by A. Harris Stone (see page 91), *The Winds of Weather* is written for upper elementary children and is clearly illustrated.

Listen to, watch, or read weather forecasts — on TV, radio, or in daily newspapers. Compare them. How often are they correct?

Make some of your own weather instruments. *Mini-climates* and *Outdoor Education Equipment* (see pages 72 and 30 for reviews) have excellent, clear directions for rain gauges, barometers, and other instruments.

Visit the U.S. Weather Bureau in your area (frequently located at the airport). Call ahead and see if you can get a guided tour.

Learn how to read a weather map. What do the symbols ∼∼◢ or Ⓗ mean? Make a map of your area, drawing in the daily changes, or purchase a chalkboard weather map of the United States from Instructo Corporation (Paoli, PA 19301) for $7.95.

Keep a record of the temperature with an outdoor thermometer. Take the temperature reading at the same time each day for a month and make a graph showing your results. Find out the highest and lowest temperatures for that month in your area from your local U.S. Weather Bureau.

the ocean

ABC's of the Ocean
Isaac Asimov

Walker and Company
720 Fifth Avenue
New York, New York 10019
$4.50

Did you know that "xiphosurus" is the scientific name for the horseshoe crab? Or that "hadal" is a word for the deepest parts of the ocean? In this fascinating book, Isaac Asimov defines two oceanographic terms for each letter of the alphabet — not all of them as unusual as the examples above! Each entry is clearly written, easily understandable, and illustrated with an excellent drawing or photograph.

This is the best general information book we've discovered on this subject. It is neither overwhelmingly complex and intimidating nor so simplified as to be condescending, and will delight adults and children alike.

The Life Nature Library and Our Living World of Nature series have volumes dealing with the ocean. They both have superb photographs of all kinds of marine plants and animals, as well as detailed information on the sea's formation, floor, currents, and so on. See page 32 for a list of the titles in each series and their sources.

The most accessible part of the ocean is, of course, a beach! In addition to the fun of playing in the sand and swimming, there are lots of fascinating discoveries that can be made in and around the ocean — especially on a beach at low tide or in the tide pools of a rocky coast.

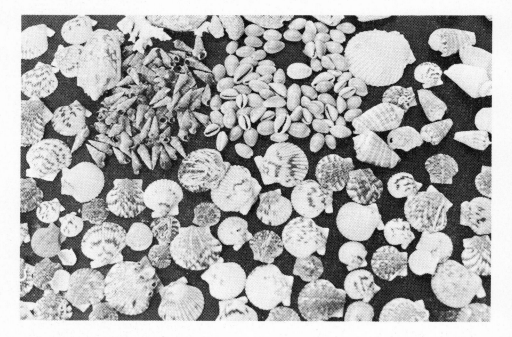

The Beachcomber's Book
Bernice Kohn

The Viking Press
625 Madison Avenue
New York, New York 10022
$1.25

This paperback children's book is chock-full of all kinds of craft ideas and interesting information based on the almost inevitable beach "treasures" that kids collect — from shells to seaweed.

It gives clear directions for sand painting, pebble mosaics, shell chimes and mobiles, beach plum jam, and bayberry candles! The line drawings are excellent, and some common shells and seaweeds are identified in a handy appendix.

Science on the Shores and Banks
Elizabeth K. Cooper

Harcourt Brace Jovanovich
757 Third Avenue
New York, New York 10017
60¢

Whether you want to explore a tide pool, become a "fish watcher," collect shells, or study some "crusty crustaceans," this book is for you! A relaxed style, cleanly drawn illustrations, fascinating experiments and activities, and intriguing information about the plant and animal life that abounds in, on, and near water make this an excellent resource. (See page 32 for other natural history titles by this author.)

The Art and Industry of Sand Castles
Jan Adkins

Walker and Company
720 Fifth Avenue
New York, New York 10019
$4.50

This book is a bit of beautiful magic! It encourages kids' (and adults'!) natural imaginings of life in medieval times, combining sundry tidbits of castle lore and practical sand-castle-building guidelines in a unique format. With wonderful wit, captivating drawings — both realistic and fanciful — and handwritten text, Jan Adkins has produced a truly delightful classic!

dinosaurs

Children of all ages are intrigued with dinosaurs. According to Herb Kohl, many young children

are obsessed with prehistoric animals. They love to play with plastic dinosaurs and in fantasy assume the size and power the creatures are supposed to have had. I think the fact that dinosaurs are extinct helps also, since real creatures could easily be lurking in a closet or in the woods or around the corner. Powerful extinct animals provide an ideal world for young children to experiment with power and violence and conflict.

—*Math, Writing, and Games,* page 100
(see our review on page 18)

Even older kids are fascinated by prehistoric creatures; building giant dinosaur models, learning all those long, complicated names, making books about them — all are tasks tackled with enthusiasm. Reflecting this ever-popular interest, there are lots of children's paperbacks available in bookstores — Scholastic Book Services (see page 298 for address) has at least six different titles on fossils, dinosaurs, or early man!

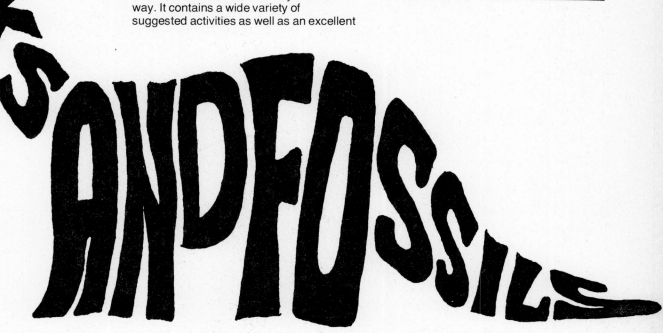

Science Teachers' Association of Ontario

*Donco Quality Printers
212 Division Street
Kingston, Ontario K7K 3Z1, CANADA
$2.83*

Rocks and Fossils is one of the best guides in this series from Canada (see page 28), interrelating the study of rocks, fossils, and dinosaurs in a very natural way. It contains a wide variety of suggested activities as well as an excellent collection of charts, diagrams, and background information. The drawings of fossils and dinosaurs are particularly good, including a comprehensive geological time line.

Here are a few activity ideas to try if your kids develop "dinosaur-mania":

Pretend you *are* a dinosaur and write about your life and adventures. Who are your friends and enemies in the dinosaur world? What do you do to protect yourself? What do you like to do best — play in the water? Have a mud bath? Take long naps? Feast on a huge supply of your favorite food?

Role play a fight between two dinosaurs with a friend — perhaps a stegosaurus and an allosaurus.

After you've learned about several different kinds of prehistoric animals, try making up a crossword puzzle for your friends or family to solve. See page 287 for an easy way to do it.

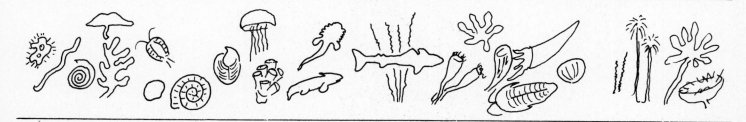

BASIC KINDS OF DINOSAURS

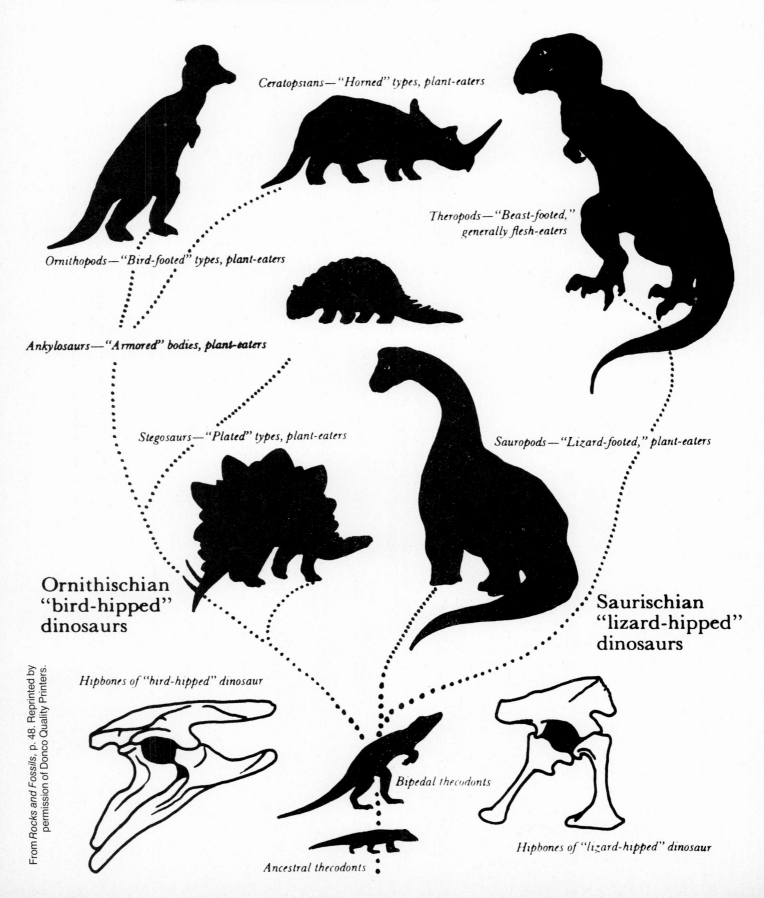

Ceratopsians—"Horned" types, plant-eaters

Theropods—"Beast-footed," generally flesh-eaters

Ornithopods—"Bird-footed" types, plant-eaters

Ankylosaurs—"Armored" bodies, plant-eaters

Stegosaurs—"Plated" types, plant-eaters

Sauropods—"Lizard-footed," plant-eaters

Ornithischian "bird-hipped" dinosaurs

Saurischian "lizard-hipped" dinosaurs

Hipbones of "bird-hipped" dinosaur

Bipedal thecodonts

Hipbones of "lizard-hipped" dinosaur

Ancestral thecodonts

From *Rocks and Fossils*, p. 48. Reprinted by permission of Donco Quality Printers.

Jerry McQuaid - DINOSAURS

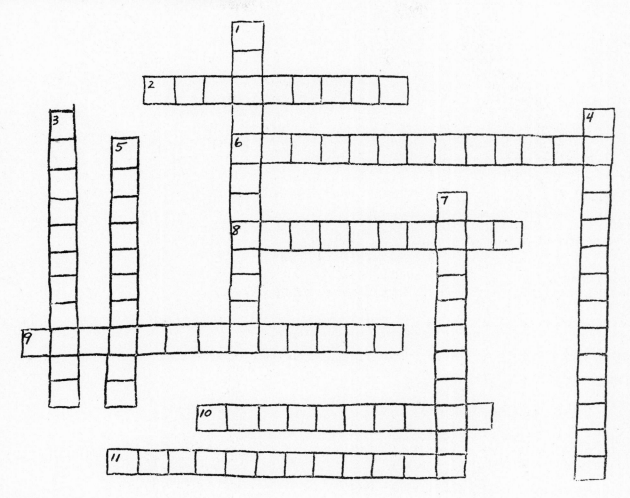

ACROSS

2. This puzzle is about _____.
6. Most famous meat-eating dinosaur.
8. Fierce Jurassic dinosaur.
9. Biggest dinosaur.
10. Jurassic period's biggest bird.
11. Biggest fish of Jurassic period.

DOWN

1. Most common dinosaur.
3. Plated dinosaur.
4. Parrot beaked dinosaur.
5. Longest dinosaur.
7. Three-horn face.

fossils

Fossils are freaky, fascinating things to kids (and many adults!) — the idea of being able to hold or touch something actually formed millions of years ago is awesome and exciting. And fossils are easier to find than you might imagine!

Whenever you see freshly broken rocks that have been exposed to view (maybe dug up during road construction or at a local quarry), take a closer look. Any sedimentary rock is likely to contain fossils of some kind, and most of the eastern United States was once under water. Check with your state Chamber of Commerce or Geological Survey Department (also any major universities) for information about the most likely sites for fossils in your area.

Have your kids make their own fossil prints with plaster of Paris (see page 71) — try a leaf, a shell, a baseball, or a footprint!

evolution

Life Story
Virginia Lee Burton

Houghton Mifflin Company
1 Beacon Street
Boston, Massachusetts 02107

In this simply beautiful book all the world's history — from its earliest beginnings to yesterday morning — unfolds as an enthralling drama that readers of any age can pore over for hours. Virginia Lee Burton, author of *Mike Mulligan* and *The Little House* (see page 297), displays her usual artistry in presenting an overwhelming subject in a way that children can understand.

Life Story is the only book we've seen that covers the entire evolutionary process in a simple yet visually dramatic fashion. The text is easy to read and even young children will be able to appreciate the story of our planet as told by Ms. Burton.

The story of the origins and evolution of humankind is far from complete, and resources in this field are rarely available for children (although you might try your local natural history or science museum). Here are some activities that should give your kids a feel for what early people might have experienced:

Try making an arrowhead or hand ax by chipping it with a harder stone. This is sure to be frustrating, but will give you a real appreciation of our ancestors' accomplishments!

Invent your own language — oral or written — and teach it to a friend. Read Rudyard Kipling's "The First Letter" or "How the Alphabet Was Made" ("Just So" stories) for some intriguing ideas — or learn some other present-day alphabets (e.g., Russian, Arabic, Chinese).

Read *Beginnings* (see page 268 for review) for some ancient stories about how the world and people began. Try to make up your own creation myth.

astronomy

Astronomy has always held a special fascination for me. As a child, I often went outside on a clear night with my father . . . to hear and learn the legends about the constellations, watch meteor showers in August, look at the moon and planets through a small telescope, and become familiar with the names of the major stars. For this introduction to the wonders and sheer beauty of the heavens I shall always be grateful, since even now there is nothing more breathtaking to me than seeing Venus and the first crescent moon just after sunset on a clear spring evening.

Whether you are lying on a blanket in your own backyard, walking along a deserted beach at night, or just stopping to watch the moon rise a thousand miles from home . . . the nighttime sky is always there to delight and thrill you and your children. The resources, information, and activities suggested in this section are only a beginning!

ABRAMS PLANETARIUM
SKY CALENDAR JUNE 1975
Information for helping teachers and students observe the sky

Sunrise and sunset, East Lansing--Sunrise: June 1 6:02 a.m.; June 16 5:59 a.m.; June 30 6:03 a.m. EDT
Sunset: June 1 9:09 p.m.; June 16 9:18 p.m.; June 30 9:20 p.m. EDT

SUNDAY	MONDAY	TUESDAY	WEDNESDAY	THURSDAY	FRIDAY	SATURDAY
1 Moon, near Last Quarter, is about 90° west of sun in morning sky. For positions of Venus and Saturn in evening sky see this month's map.	**2** This evening Venus lines up with Castor and Pollux and is 5 1/2° to the left of Pollux. Saturn 10° lower right of Venus.	**3** Look at Saturn with binoculars. Note faint star nearly 1° to upper left of Saturn. Watch star and planet next 7 days (see June 10).	**4** 1 hr before sunrise: [Mars, Jupiter] (planets 7° apart)	**5** 1 hr before sunrise: [Mars, Jupiter] (planets 6° apart)	**6** Arcturus passes due south near end of evening twilight. "Follow the arc (of the Big Dipper's handle) to Arcturus, and drive a spike to Spica."	**7** Last chance to see moon easily until June 11. Look low ENE 1 hour before sunrise. Mars and Jupiter about 5° apart this morning.
8 When sky has darkened, look about 4° upper left of Venus for the Beehive Cluster in Cancer. Use binoculars. Venus very close to cluster June 12.	**9** New Moon, not visible. Moon sets with sun, and dark side is toward us. -- Capella very low NW to NNW 1 hr after sunset.	**10** Tonight Saturn is one-tenth of a degree north of 3.5-magnitude Delta in Gemini. Use binoculars to see star.	**11** 1 hr after sunset: [Venus, Castor, Pollux, Saturn]	**12** 1 hr after sunset: [Venus, Castor, Pollux, Saturn]	**13** 1 hr after sunset: [Regulus, Venus]	**14** 1 hr after sunset: [Regulus, Venus]
15 This month's map represents the sky about 1 hr after sunset tonight. See map for tonight's positions of Venus (20° lower right of Regulus) and Saturn (8° from Pollux).	**16** Mars and Jupiter appear closest this morning, only 1/2° apart. Pair rises in E 3 hrs before sunup and is best 1 hr before sunup. Evening: Moon, near First Quarter, about 90° east of sun at sunset.	**17** Bright star near moon tonight, to the east of it, is Spica. By tomorrow night moon will have moved 14° to the east of tonight's position. Spica will then be to west of moon.	**18** Venus reaches greatest elongation (maximum angular distance from sun at this apparition, 45°). Through telescope immediately after sunset, Venus looks like tiny half moon.	**19** Altair now rises at about sunset. As sky darkens, use this month's map to locate Vega, Deneb, and Altair in eastern sky. They form the Summer Triangle, so named because it is visible all night in early summer.	**20** Regulus 15° upper left of Venus. Watch Venus approach Regulus until July 8. Saturn now sets only 1 1/4 hrs after sun and is difficult to observe. Saturn behind sun July 15.	**21** Sun enters Gemini (Castor and Pollux disappear near end of June). Summer Solstice: Sun rises and sets farthest north. Highest midday sun of year. Evening: Red Antares south of moon.
22 Venus is nearing the end of its reign as the "evening star." In 7 weeks it will set only 1/2 hr after the sun and be difficult to see. Watch for changes thru telescope and binoculars until then.	**23** Full Moon rises in SE sky as sun sets in NW. Moon in Sagittarius, halfway around zodiac from sun's place. Bright moon makes Sagittarius hard to see. Wait a few days.	**24** Moon rises about 40 min after sunset (as seen from latitude 40° north). Note moon's reddish color and apparently large size as it first appears.	**25** Moon rises about 1 hour and 20 minutes after sunset, well before twilight ends. Notice that the moon no longer appears full to the unaided eye.	**26** Moon rises about 1 hour and 50 minutes after sunset, shortly before the end of evening twilight. Moon now remains visible for several hrs after sunrise.	**27** Beginning tonight the moon rises after the end of evening twilight. For part of the evening the sky is dark, good for viewing the Milky Way.	**28** Next month's map represents the sky about 2 hrs after sunset tonight. Use binoculars to look for star clusters and nebulae in Scorpius and Sagittarius.
29 1 hr before sunrise: [Jupiter (35° up in ESE), Mars] (planets 7° apart)	**30** Regulus 6° upper left of Venus. [Regulus, Venus]					

June Planet Summary: Morning Planets: Brilliant yellowish Jupiter and reddish Mars appear close together all month in the eastern sky before sunup. Jupiter appears 12 times as bright as Mars. On June 1 Mars is 9° upper right of Jupiter. On June 15-17 they fit within a 1° telescope field (see June 16). On June 30 Mars is 8° lower left of Jupiter. For most of June the two planets can be viewed together within the field of 7-power binoculars, which also show the brightest satellites of Jupiter.

Evening Planets: Venus is the brilliant "evening star" in the western sky at dusk. It sets over 3 hrs after sunset June 1, decreasing to 2 1/2 hrs by June 30. Venus continues moving rapidly (1° per day) against background stars; on June 2 it is to the left of Castor and Pollux, and at month's end it is approaching Regulus. Getting 750,000 miles closer to earth as each day passes, Venus grows noticeably in size this month when viewed through a telescope. But less of its sunlit side is turned toward us as it begins to swing between earth and sun. A good time for viewing the phase of Venus through a telescope is shortly after sunset, before the sky darkens much. **Saturn** below Pollux. See Jun 1-3,10-12,15.

Written by Robert C. Victor

Subscription: $2.00 per year, from Abrams Planetarium

Magnitudes of the Planets: Venus -3.9; Jupiter -1.9; Saturn +0.4; Mars +0.8
Motions of the Planets: Venus 29° eastward, from Gemini through Cancer into Leo. Mars 22° eastward, and Jupiter 5° eastward, in Pisces. Saturn moves 7' (minutes of arc) per day eastward in Gemini during first half of June.

Astronomy
Examining Your Environment

Winston Press
25 Groveland Terrace
Minneapolis, Minnesota 55403

"We want you to get involved with the universe!"

With this introductory sentence, the emphasis of this book is accurately established. One of the Examining Your Environment series (see page 28 for complete list of titles), *Astronomy* is replete with information and activity ideas geared to a firsthand exploration of the skies.

It includes a handy star chart (to be cut out and put together by kids) as well as striking illustrations of the constellations, clear instructions on how to make an astrolabe or a simple eight-power telescope, and suggested moon-watching activities. This book is the only easily readable, activity-oriented source we've found for a well-rounded introduction to astronomy for kids.

Space Puzzles: Curious Questions and Answers about the Solar System
Martin Gardner

Simon and Schuster
630 Fifth Avenue
New York, New York 10020
$4.95

How many times does the moon rotate on its axis in one complete revolution around the earth? Are there really canals on Mars? What are three ways artificial gravity can be created inside a moving spaceship?

The answers to these and other tantalizing questions are found in this fascinating book. Each section contains a short introduction, intriguing puzzles, and lively, informative answers for astronomy buffs of all ages!

materials

One of the nicest things about astronomy is that you need so little in the way of materials or equipment to enjoy and explore the heavens.

A star-finder chart is almost essential for locating and identifying major stars and constellations. One that kids can put together for themselves is included in *Astronomy* (reviewed on page 81). You can also obtain one for seventy-five cents postpaid from:

Edmund Scientific Company
555 Edscorp Building
Barrington, New Jersey 08007

Edmund also has a "make your own star chart" package — twenty-five cut out–put together charts for one dollar postpaid.

Another extremely valuable aid to sky watching is the "Sky Calendar" published by Michigan State University. This unique calendar appears monthly in *Science and Children,* a magazine published by the National Science Teachers Association (NSTA). The calendar can also be ordered directly from:

Abrams Planetarium
Michigan State University
East Lansing, Michigan 48823
$2 / yearly subscription

The sky calendar's special value is its detailed information on planet visibility, but it also includes notes on special events, such as meteor showers and lunar and solar eclipses.

Telescopes add an exciting dimension to viewing the sky at night. With a three-inch reflector (available for about forty dollars from Edmund Scientific), you can see Saturn's rings, the giant moons of Jupiter, double stars, craters on the moon, and much more.

Astronomy has clear directions for building a small telescope right in its text. In addition, Edmund has a simple eight-power telescope "kit" for three to four dollars. In any case, building your own telescope is a valuable learning experience — giving an incomparable understanding of how and why it works, as well as a strong sense of personal accomplishment.

daytime astronomy

Daytime Astronomy
Elementary Science Study

McGraw-Hill Book Company
1221 Avenue of the Americas
New York, New York 10020
$4.95

This ESS teacher's guide suggests a wide variety of activities — making sundials, exploring shadows, creating models of the earth and moon — aimed at an understanding of the relationship between the sun and the earth based upon firsthand evidence collected by kids. It also contains a list of handy materials, a "calendar of special events," and loads of supplementary information.

One teacher has his students begin with the assumptions that the earth is flat and that the earth is the center of the universe, and they must persist with these assumptions until they have accumulated enough evidence to disprove them (page 1).

Look at the position of the sun at different times of the day. Mark its positions with tape on a window. Where does it rise and set? When is it highest in the sky?

Play "shadow tag" — person who is "it" has to step on another person's shadow to tag.

Go outside at different times on a sunny day. Have a friend trace your shadow. Can you "fit into it" when you return an hour later? Why not? Which way has your shadow moved? Which way has the moved?

Mount a "shadow stick" on a piece of board. Trace the line of the stick's shadow at one-hour intervals throughout the day, and mark each line drawn with the time. The shortest line points in which direction?

Use your shadow stick as a sundial. Can you tell the time by the length and direction of the shadow? How does a change in season affect its accuracy?

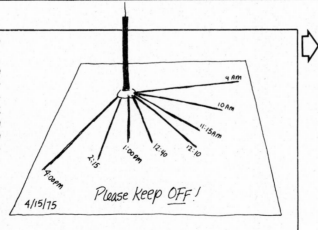

9 AM
10 Am
11:15Am
12:10
12:40
1:00 pm
2:15
4:00pm
4/15/75
Please Keep OFF !

See page 176 (Math) for more detailed activities with sundials.

Using a globe, mark your town with a nail attached with clay. Stand the globe in a coffee can or other support so that the nail is on top and the north pole faces north. The globe is now facing the sun exactly the same way the earth is. Where on the globe is the sun rising? Where on the globe is the sun directly overhead (no shadow)?

Using a ball ¼ the size of your globe, can you create a "solar eclipse"?

our moon

Where Is the Moon?
Elementary Science Study

*McGraw-Hill Book Company
1221 Avenue of the Americas
New York, New York 10020
$4.98*

Did you see the moon last night? Where was it? What did it look like? Will it look the same tomorrow night? Next week? Are there times when you can't see the moon at all? Have you ever seen it in the day-time?

These and other questions are asked and answered by children's own observations in this ESS unit. After a couple of months of regular moon watching — drawing pictures, "fisting" its changing position,* seeing it wax and wane — children will begin to notice an order and rhythm to the moon's appearances that will enable them to predict where it will be and what it will look like.

In addition to basic information and suggested questions to stimulate children's observations, the guide also includes a reference chart of the visibility of Venus and Jupiter up to 1983. This is especially useful for determining months that the moon can be seen in conjunction

Monday Oct. 21, 1974. three fists high 7:00

I think the Moon will be full in two days.

with these bright planets, which adds an exciting dimension to moon watching.

How long after sunset does the new crescent moon set?
Is the moon waxing or waning when it can be seen in the afternoon?
Does the moon really change shape?
In which part of the sky is the moon never seen?
What is a harvest moon?
What are the dark patches on the moon?
What causes a lunar eclipse?
What does "the new moon in the old moon's arms" mean?

It takes nine fists to go from the horizon to straight overhead, no matter how tall you are. Keep arms and back straight.

*how to "fist"

The Moon in Fact and Fancy
Alfred Slote

*World Publishing Company
2231 West 110th Street
Cleveland, Ohio 44102*

This is an interesting book containing several fascinating folktales from around the world that explain lunar phenomena, as well as related scientific explanations.

The *Old Farmer's Almanac,* available in many local stores, is an excellent source of data on when the moon rises and sets, when to expect particular phases, and so on. It also gives times when the sun rises and sets for any particular day of the year.

planets

	average distance from sun in miles	diameter (in miles)	period of revolution	period of rotation	known moons	your weight (multiply by...)
Mercury	35,960,000	3100	88 days	57 days	0	0.27
Venus	67,200,000	7700	225 days	247 days	0	0.85
Earth	92,900,000	7918	365¼ days	23 hrs, 56 mins.	1	1.00
Mars	141,500,000	4200	687 days	24 hrs, 37 mins.	2	0.38
Jupiter	483,400,000	89,000	11.86 years	9 hrs, 55 mins.	13	2.64
Saturn	886,200,000	71,500	29.5 years	10 hrs, 14 mins.	10	1.17
Uranus	1,783,000,000	30,000	84 years	10 hrs, 45 mins.	5	0.92
Neptune	2,790,000,000	27,700	164.75 years	15 hrs, 45 mins.	2	1.12
Pluto	3,670,000,000	3600(?)	248.5 years	6.4 days	0	?

stars

constellations

Polaris is a very valuable star to know. Because it is over the north pole of the earth, it is called the North Star and does not appear to move across the sky. It is not a particularly bright star, but can be located easily by following an imaginary line drawn from "the pointers" — two stars in the cup of the Big Dipper (see below). When you have learned to find Polaris, you will never be lost at night — if you face the North Star you are facing due north!

Did you know that the Big Dipper is really part of a larger constellation called Ursa Major (or the Big Bear)? It also has a companion, Ursa Minor (the Little Bear), whose tail (or dipper handle) ends with Polaris.

These constellations never rise or set in the northern hemisphere, but swing around Polaris as the year progresses. An American Indian tale explains their seasonal positions as being inside (under) or outside (over) their cave. Polaris is the cave's mouth, and if you look at these constellations in winter you will see that the bears are indeed hibernating!

Patterns in the Sky: The Story of the Constellations
W. Maxwell Reed

*William Morrow and Company
Lothrop, Lee and Shepard
105 Madison Avenue
New York, New York 10016
$4.75*

This is a collection of Greek and Roman myths surrounding twenty-five familiar constellations — how they got their names and why they were put in the sky in the first place. It includes sky charts and considerable background information, as well as the mythological stories.

Although *Patterns in the Sky* is easily readable, I would strongly recommend learning the stories and telling them to your kids in your own words. This is particularly enjoyable when you're outside at night trying to find the constellations together — of course!

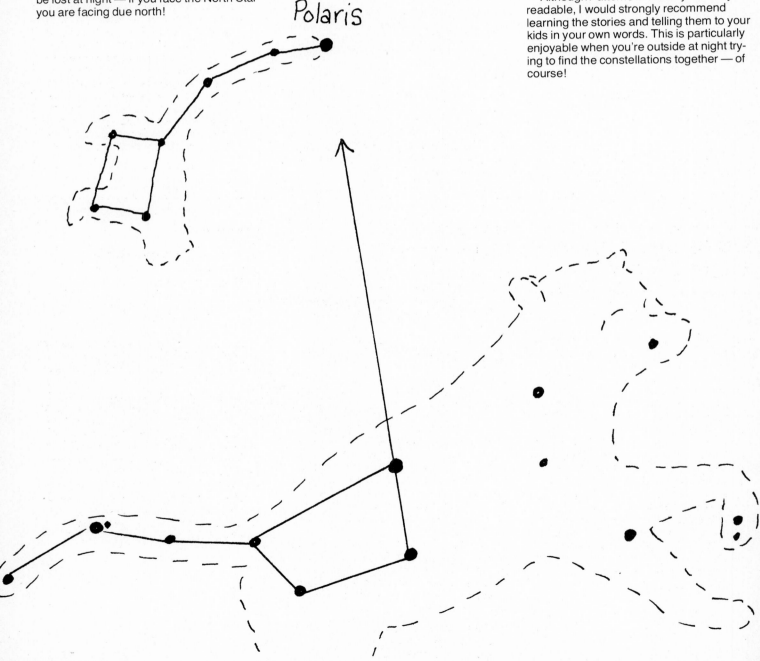

Polaris

three ways to bring the stars indoors

You need a small cardboard tube, black paper, and a pin. Trace the tube opening on a piece of black paper. Poke holes with the pin to represent the stars of a single constellation. Cut around the traced circle, leaving about a quarter-inch border. Cut slots in the border, fold them over the end of the tube, and tape. Look through the other end of the tube. Make several and see if you can identify the constellations.

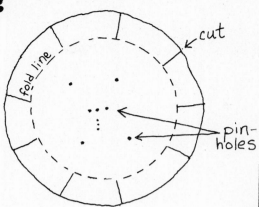

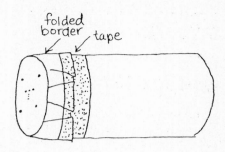

Junior Planetarium

Steven Manufacturing Company
224 East Fourth Street
Hermann, Missouri 65041
$15

This commercial "Junior Planetarium" projects more than sixty constellations and hundreds of stars on the walls and ceiling. It stands fourteen inches high and is made of plastic; it can be adjusted to show the stars at different seasons as well as in different positions in the sky. Our family had one and we all thought it a terrific aid to star identification!

Since an umbrella has the shape of the inside of a sphere, it can be used to make a simple planetarium. Scrounge around for a large, opaque umbrella (preferably black). Mark Polaris, the North Star, with chalk on the inside of the umbrella. Using a star chart, fill in the major constellations in their proper positions relative to Polaris (using chalk to represent the stars). Then poke holes where you've marked the stars. In a darkened room, place a bright light under the umbrella — the stars and constellations will be projected on the ceiling and walls.

imagination unlimited

Kids as well as adults are fascinated by the unknown. In the field of astronomy, so much is unknown that speculation is rampant and it provides a perfect subject for stretching one's imagination!

Science fiction writers have predicted much of what we accept as commonplace today. True science fiction sticks to and extrapolates from existing, known scientific facts — try encouraging your children to write imaginative science fiction stories of their own, based on the facts they know. Life on other planets in our solar system obviously does not exist "as we know it" — if it did exist, however, could you picture its form? Can you design a robot and describe its practical uses in the future? (Become familiar with Isaac Asimov's famous First Law of Robotics, for a start!)

Franklyn M. Branley

A Book of Astronauts for You
A Book of Flying Saucers for You
A Book of Moon Rockets for You
A Book of Outer Space for You
A Book of Stars for You
A Book of the Milky Way Galaxy for You

Thomas Y. Crowell Company
Department of Books for Children and
*   Young People*
666 Fifth Avenue
New York, New York 10019
$4.50 each

This series of easy-to-read children's books serves as an excellent introduction to many aspects of astronomy not usually written about for kids. The books present clear, factual information in an interesting, understandable style. In addition, each book is amply illustrated with photographs and drawings that make the subject "come alive."

In *A Book of Flying Saucers for You,* the author discusses both fact and fantasy surrounding UFO sightings, leaving the reader with plenty of food for imaginative thought. For more information on this intriguing subject, write to:

Center for UFO Studies
2623 Ridge Avenue
Evanston, Illinois 60201

Powers of Ten

University of Southern California
Division of Cinema
School of Performing Arts
University Park
Los Angeles, California 90007
rental: $10 for 1–3 days

That truth can blow the mind fully as well as science fiction is demonstrated by this powerful little film about the proportions of the universe.

Using a familiar technique — zooming — but taking it to its greatest extremes, the camera retreats outward from the hand of a sleeping man to the furthest reaches of the universe and then returns to the hand only to continue inward through cells and atomic structure. The sense of huge dimensions of time and space is overwhelming; I felt literally carried away on a voyage into realms that we can barely imagine. A double-whammy, and a superb educational experience!

science

While professional science grows in complexity, the experiences we design for teaching science to children are becoming progressively simpler. Maybe you could call this a "return to basics." In any case, it's a recognition that kids need to look at strange granules through a microscope or feel the pull of a magnet more than they need to study a comprehensive textbook, however "modern" it may be. They will learn best if they can investigate the world around them in the same way a real scientist would; that is, by looking at it, touching it, or *doing* things with it. The activities and resources in this section have been chosen from that point of view.

general resources

general science supplies

equipment: bought or borrowed

microscopes (see Edmund Scientific catalog; their address appears below, right)
slides
hand lenses or other magnifiers
tweezers

hot plate
stopwatch
thermometer
scales or balances
timer

cooking and chemistry

measuring cups
measuring spoons
bowls
spoons, stirrers, knives, beaters, forks
cans
bottles
plastic dishes and storage containers
cooking pots
tall plastic pitcher
variety of kitchen chemicals:
    vinegar, baking soda, flour
    sugar, salt
    vegetable oil, food coloring

electricity and magnetism

bell wire
uninsulated wire
D-cell batteries
black plastic tape
screw-in flashlight bulbs
bulb holders
magnets (see pp. 118–119)
large nails
thin scraps of metal
pie pans
rubber bands

general materials: mostly scroungeable

small plastic bags
plastic sheeting
plastic storage containers
plastic dishes and pails
cardboard paint pails
plastic and paper cups
milk cartons
paper towels
cardboard or other trays
cloth (old sheets, etc.)
paper plates
Styrofoam trays and packing pieces
oaktag
string, cotton braided or nylon
thread
clothesline
clothespins
cardboard sheets
cheesecloth or fine netting
cotton
wire screening
glass sheet
aluminum foil
waxed paper
paper of all types; graph paper
wire of all types
scraps of wood
toothpicks
plaster of Paris
pipe cleaners
modeling clay
tongue depressors, Popsicle sticks, or
    coffee stirrers
olive or Alka-Seltzer bottles
tin cans (especially large ones)
steel wool
straws
sand
shoe boxes
rubber bands
assorted weights
corks and stoppers
common pins
nails, nuts and bolts
balloons
marbles
Elmer's glue
matches
candles
alcohol
measuring cups
tape

water

plastic squeeze bottles
medicine droppers
medicine cups
plastic sheeting
plastic tubing
stoppers
funnel
sponges
liquid detergent

commercial sources

There are many scientific supply houses, but we have found that the few sources noted below are usually adequate for most needs. For the most part, the kinds of activities we suggest depend on scrounged, handmade, or locally purchased supplies.

Edmund Scientific Company

55 Edscorp Building
Barrington, New Jersey 08007
(609) 547-3488

Generally recognized as the best all-around source for scientific supplies and equipment, they can satisfy almost every kind of need at reasonable prices. Write them for a catalog.

Both American Science and Engineering (AS&E) and Selective Educational Equipment (SEE) sell materials designed for or made to be compatible with ESS kits. While McGraw-Hill is the major source for the kits themselves, these other two sources will also sell individual items from kits and other basic science materials. (See general description of ESS and addresses, page 34.)

Also see *Educators Guide to Free Science Materials,* reviewed on page 91.

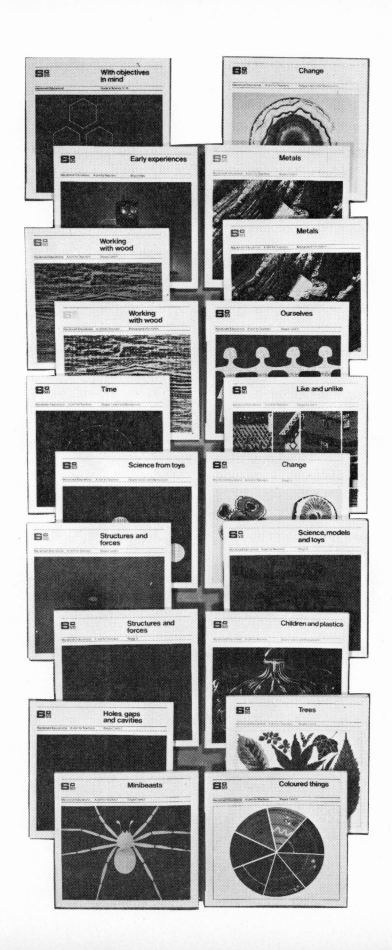

books

One of our assumptions is that any adult who enjoys doing science with children can be resourceful enough to pull together the appropriate equipment or materials without buying expensive kits or using ready-made programs. Below is a selection of books that we have found to be useful general aids for people who like to work this way.

Science 5/13
Macdonald Educational

Purnell Educational
850 Seventh Avenue
New York, New York 10019
or
Children's Museum
The Jamaicaway
Boston, Massachusetts 02130

We have found this series of British guides the most valuable general resource for science of any we've used. Only recently made available in this country, they're a must for any creative elementary teacher and worthwhile for parents to consider, too. More good activities can be gleaned from these books than can be used in a lifetime. The Children's Museum will sell you single copies; Purnell doesn't like to. A selection of activities from several guides has been compiled in the *Junior Science Source Book,* available from Purnell.

Investigating Science Series
Laurence B. White, Jr.

> Investigating Science with Nails
> Investigating Science with Coins
> Investigating Science with Rubber Bands
> Investigating Science with Paper

Addison-Wesley Publishing Company
2725 Sand Hill Road
Menlo Park, California 94025
$3.75 each

White has a knack for infusing simple experiments with an air of magic. Part of the magic is that he explores fundamental scientific principles using the most common of materials. Sometimes his explanations are a trifle long-winded, yet they are clear and written in a language even young readers will understand. He has just published another series of four books, designed for the youngest readers, entitled *Science Toys, Science Puzzles, Science Tricks,* and *Science Games.*

Science Inquiry Project Series
A. Harris Stone et al.

Prentice-Hall
Educational Book Division
Englewood Cliffs, New Jersey 07632

Compare these with White's *Investigating Science* series if you're looking for something in this vein. They're parallel in general aim, but the important difference is that Stone's books ask rather than tell. In fact, there is no explanation; the text of each book is made up almost entirely of questions, inviting kids to find out by trying out, and then form their own conclusions. See pages indicated below for reviews of individual titles.

> *Animals Are Like This,* p. 54
> *The Chemistry of a Lemon,* p. 103
> *The Chemistry of Soap,* p. 103
> *Crystals from the Sea: A Look at Salt*
> *Drop by Drop: A Look at Water*
> *Have a Ball,* p. 123
> *The Heat's On!,* p. 110
> *Microbes Are Something Else*
> *Plants Are Like That,* p. 63
> *Puttering with Paper*
> *Rocks and Rills: A Look at Geology,* p. 70
> *Take a Balloon*
> *Turned On: A Look at Electricity*
> *The Winds of Weather,* p. 73

Teaching Science with Everyday Things
Victor E. Schmidt and Verne N. Rockcastle

McGraw-Hill Book Company
1221 Avenue of the Americas
New York, New York 10020

We like the authors' taste for simple experiments designed to teach important principles. They prove that meaningful science can be learned from whatever's handy as long as you know what to do with it. Parents who want to do their own teaching will find the book invaluable. It's available in paperback.

Educators Guide to Free Science Materials
Mary H. Saterstrom, editor

Educators Progress Service
Randolph, Wisconsin 53956
$10.25

A handy book if you like to send away for things. It has a huge collection of sources for free films, filmstrips, tapes, videotapes, booklets, charts, magazines, exhibits, and informational packets. Every item is well annotated. There are full indexes and even a few model study-units that call upon selected resources.

New Unesco Source Book for Science Teaching

Unipub
P.O. Box 433
Murray Hill Station
New York, New York 10016

You might also find this in its older edition, *Seven Hundred Science Experiments for Everyone* (Doubleday), a more descriptive title. It's a very good single-volume collection of specific experiments appropriate to children of all ages, though written for adults. Clear diagrams, too.

Guppies, Bubbles, and Vibrating Objects
John McGavack, Jr., and Donald P. LaSalle

John Day Company
257 Park Avenue South
New York, New York 10010
$7.50

Designed as a complete guide for a primary science program, this is a series of carefully laid out lesson plans on a variety of appealing topics along with an extensive overview about getting it together. In other words, strictly for teachers. It's oriented to hands-on learning using fairly inexpensive equipment. The text is enlivened by a generous number of photographs showing kids working through the activities.

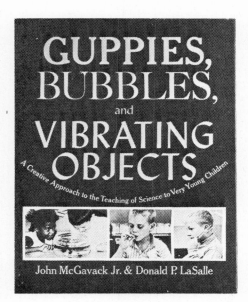

What Makes it Go? Work? Fly? Float?
Joe Kaufman

Golden Press Division
Western Publishing Company
1220 Mound Avenue
Racine, Wisconsin 53402
$4.95

This picture book is as useful for young kids as *The Way Things Work* (see page 128 for review) is for older readers. Its appealing and informative illustrations closely resemble those in Richard Scarry's books (see *What Do People Do All Day?,* page 297). Cartoon diagrams of household appliances, vehicles of all types, escalators, and even musical instruments reveal all the working details clearly, and there is an accompanying text for adults to read aloud. Golden Press also has an extensive series of kids' science books on specific topics, many of which are very good. Write them for a catalog.

See also:
Science Teachers' Association of Ontario booklets on a wide range of scientific concepts, reviewed on page 28.

Examining Your Environment series, reviewed on page 28.

Elementary Science Study teacher's guides; general review, page 34.

water

Water is omnipresent; one could hardly imagine life, or even a world, without it. It's in our bodies, in the food we eat, in the air we breathe. We dam it up and do work with it, admire its beauty in waterfalls and raindrops, or play with it in oceans, streams, and pools. Kids' natural delight with water in all its forms makes it a wonderful general resource for science study. You can start with something as simple as observing the behavior of drops and tiny streams.

drops

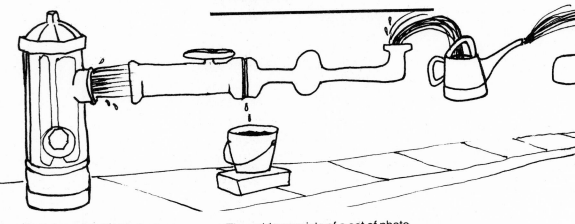

Drops, Streams, and Containers
Elementary Science Study

McGraw-Hill Book Company
1221 Avenue of the Americas
New York, New York 10020

If the right objective is finding materials that let kids make wonderful discoveries by just "messing around," then these are ideal. With not much more than an eye-dropper, some jars of water, and a piece of waxed paper, a child is off to some first-class scientific adventure.

One little girl concentrated on drop piles of different sizes. She had big round ones, little tiny ones, and flat pools. This kept her busy for about a half hour until she suddenly discovered the optical effects. "It looks bigger" resulted in many experiments with different-sized drops and different-sized letters in the newsprint. Eventually she got an air bubble in her drop: "Look, I've got a bubble in a bubble!" Much excitement, and friends called over to see this wonder. . . . "And now it's smaller. Can you see that it looks smaller?" So she was off again and, when I left the room, was still investigating this newfound wonder (Introduction, page 4).

The guide consists of a set of photo cards showing individual activities and questions. A kit is available, but seems particularly unnecessary since all the items can be collected more cheaply on your own.

The activities below are adapted from this guide and from *Kitchen Physics* (see review on page 95).

A lot of what you can find out about drops calls for looking at the interaction between droppers, drops, and surfaces.

With an eyedropper, see how big a drop you can pull around on a piece of

waxed paper	Try	a pin
aluminum foil		a straw
paper towel		a paper clip
a sheet of glass		

Do the individual drops that you make on each of the surfaces look the same?

Experiment with the drops a straw makes.

Look through a drop at

a grainy piece of wood (even a table-top)
the letters on a newspaper
the back of your hand

How does the drop change what you see?

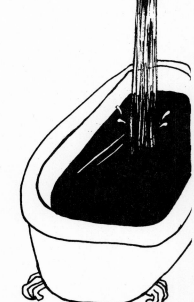

Reprinted from *Kitchen Physics Teacher's Guide.* © 1967, pp. 15, 25. Reproduced by permission of the Elementary Science Study of Education Development Center, Inc.

DROPS OF VARIOUS LIQUIDS ON WAXED PAPER

DROP OF WATER
DROP OF SOAPY WATER
DROP OF ALCOHOL
DROP OF COOKING OIL

WATER DROPS ON WAXED PAPER

1 DROP   5 DROPS   10 DROPS   20 DROPS

DROPS OF VARIOUS LIQUIDS ON ALUMINUM FOIL

DROP OF WATER
DROP OF SOAPY WATER
DROP OF ALCOHOL
DROP OF COOKING OIL

WATER DROPS ON ALUMINUM FOIL

1 DROP   5 DROPS   10 DROPS   20 DROPS

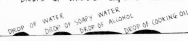

DROPS OF VARIOUS LIQUIDS ON GLASS

DROP OF WATER
DROP OF SOAPY WATER
DROP OF ALCOHOL
DROP OF COOKING OIL

WATER DROPS ON GLASS

1 DROP   5 DROPS   10 DROPS

streams

Plastic bottles with narrow spout openings are the best equipment for discovering how small streams of water (or other liquids) act.

Bottles to scrounge:

> detergent bottles
> glue bottles
> baby bottles
> any of above bottles,
>   replacing screw-on top with
>   rubber stoppers with holes
>   of various sizes in them.

How fast can you empty a bottle with a narrow opening?

Try making a stream land without noise.

When does a stream break up into drops?

Can you measure the length of an unbroken column?

Punch small holes in the sides of a bottle.

How can you get a stream to make the biggest arc? (Do this over a sink or outdoors.)

Measuring the unbroken column.

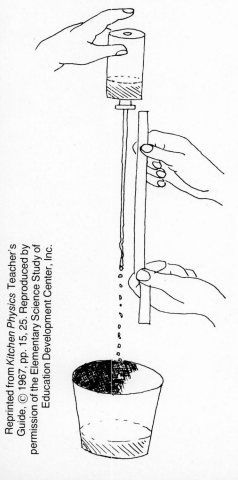

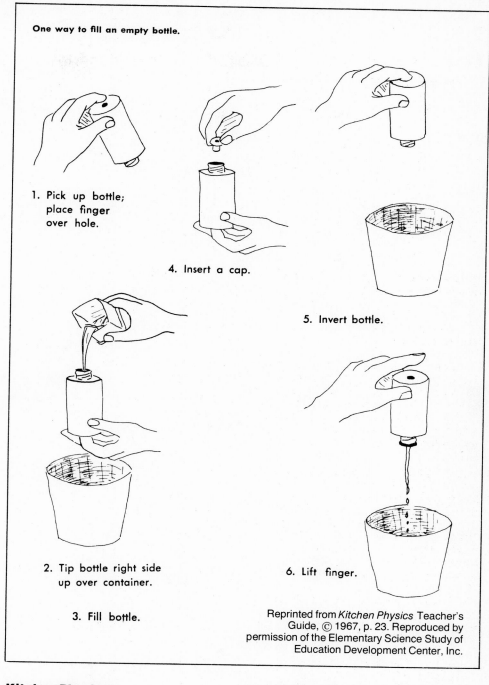

One way to fill an empty bottle.

1. Pick up bottle; place finger over hole.

4. Insert a cap.

5. Invert bottle.

2. Tip bottle right side up over container.

3. Fill bottle.

6. Lift finger.

Kitchen Physics
Elementary Science Study

McGraw-Hill Book Company
1221 Avenue of the Americas
New York, New York 10020

Observing the behavior of water in drops and streams moves into the big league with *Kitchen Physics*. Intended mainly for older kids (aged eleven to thirteen), the activities call for a little more sophisticated equipment and a lot more careful thinking about what's going on in the experiments. Explanation and prediction of phenomena are now called for. A theme-note that you hear repeatedly in ESS-designed guides is sounded here again: let kids explain what they see *in their own words.*

"Water is grabbier."
"Soap is thinner."
"Soapy water is heavier, so it sticks together better."
"Water has more togetherness."

surface tension

The skinlike effect (surface tension) of liquids usually surprises kids. Here are some ways to observe it.

holey scow *

Use a lightweight aluminum pan — the kind baked goods or frozen dinners are packed in — and a sink or tub full of water.

Will this scow float even if punched with holes?
If so, can it still carry a load of paper clips or small pebbles?
How much weight can a holey scow carry before sinking?
How numerous, or large, can the holes be before it sinks?

Have children look through a magnifying glass at the water in the larger holes. How is its surface shaped?

*From *Teaching Science with Everyday Things* by Victor E. Schmidt and Verne N. Rockcastle, page 34. Copyright 1968 by Victor E. Schmidt and Verne N. Rockcastle. Used with permission of McGraw-Hill Book Company.

" floating " paper clips

Older children who are a little more dexterous can try floating a paper clip on the surface of a cup of water filled to the brim. (Water container must be free of soap.)

Will the clip sink if you push it under? What happens if you add a little soap to the water before placing the clip?

FIGURE 21. Placing a paper clip on water with a wire cradle or table fork.

1. Unfold a paper clip.

2. Bend up one end to make a wire cradle.

3. Use wire cradle to place another paper clip on water.

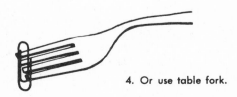

4. Or use table fork.

Reprinted from *Kitchen Physics* Teacher's Guide, © 1967, p. 42. Reproduced by permission of the Elementary Science Study of Education Development Center, Inc.

---

other floating things

"Nice? It's the only thing," said the Water Rat solemnly, as he leant forward for his stroke. *"Believe me, my young friend, there is nothing – absolutely nothing – half so much worth doing as simply messing about in boats."*

— from *The Wind in the Willows*, Kenneth Grahame

If the kids you're working with really get off into boats there are a lot of things you can do that will interest them, especially using homemade toys and test models.

Put an empty tin can in water. How does it float?
Does a *piece* of tin — say a can top — float? (Drop it in on its edge.)
Why does a can float?
(Try explaining *that* without quoting Archimedes. A British teacher came up with this: "The simplest explanation is that an iron ship is not all iron but a mixture of air which floats and iron which sinks and it is the air which 'wins.' ")

the flow of water

Water Flow
Elementary Science Study

McGraw-Hill Book Company
1221 Avenue of the Americas
New York, New York 10020

Kids get naturally caught up in this sort of thing. Using plastic tubing, juice bottles, and connectors set up on a frame, they can put together intricate systems for water to flow through. They can learn to control and predict how it flows, and the insights extend beyond the water into such things as how electric current travels in circuits. The materials lend themselves to self-initiated experimenting, helped out, if you want, by a well-designed set of idea cards available separately from the guide.

One of the best-conceived guides ESS has done, this gives plenty of clear information and illustrations for organizing the activities indoors or out. The authors had a small group of fifth or sixth graders in mind, but it would be appropriate for even a single child of anywhere from nine to fourteen.

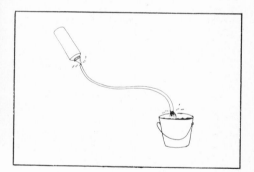

The simplest way to experiment with the basic idea of water flowing through a system is to provide a long stretch of plastic tubing, a narrow-spout bottle, and a few big containers (dishpan, pail), and then ask:

"How many ways can you get water from one end of a long tube to the other?"

"How can you speed up the flow of water? Slow it down?"

Will a ball of modeling clay sink in a container of water?
(What kids — and maybe some of the rest of us — discover is that it depends on how you shape the stuff.)

If this kind of activity provokes further questions, you might try the ESS *Clay Boats* teacher's guide for some well-planned methods of working with clay and related materials in order to find out how things float.
Then you can go on to investigate:

keels
shapes and streamlining
use of sails (you can get a trade wind with a fan, indoors)
reading about actual accounts of voyages

Running Water
Examining Your Environment

Winston Press
25 Groveland Terrace
Minneapolis, Minnesota 55403

The whole Examining Your Environment series turns us on, but this particular selection leaves our enthusiasm overflowing. It's superbly illustrated, for one thing, and it's got some wonderful ideas for exploring the flow of water in all the places you're used to seeing it but never *thought* about seeing it. Faucets, sprinklers, plumbing, gutter pipes, the front lawn of your house, and the street in front of that are all drawn into one set of investigations that will lead you to wonder why you bother to have your kids in school.

Other than a few easily homemade measuring instruments, such as the water-force gauge, nothing the authors suggest calls for fancy equipment or elaborate preparation. It is readable by kids as well as adults.

plumbing

What is the pathway of water in a building?
How many water outlets are there in your house? School?
How many different sizes (diameters) of pipe did you find?

How much piping is there for hot water? Cold water?
How much piping is there for fresh water? Wastewater?
What is the most noticeable difference between freshwater pipes and wastewater pipes?

What is the purpose of the tank ball?
Why does the tank ball float even though it is made of metal?
How is the water turned on? Turned off?
How much water does the tank hold?

—adapted from *Running Water,*
pages 2–3, 6–7

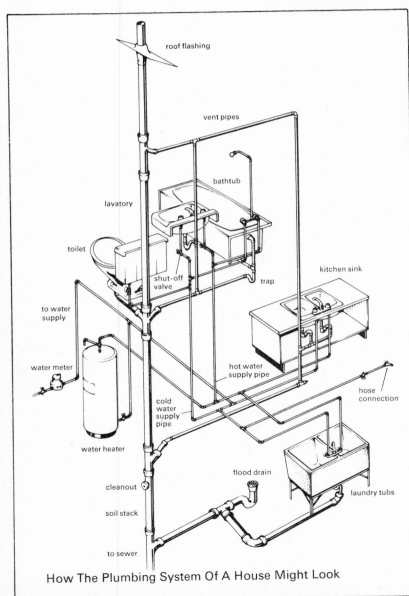

How The Plumbing System Of A House Might Look

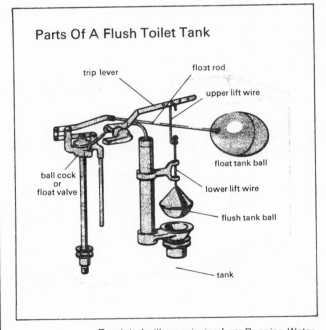

Parts Of A Flush Toilet Tank

Reprinted with permission from *Running Water,* pp. 3, 7, © 1971, Holt, Rinehart and Winston of Canada, Ltd., distributed in the U.S. by Winston Press.

water consumption

How much water gets used up around a house in an average day?

This is no insignificant question, as we live at a time when soaring population will most certainly lead to shortages of water, even for daily needs.

Here are some ways your kids can make some surveys of their own family's water consumption:

Water Used By	Ways to Measure It
a toilet	Calibrate a pail by (a) sticking a piece of waterproof adhesive tape vertically down the inside, and (b) filling it a quart at a time, making marks with a pencil on the tape after each quart. Then close the shutoff valve on the pipe leading to the toilet, flush it, refill it with the calibrated bucket, and record amount.
a bathtub	Calibrate the tub by sticking a waterproof piece of tape vertically down the inside, near the drain. When you take a bath, draw the water a gallon at a time into the bucket and pour it into the tub, making a mark on the tape for each gallon. Which takes more, a shower or a bath? (To measure shower, put in the plug.)
a washing machine or dishwasher	Try consulting the book of instructions that came with the machine, first, or call your appliance dealer for information. Otherwise, you could try to deduce how many times the machine fills and then use the calibrated pail method.
a hose or sprinkler (watering lawn, garden; washing car, etc.)	Put the end of the hose or inverted sprinkler into a calibrated pail and record the length of time it takes to collect a gallon. How much water does the hose discharge in a minute? An hour?
all household needs in a single day	Read the house water meter at the beginning and end of the day.

— paraphrased from *Teaching Science with Everyday Things*, page 36 (see our review, page 91)

cooking and chemistry

As most of the activities and reviews in the next few pages will prove, the kitchen is a rich environment for kids' learning. Here they can mess around and discover things from a large variety of intriguing materials and available equipment. The kind of science they get into with this stuff is exactly what the 1960s' curriculum reform movement had in mind. It represents a perfect hands-on, real-life, self-discovery mode of education, and kids eat it up, literally and figuratively.

activity books

The Kids' Kitchen Takeover
Sara Bonnett Stein

Workman Publishing Company
231 East 51st Street
New York, New York 10022
$4.95

We can describe this only in glowing terms; it has to be an ultimate achievement among many efforts to capitalize on the kitchen as a home learning center. Far more than a cookbook, it is a wonderfully appealing collection of craft ideas (tie-dyeing, candle making, fish prints), science experiments (water equalizer machine, invisible ink), nature study (sea urchins, gourds), and, of course, recipes and experiments for cooking (would you believe "burnt berry jelly" or "fake bread"?). As some of the above examples illustrate, activities are not limited to the kitchen, but in the author's view it serves as a well-supplied work space and resource center, a place to find most of what you need to do any of these engaging things. Like other Workman books (see general review, page 16) it is a model of visual delight and sensible format. What a terrific book!

Cure For Hiccups

No one is sure why this works, but it does. When you can't get rid of hiccups, eat a spoonful of granulated sugar. The hiccups will stop as soon as the sugar is in your mouth, even before you swallow it.

Two Ways To Stop Burns From Hurting

Long ago people used to keep an aloe plant growing on their kitchen windowsills to treat burns. Herb nurseries are the most likely place to find an aloe now. Should you have an aloe plant in your kitchen and you happen to get a burn, squeeze the leaves to get the juice, then wipe the juice on the burn. Aloe juice is a

An aloe plant

common ingredient in sunburn ointments.

Today most people have baking soda in the kitchen. If you get a burn, mix regular baking soda with water to make a thin paste. Spoon the paste liberally onto the burn. It will relieve most of the pain right away. When it starts to hurt again, rinse off the first paste, which is probably a little dry, and put more on.

Science Experiments You Can Eat
Vicki Cobb

J. B. Lippincott Company
East Washington Square
Philadelphia, Pennsylvania 19105
$1.95

The author presents an ordinary kitchen as a unique laboratory in which a great deal of basic chemistry can be learned over boiling pots of grape jelly or a plateful of spinach. Chapters are organized by grouping food experiments that demonstrate fundamental concepts. For instance, the subcontents under "Suspensions, Colloids, and Emulsions" are:

Borscht Cocktail: Separating
    Suspended Particles
Liquid Food and the Tyndall Effect
Salad Dressing: A Liquid Suspended in
    a Liquid
Mayonnaise: A Stabilized Suspension
Strawberry Bombe: A Frozen Emulsion

Pretty advanced stuff from such commonplace resources, but then, that is the special genius of the book. It should be clear that this is not for getting kids interested in cooking, but rather for helping kids who have already had a lot of experience in that realm learn some chemistry from it. Charmingly illustrated and written for kids to read (older ones, that is), it is well recommended by those who have tried it out.

Illustrations copyright © 1972 by Peter Lippman. Reproduced by permission of J. B. Lippincott Company.

LEMON FIZZ: A REACTION FORMS A GAS

Some reactions form gases as products. When the reaction takes place in a liquid, the bubbles rise to the surface and can be easily observed.

MATERIALS AND EQUIPMENT

baking soda   2 glass tumblers
water   2 spoons
lemonade

PROCEDURE

Fill one glass half full of water. Stir in ½ teaspoon of baking soda. Does it dissolve easily? Is there any reaction? Use red cabbage indicator (Chapter 2) to test this solution to see if it is an acid or a base.

Fill the second glass half full of lemonade. (Test the lemonade with the indicator.) Use a clean spoon to put ½ teaspoon of baking soda in the lemonade. How can you tell there is a reaction? Drink the lemon fizz quickly before all the bubbles escape into the air.

From *Science Experiments You Can Eat*, p. 73.
Text copyright © 1972 by Vicki Cobb.

Creative Food Experiences for Children
Mary T. Goodwin and Gerry Pollen

Center for Science in the Public Interest
1779 Church Street
Washington, D.C. 20036
$14

Our national consciousness of nutrition has been slowly deadened by convenience foods. Soda pop, snack foods, and hamburgers-to-go constitute the regular diet for a bigger proportion of kids than we care to admit. Teaching what foods do to people and how to eat well are what this book is about. It is not an exciting book: businesslike lesson plans, lack of illustrations, and typescript format. Yet there are excellent teaching ideas and worthwhile suggestions for integrating food experiences with other parts of a school curriculum. We recommend it as a good general resource if you're going to do a lot with cooking.

The Chemistry of a Lemon
A. Harris Stone

The Chemistry of Soap
A. Harris Stone and Bertram M. Siegel

Prentice-Hall
Educational Book Division
Englewood Cliffs, New Jersey 07632
$4.95 each

Stone's books are good science books in general (see review, page 91), but these two in particular are favorites with a lot of people. The most common materials become main sources for wide-ranging chemistry lessons that even young kids will enjoy learning. In each book the text is largely interrogative, the aim being to help kids approach scientific investigations in the same way that a professional chemist would: posing questions and then performing experiments to look for answers. Format, prose, supplies, and illustrations are all simple enough to make this kind of chemistry readily available to kids.

The Good for Me Cookbook
Karen B. Croft

Karen B. Croft
741 Maplewood Place
Palo Alto, California 94303
$2

Another book that grew out of teaching experience in a nursery school, this has a delightful set of recipes that utilize natural foods and represent an interesting cross section of ethnic cookery. The handmade text written in calligraphic form includes artwork by the author and by children whom she taught.

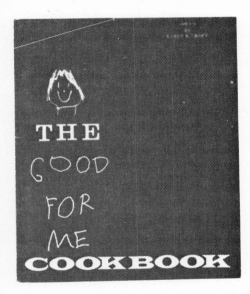

Kids Are Natural Cooks
Parents' Nursery School

Houghton Mifflin Company
Children's Book Division
2 Park Street
Boston, Massachusetts 02107
$4.95

So far, this has been my favorite cookbook to use with my kids. Without it, we would not be eating our own granola, among other things. By working out each of the cooking activities with their nursery school kids, the authors developed a sure-fire set of recipes and a marvelously sensible way of writing them down that combines directions, ingredients, and diagrammatic illustration in a single flow. The contents are organized by seasons, so that in the fall, for instance, you can start making:

~ Pumpkin spice Custard ~

Beat 2 eggs.
Add: 1 can (1 lb.) pumpkin, (about 3 cups).
          ½ c. milk or cream
          2 heaping Tablespoons honey
          1½ t. cinnamon
          ½ t. vanilla extract

Spoon into individual custard cups. Set the cups in a large baking pan with about 1 inch of cold water. Bake at 350° 50 minutes.

~ Children can do most of the work for this recipe (stirring, spooning into custard cups). Show them the difference between fresh and canned pumpkin, if possible ~

Apples into applesauce
Pumpkins into pies and breads
Grains ground into flours, baked into
    breads and cakes
Nuts ground into spreads
Seeds — cooked and sprouted
Leaves dried for tea

— from the table of contents

It's also nice to know that proceeds from the sale of this book still return in part to the Parents' Nursery School.

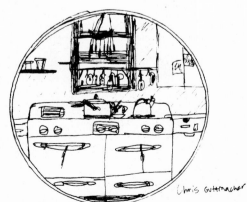

Kitchen seen from porthole No. 2

Chris Guttmacher '75

identifying kitchen powders

Here's one good way to set up experiments from which kids of at least eight can do some meaningful chemistry. You need only commonplace materials and simple equipment in quantities sufficient for the number of kids you're working with.

Assemble the following:

plastic medicine cups or small paper cups
aluminum foil
spoons
flat toothpicks
wooden clothespins
hand lens or microscope
candle or can of Sterno
newspapers or plastic sheet, sponges, and dustpan with brush
large cans or buckets
eyedropper

at least four of these powders:

granulated sugar
salt
baking soda
cornstarch or laundry starch
powdered milk
flour
plaster of Paris

in addition to:

iodine (small amount diluted in generous supply of water, since it's poisonous)
white vinegar

Put each of the powders into a container of suitable size, put numbers on them, but don't otherwise identify the materials for the kids doing the experiments.

For the first stage, let the kids try to figure out what the powders are by using any simple tests they can think of. These chemicals are all safe for blowing, tasting, smelling, feeling, or examining under a lens.

The kids can keep a record of their findings on a simple chart numbered like the powders.

Once they have made these preliminary attempts, challenge them to devise more exacting tests so they can be surer of what they think the powders are. Set out other materials, but direct them as little as possible. From this point on, though, things will

be neater and more economical if they put small quantities of the powder in the individual cups. They might try:

mixing powders with water
reexamining them under a microscope, dry and wet
looking for variations of color and texture

and then also try:

mixing powders with vinegar
putting drops of iodine on them with the eyedropper
heating small quantities on a square of tinfoil held with a clothespin over a flame

The preceding investigations should all be performed without mixing powders together, as this would seriously confuse the results.

If they have done these experiments carefully, kept records, and compared notes with one another, the kids should now be able to predict what each of the tests will consistently show. In the last stage you can try mixing various powders together and ask the kids to use their knowledge of testing to identify the contents.

And now, have fun cleaning up!

For more refined guidance, get a copy of the ESS teacher's guide *Mystery Powders,* from which these activities were adapted. (See page 34 for ESS materials and ordering information.)

heat

All natural forms of energy inspire a sense of wonder, but there is a special enchantment in heat. Consider a blazing campfire, warm sunrises, the glow of a candle. Because we have to instill an awareness of its dangers (from open flame, excessive sun, hot surfaces), children are usually discouraged from experimenting freely with many types of heat. There are plenty of safe ways to satisfy their curiosity, however, and they need to know that things hot and cold behave as predictably as the other elements.

Candles are one good place to start (at least with children over eight), because they have a lot of appeal and there are many good activities to do with them.

See page 108 for candle-burning activities

candle burning

Drip melted wax from candle onto tin-foil plate and affix candle to plate. Fill plate with approximately ½ inch of water. Set inverted glass jar over candle, into water.

How long will the candle continue to burn?
What happens to the level of water in the jar?
Why does the candle go out?

Try cooling the glass in a freezer first, and place it over the flame for two seconds. Where does the water come from that forms inside the glass? (Careful!)

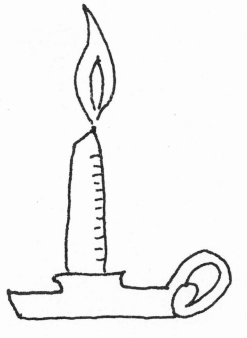

The Burning of a Candle
Science Teachers' Association of Ontario

*Donco Quality Printers
212 Division Street
Kingston, Ontario K7K 3Z1, CANADA*

As everyone knows who has lived or worked with young children, open flame holds a special fascination for them. I'm convinced that pyromaniacs are people who have been denied the unique pleasure of burning up whole boxes of wooden matches, one by one. For that reason, among others, I am a strong advocate of (carefully supervised) experiments with flame, in spite of the risks and worried fire marshals. Just be sure you have water, fire blankets, or extinguishers, and that the children know a few things about putting out fires quickly, treating burns, and so on. (For instance, it's good to know that putting a burning injury under cool water as fast as possible minimizes the damage.)

This Ontario booklet is especially appropriate if you are also doing some candle making, but you can get along fine with commercial candles, too. It provides an excellent starting point for work with flame, stressing simple observations and basic questions.

paper boiler

This is a fascinating little experiment, which can be performed well only on homemade equipment.

To make the stove, remove both ends from the can and punch several draft holes at one end with a punch opener. Drip wax into the pie pan and set the candle on it. The candle should be 1 inch shorter than the can. Place can over candle and a 5-inch-square piece of wire netting on top of the can.

To make the boiler, a 5-by-7-inch piece of coated paper should be folded 1½ inches from each edge, the squares at each edge folded diagonally, and the sides wrapped around the ends so that they can be fastened with a paper clip as shown.

Fill the container with no more than ½ inch of water and place it directly on top of the stove.

So long as there is water in the boiler, the candle flame cannot heat the paper to its kindling temperature. The water limits the temperature to which the flame can raise the paper, even though heat is added to the container and its contents.

— adapted from *Teaching Science with Everyday Things,* page 144
(reviewed on page 91)

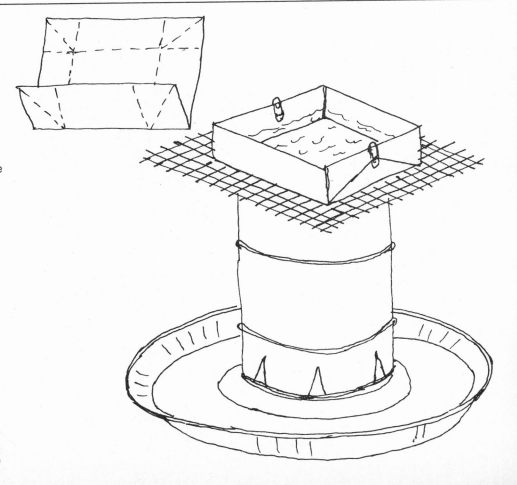

other stove experiments

Substitute another aluminum plate for the wire netting on top of the stove and try placing a variety of combustible materials in it to see how easily they burn.

photo negative
cotton
paper with high rag content
wood
coal

Find the time it takes for each substance to start to burn, smolder, or smoke. Graph the results.

To get a better idea of how a furnace or stove works, wrap a piece of masking tape around the bottom of the can, covering all the punched draft holes. Place a square of glass on top of the can. After the candle is lit, strip off the tape from one hole and note the effects on its flame. Gradually uncover more holes. How does this change the flame?

You can also try replacing the candle with some of the combustible materials used in the experiment above, placed *inside* the can. Ignite the material and experiment with tape as before.

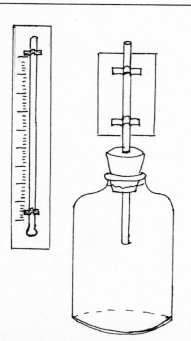

water thermometer

One way to get a clear idea of how predictable heat energy can be is to make measurements of it with thermometers. To understand how thermometers record fluctuations in heat, it's a good idea for kids to construct their own.

Constructing and using this thermometer takes the mystery out of the instrument — it's nothing more than a system for watching a fluid expand or contract with changing temperature. It's the oldest known means for measuring these changes.

Find a bottle with an opening that makes a tight fit with a cork you have available. Make a hole in the cork to fit a plastic straw. (You can heat a nail of the right size with a candle flame and burn the hole through.)

Fill the bottle *to the brim* with colored water and push the cork with the straw inserted in it down into the opening, thus forcing some of the water up the straw. If things aren't perfectly snug (no air should get in or out), seal with melted wax or plasticine.

If you're going to use it over a long period of time, put a few drops of oil into the straw to keep the water from evaporating. If you want to use it for measuring temperatures colder than the freezing point, add 25 percent alcohol to the water.

To calibrate, tape an index card onto the back of the straw, and put a mark even with the level of fluid. As the temperature rises or falls, record other marks to show changing levels. You can match calibrations with those of a standard thermometer by placing the two side by side and marking temperatures on the card as changes occur.

How can you use the thermometer to find out which is the warmer of two pots of water?

What happens if you place the device in a pot of boiling water for five minutes?

What is the range of temperatures outside a building over a period of one week? One month?

Thermometers
Science Teachers' Association of Ontario

Donco Quality Printers
212 Division Street
Kingston, Ontario K7K 3Z1, CANADA

For some reason there are two Ontario booklets with this same title, but we recommend only the one ordered as #73135, since the other is textbookish and uninventive by comparison. While not very extensive, this has the best detailed information and activities for work with thermometers specifically. Use it in conjunction with one of the more general books on heat (see reviews next page).

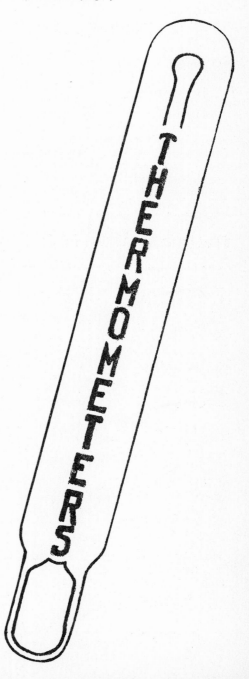

heating materials

Children are often not aware of the subtle ways in which metal and other materials show the effects of heat. They're fascinated to learn that the Empire State Building grows several inches every summer or that those funny sets of teeth in a bridge allow it to expand and contract according to changes in temperature. Some of the following books and activities can help kids learn about these effects at first hand.

Experiments with Heat
Harry Sootin

W. W. Norton and Company
55 Fifth Avenue
New York, New York 10003

This is a good basic source book for experiments in heat, although it leans toward older children. It generally avoids special equipment and elaborate investigations of simple principles, relying instead on activities using materials from home or hardware store. You will probably want to avoid sections like "Specific Heat" or some of the more advanced measurement calculations that frequently appear. I liked Sootin's rubber band experiment: If you put one gently against your lips and stretch it suddenly, you feel some heat, thus demonstrating that rubber behaves in contradiction to most other materials, which cool down when expanded. You'll have to let Sootin explain why. (Maybe that's why I like to chew erasers?)

The Heat's On
A. Harris Stone and Bertram M. Siegel

Prentice-Hall
Educational Book Division
Englewood Cliffs, New Jersey 07632

This is one of Stone's inquiry science books, and like the others, simple to use. (See review of series, page 91.) It's less sophisticated than Sootin's *Experiments with Heat* (above), both in concepts and equipment, but it covers the same range of activities. Better for younger children.

metal expansion

Here's a neat little device for learning about the expansion caused by heat in solid materials.

Attach a thin wire (copper is best) to a nail in the wall or some other support so you have about five feet of it hanging free. To make the wire taut, suspend a weight from the bottom (a hammer is handy), and adjust the height so that the lower end is hanging just above the floor.

Now heat the wire by moving a candle flame slowly up and down its length. When the wire is heated, the weight will move toward or touch the floor.

You can measure the expansion by placing a strip of paper on the wall behind the weight and marking variations in height, or by constructing the more sensitive device shown at bottom of page.

Now you can wrestle with this old problem: Are you measuring heat, or temperature?

If you get stuck, try making two water thermometers with different-size bottles, and put them both in boiling water. Does one take longer than the other to reach the same level in the straw? Why?

— adapted from *Experiments with Heat,* pages 10–11 (reviewed on page 110)

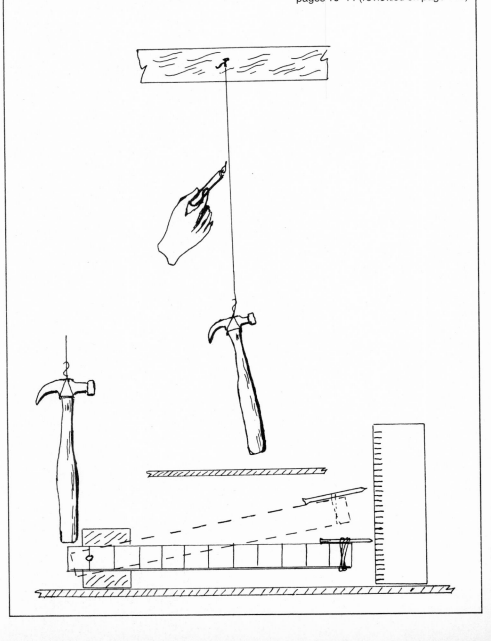

metal heating

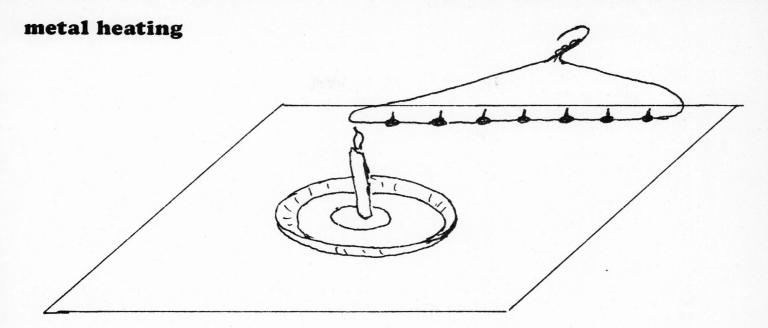

The heat-conducting properties of metals can be tested out with this (and variations of this) simple experiment.

Using your candle, melt droplets of wax at equal intervals along a heavy wire or rod. (A coat hanger without paint works well and provides its own handle. Lay it flat on a table for this operation.) While the wax is still soft, "glue" a tack to each droplet. Heat just one end of the wire over a candle and watch the tacks drop off one by one as the heat travels down the rod. By noting the time it takes each tack to drop you can come to some conclusions about the rate of heat conduction in the wire.

Try the same thing with other kinds of metals, other diameters and lengths of rods.

What kind of metal conducts heat fastest?
How long a wire can you heat this way?

melting and freezing

One way to study heat is to observe its absence. Here are some resources and intriguing activities for exploring what happens when things are cold.

There's a wealth of further activities in *Snow and Ice,* one of the guides from the Examining Your Environment series (see page 28 for general review). Also see *Snow Stumpers* (page 32) for some interesting puzzles about patterns of freezing and melting.

Ice Cubes
Elementary Science Study

McGraw-Hill Book Company
1221 Avenue of the Americas
New York, New York 10020

Another one of the ESS booklets that requires no other equipment than what you can find in your own kitchen. (They sell a kit, too, but you can do without it.)

It lays out nicely systematic, scientifically controlled experiments, laced with interesting comments made by children as they worked. Using it helps in figuring out how any one activity can flow smoothly into others, or predicting what problems and questions the young experimenters are likely to encounter.

melting ice cubes

Maybe the easiest way to be aware of living in a world of heat is to sit and watch an ice cube melt.

Next step is to set the task: "Find some way to make ice melt faster." (If you want, especially with older kids, make the conditions that crushing the ice or using artificial heat is not allowed.)

Did some people try using the heat of their bodies?
What happens if you rub your hands together before holding the ice cube?
Did anyone think of placing the cube on dark objects? On other objects that trap heat?

build a better ice cube keeper

Reversing the task of melting cubes, how can you keep ice unmelted, without refrigeration? How long can you keep it?

I'm tempted to say that children really warm up to this task, but obviously that wouldn't be appropriate. All sorts of materials can be used:

pieces of Styrofoam
corrugated cardboard
cloth
egg boxes
aluminum foil
sawdust

That is — anything that has some insulating qualities or that can be tested for those qualities.

other experiments

Now you'll want to try a whole series of other variations on the ice-melting theme, the best source for which is the ESS *Ice Cubes,* from which these activities are adapted.

Freeze water in a variety of plastic containers; make pancakes, cylinders, thin tubes, cakes with holes in the middle. Try balloons. How does the shape affect the rate of melting?

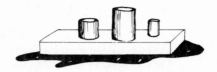

Do different substances freeze faster than others? Try milk, soda, syrup, etc. What happens when you add salt to the water?

Place different objects on top of a slab or block of ice. What happens to the objects on the ice? Do some sink into the ice faster than others? How do you account for some behaving differently from others?

electricity and magnetism

The electronic age is steadily plugging us in to a web of complex circuitry: television, computors, and vast communications systems are involved with practically everything we do. Most of it is too sophisticated for the average adult to understand, to say nothing of children. Yet all of it depends on some basic operating principles of electricity and electromagnetism that even young kids can fathom if they get a chance to play around with simple circuits and related equipment. For kids, feeling a spark of static electricity or hitching up a few wires, a bulb, and some batteries is exciting stuff. At least part of the excitement comes from knowing these things are representative of the powerful electronic network that hums all around them.

Safe and Simple Electrical Experiments
Rudolf F. Graf

Dover Publications
180 Varick Street
New York, New York 10014

This is certainly one of the handiest experiment books for electricity and magnetism. (Almost half the book is devoted to magnets; I don't understand why this isn't indicated in the title.) They have struck a nice balance between explanation and straight directions. Diagrams are full and clear, directions easy to follow, and raw materials are the simplest available.

The book is divided into three categories of nearly equal size: "Static Electricity," "Magnetism," and "Current Electricity and Electromagnetism." It does lack an index and there is no clear pattern to the way experiments are presented, but kids can leaf through and say, "I want to do *that*."

Harry Sootin

Experiments with Electric Currents
Experiments with Magnetism
Experiments with Static Electricity

Grosset and Dunlap
51 Madison Avenue
New York, New York 10010

This is a lot more expensive way to cover the same field that *Safe and Simple Electrical Experiments* does, but Sootin's books are heavier in background explanation and have the advantage of experiments laid out in a carefully organized sequence. If you're really seeking to "teach the principles," albeit through experimental discovery, use these. They are probably better for school use because of both the presentation and their sheer durability. Try getting them from libraries first.

pie-pan generator

Everybody has experienced the shocks you get on a dry day in the winter scuffing across a rug and then touching something metallic. Here's a way to generate larger charges and capture them for use.

Stretch two rubber bands at right angles to each other across an aluminum pie pan.

Rub flattened plastic bag briskly with *wool* cloth, and hold the bag up by one edge.

Lift the pan by the rubber bands and, keeping all parts of your body away from the metal, hold the pan against the bag.

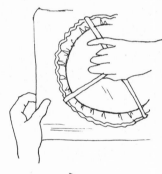

While it is in this position, touch the pan briefly with the tip of your finger.
Do you *hear* the charge?

Without touching the metal again, take the pan away from the bag and bring it to your nose.
Can you *feel* the charge?

In a dark room, try holding a fluorescent bulb at one end and touching the other to the charged pan.
What happens to the bulb?

This is how the charges are transmitted. (Look again at the diagrams as you read.)

1. Plastic receives (−) charge as it is rubbed with wool;
2. (−) charge in the plastic causes negative electricity in the metal to jump to your finger (pan is left with (+) charge);
3. (−) charge jumps from your nose back to the metal.

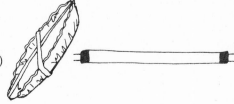

— adapted from *Teaching Science with Everyday Things,* page 119
(reviewed on page 91)

can static be current?

Remember the puzzler about *temperature* versus *heat*? (See page 110.) Here's another one: What is the difference between *static* and *current*? It's really the same thing as asking what the distinction is between two kinds of water, *still* and *flowing*.

Check it out this way:

Place a fluorescent bulb (even a burned-out one is okay) on a box so that one end touches something large and metal, such as a radiator or water pipe. Touch a charged pie pan to the other end. What happens?

Now try fastening one bared end of a wire to the prongs on the tube, and suspend the wire from rubber bands held by some kids or by strings fastened overhead. Charge the pan again and touch it to the other bared end of the wire.

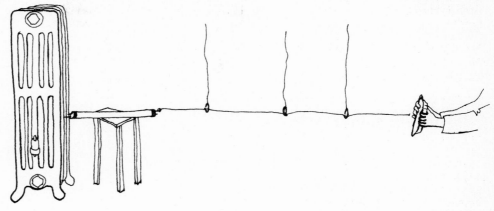

Can you make some deductions about the behavior of electricity?
What is it when it's in the pan, current or static?
What is it when it's in the wire? In the bulb?
How long can the wire be?
Can you use other kinds of wire?

Will string, thread, rubber bands linked together, or a long strip of foil work in place of wire?
What happens when you *wet* string?

— adapted from *Teaching Science with Everyday Things*, page 120
(reviewed on page 91)

circuits

Teacher's Guide for Batteries and Bulbs
Elementary Science Study

McGraw-Hill Book Company
1221 Avenue of the Americas
New York, New York 10020

Nobody has been able to match the ESS method for teaching kids to make a thorough investigation of a subject. (We're not getting a commission; we really believe this!) Here is real discovery stuff, not an "I know this works but see if you can do it yourself" approach.

In this unit kids design and construct numerous basic circuits with the simplest components, methodically testing, predicting, testing as they go. They take things apart to see how they function; they draw diagrams and invent terms that they can understand. The whole process has been refined through extensive classroom trials; it's reliable.

light a bulb

First experiments that kids do with batteries and bulbs ought to be done with *little or no direction* from more experienced people.

Provide them with:

standard flashlight D- or C-cells
odds and ends of bare wire and single-strand insulated wire
thin strips of aluminum cut from pans or cans (you can use regular scissors to cut)
masking tape or rubber bands
flashlight bulbs

Set the task:

See if you can get a bulb to light, using these materials.

Ask some questions:

Will the bulb light if it is held by itself against the top of the battery? The bottom?
Can the bulb be lit even if it does not touch the battery?
What happens if you use more than one battery?
Can you design a setup that makes it easy to switch the light on and off with just your finger?
Can you make a handy night-light to put beside your bed?

building bigger circuits

The idea of an electric circuit has now been introduced: a continuous loop of materials through which electricity flows. (If you've done some *Water Flow* experiments [see pages 97–98], you might ask the kids to think about some of the resemblances.)

Here are a few designs for homemade bulb holders and switches that you can put into your circuits.

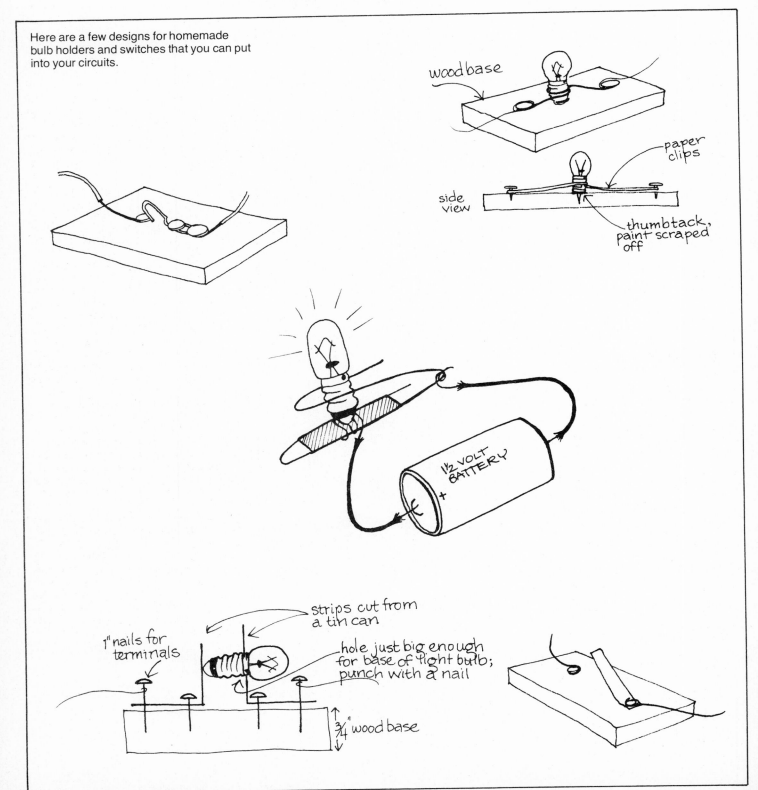

wood base

paper clips

side view

thumbtack, paint scraped off

1½ VOLT BATTERY

strips cut from a tin can

1" nails for terminals

hole just big enough for base of light bulb; punch with a nail

¾" wood base

The next step is to explore more complex circuits, opening and closing them, controlling them for different purposes.

The same materials supplied for lighting a bulb can be used, along with small blocks of wood and thumbtacks for constructing "circuit boxes." The kids should be shown how to strip insulated bell wire with a wire stripper.

Some more tasks:

Make a good bulb holder on a block of wood.
Make a switch on a wood block that can conveniently complete (close) or break (open) a circuit.
Put together a whole circuit using these devices, batteries, and wire.

Some more questions:

Can a circuit be connected with string?
What differences do you find in using insulated (covered) wire instead of bare wire?
Does it matter how long the connecting wires are?
Does it matter where you place the batteries in the circuit? Where you place the switch?

mystery circuits

Once the kids have had some experience with basic bulb, battery, and wire circuits you can open the doors into the world of circuitry a little wider (Marshall McLuhan, we're on our way!) with these little boxes.

Materials:

shoe boxes (or other boxes of similar size)
brass paper fasteners
bell wire
wire stripper
a nail
masking tape
Fahnestock clips — optional
battery
bulb and holder
wide rubber bands

Using a nail, punch 6 to 8 holes in the top of a shoe box, and number them.

Put a paper fastener through each hole so the head stays on top. (At this point, if you want to use Fahnestock clips, place one through the extended tips of a fastener and bend the tips over to hold the clip in place on the underside of the cover.)

Strip an inch of insulation from each end of 4 or 5 box-length pieces of bell wire.

Connect the wires in a pattern like the one shown, or any variation of it. Use just 4 or 5 wires inside any one box.

Put the lid on the box and seal it with tape.

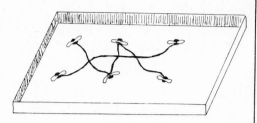

If you have batteries, bulbs, and wire lying around you can simply ask the experimenters : "How can you find out which buttons are connected with wires inside the box without opening it?" and then see if they can use their previous experience with simple bulb and battery circuits.

In any case, they will need to construct a testing device like the following to solve the problem. By connecting the two free ends of the tester to pairs of buttons they can work out the mystery of the circuit pattern and make a diagram to record their findings.

Many, more complex circuits — involving buzzers, lights, electromagnets — can be constructed inside such boxes as the kids gain sophistication with the materials (see *Batteries and Bulbs,* pages 65 ff).

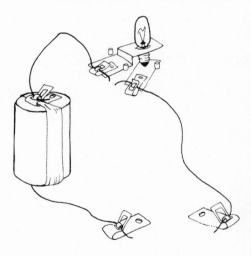

Use of the boxes should come after the kids have worked with the same components in the open and have developed a clear understanding of how they work. As this may suggest, the boxes provide a good means for evaluating in a concrete way what the kids have learned (see *Batteries and Bulbs,* page 67). Also, they serve as a crude model of complex, manufactured circuitry.

more powerful stuff

Young kids' direct experimentation with electricity obviously needs to be confined to whatever batteries will power, but there are some ways to learn about more complicated electrical stuff. By taking apart old appliances, for instance. Stores and trash heaps will often yield things like broken toasters, radios, phonographs, hair dryers, and a variety of small motors. Kids love to look inside or just play around with all the different components they find. Wires, resistors, magnets, loudspeakers, and bits of circuitry can be fashioned into imaginary machines or assembled as intriguing junk sculptures. Caution: cut off all plug cords and avoid TV sets altogether (they have some dangerous parts).

"Printed" circuits have come into general use in the last few years and are fascinating to look at by themselves. Besides those to be found inside used radios, you might get hold of some from an electronics manufacturer. See if kids can find a relationship between them and the simple battery circuits they have made.

And then there's electric trains. Kids still love them, even though nobody travels on the real thing much anymore. Since transformers reduce house current to a level that's safe to handle, kids can not only control the trains but also wire up all manner of switches, lights, and miniature equipment. There's high incentive to wire up things so they *work,* and, unless Mom or Dad takes over, kids have to learn how to make the right things light, or prevent short circuits, for instance.

For older kids who want to get into much more sophisticated stuff, commercially available kits offer a pretty good, albeit expensive, way to learn how electrical systems work. One series is sold by Science Fair of Tandy Corporation Company, Fort Worth, TX 76107. Write them for a catalog or look in an electronics store. Also check the Edmund Scientific catalog (see page 90) for what they may have available.

magnetism

some magnets

Experiments with magnets are good companions to those with electricity, since the two forces are partly related (electricity can create a magnetic field). Even very young children are fascinated by the magnet's ability to attract or repel things. No one can fail to have his or her sense of wonder provoked by seeing iron filings dance themselves into symmetrical patterns under the control of a magnetic field.

To get an idea of the different faculties magnets have according to their design, it's a good idea to have a big variety available. The best source we know is Edmund Scientific (see page 90).

20/21   magnets G-1

How are you doing?

1. Will these magnets __attract__ or __repel__ each other?

   a.   [S   N] [N   S]

   b.   [S   N] [S   N]

2. Name __3__ things that are __magnetic__.
   Name __3__ things that are __not magnetic__.

3. How can you show that the __2 poles__ of a U-Magnet are different?

SAM card. Part of the SAM card series deals with magnet activities (SEE, $3.35 / set of 29 cards). SEE also has an assortment of magnet equipment for $16.25.

Mickey's Magnet
Franklyn M. Branley and
Eleanor K. Vaughan

*Thomas Y. Crowell Company
Department of Books for Children and
   Young People
666 Fifth Avenue
New York, New York 10019*

A lot of people seem to like this beginning reader's account of a little tot's discovering how magnets work — maybe because the adults in the story show a good sense of when, and when not, to intervene.

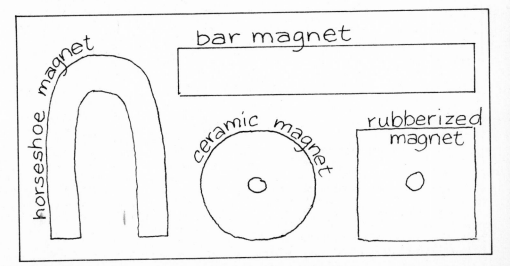

electromagnet

Start with the simplest arrangement for exploring the relationship between electricity and magnetism. It *is* rather mysterious, but it does not need to be complicated! (A good explanation of what's happening in electromagnets can be found in Laurence B. White's *Investigating Science with Nails,* pages 52–60; see our review on page 91.)

Use a 6-to-8-inch length of bell wire and a D-cell. Holding the two bared ends of the wire against the poles of the battery, bring the loop of wire close to a small pile of iron filings. The filings will jump and stick to the wire. (Do not leave the wire connected for more than a few seconds.)

Now you can increase the strength of this magnetic field and make definite poles this way.

Take a longer insulated wire (8 to 10 feet) and a 3-inch nail. Strip 1 inch of both ends of the wire, and wind all of it around the nail, leaving about 6 inches at each end of the wire free. (The winding does not have to be neat.)

Have the child hold one wire tip against the top of the battery and the other at the bottom, and then use an end of the magnetic nail to pick up paper clips, staples, or filings.

Note: If the wire is left connected for more than a few seconds at a time the battery will soon be drained.

If you do not have enough wire available, you can use a long strip of aluminum foil cut from a roll, but it must be wound on the nail together with a similar strip of plastic.

Experiments can be aimed at discovering relative strengths of different designs, and other features of the magnets.

Does the number of turns of wire or foil affect the magnet's strength?
How does the number of batteries affect the strength?
What about the kind of metal in the core? (Try aluminum nails, rods of other metals.)
Are there two poles, as in nonelectrical magnets?
Does reversing the wires on the battery affect the poles on the magnet?

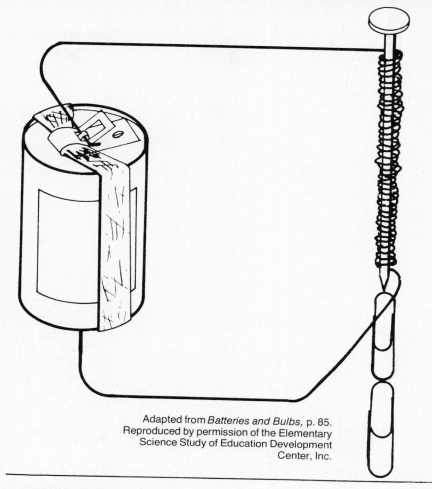

Adapted from *Batteries and Bulbs*, p. 85. Reproduced by permission of the Elementary Science Study of Education Development Center, Inc.

compasses

Homemade Compass

By building their own, kids will get a better understanding of how a compass works than they will by playing with a manufactured one.

To make a compass, begin by spreading apart the prongs of a metal bobby pin so that they are in a straight line, except for a small bend at the center. Then hold it by the bend and stroke it about fifty times on a strong magnet. (See magnets, page 118.) Rub its entire length, from tip to tip, on *one* end of the magnet only, and always in the same direction. Lift after each stroke. Test the bobby pin to see if it will pick up a paper clip; if so, it is sufficiently magnetized.

Tie a thin thread to the bobby pin at the center so it can swing freely and level. Tie the other end onto a pencil as a means of suspending the pin inside a glass jar. Be sure the whole apparatus is yards away from any magnets or metallic objects (including watches!).

After it has spun freely for a few moments and come to rest, mark the tip that points northward (in the direction of midday shadows) with a dab of nail polish or a small paper sticker.

The north-seeking quality of a compass needle will be more clearly demonstrated if several of these devices are made and used at the same time. (Keep them several feet apart.)

Will the bobby-pin compass work as well if the jar is filled with water? Are there any advantages to this method?

— adapted from *Teaching Science with Everyday Things*, page 111 (reviewed on page 91)

A Gnomon

The earliest mariner's compasses, known as "gnomons," consisted of a magnetized steel needle pushed through a small chunk of wood and floated on the surface of water in a container. When the north-seeking tip came to rest, the skipper proceeded accordingly.

To make your own, balance a magnetized needle on a thin cork (the lining of a soda-pop bottle works well) and float the arrangement in a plastic or glass container. If you put a small amount of detergent in the water it will help keep the cork and needle from floating over to the edges. (See Floating Paper Clips, page 96.) Give the cork a gentle spin, and watch it come to rest in a north-south position.

You can "calibrate" it by drawing a circle on a piece of paper with "N," "S," "E," and "W" and placing this beneath the container, lining up "N" with the north-seeking tip of the needle.

— adapted from *Safe and Simple Electrical Experiments,* pages 55–57 (reviewed on page 114)

SAFE AND SIMPLE
ELECTRICAL
EXPERIMENTS

RUDOLF F. GRAF

164 ILLUSTRATIONS

mechanics

Kids develop an early fascination with things that work: washing machines, telephones, road graders, clocks, rockets, and all manner of toys (including many modeled after real-life machines). They want to know *how* they work, which sometimes can be explained or demonstrated, but also *why* they work, which makes a lot of adults start sidestepping and pointing to encyclopedias. The best way to deal with "why" and even some of the "how" is to let kids handle and study the simplest mechanical devices — things like pendulums.

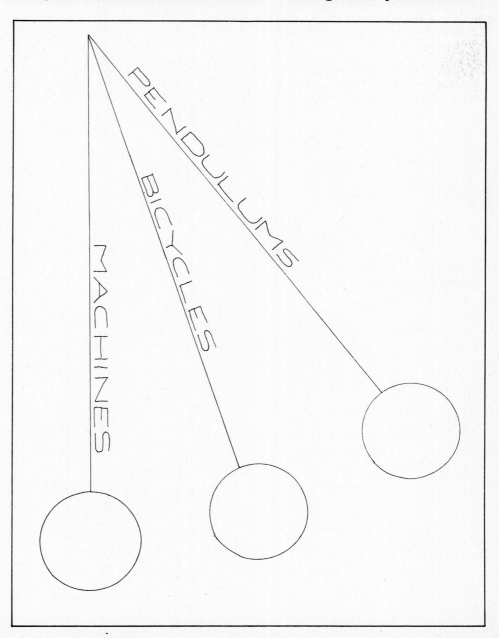

pendulums

Pendulums
Elementary Science Study

McGraw-Hill Book Company
1221 Avenue of the Americas
New York, New York 10020

Pendulums
Science Teachers' Association of Ontario

Donco Quality Printers
212 Division Street
Kingston, Ontario K7K 3Z1, CANADA

Ontario's booklet is cheaper and assumes homemade or scrounged equipment. They're not as thorough as the ESS teacher's guide but they do have a number of activities that ESS doesn't. The ESS guide has the additional advantage of good photos and diagrams. If you want a maximum number of ideas but you don't want to buy equipment, get them both.

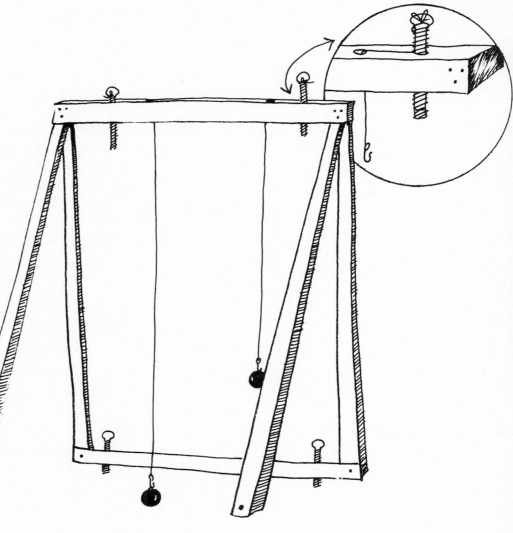

DETAIL

pendulum apparatus

Grandfather clocks, swings, an apple on a tree: it's easy enough to find things that hang and swing, and they suggest a lot of questions about basic laws of motion.

To get kids playing with these questions, let them start with the simplest versions they can make.

Then, to make a more controllable apparatus:

1. See what you can collect in the way of small weighty objects that can be easily suspended. Have several of as nearly the same size as possible.

    golf balls
    small rubber balls
    tennis balls
    wooden balls (from toys)
    croquet balls
    plasticine
    fish-line sinkers
    ball bearings
    can with nuts or washers
    sections of dowel
    washers

Or, order some from AS&E. (They have other pendulum supplies, as well.)

2. Balls can be suspended by drilling pilot holes and inserting small screw eyes, then tying on lines, or gluing line directly to ball with epoxy glue. Use fish line or nylon thread.

3. Make a frame: the ESS design has a thumbscrew for winding up the line to raise and lower the pendulum. You can suspend it from the ceiling. A stepladder works fine, too, especially for long suspension lines.

4. Hang two pendulums next to each other from the same overhead support to allow comparisons between the two as you make variations in weight, amplitude (horizontal distance pendulum swings), frequency (number of swings per unit of time), and so on.

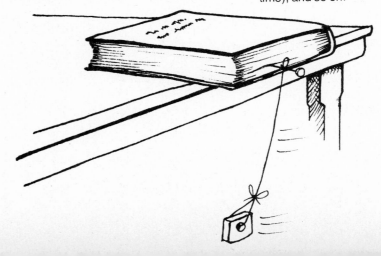

roquet

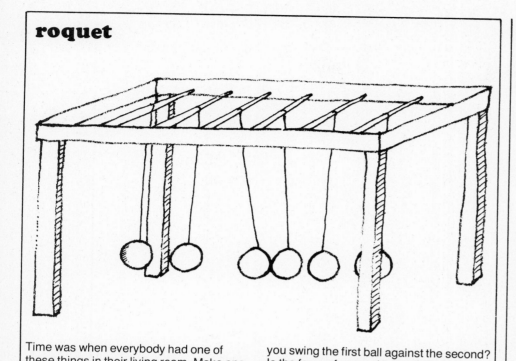

Time was when everybody had one of these things in their living room. Make one of your own design. It's a good extension of pendulum activity. What happens when you swing the first ball against the second? Is the force of one swinging ball transmitted equally down the line?

principles of pendulums

Start swinging!

The first activities with pendulums should occur with as little guidance as possible.

Can you get two balls to swing together? Will they stay together for ten swings? Twenty?

What happens when you try two balls of the same size but very different weights (wooden ball and steel ball; Ping-Pong ball and golf ball)?

How else can a pendulum swing besides straight back and forth?

Try setting up an inverted golf tee or a piece of chalk and knocking it down with the return swing of the bob only.

What happens when you set up a whole row of pegs and let the pendulum swing in a circular motion?

have a ball

playing the angles

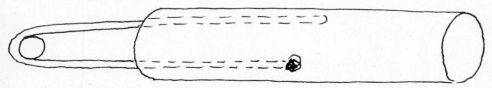

Use a section of mailing tube (experiment with the length) and tie a sturdy piece of rubber band inside it to make this variation of a slingshot. Find a rubber ball of the right size (smaller) to be launched through the tube. Coat the ball with chalk dust so that it will leave a mark when it strikes a surface.

Where does the ball hit the wall if you make a level shot from about five feet away?

As you move back, where do the chalk spots on the wall occur?

If you hold the tube at a different angle, does it change the height at which the ball strikes the wall?

Have a Ball
A. Harris Stone and Bertram M. Siegel

Prentice-Hall
Educational Book Division
Englewood Cliffs, New Jersey 07632

Variation
Science Teachers' Association of Ontario

Donco Quality Printers
212 Division Street
Kingston, Ontario K7K 3Z1, CANADA

Have a Ball is Stone at his best. The book has its title's character, a happy coincidence of things that are fun to do and serious learning. With luck, your kids won't even know they're studying physics. Balls of all kinds — baseballs, golf and croquet balls, and ball bearings — are 90 percent of the equipment. Anybody could get along with this just fine.

If you want something a little more pedestrian, a regular unit, you can try Ontario's *Variation*, where you get:

"Does the material of which the ball is made affect the height it will bounce? Does the weight of the ball affect the height which the ball will bounce?," and so on.

Most of these activities have to do with balls, yet the principles of variation they demonstrate can be applied to differences in body dimensions, and other aspects of biological diversity.

From what height must a baseball be dropped so that it will tear through a piece of waxed paper that has been tightly stretched over a frame?

Does doubling the distance that the ball falls double the number of waxed paper sheets it can tear?

Do other kinds of paper tear when the ball is dropped from the same height?

Which has the greatest effect on the number of sheets of paper that can be torn — the height from which the ball is dropped, or the weight of the ball?

— from Have a Ball, pages 12–13

Gabby Street, a baseball player, once caught a baseball thrown from the top of the Washington Monument, which is over 500 feet high. How fast was the baseball traveling when he caught it at ground level?

— from Have a Ball, page 51

simple machines

I've scanned our sources for a rugged, inexpensive set of pulleys, and can't find any. If you know of some or can think of a way to improvise them, let me know so I can stock my room.

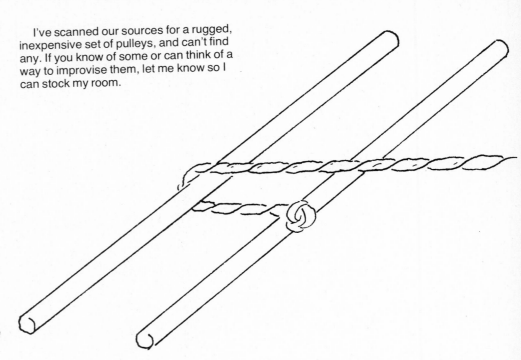

Simple machines turn me on almost as much as fine tools do; I would like to have a room full of them, just to admire and play with. I happen to be a particular fan of pulley systems, especially block-and-tackle (a term that rings of medieval England). I can remember having a long argument with someone about whether you can pull yourself over a beam with a rope. (Can you?)

The simplest way to experience what a pulley does is to place two chairs a short distance apart, back to back, and put a child in each. Then make a rope-and-broom-handle system as shown, and have somebody pull.

What happens if you make several more turns around the two poles and then pull?

rope machine

I don't know if this is accurately classified as a tool or as a machine, but it's terrific.

Steven Caney's directions aren't easily condensed, so they're reprinted here in full (*Toy Book,* pages 115–117 — see our review on page 196). I'll simply add the suggestion that for "wood stripping" you

use a 30″ × 2″ × 1″ piece of fir or hardwood. The screws and hooks will quickly loosen up in softwood.

Rope machine

Did you ever wonder how rope is made? Maybe it's not one of the great mysteries of life, but fun to know anyway. The ROPE MACHINE is a hand version of the big machines used in rope factories—the process has been the same for thousands of years. The time it takes to construct the rope machine is well worth the fine results it will produce. You are making a tool. Once you have built the machine, any amount and type of rope can be made, and the results come fast. You can make fat or thin ropes, decorative ropes of multicolored yarns, strong work ropes, long or short ropes, or ropes for braiding. You might try belts or jump ropes too.

MATERIALS	TOOLS	
wood stripping	saw	ruler
3 wood screws	drill	sandpaper
3 screw hooks	pencil	screwdriver

CONSTRUCTION

As long as the ROPE MACHINE works right mechanically, it doesn't matter how you have

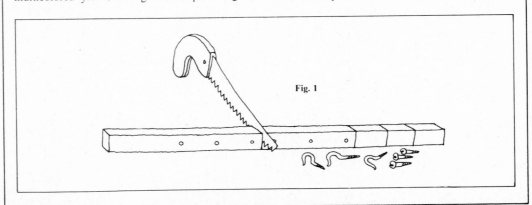

Fig. 1

built it, or what it looks like. So feel free to substitute your own ideas and materials.

Mark off a length of wood stripping into two pieces approximately 13 and 8 inches long, and three pieces, each 2 1/2 inches long. Drill holes where you see the small circles in Fig. 1 (six in all). The drilled holes should be generously larger than the thickness of the wood screws and screw hooks. Cut the wood stripping to size, sand smooth, and assemble the parts as shown in Fig. 2. The wood screws and screw hooks fit loosely through the drilled holes, and fasten securely in the three short center blocks. Don't tighten the screws and hooks all the way. When completed, the ROPE MACHINE should easily rotate all three hooks in unison.

ROPE MAKING

The instructions for making rope might sound complicated, but the process is quite simple. Refer to the illustrations so that you don't get lost in the words.

Any combination of yarn, string, or thread can be used to make rope. Yarns of different color

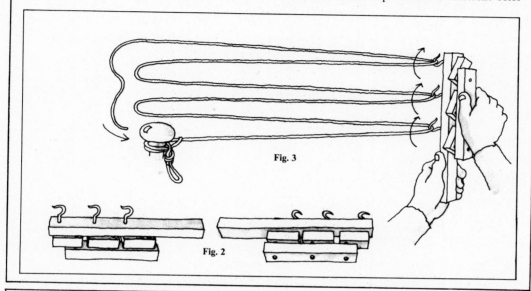

Fig. 3

Fig. 2

and thickness can be strung side by side on the ROPE MACHINE to create fat or thin ropes, or interesting textures and designs. You need to start with yarn about eight times the length of the finished rope you want to make. If you are combining yarns, tie the ends together in a loop that will slip over a door knob. Either way, string up the yarns as shown in Fig. 3: door knob to first hook, to door knob to second hook, to door knob to third hood, to door knob, making a loop to slip over the knob. (You can repeat the stringing a second or third time to make fatter ropes.) It's easier if someone can hold the ROPE MACHINE, or else place it on a chair and run the yarns back of the chair. The ROPE MACHINE should be held about one third further from the door knob than the length of rope you want to make.

Keep the yarn taut, and crank the machine in a clockwise direction. You'll have to move forward while cranking because the twisting takes up some of the yarn's length. Keep cranking until the twists are tight, but don't let the strands kink. The more turns you make, the tighter the finished rope will be. Have someone hold the ROPE MACHINE, or place it over the chair back, Fig. 4.

Carefully remove the yarn from the door knob, and with your other hand grab the three strands of twisted yarn. Keep the strands taut while pulling the end and twisting the three parts together in a counterclockwise direction. Continue until the full length of rope is made. Hold the rope tightly while removing the yarn from the hooks. Tie both ends of the rope in a single knot to prevent unraveling. You can snip off the loop ends to make a tassel.

The rope is complete.

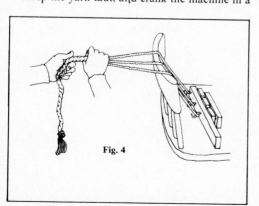

Fig. 4

Drawings by Arielle Mather. Copyright © 1972 by Steven Caney. Reprinted by permission of Workman Publishing Company from Toy Book.

racing spool

Steven Caney (see *Toy Book,* page 98; reviewed on page 196) says you can't make just one of these. It must be the simplest self-powered toy ever invented.

Put a rubber band through the hole of a large wooden spool and loop it around a carpet tack hammered into one end. Place a washer over the loose end of the rubber band and then push a pencil or short stick through the remaining loop. Wind it up, put it down on the floor, and let 'er go.

Does it behave differently on a rug, a smooth floor, or on the grass?
Would cutting some notches on the edges of the spool make it go better?
What happens if you use a fat rubber band? A skinny one?

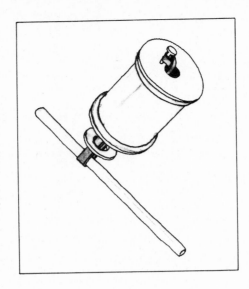

Drawing by Arielle Mather. Copyright © 1972 by Steven Caney. Reprinted by permission of Workman Publishing Company from *Toy Book.*

bike mechanics

Bikes are ideal for finding out all sorts of things about mechanical systems and energy. Finding one to take apart should be no problem — every family with kids has at least one retired specimen lying around; otherwise, bike shops tend to be cooperative in donating something they don't want to fix, or selling one for a low price. The activities shown on the following pages can all be done with bike wheels alone.

For many other activities of this kind, see *The Bicycle,* one of the booklets put together by the Science Teachers' Association of Ontario (address, page 28).

wheels and spokes

Is the length of the spoke related to the distance around the rim?

Ask your kids to use string and a ruler to measure the length of the spoke and the distance around the outside of the tire. Find how many times the length of the spoke will fit into the length of string.

Lay the wheel on its side with a piece of mural paper on the floor underneath. Tape a pencil vertically to one of the spokes about two or three inches from the hub. Rotate the wheel so that the pencil traces a circle on the paper. Use a piece of string to measure this line. Then slide the pencil toward the rim, a distance that is exactly twice the original distance from the hub. Rotate; measure the line. Continue tracing circles by moving the pencil outward, doubling the preceding distance each time. You can plot the two measurements on a graph to see what kind of relationships you get.

(Optional) Insert a dowel into the hub, and pull the wheel across the paper as someone rotates it. What kind of pattern do you get?

———————————

How do spokes support a wheel rim? If you remove the tire and inner tube from a wheel rim you can undo the screws that attach the spokes and so remove the spokes.

Experiment with tightening or loosening various combinations of spokes. Can you make a wobbly wheel? Using a pencil with a large eraser as a hammer to test the sound spokes make, what changes in sound occur as you tighten and loosen the spokes?

Experiment with removing spokes one at a time from different sides of the wheel and spin the wheel after each spoke is removed. What is the smallest number of spokes a wheel can have and still turn? What happens if you remove a lot of spokes from one side? Can you figure out a testing device to see how much weight a wheel will support as a given number of spokes are removed?

bicycle wheel pendulum

Tie four strings or wires to a bicycle wheel so that it can be suspended horizontally from one point overhead. Suspend a second wheel underneath and parallel to the first by four more lines.

Now you can rotate and then release either wheel and watch what happens. Try to do something to one of the wheels to make the other do exactly what you want it to.

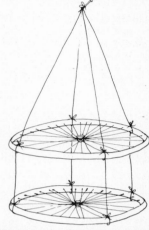

how everything else works

Ah, the great world of technology. Or, I suppose, ugh, the world of mechanized living. I have my share of qualms about humanity's becoming enslaved by its own machines, yet I could cheerfully spend three solid weeks in the Smithsonian Institution, the Franklin Institute, or any one of the other great museums of man's inventions. We are a pretty ingenious lot, after all, especially when it comes to getting something else to do our work for us.

The books reviewed on these pages represent a few examples of what's in print that may serve in place of a museum trip, but there are many other excellent (though often expensive) volumes to choose from that we couldn't include. These are the kind of books you can sit and pore over for hours, even if you're very young and care about only the illustrations.

The other major alternative for the machine worshiper is to visit factories, any and all that will let you in with kids. The variety of machines and processes you can see is nearly unlimited. Around where I live we've visited the Parker Brothers games factory, bread factories, newspaper presses, bottling plants, and working replicas or restorations of old industries such as mills, cottage crafts, and such.

bicycle wheel gyroscope

Cut two pieces of garden hose or heavy plastic tubing about six inches long and slip these over the threaded parts of the axle to serve as handles.

Have a person hold the wheel vertically by these handles and sit on a swivel chair or small table equipped with casters. Someone else can give the wheel a rapid spin. As it spins, the person holding the wheel can turn it slowly to a horizontal position and experience what happens.

Try other movements.

You will probably want to finesse the explanation for this phenomenon as it is far too complicated for children, let alone you and me, to understand in short order. If you want to be a diehard about it, though, consult *The Way Things Work,* volume one, pages 458–459 (see review on page 128).

What happens if you fasten a weight in one place on the rim? (Try a blob of plasticine.)

motors, engines, and machines

Of all the devices invented for converting natural resources into energy, those using water intrigue me the most; somehow they always make an impressive demonstration of man's native ingenuity in getting machines to do his work for him. The story of the steam engine is a wonderful example.

"I had gone to take a walk on a fine Sabbath afternoon," wrote James Watt, an instrument maker of Glasgow, remembering a day in May of 1785 which was to be crucial in his career. "I had entered the Green and passed the old washing house. I was thinking of the engine at the time." Watt had been asked by Glasgow University two years before to rebuild a model of the Newcomen steam engine. The Newcomen engine was in turn an improved version of Savery's pioneer engine. Noting the inefficiency caused by the rapid heating and cooling of Newcomen's cylinder, Watt had been searching for a solution to the problem. On this memorable day he found it. "I had not walked farther than the Golf house," he wrote, "when the whole thing was arranged in my mind." Four years later Watt patented his idea of a steam condenser outside the cylinder, allowing the latter to remain hot. Here was the most important single invention ever applied to the steam engine, and it can be said that from this invention, and from Watt's flash of intuition on Glasgow Green that produced it, stemmed the entire industrial revolution in full tide. And the industrial revolution has changed the face of our world.

— Robert Soulard, *A History of the Machine,*
page 43 (reviewed on page 128)

I hope all the educators who devote their time to creating behavioral objectives and sequential lesson plans will take note of Watt's thinking process. What does it say about our schools that many of the world's great inventors did most of their learning outside them?

about technology

Simple Working Models of Historic Machines
Aubrey F. Burstall

*The M.I.T. Press
28 Carleton Street
Cambridge, Massachusetts 02142*

Although the subtitle adds, "easily made by the reader," I am not recommending the

book for use in that way, as it really assumes a high degree of competency with tools. Even so, it represents just the right way to go about studying old machines. I would want to have it around if my kids were delving into the mysteries of "how things work," especially if they tended to think of machines as assembly-line products.

The author, who sounds like a real machine-shop craftsman of the old school, offers his designs for working models he has built of technologically primitive but fascinating devices ranging from a simple bow drill to a "Chinese South-pointing Chariot." Historical notes accompany each plan. Maybe you can get some able high-schoolers to construct some of them and do demonstrations for younger kids.

The Way Things Work: An Illustrated Encyclopedia of Technology, 2 volumes, and Special Edition for Young People
T. Ludewijk et al.

*Simon and Schuster
630 Fifth Avenue
New York, New York 10020*

These volumes have become indispensable reference works for all tinkerers, which includes most children. (Used to be just boys, right?)

A blurb on the cover reads, "From the ballpoint pen to the computer, from the Polaroid Camera to the Atomic clock [*sic*], with 1071 two-color drawings and diagrams," and the newer second volume has doubled that promise. The text, unfortunately for our purposes, is abstruse and full of unfamiliar technical terminology. The Special Edition for Young People partly overcomes this limitation by editing out much of the heavy jargon and streamlining the syntax, but it still assumes sophisticated reading skills, and is considerably abridged, as well. Since the diagrams are the most valuable feature, I would recommend getting the original two volumes if the main users are going to be children under twelve.

A History of the Machine
Robert Soulard
New Illustrated Library of Science and Invention

*Hawthorn Books
260 Madison Avenue
New York, New York 10016*

This book, like others in the set, must be the next closest thing to walking into the Museum of Technology at the Smithsonian Institution. Beautifully illustrated with full-

color and black and white reproductions, many from old manuscripts, it is a lucid, scholarly survey of the development of the machine since the crudest hoe. Get it so that kids can pore over the pictures and fantasize their own inventions, but also so that you can read it and give them some account of how things used to work.

We haven't seen any of the others in the series, but the book jacket promises they are all of the same design and quality. The series includes:

A History of . . .

Rockets and Space	*Electricity*
Ships and Seafaring	*Land Transportation*
Flight	*Physics*
Weaponry	*Communications*
Astronomy	*Chemistry*
	Medicine

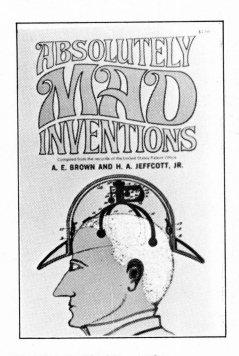

Absolutely Mad Inventions
A. E. Brown and H. A. Jeffcott, Jr.

*Dover Publications
180 Varick Street
New York, New York 10014*

This is a compilation of unbelievable designs submitted to the U.S. Patent Office around the turn of the century, which must have been a prime era for Rube Goldbergs in earnest. Would you believe a device attached to the bottom end of a hen to mark the eggs as they come out? Original drawings and excerpts from the accompanying specifications make up the text. The authors note that complete copies of the original patents may be obtained for fifty cents from the Patent Office in Washington, just in case you want to try duplicating some of these madcap efforts.

math

Measurement

Logic and probability

Shapes

general resources

It is a place full of "things": games to be played, tools and equipment for experimentation, blocks for building beautiful structures, patterns, concepts; boxes and bottles, shapes of all kinds; scales and balances, rulers, measuring devices in standard and nonstandard units; papers and pencils and crayons and marker pens; spools, little toy cars, trains, dried beans, peas, rice, salt, sugar, coffee, cups, spoons — to name just a few. It is a place where one can learn just about all he [or she] wants to know about numbers, and what happens "if." . . .

— from *Learning to Think in a Math Lab,*
page 1 (reviewed on page 132)

Although Manon P. Charbonneau is referring to a math lab, her description could as easily be applied to a classroom or home learning center where math experiences are encouraged. It would be virtually impossible to list all the stuff that would be handy to have around for exploring maths, but this passage should give you a feel for the kinds and variety of things to look for.

Our emphasis in this chapter, as throughout our book, is the active involvement of children with materials of all kinds. Although math is an area in which there are an unusual number of specialized, excellent manipulatives available, it is just as valid (and in some cases more so) for kids to explore maths with scrounged or household items.

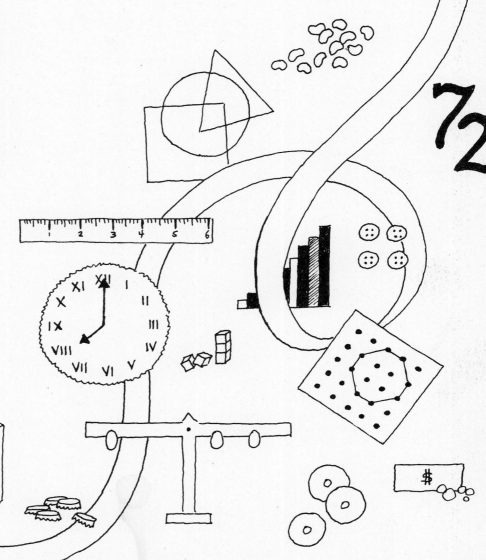

activity books

Nuffield Mathematics Project

John Wiley and Sons
605 Third Avenue
New York, New York 10016

This is basically a beautiful set of teacher's guides for working with children aged five to thirteen. The guides provide myriad suggested activities that lead to math discoveries, and are profusely illustrated with examples of children's work — including graphs and tables they've made to record and describe their own investigations. Each guide stresses the interaction of children, mathematics, and the environment in a natural way.

In addition to the teacher's guides, the Nuffield Maths Project has produced quite a few activity and problem card sets specifically for use with eleven-to-thirteen-year-old children; several "general guides" for teachers, which serve as references and outlines of the approach and concepts; and a guide for parents that answers questions about the method and philosophy behind the project. Send for a complete description of Nuffield materials and prices from the American distributor, John Wiley and Sons.

The core guides are organized by three main topics: ●Computation and Structure, ▼Shape and Size, and ■Graphing. Each guide is interrelated to the others, and the same concept is met over and over again — treated in a different way at every stage. These cost approximately four dollars each.

The "weaving guides" are single-concept books that give detailed information on a specific project. They show the incredible amount of maths that can be learned in all areas!

Math Dimension
John Lettau and Bill McConnell

L & M Educational Enterprises
Box 88
Santa Maria, California 93454
$4.50 each

This series of three activity handbooks includes a wide variety of math games, puzzles, worksheets, patterns, and problems. Reproduction permission is granted to individual teachers for classroom use, but the activities would be valuable (and fun!) for kids at home as well. Most of the games, puzzles, and other challenging exercises in these books can be done either independently or with only one other person; they are often ideal for kids and grown-ups to tackle together!

Learning Mathematics through Activities
S. Jeanne Kelley

John Wiley and Sons
605 Third Avenue
New York, New York 10016
$3.50

This is "a resource book for elementary teachers" and seems uniquely valuable. It contains directions for making your own math equipment; lots of specific activities for learning about sets, number relationships, arithmetic operations, geometry, and measurement; and very handy, comprehensive appendixes to commercial manipulatives, resource books, and publishers or suppliers.

We have not yet seen a more complete and easy-to-follow resource guide for teachers (or parents) who want to create a concrete, materials-oriented math program!

Learning to Think in a Math Lab
Manon P. Charbonneau

National Association of Independent
Schools
4 Liberty Square
Boston, Massachusetts 02109
$2.50

"Despite what many experts in the field of education say, I firmly believe that children do not learn in an organized way . . . in a way organized by adults" (page 3).

This is an exceptional book. As a guide to setting up a math lab — with suggested attitudes, materials, and activities — it is superb. It is also a statement of educational philosophy, a personal account, and a guide to helping kids both learn and enjoy experiences with mathematics. The writing style is warmly informal, yet the book is chock-full of very practical ideas for getting started as well as for maintaining kids' interest in math.

Freedom to Learn
Edith E. Biggs and James R. MacLean

Addison-Wesley Publishing Company
2725 Sand Hill Road
Menlo Park, California 94025
$6.36

An active learning approach to mathematics is one that "presents a wide variety of opportunities, an approach that encourages [children] to ask questions and to find the answers, an approach that fosters the use of physical materials" (Foreword). This book is written for teachers, and contains a wealth of information on just how to go about creating an active learning environment.

There is a section on "classroom needs" (space, storage, equipment, etc.) as well as a wide variety of specific activities for learning everything from arithmetic to spatial relationships. *Freedom to Learn* is well written, easy to understand, and profusely illustrated with photographs, diagrams, and examples of children's work.

The I Hate Mathematics! Book
Marilyn Burns

Little, Brown and Company
34 Beacon Street
Boston, Massachusetts 02106
$3.95

Sidewalk squares, ice cream flavors, dots, doing dishes, popcorn, birds, bananas, and handshakes — what do all these things have in common? They are all related to everyday experiences, and are all used in this fascinating, funny book to make mathematics come alive! This book was especially written for kids (or grown-ups!) who think they hate math; but we think math-lovers of all ages would enjoy it just as much!

Designed for kids and grown-ups together, and illustrated with delightful line drawings, this book is part of the Brown Paper School series. The authors believe learning happens only when it is wanted; that it can happen anywhere and doesn't require fancy tools. This book and the others in this series (see pages 14 and 174) are dedicated to anyone who thinks so too.

Aftermath
Dale Seymour et al.

Creative Publications
P.O. Box 10328
Palo Alto, California 94303
$4.50 each

This four-book series of creative activity books has been recently revised and extended. Each book contains more than a hundred pages of cartoons, humor, designs, puzzles, codes, and games to enliven your math program at school or to play with at home. One possible weakness is that so many of the activities are repeated throughout each book; for example, an awful lot is done with mazes and patterns.

HEY GANG! I CALL THIS PUZZLE **TINKERTOTALS**, BECAUSE IT LOOKS LIKE IT WAS MADE FROM TINKERTOYS.

THE THREE NUMBERS IN A LINE SHOULD ADD UP TO THE SAME NUMBER.

HERE'S AN EXAMPLE OF A COMPLETED TINKERTOTAL.

ANY WAY YOU GO, IT ADDS UP TO NINE!

AMAZING!

CAN YOU COMPLETE THESE **TINKERTOTALS**?

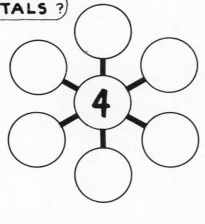

USE THE FIRST SEVEN COUNTING NUMBERS.

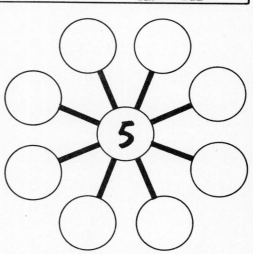

USE THE FIRST NINE COUNTING NUMBERS.

USE THE FIRST ELEVEN COUNTING NUMBERS.

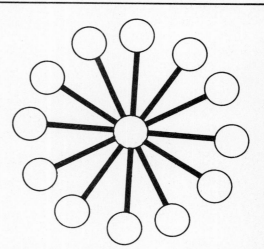

USE THE FIRST THIRTEEN COUNTING NUMBERS.

MOVING MATCHES

I.

MAKE 5 TRIANGLES
WITH 9 MATCHES.

II. MOVE ONE MATCH TO
FORM A TRUE EQUATION.

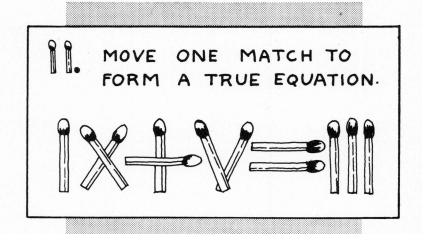

III. 17 MATCHES:
REMOVE 6 TO LEAVE 2 SQUARES.

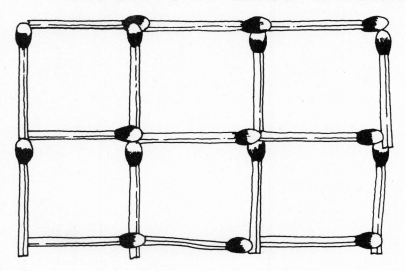

GOT A MATCH?

IV. MOVE ONE MATCH
TO FORM A TRUE
EQUATION.

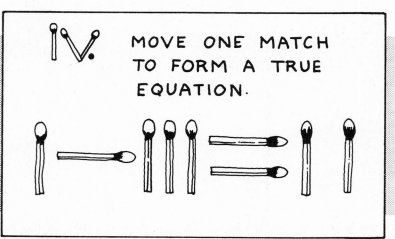

Reprinted from *Aftermath I,* p. 27, and *Aftermath
II,* p. 12, with permission of Creative
Publications, © 1975.

Fun and Games with Mathematics
James Haugaard and David Horlock

Activity Resources Company
Box 4875
Hayward, California 94545
$9.95

This giant book of "fun and games" is unbeatable for its variety and sheer quantity of ideas and activities! It comes in a bulky, three-ring loose-leaf binder and its contents include these topics:

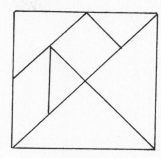

The Tangram

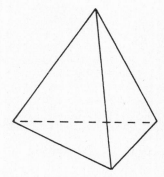

Polyhedra

Games, Puzzles and Patterns

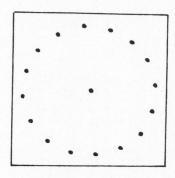

The Geoboard

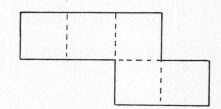

Pentominoes

Enhancing the Times Tables

x	y
2	12
5	30
6	?

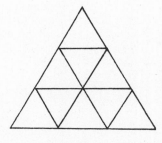

Fun with a Twist of Geometry

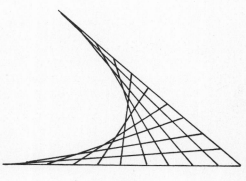

Aestheometry

1, 17, 23 / 4, 12, 106

These Are, These Aren't

activity cards

There are dozens of math activity card sets around. Most of them cover the whole gamut of math activities — number, sets, measurement, geometry, and logic. The following is an annotated list of several activity card sets that we like for one reason or another; since classroom styles, needs, and preferences are so varied, it's impossible to recommend only one! You will need to write to the publisher for prices and more detailed information about those that interest you.

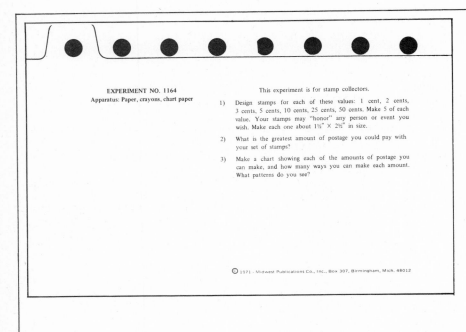

EXPERIMENT NO. 1164
Apparatus: Paper, crayons, chart paper

This experiment is for stamp collectors.

1) Design stamps for each of these values: 1 cent, 2 cents, 3 cents, 5 cents, 10 cents, 25 cents, 50 cents. Make 5 of each value. Your stamps may "honor" any person or event you wish. Make each one about 1½" × 2½" in size.

2) What is the greatest amount of postage you could pay with your set of stamps?

3) Make a chart showing each of the amounts of postage you can make, and how many ways you can make each amount. What patterns do you see?

© 1971 - Midwest Publications Co., Inc., Box 307, Birmingham, Mich. 48012

Cloudburst

Midwest Publications Company
P.O. Box 129
Troy, Michigan 48084

These 6″ × 9″ cards are also available in book form. Their unique feature is a "key sort system" for locating cards in a particular area.

Reprinted by permission of Midwest Publications Company, Inc., © 1971.

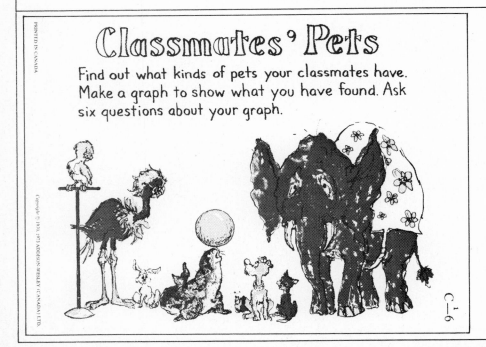

Classmates' Pets

Find out what kinds of pets your classmates have. Make a graph to show what you have found. Ask six questions about your graph.

PRINTED IN CANADA

Copyright © 1970, 1973 ADDISON-WESLEY (CANADA) LTD.

C-1-6

Developmental Math Cards

Addison-Wesley Publishing Company
Sand Hill Road
Menlo Park, California 94025

These 8½″ × 11″ cards are colorful, easy to read, and most of the activities utilize common, everyday materials (string, counters, newspaper, playing cards, etc.). They are organized by grade level, approximately forty cards per grade.

Reprinted by permission of Addison-Wesley (Canada) Ltd., copyright © 1973.

MATERIALS: a well-travelled street

MAKE A SURVEY OF THE CARS GOING BY NEAR THE SCHOOL.

GRAPH THE COUNT OF CARS BY COLOR.

WHICH IS THE MOST POPULAR COLOR?

WRITE A STORY ABOUT WHAT YOU DID AND WHAT YOUR GRAPH SHOWS.

Maths Mini-Lab

SEE
3 Bridge Street
Newton, Massachusetts 02195

Although not visually enticing, these 5″ × 8″ cards have good environmental math activities. The cards are available with or without a set of related, miscellaneous materials.

14

A man saw a clock face in a mirror:

What time was it? Are there any times at which the clock and its mirror image appear exactly the same?

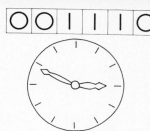

Nuffield Problem Cards

John Wiley and Sons
605 Third Avenue
New York, New York 10016

While these three card sets are designed for eleven-to-thirteen-year-olds, many of the activities (especially those in the green set) would be fun and challenging for kids of nine or ten. The cards are relatively small, about 4½″ × 6″.

9/12 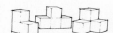 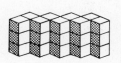 soma™cubes B-6

1. Try these:

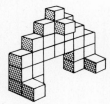

Tell about them!

SAM cards

SEE
3 Bridge Street
Newton, Massachusetts 02195

These are a set of 5″ × 8″ cards (laminated on one side) that are designed for use with specific equipment — geoblocks, Cuisenaire rods, math balance, etc. Cards and equipment are available separately.

games

Math Card Games
Walter Rucker and Clyde Dilley

Creative Publications
P.O. Box 10328
Palo Alto, California 94303
$4.95

Thirty Math Games for the Elementary Grades
Richard M. Sharp et al.

Fearon Publishers
6 Davis Drive
Belmont, California 94002
$2.50

Throughout this chapter, we recommend a variety of commercial games that are particularly good for reinforcing math skills. Making your own games, however, is much more valuable (and fun!) for both you and your kids. These two books are excellent resources for creating your own math games.

Math Card Games is a compilation of over forty games — mostly for learning basic facts, computation skills, and fractions. Each game includes major concepts to be learned, cards to be made, and rules of play. An essential source book for anyone interested in card games as an aid to learning is *Deal Me In!* by Margie Golick (see page 18 for review).

Thirty Math Games for the Elementary Grades contains a selection of original board game ideas. The objectives, playing directions, and materials needed (including a game-board diagram) are presented in a clear, attractive format.

sources

There are many, many sources of math materials throughout the country. Most of the standard games and equipment used for learning and/or reinforcing math skills are found in at least a dozen places. Still, we seem to always come back to a few places that have a wide variety of high-quality, reasonably priced items. Probably our two most frequently used sources are Creative Publications and SEE.

CREATIVE PUBLICATIONS

P.O. Box 10328
Palo Alto, California 94303

Creative Publications has exclusively "mathematics curriculum materials." Their catalog is colorful and inviting, and they offer a comprehensive selection of excellent materials, games, and books. If we had to choose just one supplier for good math stuff, Creative Publications would definitely be that source. They have lots of metric materials and even a selection of game-making materials (dice, blank cards and playing boards, etc.).

The following is a list of other suppliers whose math manipulatives are worth considering. They usually have a smaller selection of products than Creative Publications or SEE.

Activity Resources Company, P.O. Box 4875, Hayward, California 94545
  Mostly books, guides

Cuisenaire Company of America, 12 Church Street, New Rochelle, New York 10805
  Cuisenaire rods; some games, books

Leicestershire Learning Systems, Box 335, New Gloucester, Maine 04260
  Primary manipulatives

Midwest Publications Company, P.O. Box 129, Troy, Michigan 48084
  Mostly books, guides

Scott Resources, 1900 E. Lincoln, Box 2121, Fort Collins, Colorado 80521
  Originators of good materials

3 Bridge Street
Newton, Massachusetts 02195

SEE develops and sells primarily math and science materials. They have an excellent supply of British teaching aids as well as their own original products, activity cards, and so on. They are extremely selective in their choice of items, and are very responsive to feedback. SEE encourages full use of their materials through detailed, thorough descriptions (e.g., suggesting in their catalog that the back of their 100 number board could be used as a pegboard or geoboard!), and suggests ways to improvise, adapt, or even create your own materials.

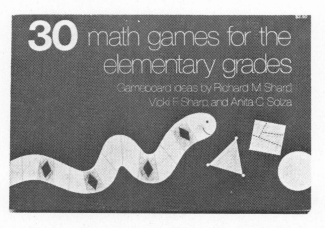

everyday math

Math is all around us, and is a part of the everyday experiences of kids of all ages. Counting, sorting, classifying, measuring, weighing and making things balance, exploring capacity with sand and water play — all these are activities with which children are familiar.

We think it's important to encourage this kind of exploration — in school as well as at home. These few pages suggest two of the many ways of learning about math through everyday materials and activities.

Each of the activities — creating a play store and cooking with kids — necessitates the use and understanding of a variety of interrelated math skills. The activities are also interdisciplinary — involving language, science, and even social studies along with mathematics.

play store

Handling and playing with money is a natural, real way for kids to become involved with the whole world of math — from counting and computing to basic economics. Most kids are already familiar with the value of money to some extent by the time they're in school — needing lunch or milk money, receiving an allowance, or being paid for errands or odd jobs done around the house.

One of my fondest childhood memories is of setting up and "playing store" — with a great deal of help and encouragement from my incredibly creative mother. The project went on for several months; and my mother saved empty bread bags, gum and candy wrappers, cans, and boxes of everything from soap powder to Cheerios! I still think this kind of project is an excellent way for children to explore a wide range of math activities in a meaningful, concrete way. Items that do not come in packages could be represented by pictures cut out of a magazine and pasted onto sturdy cardboard. Try making fruits and vegetables out of papier-mâché; or use weeds and leaves to make green vegetables. The following ideas illustrate the rich possibilities involved in setting up a store in home or classroom (we used the back of our garage).

Jean bought some ice cream for 79¢ and 2 boxes of cookies for 49¢ each. She gave you, the cashier, $2. How much change should she receive?

How can you package or display a product to appeal to your customers? Make a survey of what catches people's eyes — color? Design? Shape of container? Look for advertisements of your products on TV or in newspapers.

Design your own package for an item in your store.

How would you design a package for "pure air"?

Unit pricing is now required by law in all markets. If you are selling 7 oz. of tuna fish for 69¢, what is the cost per ounce? "Unit price" all the items in your store — try comparing unit prices for different brands of the same product.

How will you price the items you sell? Some packages may still have prices on them. Visit a local market or grocery store for some ideas (if you speak to the manager ahead of time, you might even get a tour). What is a "fair" price? What do supply and demand have to do with pricing?

Use a grocer's scale to weigh out 5 lbs. of potatoes (medium-sized rocks would do) or 1 lb. of hard candy (pebbles in tinfoil or candy wrappers). All kinds of scrounged items — buttons, bits of chalk, clothespins, beans, etc. — can be used for things that need to be sold by weight.

Have a big SALE! Slash prices! How much would each item in your store cost if you cut prices by 20 percent? Half? Make out special coupons so your customers will save money on products you want to get rid of.

Toy Money

Play money is available in many local "five and tens." If you cannot find any locally, you can write to:

J. L. Hammett Company
Hammett Place
Braintree, Massachusetts 02184

Hammett's has several toy money "kits" ranging in price from $1.25 to $11.95.

Kids can, of course, make their own or scrounge it from incomplete Monopoly sets. One way of creating play money in bulk is to have your kids design different denominations on a single sheet of paper, then make Xerox copies. Or simply use beans or buttons of different sizes for coins.

Cash Register

New England School Supply / Milton
   Bradley
P.O. Box 1581
Springfield, Massachusetts 01101

These people have two inexpensive cash registers for kids. Although a shoe box would do nicely for storing toy money, somehow there's a special delight in using a "real" cash register in running a store!

> For older kids, or for children who've been "playing store" for a while, try creating a real shop! This might be an ideal way for kids to earn their own money — used books or toys or games or puzzles, child-made cakes or lemonade, all those gerbil babies you don't know what to do with . . . the possibilities for "products" are as endless as your kids' imaginations!

cooking

You can't ask for a better way to combine fun and learning than cooking with kids. Boys and girls of all ages love to "mess around" in the kitchen, experiment with recipes, and gobble up the (hopefully) yummy products! See our reviews of cookbooks for kids on pages 102–104.

If you're working at home, you'll have all the necessary tools and most ingredients handy (although it would be a great exercise to have your kids shop for their own ingredients for a particular recipe). If you want to cook with kids in school, you'll need access to a stove for baked stuff — though a hot plate will do nicely for a lot of things. Have an assortment of pots and pans, measuring cups and spoons, scales, utensils, bowls, and so on, available. It would also be handy to have some basic ingredients around (e.g., salt, sugar, flour) — unless you have a refrigerator, you'll need to get things like milk, butter, and eggs as required for specific recipes.

Here are a half dozen activities you might try that will add to the learning involved when your kids get into cooking — with or without your assistance!

> Sort an equal volume of different cooking ingredients by weight (or vice versa). Which is heavier — a cup of flour or a cup of sugar? Which takes up more space — 4 ounces of butter or 4 ounces of mayonnaise?
>
> ---
>
> If you add ½ cup of water to ½ cup of flour, do you get 1 full cup of mixture? Why not? How about weighing each, then comparing the total weight before and after mixing.
>
> ---
>
> Melt ¼ cup of butter (or margarine) in a saucepan. Pour the melted butter back into the measuring cup. What happens? Why?
>
> ---
>
> How much is "a pinch" of salt? Compare your pinch to that of a grown-up. Can you figure out a way to measure a pinch? How many grains of salt are in a pinch? Can you find out without counting them?
>
> ---
>
> Make your own collection of favorite recipes and bind them into a personal cookbook (see pages 292–294 for bookbinding techniques).
>
> ---
>
> Make some bread and investigate the "rising" properties of yeast. How long does bread dough take to double its size? What happens when you punch it down — and why? Try weighing the dough at each stage of its preparation — even after cooking; what do you notice?

computation

From *How You Make Choices*, p. 7 (book four of The Process of Choice series), reprinted by permission of Group for Environmental Education, Inc., © 1973.

counting

numerals

Counting is one of the first steps toward an understanding of number relationships, and counting experiences for kids are everywhere — from a collection of buttons to cars at a busy intersection! Learning to count from one to ten in different languages — past and present — can be fun as well as educational, and a super way to integrate math with language and social studies. The variety of representational symbols (1, I, ⁄ . . .) is fascinating and helps kids to understand that the symbols themselves are arbitrary.

I II III IV V VI VII VIII IX X

1 2 3 4 5 6 7 8 9 10

一 yet
二 nyee
三 sam
四 see
五 mm
六 lok
七 tik
八 bak
九 giu
十 sip

Moja Means One
Muriel Feelings

The Dial Press
1 Dag Hammarskjold Plaza
245 East 47th Street
New York, New York 10017

This is a delightful and informative Swahili counting book. Muriel Feelings, who has lived and taught in East Africa, has written it for two reasons: to familiarize American children with some basic aspects of East African life, and to teach them to count from one to ten in Swahili. Her husband, Tom Feelings, has created a carefully detailed double-spread painting for each number, ranging from a fireside storytelling scene to the types of clothing East African men and women wear. For each number, there is an appropriate number of objects to count within the soft-hued picture.

This lovely book does an excellent job of combining basic counting activities with learning about a fascinating culture. The Feelings have created a companion book, *Jambo Means Hello,* that is equally valuable.

graphs

Creating graphs to pictorially represent things counted is fun and easy for kids of all ages. Personal surveys lend themselves beautifully to graphing activities. Children choose a subject (favorite TV programs, number of siblings, kinds of pets — the list is endless!), then ask friends, classmates, or family members to indicate a response. Or, to make it even simpler, the child can choose the categories within a subject from which others must select.

The responses can then be represented on a graph (bar graphs are best for beginners). One-inch or half-inch graph paper is ideal for use with young children, especially for coloring or decorating individual spaces within the graph.

An excellent follow-up activity can involve word problems, addition and subtraction, fractions, or percentages — any number of computational activities depending upon ability level.

Have kids read each other's (or their own) graphs and formulate questions based on the information shown. On the sample birthday graph below, such questions can range from "Which month shows the most birthdays?" to "How many more people have birthdays in March than in September?" to "What percentage of the group has birthdays in the month of February?" The next step, of course, is to solve the problems generated!

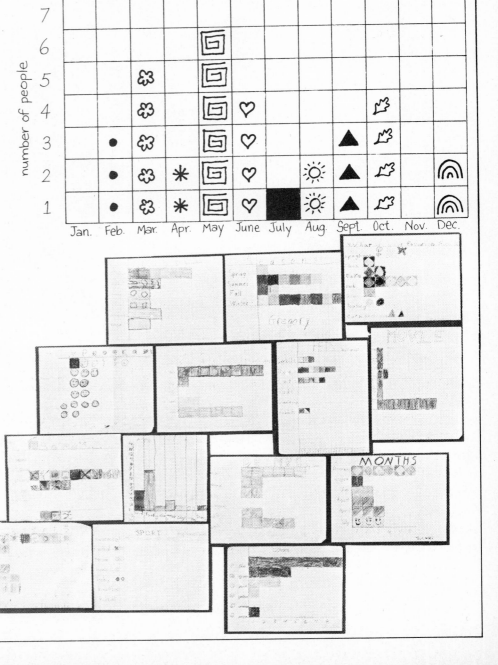

BIRTHDAYS IN OUR CLASS

abacuses

The abacus has been used as a computing device for thousands of years! It is a very handy piece of equipment for all kinds of number activities, and is especially useful for making place value concrete and visual. There are three basic commercial styles:

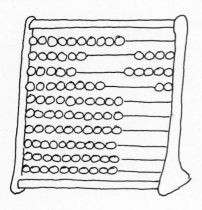

bead frame abacus

SEE, $6.20

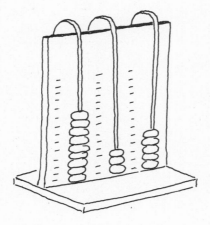

loop abacus

Creative Publications, $6.75

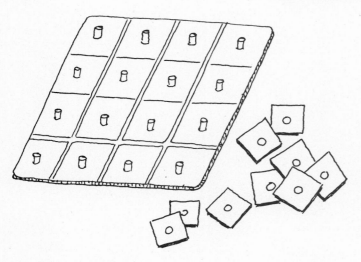

abacus board

Creative Publications, $1.00
   100 tablets (20 each of 5 colors),
   $2.50

Multibase abacuses are also available, but base 10 is most commonly used with elementary children.

The principles are quite simple. Each row of beads represents a place value position (ones, tens, hundreds, etc. — depending upon the number of rows). Thus, on a loop abacus, 935 would be expressed as shown on the loop abacus at left. When numbers are added or subtracted, there is a physical necessity to "carry" or "borrow" because of the ten-bead limit per row! Using an abacus, kids will be able to clearly *see* the reason behind such exchanges.

It would not be too difficult to create your own abacus. Use large beads (½″ diameter for easy handling; 10 per row), wire hangers, and 4 strips of wood to make the frame (wide enough to stand up or attach to a backing; length is variable).

1. Drill small holes in 2 of the pieces of wood, about 1″ apart for ½″ beads.

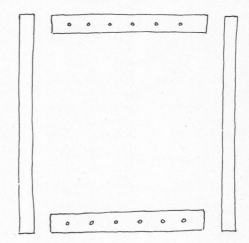

2. Fasten the frame together with glue or nails.
3. String 10 beads on each piece of straightened wire; wire should be at least 8″ long.

4. Poke the wire through the holes in the frame, and fasten by bending the ends.

arithmetic activities

A palindrome is a number (or word!) that reads the same both forward and backward, such as 12321. It's easy and fun to create palindromes — as well as good practice in addition! Just take any number, reverse it, and add the two together. If the answer is not a palindrome, repeat the process until it is!

$$
\begin{array}{r}
426 \\
+624 \\
\hline
1050 \\
+0501 \\
\hline
1551
\end{array}
$$

Here is a cooperative family game for traveling on long trips, which my father taught me long ago and which I still play! As cars go whizzing by you (or vice versa), look at the numbers on the license plates. Add up the digits (ignore letters, of course), and keep adding until you're left with one digit.

$$6325 \text{ AS} = 6 + 3 + 2 + 5 = 16 = 1 + 6 = 7$$

The object of the game is to find license plates whose numbers add up to 1, 2, 3, 4, 5, 6, 7, 8, 9 — in order. The whole family should look for a "1" — when it's found, all proceed to search for a "2" — and so on. The game is won if you succeed in reaching "9" before you arrive at your destination! (A tip for quick adding — 9s don't count! Try it — 8934 gives the same one-digit "answer" as 834.)

Do your kids have trouble multiplying by 9? Here's an easy way to multiply 9 by any number from 1 to 10. Hold your hands open facing you. Start counting your fingers from the left until you reach the number you want to multiply by 9 — put that finger down (for example, if you're solving 4×9 you put your fourth finger down). The raised fingers to its left represent tens; those to the right represent ones!

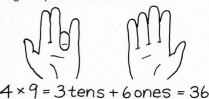

$4 \times 9 = 3$ tens + 6 ones = 36

equipment

100 Number Board
Midwest Publications, $7.95

The 100 number board, available from a variety of sources, is a useful manipulative device for counting, grouping, and patterning numbers. Activities may include counting in units (2s, 3s, 5s, 10s) up to 100, isolating odd and even numbers, adding and subtracting, and building numerical sequences.

A set of a hundred numbered plastic tablets accompanies the 10 by 10 grid, and Midwest Publications includes twenty-five blank tablets to extend the activities possible. A booklet of tear-out activity cards, *Math Experiments with the Number Tablets* ($2.30), is also available from Midwest.

EXPERIMENT LR 3

| 1 | ● | 3 | ● | 5 | ● | 7 | ● | 9 | ● |
| 11 | ● | 13 | ● | 15 | ● | 17 | ● | 19 | ● |

1) You will need some lima beans or something to cover the numbers.

2) Starting with 2, cover every other number with a bean.

3) You have covered all the **EVEN NUMBERS**.
The numbers you can see are **ODD NUMBERS**.

EXPERIMENT MR 10

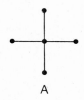
A

B

C

1) Copy the above diagrams (enlarged) on to three sheets of paper.

2) The puzzle is to place the first 5 numbers on the dots in A, then the first 7 numbers on the dots in B and then the first 9 numbers on the dots in C, so that the lines in A add to the same totals, the lines in B to the same, and in C.

3) If you see the trick of how to do this, can you put numbers 6-12 in B to give the same totals on lines and 13-21 in C to give the same totals on lines?

Reprinted from *Math Experiments with the Number Tablets* by permission of Midwest Publications Company, Inc., © 1972.

21/24 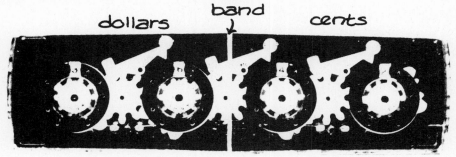 see·calculator tm   G-1

1. Use the <u>rubber band</u> around your Calculator as a <u>decimal point</u> like this:

dollars   rubber band   cents

2. Show $36.42 on the Calculator.
Add $25.79. Make up your own money problems.

3. Move the rubber band to another place. Try making up some problems with decimals.

5/24   see·calculator tm   B-1

1. Now let's look at the numerals in the <u>tens</u> circle.

2. Show <u>15</u> in the windows.

Add <u>6</u> to it in the <u>ones</u> circle.

What happened?

 15 + 6 = ☐

SEE–Calculator
SEE, $1.90 each

The special value of this item is that its operation is totally visible! Children are intrigued by the movement of the gears and can clearly follow the mechanism of this simple calculator. Of course, it can also be used for addition and subtraction, place value study, and more. SEE has a complementary set of twenty-four activity cards (5″ × 8″) for $3.60 per set.

Napier Rods

Napier rods are a handy aid to multiplication. They are available from a variety of sources, but are simple to make. Reproduce the grid at right, then cut it into vertical strips and mount each strip on cardboard or a Popsicle stick.

The way these rods work is best shown by example. To find 6 × 73, place these rods side by side: index, 7, and 3. The following sketch shows the portion of these rods that gives the solution. Simply add the digits from right to left, along the diagonal: 6 × 73 = 438.

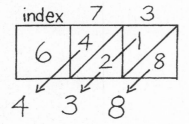

index	1	2	3	4	5	6	7	8	9	0
1	0/1	0/2	0/3	0/4	0/5	0/6	0/7	0/8	0/9	0/0
2	0/2	0/4	0/6	0/8	1/0	1/2	1/4	1/6	1/8	0/0
3	0/3	0/6	0/9	1/2	1/5	1/8	2/1	2/4	2/7	0/0
4	0/4	0/8	1/2	1/6	2/0	2/4	2/8	3/2	3/6	0/0
5	0/5	1/0	1/5	2/0	2/5	3/0	3/5	4/0	4/5	0/0
6	0/6	1/2	1/8	2/4	3/0	3/6	4/2	4/8	5/4	0/0
7	0/7	1/4	2/1	2/8	3/5	4/2	4/9	5/6	6/3	0/0
8	0/8	1/6	2/4	3/2	4/0	4/8	5/6	6/4	7/2	0/0
9	0/9	1/8	2/7	3/6	4/5	5/4	6/3	7/2	8/1	0/0

Math Balance
Creative Publications, $7.95

This is a very handy item that encourages exploration of basic arithmetic operations, solves algebra problems, and demonstrates the commutative (8 + 3 = 3 + 8) and associative (6 + 5 = 6 + [2 + 3]) laws. One side of the beam is numbered from 1 to 10, starting at the center, and the reverse side is blank. Self-adhesive labels are supplied to mark each peg on the blank side of the beam with other values (e.g., fractions, money, length, positive and negative numbers). The balance comes with twenty uniform plastic weights and special peg caps to keep the weights from falling off or to extend peg capacity.

SEE has a set of activity cards for the math balance that seem quite good. They are $3.50 per set of twenty-one cards; balance and cards together are $11.50.

SAM cards reprinted by permission of SEE, Inc., © 1972.

12/21  math balance B-4

1. Put a weight on numeral <u>10</u>.

2. Without doing it, can you tell where <u>2</u> weights ⬭⬭ should go to balance the beam?

   Where should <u>3</u> go? ⬭ ⬭ ⬭

   Where should <u>4</u> go? ⬭ ⬭ ⬭ ⬭

   Where should <u>1</u> go? ⬭

3. Try this again. Start with a weight on <u>9</u>.

13/21  math balance C-1

You can <u>multiply</u> with the balance!

1. Hang <u>2</u> weights on the same numeral.
2. On the other side hang a weight to balance the beam.
   Here is a way to record your results:

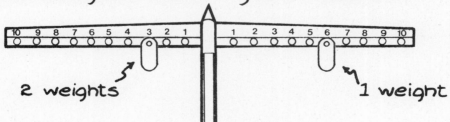

2 weights   1 weight

<u>Left</u> side <u>Right</u> side   <u>Left</u> side <u>Right</u> side
2 × 3 = 6   or   3 + 3 = 6

Cuisenaire Rods

Cuisenaire Company of America
12 Church Street
New Rochelle, New York 10805

Cuisenaire rods make numbers and their relationships concrete and meaningful to children. They have been used with children of all ages in classrooms throughout the country, and a key to their success is the use of color and length as their only distinguishing characteristics, giving them incredible flexibility.

These attractive colored rods can be used for helping kids do and understand arithmetic operations, odd and even numbers, fractions, factors and prime numbers, algebra, ratio and proportion, word problems, and much more! *Using the Cuisenaire Rods,* by Jessica Davidson ($7.95), is a photo/text guide and invaluable aid to anyone using rods for teaching math skills. The directions, explanations, and pictures are clear and easy to follow.

The Cuisenaire rods come in several classroom or math lab sets for school use. The smallest package of rods only (for possible use at home) is a single box of 155 rods for $7.95. Send for a catalog of prices of school sets and related materials.

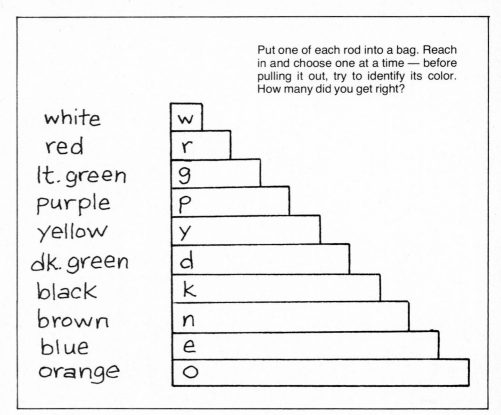

Put one of each rod into a bag. Reach in and choose one at a time — before pulling it out, try to identify its color. How many did you get right?

white   w
red   r
lt. green   g
purple   P
yellow   y
dk. green   d
black   k
brown   n
blue   e
orange   o

These rods all add up to ten, or equal one orange rod!

Multibase Arithmetic Blocks
Creative Publications, $72.50 / base 10 set

We know these materials as Diene's blocks, but our only known source identifies them as "Multibase Arithmetic Blocks." They can be used to provide experience with several different bases, place value, and measurement of length, area, volume, and mass. Although applicable only to classroom use, primarily because of cost, these natural hardwood blocks are one of the most valuable aids to concrete, manipulative math activity.

Sets are available in bases 2, 3, 4, 5, and 10. Each base 10 set includes two hundred unit cubes (one cubic centimeter) thirty longs (representing ten units each), thirty flats (one hundred units), and five blocks (one thousand units).

Ronnie and Andrew are playing "Make 1000!" — a game using base 10 blocks and two dice (one large green die, one small white die). Players take turns rolling the dice, then taking the number of unit cubes corresponding to the number on the small die, and the number of longs determined by the number on the large die. It's necessary to constantly exchange unit cubes for longs, and longs for flats, until one player has ten flats, which can be traded in for the thousand block.

SEE–Slide
SEE, $1.50 each

Here is a simple ten-inch slide rule, specially designed for use by elementary age children, which is both easy to use and easy to understand. A child can add, subtract, multiply, and divide on this one rule, which has both linear and logarithmic scales.

The slide is reversible, and the blank back provides an excellent writing surface so that you and/or your kids can create your own scales. Although you can make your own slide rules from cardboard, this sturdy plastic one seems well worth the price.

Metric Multibase Mathematics
Verda Holmberg, Mary Laycock, and Betty Sternberg

Activity Resources Company
P.O. Box 4875
Hayward, California 94545
$5

Here is a solid, simple, and composite approach to learning basic mathematical operations. If you've been searching for a single method that allows children to work with concrete materials and discover their way into the basic principles of computation, place value, bases, fractions, geometry, and logic, then this might be just what you want. Appropriate for kids eight to twelve, it's metric based to boot.

Using only a set of multibase blocks (other names: metric multibase blocks, Diene's blocks, or Cuisenaire cubes, square, and rods) and a succession of grids or patterns, kids lay out combinations of blocks according to the options presented to them in the diagrams. This way, they have a clear visual perspective on what's happening for any operation they're working with. The book includes actual scale designs for making your own blocks, if you're so disposed.

Chip Trading

*Scott Resources
Creative Publications*

Chip Trading helps children learn basic math skills by means of a series of games, activities, and problems — all presented in spiral-bound activity-card booklets. Each of the four whole-number operations is developed from the concrete stages involving the trading of colored chips. The materials are particularly well suited to gaining an understanding of place value.

There is a whole series of school sets available; send for a catalog from one of the sources for complete information. The activity booklets are $4.50 each, and a "starter set" with teacher's guide and basic materials for four kids is available for $14.95.

Photo from *Chip-Trading Activities,* reprinted by permission of Scott Resources, © 1975

games

Using games in home or classroom is an ideal way of reinforcing math skills — especially those that involve practice of arithmetic operations. Most of us accept the value of kids' learning the "times tables," for example, but who can forget those grueling homework assignments of fifteen to fifty problems per night? Aagh! Playing games can accomplish the same ends without any of the agony. Games are *fun*, and make learning as interesting as it should be.

commercial

There are literally hundreds of math games on the market. The following is an annotated list of some commercial games we've used and found particularly stimulating to kids. Most of them are difficult to duplicate or not worth the time and expense.

Checkermatics
SEE, $14.75

Here is a set of fifteen checkerboards with arithmetic problems in alternate squares. The playing disks are clear plastic so you can see the problem being jumped. Rules are variable — try making an ordinary checkerboard into a Checkermatics-type board.

Cover Up
SEE, $3.75

This is a strategy/addition game that involves throwing a pair of dice and covering any combination of numerals whose values total those shown on the dice — it can even be played as solitaire!

Foo
Cuisenaire Company of
   America, $4.95

This intriguing math game consists of seventy-eight cards and four playing frames. Cards are marked with numbers and operation symbols. Players are dealt seven cards and try to arrange them to create multiples of twelve, drawing and discarding cards until one person is successful.

In Order
Midwest Publications, $11.95

This is a kit of materials for easy assembly of thirteen different card games at a variety of levels. The basic game uses a deck of forty-two numbered cards that have to be placed in a rack in the order dealt — then rearranged through a series of strategic plays so that the numbers are consecutive.

Krypto
Creative Publications, $1.25

This card game is for older kids. Players have to create an "object number" using numbered cards dealt to them in various combinations.

Numble
Creative Publications, $5.25

This Scrabble-type game can often be found in local department stores. Tiles numbered 0 to 9 are laid out in ascending or descending order to make totals divisible by three. Basic arithmetic practice, luck, and strategy are all part of the play.

Operations Bingo
Creative Publications, $7.95

Instructions for twelve different Bingo games are included in this whole-class set of materials.

Prime Drag
Creative Publications, $3.95

This is a very popular game with upper elementary kids. The objective is to have players identify primes and composites on a "drag strip" board.

Tuf
SEE, $10.00

A near-classic math game, Tuf involves forming number sentences and equations with numbered and/or operational cubes. Players compete with each other and with a timer. Tuf is a fast-paced, exciting game for any age level, particularly since all players are active simultaneously (no waiting for turns). SEE has a set of twenty activity cards and twelve blank cubes (for extending the game possibilities) that can be purchased separately or with the standard game.

homemade games

Making your own skill reinforcement games (or having your kids make them!) is of course the best way to have games that fit your kids' particular needs. A few "essential materials" are listed below; please refer to pages 18–22 for sources and a more complete treatment of the wide variety and "how to" of homemade games.

blank cards
wooden or cardboard disks
checkerboards
file folders for making playing boards
counters or chips
blank ½" cubes for making dice
an assortment of sturdy containers

Some classic games that are ideal for adaptation:

Bingo
Concentration
Go Fish
Rummy
War
any favorite board game

A basic game form uses playing cards — usually thirty to fifty-two per deck. Multi-Match is simple to make and adapt to any math skill, and the cards can be used for at least three popular games (or any game that involves pairing or matching).

You need to make forty playing cards — half of which are multiplication problems, the remainder, answers. It's best if there are no duplicate answers (e.g., $4 \times 3 = 12$, but so does 6×2). The following pairs were used with fourth graders:

4×3	12	5×8	40
5×4	20	7×6	42
6×4	24	8×6	48
5×5	25	7×7	49
3×9	27	9×6	54
4×7	28	8×7	56
6×5	30	9×7	63
4×8	32	8×8	64
7×5	35	9×8	72
4×9	36	9×9	81

To play:

Concentration

All cards are laid face down. Players take turns turning two cards face up — matches (problem + answer) are kept. Winner is player with the most pairs when all cards are taken.

Go Fish

Players are each dealt five cards; the remainder of the deck is placed face down in a pile. Each player tries to create matches by asking opponent for an answer or a problem, depending upon card in hand (e.g., if a player holds 6×5, opponent might be asked, "Do you have 30?"). If so, opponent hands over the card and player goes again. If not, player must "go fish" and pick a card from the pile. Winner can be person with most pairs or person to get rid of all cards first.

War

All cards are distributed evenly among players. Players simultaneously turn up the top cards on their piles. Highest number takes all face-up cards. If a problem and its answer are turned up, "war" is declared: players put two cards face down, turn third card up — highest number takes all cards played. Winner is person with the most cards at the end of a set time limit — or play can continue (forever?) until one person has all the cards!

---

fractions

Here are several fraction activities, each utilizing a different set of materials. Almost any math unit can be presented with such a variety of commercial and homemade materials.

Pattern Block* fractions

*See page 182 for review of Pattern Blocks materials.

How many blue rhombuses will fit on a yellow hexagon?

If the hexagon = 1 whole, 1 blue rhombus = ?

How many green triangles will fit on
a hexagon?
a trapezoid?
a rhombus?

The green triangle is what fraction of the hexagon?

How much is 1 hexagon + 1 trapezoid + 2 rhombuses + 3 triangles?

3 green triangles = 1 red trapezoid = ½ hexagon

Can you discover another way of expressing what fraction of a hexagon = 3 green triangles?

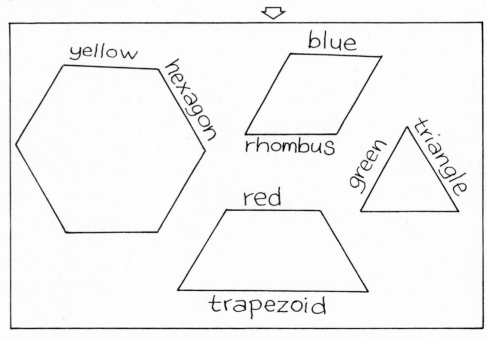

jumping fractions

Here is a homemade game that was the all-time favorite of my fourth grade class last year! Use a standard checkerboard and sixty-four wooden or cardboard disks (see page 20 for sources of game materials). Each disk should have a pictured fraction on one side, and a written fraction on the other.

Place all the disks on the checkerboard, picture side up. First player removes one disk to start the game. Players take turns jumping disks, and must correctly identify (name) the fraction pictured in order to keep the "jumped-over" disk. Jumps can be in any straight line — horizontally, vertically, or diagonally. Multiple jumps are okay as long as the fraction is properly identified with each jump. The winner is the player with the most disks at the end of the game (when no more jumps can be made). Have fun!

fraction bars

Scott Resources
Creative Publications

Fraction Bars is a unique set of materials, games, and activities. The bars themselves (in sets of sixty-four) are sturdy strips of cardboard, about $1'' \times 6''$. They are divided into 2, 3, 4, 6, and 12 parts and color-coded; each bar represents a fraction. These are mixed, matched, compared, and generally played with in a multitude of ways. A series of activity-card sets (spiral bound) includes an incredibly huge variety of high-quality, fun activities to help kids learn about fractions.

Although there are many approaches to helping kids recognize, understand, and use fractions, this set of materials is the most comprehensive. It is particularly valuable for people who are unfamiliar with fractions, want an organized, complete program, and/or have neither the time nor the energy to create their own materials.

Fraction Bars are available in several sets, some of which include playing cards, game mats, dice, markers, and other materials to extend activities with the bars. Here are a few package prices:

set of bars only $ 2.75
starter set $14.95
introductory set $46.00 (for thirty kids)

A game of Flip (similar to War) using Fraction Bars

fraction rods*

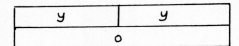

The orange rod is twice as big as the yellow rod.

The yellow rod is ½ of the _____ rod.

The brown rod is 4 times as big as the _____ rod.

The red rod is ¼ of the _____ rod.

Which rod = ½ the brown rod?

The light green rod is what fraction of the blue rod?

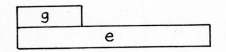

*Using Cuisenaire rods (see page 148).

The yellow rod is what fraction of the black rod?

How did you find out?

fraction dominoes

This set of beautifully designed natural wood pieces (9 cm. × 4 cm. × ½ cm.) helps kids to see the relationships among numbered, named, and pictured fractions. You can, of course, design your own; using oaktag, cardboard, or wood (for the very ambitious!) — dominoes is an extremely adaptable game. This set is the nicest commercial version we've seen.

competitive fractions

Competitive Fractions is a game for three to five players that reinforces a child's ability to recognize and add simple fractions (¼, ½, ¾). Playing pieces are based on a 4″ × 4″ square and are cut two ways. Players compete to fill a game board of whole squares by picking up fractional parts (designated by cards).

This is also a good introduction to equivalent fractions, and can be easily adapted to higher ability levels. Just cut the playing pieces into smaller fractions or create your own!

design fractions

If the shaded part = ½, color the section □.
If the shaded part = ⅓, color the section □.
If the shaded part = ⅔, color the section □.
If the shaded part = ¼, color the section □.
If the shaded part = ¾, color the section □.

Create any kind of design, curved or angular — your kids might even enjoy creating their own! Kids choose the colors they like and you can "check" just by looking at the finished color pattern!

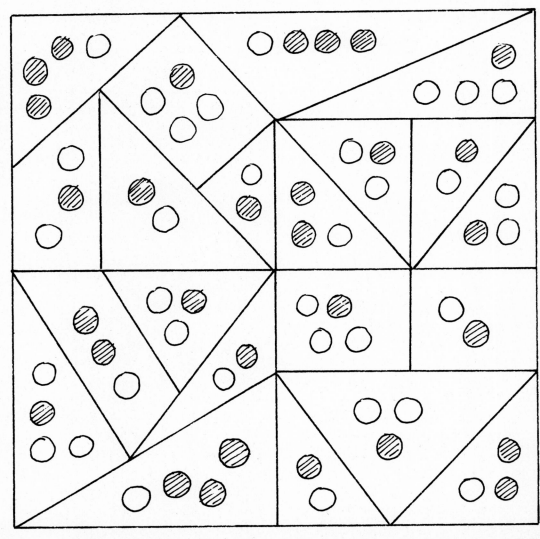

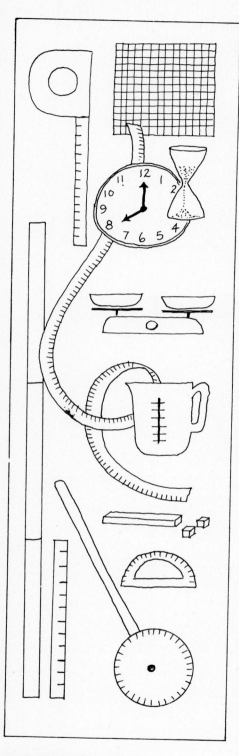

measurement

Just about anything you can touch, see, or do can be measured, which means there are plenty of activities available for Monday morning (or a rainy Saturday at home).* You're not at all limited to rulers and yardsticks, although those come in handy, too, when kids are ready for them. A whole lot of things on your shelves come into use: blocks, cubes, chips, timers, string, salt, sugar, assorted containers, and balances. Kids will gladly accept challenges to find out who has the longest reach, how fast someone can run an obstacle course, how many cubes of sugar will balance a given weight, or what the dimensions of a playing field are. Measurement becomes a valuable key for examining the whole environment and getting a sense of true scale.

*In fact, John Holt's *What Do I Do Monday?* (E. P. Dutton and Company, 1970, $6.95) has several chapters full of good ideas.

activities

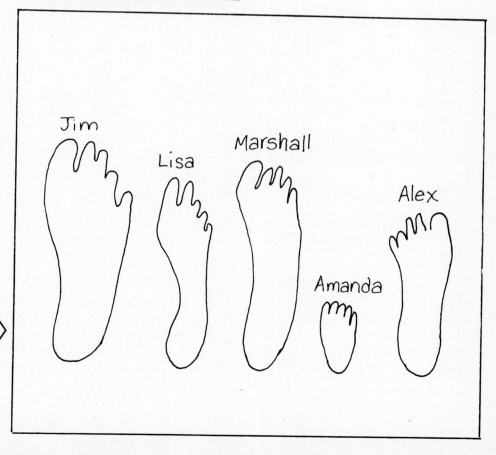

body graphs

Trace around feet (or hands, arms, legs, and whole bodies) to make a comparative picture-graph of sizes and shapes.

The same sort of thing can be done with ages, estimated weights, or other vital statistics, using cutout picture-symbols in place of body outlines. Let differences show themselves without actual measurements.

floor plans

Make floor plan–type cutouts, to scale, of all the pieces of furniture that might be in a single room. Now make several duplicates of each piece. Draw a rectangle of the same scale on a large sheet of paper, perhaps graph paper, to represent the room. You can also try making extra rectangles in a different scale.

What combination of furniture will fit into the room?
If you put in several more of one kind, do you have to leave other things out?

Will other arrangements of the same pieces fit better?
Can you estimate how much space to leave for passageways, chair sliding, doors opening?
If you had to wax the floor, where could you move the furniture to have it take up the least space?

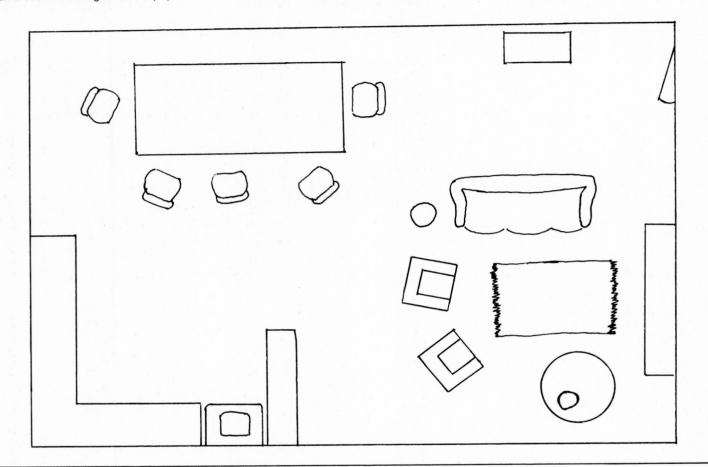

puddle measuring

Find a shallow puddle after a rainstorm or make one with a pail of water, preferably on a hard surface. As it dries, trace around its outline with a marker (chalk) every hour and record the time. (You may need to make some kind of fence around the project to protect the markings.)

How long does it take for the puddle to get half as big? To dry up?
How does the shape change?
Does the finished set of markings remind you of anything on a map?

This is a simple way to get into questions about measuring area, perimeter, and time. (Place a string around the perimeter of the puddle after each hour; compare lengths.) Graphing and mapping activities flow naturally from it, too. (Graph the shrinking area against the time.)

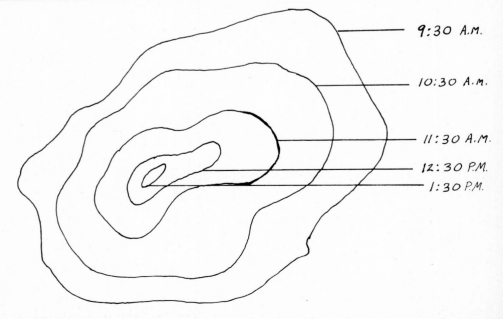

9:30 A.M.

10:30 A.M.

11:30 A.M.

12:30 P.M.

1:30 P.M.

mapping your neighborhood

You can work with three dimensions on a flat map if you first draw in streets, lots, pathways, and such, and then place side-view cutouts of buildings in their approximate positions. For simplicity, limit the map to just one block or an area equivalent to it.

You might begin by taking a walking tour of the area with your kids to make rough sketches; then sit down and make more accurate renditions. Your surveyors could collaborate on their final efforts in order to agree on relative sizes and shapes of buildings, distances between them, and placement on the drawn map. They might even get into other problems, like collecting statistics, or deciding on alternative routes for getting from one place to another and determining times for traversing each of them.

This activity may raise a host of questions that lead directly into the need for measurement, common scale, determination of area, map symbols, and so on.

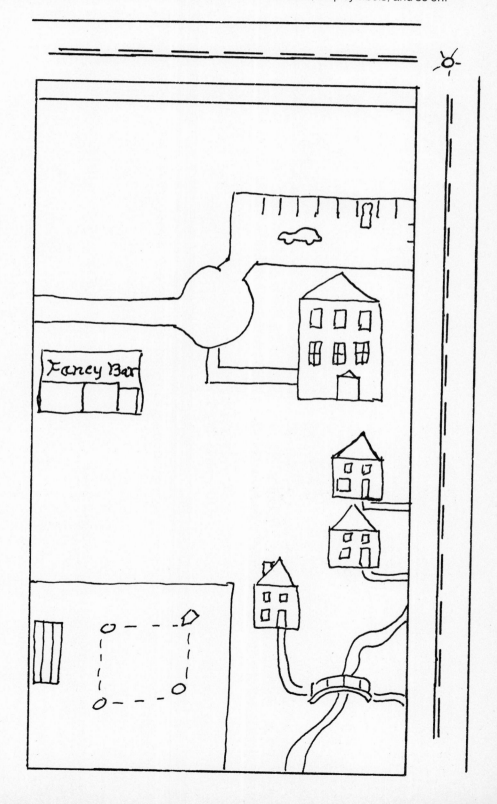

the human dimension

body parts

Measuring is basically a matter of finding something handy that can be used as a standard unit and applied to objects or spaces in order to find dimensions. Nothing is handier than your own body, of course, so why not start with that? Kids find it a very sensible, understandable, and enjoyable way to go about discovering the sizes of things around them.

body symmetry

Draw an imaginary line lengthwise through the middle of your body, dividing it into two equal halves.

Are they really equal?
When you buy a new pair of shoes, do they fit the same way on both feet?
Is one hand bigger in any part than the other?
Is your right leg longer or shorter than your left leg?

(If this intrigues you, look at pages 187–188 on symmetry.)

body parts	measurements you can make	estimate	actual count
	How many palms high is a doorway? How many handspans are there across a table? A window?		
	How many lengths of one finger are there in a chair seat? Using the span between just two finger joints, how far is it across a book?		
	Your "reach" is from the end of one extended hand to the other. How far across the room is it in "reaches"? From your elbow to the ends of your finger is a "cubit." How many "cubits" in a bench?		
	Measure the room with your feet. Measure it in paces. Which is easier to do accurately?		
	You wouldn't measure a kitchen sink with your whole body. How many lengths of you are there in a kitchen floor? In a long hallway?		
	Find objects or other people to put on the other end of your human balance. What (or who) weighs as much as you do?		
	How many somersaults long is a playing field? How many body rolls is a hill?		
	Can you measure in pulse beats how long it takes for someone to walk around a building?		

measuring people-space

The form of the whole man-made environment is determined by the dimensions of people standing, sitting, lying, moving. Here, then, is another way to look at the body as a measuring instrument.

What is a comfortable bed size?
How big is a room in relation to the people who have to use it?
How much space do people need to walk around in a bus station?

Draw an outline of a body that represents the average size of kids in a particular group, but reduce it to one-fourth scale. Do the same thing to represent an average-size adult. If possible, make outlines of the same bodies sitting, lying, running, and so on.

Attach a long piece (ten feet or more) of mural paper or wrapping paper to a wall.

Make the sheet into a large diagram showing outlines of doors, windows, sinks, room corners, and furniture drawn in proportion to the human figures. Put in measurements according to whatever units you're employing. The diagram opposite shows one way of illustrating a measuring scale.

You can do the same kind of thing using floor-plan diagrams and representing people as movable disks of appropriate sizes.

This is an extendable tool for studying the human environment in terms of the space people need and how they use it. For more people-space activities, see Volume and Capacity, page 169.

What determines how high a windowsill should be?
What is an average table height for the people of one group?
Are some pieces of furniture the right size for adults but not for children?
How wide should doorways be? What has to go through them?

7 — 9 —
6 — 8 —
5 — 7 —
4 — 6 —
3 — 5 —
2 — 4 —
1 — 3 —
    2 —
    1 —
feet

200 — 250 —
    200 —
150 — 150 —
100 — 100 —
50 — 50 —
    centimeters

From *Our Man-Made Environment, Book Seven*, p. 33, reprinted by permission of GEE!, Group for Environmental Education, Inc., © 1970.

standardized measurement

If children have had enough experience comparing sizes and shapes, seeing how things fit into spaces or fit in relation to one another, and noting basic differences of dimension, they can work into standardized measurement with a clear understanding of why it's needed and how it works. It also makes sense that they begin learning it by using their own bodies as measuring instruments, because from the moment of birth they have experienced physical dimensions through hands, feet, and whole bodies. They have a tactile knowledge of these dimensions, and translating them into the abstract medium of standardized measurement takes considerable learning of a kind that must stem from whatever innate information kids already possess.

linear and area measurement

Rods for Measuring

The kids have learned how to use their hands and other parts of their body to measure length, width, and height. They may also have discovered that individual differences in, say, width of handspan make the results of each person's measurements somewhat different.

Offer them some small rods of varied sizes — Cuisenaire rods are ideal — and suggest experimenting with these as measuring devices to substitute for hands (or feet, etc.).

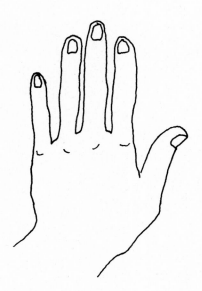

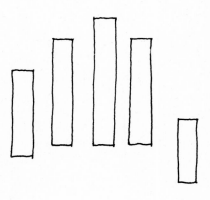

Find rods the same length as each of your fingers.
Could you measure with these instead of fingers?

If you're working with a group, it will probably happen that the finger/rod equivalents are not the same for each person. Ask them what they can do about this problem.

Do some lengths (colors) of rods appear more often than others?
Can we make up one "hand" out of the most common lengths?

The next problem will be to make a choice about using all five "finger-rods" as a set of measurers, or just one (probably the longest). The choice may depend on the age and experience of the children you're working with, but it generally makes things easier to choose one. Whatever the choice, make up names for the units of measurement.

A final step you can take is to find combinations of shorter rods that would serve to divide your standard rod(s) into sublengths, allowing greater accuracy in measurement.

Having reached these last few steps, the kids now have a standardized, partly flexible system for a wide variety of measurements.

The process of transferring from body parts to a standardized measure looks like this:

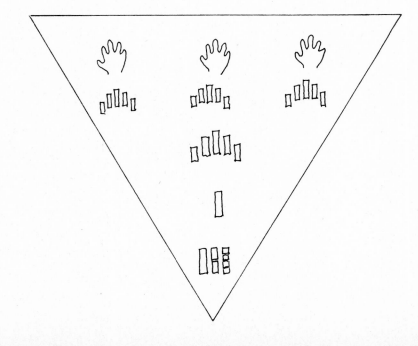

more measuring with rods

How long, or wide, is a
  table?
  chair?
  book?
  box?
Does it matter what length of
rod you choose as the basic
unit?

Build or find a rectangular
frame (box cover, tray, picture frame). How many rods
will it take to fill up all the
space inside the frame?
Does it matter what size rods
you use or how you arrange
them?

Measure the same widths
and lengths with a different
unit of measure. Can you
find more than one set of
rods that will give the same
dimensions you got the first
time? Can you see how to
use a set of basic units along
with some smaller ones to
get a more accurate mea-
surement?

Use an empty frame and line
its four inside edges with
rods in order to find the
number of units that make up
its perimeter. You will either
have to find a set of rods that
fit exactly or use a combination of basic long units and
equivalent shorter ones.

Find a large-scale architec-
tural map of part of a city or
some other map that has lots
of square corners and
straight lines. Measure
lengths and widths of buildings, blocks, and possible
routes for getting from one
point to another.

Use the rods and the map to
figure out how much area
there is in a building, block,
street, or parking lot. Can
you rearrange the rods used
to fill up one area without
changing the amount of area
you have measured? Could
you change the scale of the
map dimensions using a
smaller or larger set of rods?

If you line just one width and
one length of your frame with
rods, can you figure out how
many would fill up the whole
frame? How would they be
arranged?

Body/Standard Equivalents for Measuring Area

It takes a lot of time-consuming experiments with concrete objects to understand the concept of area measurement. If your kids are very hazy about it, go back to body measurement.

How many hands can you fit on the top of a table? A chair?

How many of you, lying down, will fit on the floor of a room?

How many bodies would it take to "fill up" a vertical area, such as a door opening?

Can you find a way to calculate how many bodies it would take to fill up one whole wall of a room?

Then substitute rectangular or three-dimensional objects to do the measuring in place of bodies. For large areas, newspapers are handy.

Finally, use a set of rods, squares or cubes, or disks.

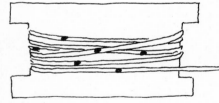

Measuring String

If your kids have become familiar with some basic units of linear measurement, they can easily learn how to use a measuring string, which is a generally more adaptable instrument than the conventional tape measure. We recommend making your string holder out of wood, but you can make it out of several layers of heavy cardboard.

Get a 50- or 100-foot length of sash cord (cotton rope at least ⅛ inch in diameter), and use felt-tip markers to mark off intervals of feet, yards, or meters. Different-size intervals can be shown by different colors. Tie it to the holder and wind it on.

How long is a field? Your front walk?

Can you use the string to measure the dimensions of a pond? How many different measurements can you come up with? (You may need a boat!)

You can measure the height of a building up to the highest window, but can you measure the height of a tree? (There might be some problems of liability!)

Height Measurer

Clinometers are a little more elaborate to make, but they are a lot of fun. They also solve those problems about measuring from the tops of trees, for instance. The clinometer is essentially an instrument to measure a vertical angle from which a linear height can be calculated.

To determine the height of an object (tree, building, pole):

1. Sight through the straw to the top of the object and determine the angle from the protractor.
2. Measure the distance from your eye to the ground.
3. Measure the horizontal distance from you to the object.
4. Represent these measurements on graph paper, according to whatever scale is appropriate.
5. If you know the angle between the object and the ground (90°), the clinometer distance between you and the object, and the height of your eye from the ground, you have all the data necessary for determining the height of the object on your graph paper.

Can you figure out the rest?

Can you see how to adapt the process to find the height of an object (a hill, for instance) when you can't measure the distance between you and its base?

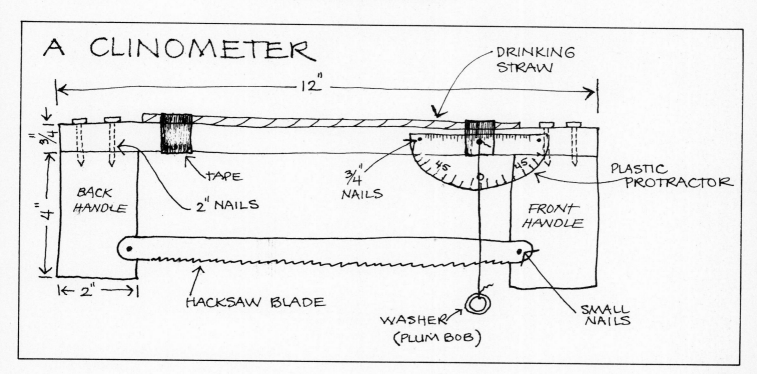

A CLINOMETER

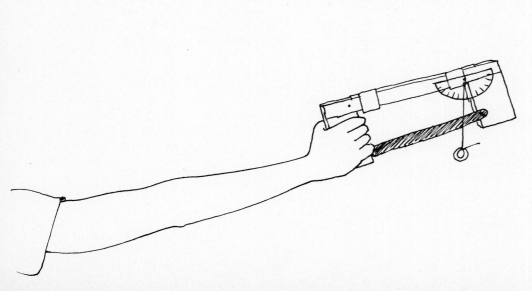

Other Measuring Tools

You don't need all these things, but this is
a fairly complete selection of devices that
get used a lot when kids are doing measuring activities.

SEE, package of 10, $2.50
Creative Publications, $.35 each

A combination metric and conventional ruler is handy. Plastic is more durable and cleanable.

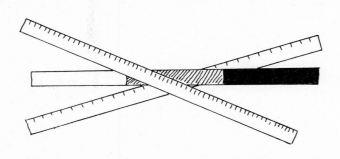

Creative Publications, $2.75 each

Yardsticks are easy to come by.
Metersticks come in a large variety.

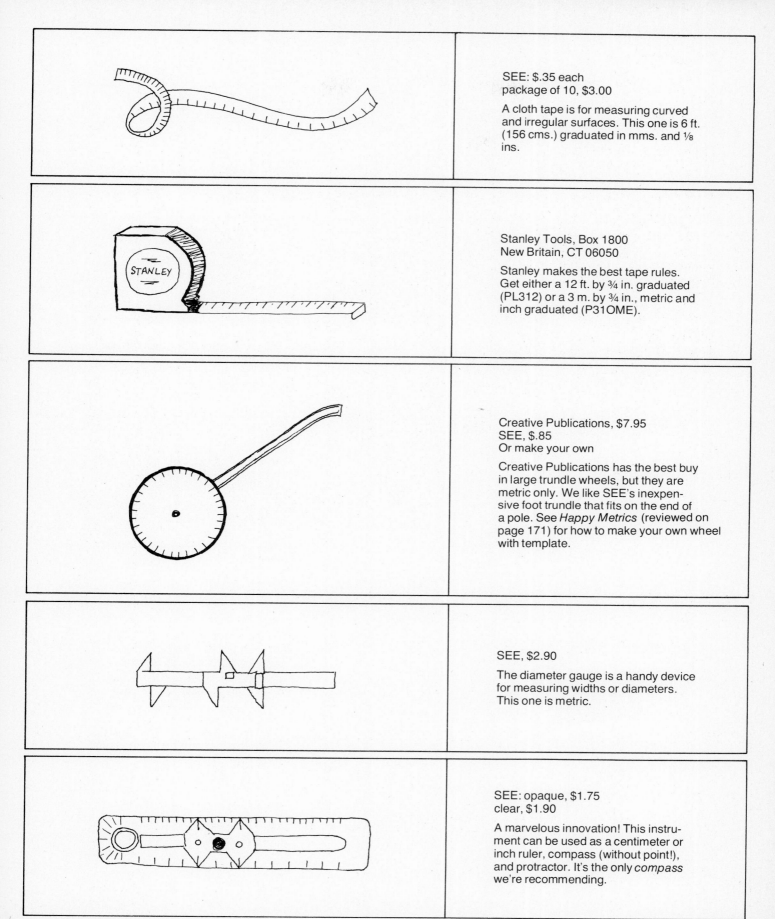

SEE: $.35 each
package of 10, $3.00

A cloth tape is for measuring curved and irregular surfaces. This one is 6 ft. (156 cms.) graduated in mms. and ⅛ ins.

Stanley Tools, Box 1800
New Britain, CT 06050

Stanley makes the best tape rules. Get either a 12 ft. by ¾ in. graduated (PL312) or a 3 m. by ¾ in., metric and inch graduated (P31OME).

Creative Publications, $7.95
SEE, $.85
Or make your own

Creative Publications has the best buy in large trundle wheels, but they are metric only. We like SEE's inexpensive foot trundle that fits on the end of a pole. See *Happy Metrics* (reviewed on page 171) for how to make your own wheel with template.

SEE, $2.90

The diameter gauge is a handy device for measuring widths or diameters. This one is metric.

SEE: opaque, $1.75
clear, $1.90

A marvelous innovation! This instrument can be used as a centimeter or inch ruler, compass (without point!), and protractor. It's the only *compass* we're recommending.

Other Tools — Continued

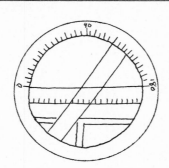

Creative Publications, $.75

The "Angle-Master" is unique; the middle rotates so that lines can be drawn at any angle.

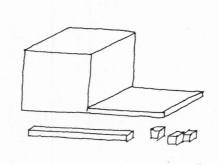

Many sources, many varieties
SEE, Creative Publications, and others

You need at least one variety of either rods, blocks, cubes, or squares. Have a large set of blank cubes and something in centimeters (Cuisenaire or multibase blocks will fill most needs).

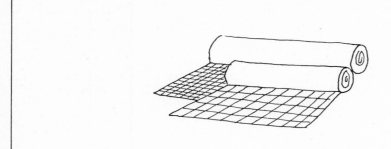

Creative Publications, roll (any grid), $16.50
Other standard paper suppliers

You should have graph paper in many sizes of grid, metric and conventional. Three basic grids are 1 cm., ¼ in., and 1 in. Creative Publications sells it by the roll.

Many sources, many varieties
Creative Publications, Sharpie:
8-color set, $6.95

For making color-coded graphs, maps, diagrams, and homemade measuring instruments, you need a set of felt-tip markers. The "Sharpie" seems to be the best for permanent marking on any surface.

volume, capacity, and weight

When you've learned how to measure the basic linear proportions of human beings and the environment they live in, what's left to work with? Stuff. There is lots of it: rocks, bricks, sand, water, marbles, wood, nails, sugar, soda pop, acorns, packages, books, pencils — all those things that fit into containers, store on shelves, or serve as the raw materials that people and nature find uses for. This is where kids get into the fascinating business of finding out how much space things take up and what they weigh. Kids of any age need to play with these concepts in many different ways and with many different materials. They especially need plenty of experience with concrete, everyday objects before they can be expected to grasp the abstract concepts involved in standardized measurement.

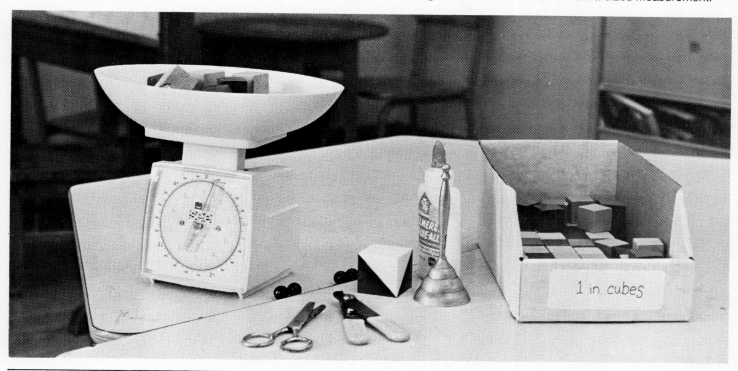

Volume and Capacity

It makes sense to start with a set of boxes of different shapes that have been selected or cut to hold equal volumes of small cubes.

1. Simply ask the kids to try filling the boxes with cubes and counting how many each container holds. You can avoid the word "volume," and speak instead of the "amount of space" the cubes fill.

2. Now let the kids use some containers of similar shape but varying capacity, so that they can begin to discover that the cubes serve as a convenient way to measure the amount of space filled in a container. They can also reassemble the blocks outside the containers in which they originally fit, change the arrangement, and refill the containers to see that volume can remain constant in spite of how the material is shaped.

3. A next step could be experimenting with differences between volume and capacity by partially filling some containers and comparing the contents with a set of blocks representing the total capacity of a container. Also, a set of cubic measurements for the capacities of various containers could be made.

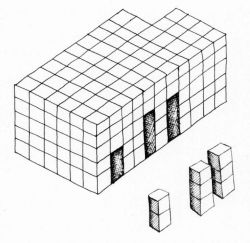

How many people do you think could fit inside a phone booth?
Could you measure the capacity of a swimming pool with people instead of water?

Capacities and volumes of people-space are measured differently, since we are usually referring to the amount of floor space they take up, along with passage for movement and breathing room. Would you think of the people-capacity of an elevator in the same way that you think of the capacity of a restaurant?

If you can get hold of a dollhouse or a small model of a building, measure the capacities of spaces in it with cubes. Then represent persons with single blocks of wood cut to appropriate scale and decide how many of them would fit comfortably in a room with a certain purpose. Finally, replace a number of cubes that represent the capacity (or volume) of that room with equivalent people-blocks. How much space do people actually take up compared to the total space available?

Weighing Stuff

You need:

a pan balance
stuff to be weighed

1. Choose or make a set of single "packages" differing in size, shape, and weight. You can stick to items from a pantry, but wrap them up to hide their identities. Using the balance, kids can be asked to make several different classifications based on weight. Some of the possibilities are shown in the diagram below.

You can do a series of the same activities with *collections:* bottle caps versus marbles, plastic spoons versus shells, and so on.

2. Supply a set of standard pound weights made from ordinary materials with different bulks, such as a bag of sand, a bag of salt, or a bag of fine sawdust. By first balancing these against a known pound weight, such as a box of sugar, and then against other objects or collections, kids will discover that they cannot infer weight from size and shape.

large/light		large/heavy
small/light		small/heavy
large/heavy		small/heavy
small/light		large/light
oblong/heavy		cubical/heavy

other games and guides

Beginnings
Nuffield Mathematics Project

John Wiley and Sons
605 Third Avenue
New York, New York 10016
$5.50

What always impresses me most about Nuffield guides is their copious illustration of children's work. You can sense, by this, a solid commitment to working patiently with children as they really think, and not as adults often glibly assume they think.

This guide, as the name implies, details a variety of early experiments with mathematical principles, focused on the study of number in the "context of measurement emerging from environmental play: volume, capacity, length, area, shape, space, time and size." The "environmental play" possibilities are extensive; cooking, music, movement, needlecraft, and model-making activities are some of those exploited for teaching basic ideas about measurement.

Inch by Inch

SEE, $7.50

A simple, carefully designed primary game, *Inch by Inch* reinforces basic measuring and measurement computation skills. Players move markers along a path graduated only in inches by throwing a die or picking up a special card that instructs them to find and measure one of the lines on the perimeter of the board. Since they need recognize only the key words "on" and "back," children with limited reading ability are able to play the game easily. SEE promises that a *Centimeter by Centimeter* is coming soon.

Made to Measure

Leicestershire Learning Systems
Box 335
New Gloucester, Maine 04260
$4.75

Here is an entertaining way of understanding area. The players compete to fill a plastic tray with a minimum number of metric-dimension "tiles." Up to three children can play at one time. A box contains three plastic trays, metric-dimension "tiles" in heavy laminated cards, metric measures, stock cards, and full instructions for play.

metrics

A government study completed in 1971 (U.S. Metric Study) recommended that the United States convert to the metric system by 1983. Are you ready? Obviously, one of the best ways to implement this conversion is to start teaching the current younger generation to "think metric." There is a rapidly increasing switch-over in many of the curriculum materials catalogs; some offer no materials at all using the customary system.

So far, our attitude as teachers and writers of this guide has been to continue using and recommending both. In effect, this is a bilingual situation in which the native language and a universal one are being learned side by side. Note that the emphasis is on simultaneous use, not on conversion back and forth.

There are now many basic guides and programs available for teaching in the metric system. One of the most useful is *Happy Metrics*.

Happy Metrics, 2 volumes
Bob Blaine and Nancy Nason

Scott Resources
1900 East Lincoln
Fort Collins, Colorado 80521
$14.95 each, with binder
$9.95 each, without binder

This loose-leaf assembly of metric activities is both comprehensive and varied. Best of all, it includes a large number of heavy cardboard cutouts for making your own metersticks, cubes, trundle wheels, game parts, and even an ingenious gram scale. The activities are a lot more imaginative than those in other guides, yet they are clear and thorough, with lots and lots of good games that would be a delight to have even if you weren't teaching metrics. Considering that most of us are just beginning to introduce metrics, volume one should do you for a long time, and with any age. I don't think it's worth spending five dollars more for the binder.

Discovering Metrics
James Galt and Company

SEE
$17.50, complete
$3.75, each set

There aren't many published resources dealing exclusively with measurement activities, but here's one and it's good. It would be highly useful for children up to ten even if you need to avoid working with the metric system as such. It follows the Nuffield approach to mathematics, and so coordinates well with books like *Begin-*nings. The large, plastic-coated color cards, which are organized in five sets (weight, length, capacity, volume, and area), present manipulative activities in a simple, clear format. They are arranged in order of difficulty, which means that abstract principles are left to the last few cards of each set. Actual metric calculations appear on only a few of the cards. My only quibble is that they make too abrupt a transition from experiments with common materials to activities with the metric scale. (By the way, I'm not recommending that you avoid using metrics — we've all got to start sometime!)

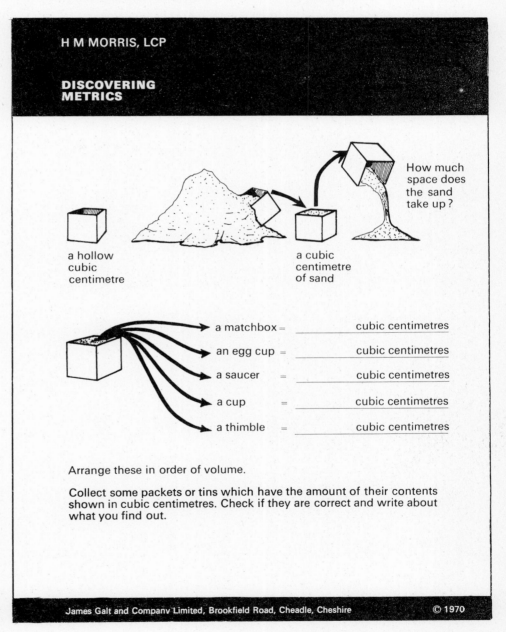

From *Discovering Metrics: Volume*, © 1970 by James Galt and Company Ltd., reprinted by permission of SEE, Inc.

time

Children learn about time through events — birthdays, meals, bedtimes, and even births and deaths. Telling time by the clock is a sophisticated skill that is really meaningful only after kids have acquired an *internal* sense of the duration, sequence, and regularity of such events. Adults, too, depend on this kind of "happening" measurement as much as they depend on time-by-the-clock.

There are some simple ways to help kids pin down the notion of what time is all about.

Help them make charts of their day's activities. Using a circular form will help illustrate a relationship to clock time. In school, it could also serve as a form of record keeping.

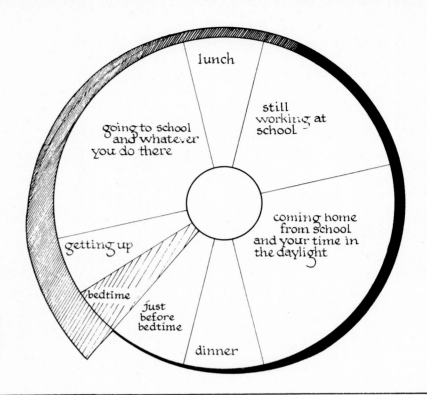

activities with time

Body Clock

Lots of people can wake themselves up by a mental alarm clock, even "setting" it for a specific time the night before. If you practice you can learn to trust it.

There are lots of other ways the body acts as a clock, too. Hunger and sleepiness both tell you from the inside when it's time to eat or go to bed.

Try keeping a chart of your own body clock, to see what your natural pattern of sleeping and working is like. You'll have to do this during a vacation when you don't have too many regular obli-gations! Just color in a square for the time you go to sleep and another for the time you wake up. After a week or so check to see what the pattern is.

There are other, less familiar time regulations in your body, too:

Did you know that your heart beats slower between 10:00 P.M. and 7:00 A.M.?
That your body temperature falls during sleep?
That your oxygen consumption peaks during your normal period of highest activity — whether you're active or not?

— from *The Reasons for Seasons,* page 51
(reviewed on page 174)

	am							Pm										am				
	6	7	8	9	10	11	NOON	1	2	3	4	5	6	7	8	9	10	11	MID-NITE	1	2	3	4	5
SUNDAY																						
MONDAY																						
TUESDAY																						
WEDNESDAY																						
THURSDAY																						
FRIDAY																						
SATURDAY																						

Time Capsule

Looking ahead, why not put together a time capsule on your birthday, New Year's Day, or maybe the day you move, so you can open it on some future day.

A shoe box is good, or even an envelope will do. In it you put:

snapshots of family, friends, and pets made during the year
school pictures of you, or one of those little photo strips you make in bus stations
a tape cassette of you and your friends together, talking and kidding around
a weekly menu from the school cafeteria
all the stuff that's in your pockets right now

ticket stubs from rock concerts, plays, events you've attended during the year
a TV guide
movie listings from the newspaper
letters you received during the year
a road map showing the route of a trip you took recently, traced with a felt-tip pen
labels off of boxes, bottles, and cans of your favorite foods
birthday, get well, and Christmas cards from the past year
your favorite magazines and comics (or parts of them)
new recipes discovered during the year

— from *My Backyard History Book*, pages 20–21 (reviewed on page 14)

Years

Visualizing time in its historical sense is easy to do with this kind of graph, especially because kids don't have so many years to remember. They will probably need to consult parents for details and sequence, though.

Use a long piece of shelf paper or some single sheets taped together. Represent birthdays as numbered vertical lines intersecting one long horizontal line; then add words and pictures to describe particular events.

The Reasons for Seasons
Linda Allison

Little, Brown and Company
34 Beacon Street
Boston, Massachusetts 02106
$3.95

Or, "The Great Cosmic Megagalactic Trip without Moving from Your Chair," as the subtitle describes it. This is one of the three in the Brown Paper School series (see general review, page 14), and there is no better description for it than what the author herself provided:

This is a book about the trip that the earth makes around the sun. It explains the reasons for seasons. Plus a whole lot more. Inside you will find stuff to do, things to make, ideas to think about, stories to read, and things to inspect, collect, and give away. Most of this book is about our place — earth. Some of it is about time and space, the invisible world, The Big Out There. All of it is in a kind of order — the kind that comes with seasons. And if you read this book and think about it some, you'll know that the order of earth life is seasonal too.

Make a large (twenty-by-twelve-inch) calendar-month grid and give it to children to decorate in their own way. One way is to change all the *numbers* into funny/lovely designs that represent something that did happen or might happen on that day. Holidays and birthdays can be included.

clocks

People have been keeping time by the sun for millennia, but there have always been the problems of what to do about cloudy days and constant adjustments for the tilt of the earth. Also, people needed something to use indoors that would be handy for measuring short intervals accurately. Humankind being rather ingenious about such things, a host of fascinating inventions came into being to answer these needs, some of them created so long ago that nobody can remember who deserves the credit. Having kids invent (or reinvent) their own time devices makes an exciting and meaningful way to learn about measuring time.

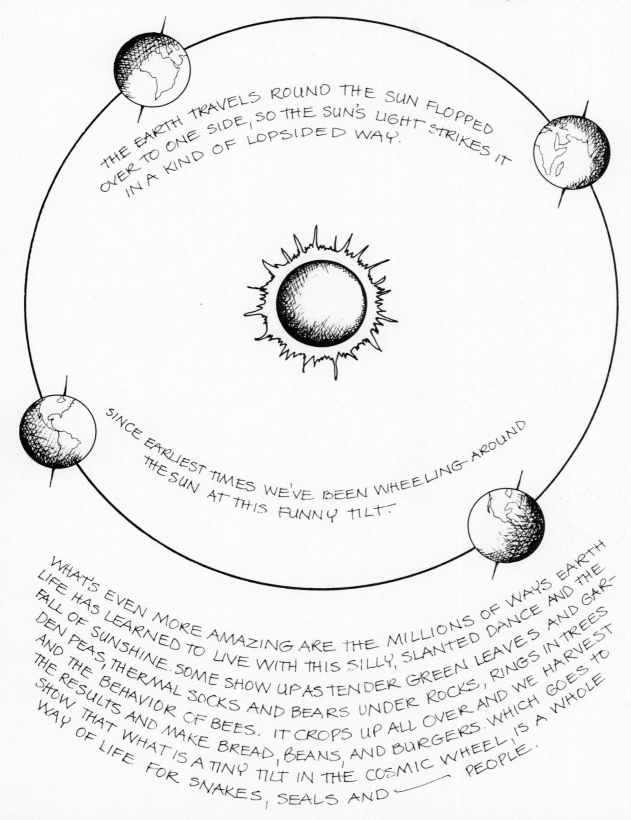

THE EARTH TRAVELS ROUND THE SUN FLOPPED OVER TO ONE SIDE, SO THE SUN'S LIGHT STRIKES IT IN A KIND OF LOPSIDED WAY.

SINCE EARLIEST TIMES WE'VE BEEN WHEELING AROUND THE SUN AT THIS FUNNY TILT.

WHAT'S EVEN MORE AMAZING ARE THE MILLIONS OF WAYS EARTH LIFE HAS LEARNED TO LIVE WITH THIS SILLY, SLANTED DANCE AND THE FALL OF SUNSHINE. SOME SHOW UP AS TENDER GREEN LEAVES AND GARDEN PEAS, THERMAL SOCKS AND BEARS UNDER ROCKS, RINGS IN TREES AND THE BEHAVIOR OF BEES. IT CROPS UP ALL OVER AND WE HARVEST THE RESULTS AND MAKE BREAD, BEANS, AND BURGERS. WHICH GOES TO SHOW THAT WHAT IS A TINY TILT IN THE COSMIC WHEEL IS A WHOLE WAY OF LIFE FOR SNAKES, SEALS AND ——— PEOPLE.

Regular Mechanical Clocks

Who invented the mechanical clock, when or where, is not known. But the development of its basic principle, in the light of contemporary knowledge, was a work of unparalleled brilliance. The inventor's reasoning might have gone something like this: if I attach a weight to a rope and pass the rope a number of times around a short cylinder or barrel that is free to revolve; if I elevate this mechanism on a framework or tower and regulate the fall of the weight so that it slowly drops a certain distance toward the ground between sunrise and sunset, unwinding the rope and turning the barrel as it drops; if I manage all this, then, by means of a toothed wheel on the end of the barrel, and other wheels geared to it, the movement of the weight could be registered by a convenient indicator, moving correspondingly around the face of a dial through the hours of a day. I could then rewind the rope on the barrel, thus raising the weight, and repeat the process the next day.

— from *Machines,* by Robert O'Brien
(Life Science Library, Time-Life Books),
pages 33, 34

Sundials

There are many different designs for sundials, including some highly elaborate ones, but almost anything that casts a shadow can be used for telling time.

Locate a tall pole (fence post, sign, tree) in a big clear space. Place a marker (a stake in soft ground; a drawn mark on a hard surface) at the tip of the shadow every hour, using a regular clock as your guide. Check it after a week, a month, a season. Is it still accurate?

Pendulum Timer

Pendulums can be fairly accurate for small time measurements.
Hang a big washer or nut by a thread from a pivot (a pin stuck into something). Experiment with the length of the thread and the distance of the swing until you can make it swing just sixty times in a minute.
With this device you can answer questions like:

How fast does sand settle in water?
How fast can toy trains or cars go in feet per second?
How many of your heartbeats are there in a minute?

More Clocks

Water clocks leave room for inventiveness, and they're fun to watch (that's important in a clock!).
It is said that a French monk invented the sand clock because his water clock kept freezing up. My private theory is that it was invented in the Sahara Desert.

Put a mark on the side of a candle, measure the distance from the top to the mark, and clock-time how long it takes for it to burn down to the mark. Keep experimenting in this way until you can mark off the candle in even intervals and know how much time each interval represents.

Can you invent a candle that has a built-in marking system?
Could you make a clock with a burning piece of string?

Time by Fire
Another very exotic alarm clock was sometimes used in China. Two brass balls were suspended from either end of a piece of string, which was placed across a burning stick of incense. In time the string burnt, and the balls fell into a bowl, making a loud enough clank to awaken people. The people could then congratulate each other on their cleverness in inventing such a sweet-smelling alarm clock.

— from *The Reasons for Seasons,* page 48
(reviewed on page 174)

shapes

We have loosely lumped all kinds of resources and activities having to do with shapes (both two- and three-dimensional) in this section. Tangrams, Soma cubes, geoboards, polyhedra and D-Stix, Pattern Blocks, attribute games and problems, symmetry — all of these are basically concerned with shapes and/or utilize shapes to give kids concrete experiences with other mathematical concepts. These include perimeter, area, fractions, sets, angles, congruence, and general problem solving. As you read through these pages, experiment with the materials and be aware of their wide application in areas other than shape recognition!

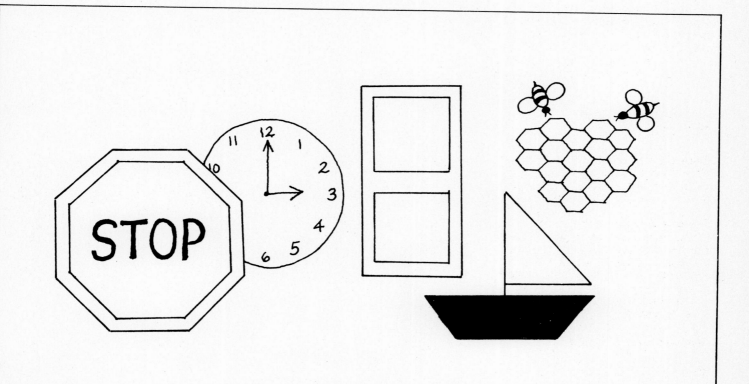

Look for shapes in the environment — in classroom or home or outdoors. How many circles can you find — clocks? Full moon? Dinner plates? How many squares — books? Sidewalk sections? Windows? Tiles? What other shapes can you find? Make a rubbing of a manhole cover, bathroom tile patterns, interesting designs in vents or gratings. How many of the shapes you see are regular? Irregular? How did you decide? Is the shape of a butterfly or a leaf regular?

Scan

This Parker Brothers game is available in many local stores. It is a fast-paced card game that requires players to locate matching shapes, colors, patterns, or positions (four games in one!). Two identical decks of twenty-four cards are used — one spread on table or floor, the other exposed one card at a time from a central pile.

Create your own Scan-type game for matching arithmetic problems, scrambled words, fractions, capital cities, and so on (see pages 18–22 for more game ideas). Use only one or two sections, rather than four, for young children.

$\frac{1}{2}$ shaded circle	stamp
Albany	8×3

$\frac{1}{2}$	atsprn
New York	24

tangrams

The tangram is a Chinese puzzle that has fascinated children and adults alike for at least two hundred years. Making your own tangram puzzle is a challenging activity; it can be made any size, but the seven pieces should bear the same relationships to one another as shown.

Tangram puzzles can be purchased from a wide variety of sources. The "best buy" we've come across is a four-inch-square plastic tangram (fifty-five cents each, or forty cents each for twenty-five or more) from:

Creative Publications
P.O. Box 10328
Palo Alto, California 94303

Creative Publications also has a set of "tangram stickers" ($2.75) that could be used for making activity cards, designs, or original problems / puzzle shapes.

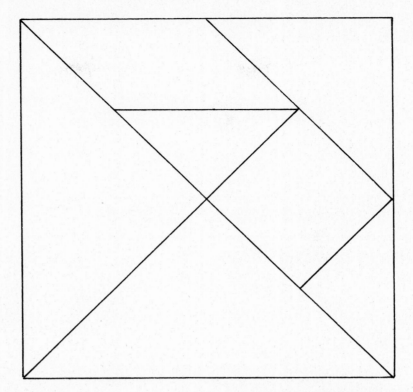

There are several tangram activity-card sets and activity books (with tear-out pages for reproduction) available commercially. Both Creative Publications and SEE have a variety of tangram materials (see page 138 for addresses), but we think the following will serve most needs quite adequately.

Tangram Cards

McGraw-Hill Book Company
1221 Avenue of the Americas
New York, New York 10020
$4.62 per set

There are a total of 121 puzzles on these activity cards, each measuring approximately 7" × 9". They progress according to difficulty and are especially designed for children by the Elementary Science Study (ESS).

Math Experiments with the Tangram
John L. Ginther

Midwest Publications Company
P.O. Box 129
Troy, Michigan 48084

This activity book is classroom oriented, and each page includes a tangram activity as well as puzzles. The pieces used make a five-inch square (rather than the four-inch square used with most activity books and cards), and include everything from making patterns to measuring angles.

Tangrams: 330 Puzzles
Ronald C. Read

Dover Publications
180 Varick Street
New York, New York 10014
$1.50

This is a collection of whimsical, intriguing tangram puzzles that can be done with any size set of tangram pieces. Alphabet letters, numerals, animals, household objects, and people are all illustrated and can be made by combining the seven tangram pieces in a variety of ways. Solutions are given at the back of the book for when you or your kids are stumped!

pentominoes

If five squares of equal size are joined in all possible ways, the twelve shapes that result are called pentominoes. They are similar to tangrams as puzzles and as enrichment in math. Shapes, area, perimeter, and problem solving are only a few of the math concepts involved in using/playing with pentominoes.

Midwest Publications (see address page 179) has the only materials we've seen that are related to pentominoes. *Math Experiments with Pentominoes* and its accompanying teacher's manual suggest a wide variety of activities using homemade or purchased pieces. "Hexed" is a puzzle game (also available in local discount stores) with colorful plastic pentominoes.

Math Experiments with Pentominoes,
    $3.95 each
teacher's manual, $1.25
Hexed, $1.80

three-dimensional shapes

space-form polyhedra

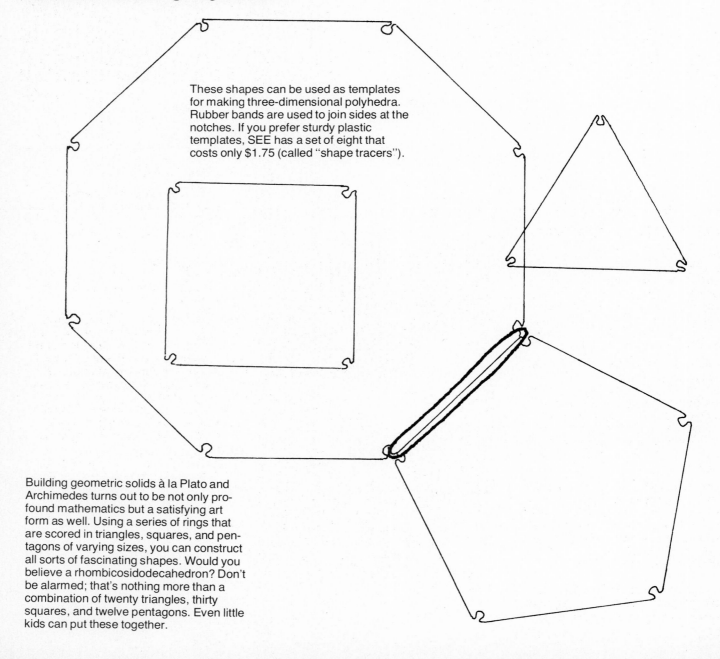

These shapes can be used as templates for making three-dimensional polyhedra. Rubber bands are used to join sides at the notches. If you prefer sturdy plastic templates, SEE has a set of eight that costs only $1.75 (called "shape tracers").

Building geometric solids à la Plato and Archimedes turns out to be not only profound mathematics but a satisfying art form as well. Using a series of rings that are scored in triangles, squares, and pentagons of varying sizes, you can construct all sorts of fascinating shapes. Would you believe a rhombicosidodecahedron? Don't be alarmed; that's nothing more than a combination of twenty triangles, thirty squares, and twelve pentagons. Even little kids can put these together.

paper plate polyshapes

You need:

  package of 100 6-inch paper plates
  rubber bands
  paper hole punch

Make a template (exact angles), the points of which meet the outside edge of the plate. Draw its outline on the plate and snip notches at each point with the paper punch. Make as many of these as you need. Bend flaps backward. To construct shapes, put any two flaps together and fasten them with a rubber band through the notches.

Photo by Jim Bottomley

straw structures

Almost any three-dimensional geometric shape can be built from straws. In fact, once a few simple construction techniques are learned, you can use straws to make unlimited kinds of structures — bridges, towers, and so on.

Materials:

  plastic straws — at least 25 per person
  string or strong thread
  alternative connecting materials, such as modeling clay, pipe cleaners, pins, or paper clips — I like paper clips, because they're neater and tighter
  a commercial kit (Construct-o-straws, SEE, $3.40) includes special plastic connectors

If you're coming at this kind of construction for the first time, experiment freely making simple, solid, basic shapes. With these materials kids quickly discover the instability of right-angle and the stability of triangular construction.

How tall a tower can you build? How long a bridge?

Then go on to building models of basic geometric solids. Where do you see some of these shapes used in the man-made world?

Building structures with D-Stix, available from Creative Publications (Junior Kit, $5.75)

tetra-kite

If you want to develop some interest in three-dimensional geometry — tell the kids to go fly a kite!

This one will fly even in a city lot.

You need:

  6 drinking straws
  light string
  tissue paper or thin plastic wrap
  glue or tape

Pass the string through three straws (you can suck it through) and tie the ends to form a triangle. Add two more to make a second triangle, and then attach the third to form a tetrahedron, the simplest and strongest straight-edged geometric shape in three dimensions.

To make it flyable, cover two sides with tissue paper, attach a three-foot tissue-paper tail, and fasten on the harness, as shown.

To make the kite fly higher, try adding two, three, or more tetra-kites to the original one.

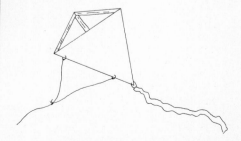

Pattern Blocks

SEE, $15.75 (with 3 mirrors)

These are a set of 250 colorful wooden shapes that lend themselves to a wide variety of activities. Counting, sorting and matching, making patterns and designs, exploring symmetry, and learning about fractions (see pages 152–154) are just a few of the possible mathematical applications.

SEE also has a set of forty-four activity cards (SAM cards, $7.25), which contain simple sentences and pictures leading children to discoveries with Pattern Blocks.

Let's Pattern Block It
Peggy McLean et al.

Activity Resources Company
P.O. Box 4875
Hayward, California 94540
$7.50

This is a handy activity book, with tear-out pages for reproduction, that has some excellent suggested activities. These include games, addition, patterns, fractions, geometry, area, and perimeter.

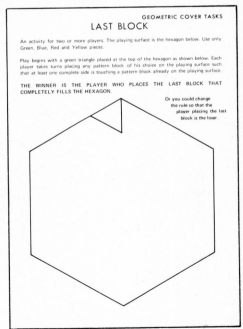

From *Let's Pattern Block It,* p. 28, reprinted by permission of Activity Resources Company, Inc., © 1973.

geoboards

A geoboard is an exciting manipulative device that allows children to visualize and play around with geometrical figures, angles, and area measurement. It is basically a square piece of wood (usually about 6″ × 6″) with nails set in a regular grid pattern. Rubber bands are then placed around the nails to create shapes and designs. Although both SEE and Creative Publications (see page 138 for addresses) have a wide variety of commercial geoboards available, they are simple to construct and children can make them with minimal adult assistance.

The materials described and illustrated on this page will give you some ideas of what to do with a geoboard once you've made one!

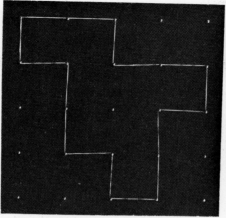
What is the perimeter of this shape?

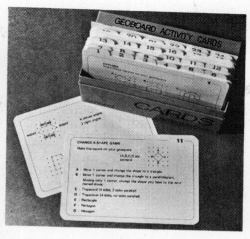
Available in Primary and Intermediate sets from Creative Publications; more than 120 activity cards in each set

---

35/56   geoboards   H-6

Use <u>1</u> <u>square</u> as a <u>square unit</u>.

1. Someone said there are 4½ <u>square units</u> of <u>area</u> inside this figure. Do you agree?   Why?

2. There are <u>12</u> <u>square units</u> of <u>area</u> inside this figure. Do you agree?   Why?

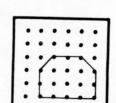

SAM card reprinted by permission of SEE, Inc., © 1972.

One of the SAM activity cards for geoboards available from SEE; set of fifty-six cards

---

Inquiry in Mathematics via the Geo-Board
Donald Cohen

*Walker and Company
720 Fifth Avenue
New York, New York 10019*
$3.50

This is a "teacher's guide" to using the geoboard that contains more than a hundred activity ideas; here are two of them:

*HOW MANY DIFFERENT SHAPE FIGURES WITH FOUR (4) SIDES CAN YOU CONSTRUCT ON THE GEOBOARD? KEEP TRACK OF THESE ON DOT PAPER.
DO ANY OF THESE HAVE SPECIAL NAMES? CAN YOU FIND ANY OF THESE*

FIGURES IN YOUR CLASSROOM, AT HOME, OR OUTSIDE? (Geo-Card 10-2)

*Kathy and Rhoda were trying to figure out how many squares they could make on the whole Geo-board (without using diagonals).
HOW MANY CAN YOU FIND?
(That's right, there are more than 16!)
(Geo-Card 33-1)*

geostrips

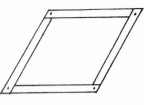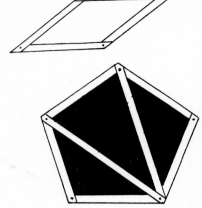

Geostrips are strips of cardboard, oaktag, plastic, or metal cut into standard lengths with holes punched at the ends so they can be joined with paper fasteners to create two-dimensional shapes. (SEE has a set of plastic geostrips for $9.40 with workcards from England.)

Children quickly discover that shapes can be altered to create new shapes. An interesting extension of this discovery is to try to make the original shapes rigid. What is the smallest number of strips (or "struts") needed to make a square rigid? A pentagon? A hexagon? Graphs can be made to record the information gained. In addition, discovery of the triangle as the shape for a rigid frame will lead to observation of its application for other structures — even three-dimensional ones, such as bridges and towers.

attribute games and problems

SEE, $9.60 (equipment only)

Attribute Games and Problems is a set of materials designed by the Elementary Science Study (ESS) to help kids develop thinking skills. It provides opportunities for children to deal with problems involving classification and the relationships between classes, groups, or sets.

The three main components of Attribute Games and Problems are: thirty-six A Blocks, sixteen People Pieces, and sixty Color Cubes. Each of these can be used in a wide variety of ways with children of all ages. SEE has all the materials available separately, as well as a set of seventy related SAM cards that suggest games and activities in easy-to-read language.

Attribute Blocks [A Blocks]

These are a set of blocks that represent three different attributes — size (large and small), shape ($\triangle$, $\square$, $\bigcirc$, $\diamondsuit$), and color (red, yellow, blue, and green).

Andrew and Alan are playing a favorite cooperative game with A Blocks. A game board (drawn on cloth for easy storage) is created by placing all the A Blocks in positions so that only one attribute is changed between adjacent positions. Draw circles around each block and label the specific changes (c = color, s = size, sh = shape) on connecting lines.

Players choose one piece at a time, in turn, and place it on the board. The object of the game is to fill every position with an appropriate block — it's a joint effort, and gets harder as you go along, when you run out of particular pieces and need to substitute.

People Pieces

This is a set of two-inch-square tiles with people on them. The tiles (People Pieces) have the following attributes: male or female, red or blue clothing, adult or child, fat or thin. The illustrated activity is from the ESS activity cards, published by McGraw-Hill Book Company (see page 34 for address).

People Pieces 8

Choose any one of the *People Pieces.* Put this piece, the key piece, on the table. Below it, make a row of all the pieces that differ from it in one way, another row of those pieces that differ from it in two ways, a third row of those that differ from it in three ways, and a fourth row of those that differ from it in four ways.

Each row is a subset of the *People Pieces* set. The subset of pieces that differ in *no* ways from the key piece contains only one piece: the key piece!

How many pieces are there in each of the other subsets?

Can you think of a good way to check whether all your subsets are correct?

Illustration: People Pieces Card 8

Key Piece

One Difference

color   sex   age   girth

Two Differences

color-sex   color-girth   color-age   sex-girth   sex-age   girth-age

Three Differences

color-sex-girth   color-sex-age   color-girth-age   sex-girth-age

Four Differences

color-sex-age-girth

Color Cubes

This set contains sixty three-quarter-inch cubes in six colors (red, blue, green, yellow, black, and white). Color cubes can be used in a wide variety of ways, as part of the Attribute Games and Problems unit or independently. You could even make and paint your own cubes! Addition, multiplication, area, volume, shapes, symmetry, and problem solving are just some of the math concepts involved in the use of color cubes.

This activity is from the ESS activity cards, published by McGraw-Hill Book Company (see page 34 for address). A variation for two players is suggested on card 11, where players need to get four cubes in a row to win.

This activity is from *Math Experiments with the One-Inch Color Cubes*, by William A. Ewbank. It is available from Midwest Publications (see page 179 for address) for $3.50, and contains a broad range of activities that extend the possible uses of ESS or other color cubes.

Color Cubes 12

This is a game for three, four, five, or six people.
Each person chooses a color and plays in turn.
The object of the game is to get three pieces in a row—

horizontally,

vertically,

or diagonally.

It is important that each player place his cube in turn.
Here is an unfinished three-in-a-row game:

Yellow will win this game unless blocked by both red and black.

This game is also interesting when played with the variation of allowing the three cubes to be stacked, one on top of another, in addition to the three other three-in-a-row possibilities.

Color Cubes card reprinted by permission of the Elementary Science Study of Education Development Center, Inc., © 1968.

MR-12

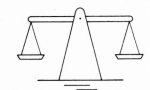

CAN YOU WEIGH?

Find 5 different objects, and guess how many cubes weigh the same as each object. Write down your guesses. How can you check?

Find out how many cubes weigh   1 ounce (oz.)
                                   1 pound (lb)
                                   1 kilogram (kg)
                                   500 grams (g)

Find the weight of one cube in g.

What do *you* weigh in cubes?

If you do not have a weighing scales, how can you make one?

other attribute materials

1, 2, 3 Think!

SEE, $2.25

This rates as both the cheapest and simplest among attribute sets, and is especially useful for children who have dif-

ficulty working with many attributes at once. It consists of 1, 2, 3 easy games played with a card deck showing only two colors, two shapes, two sizes, and "full" or "empty." If you also plan to work with more elaborate sets, it makes a good introduction or supplement.

Setsplay

SEE, $4.50

An inexpensive alternative to other attribute kits, this English-made packet in-

cludes two sets of thirty-two colorful cardboard shapes and twelve workcards (with twenty-four games and activities printed on them). You could use the shapes as templates to create additional sets.

SETSPLAY   Card 3a

colour & shape links

A game for 2 or 4 players.

If 2 are playing they take 16 shapes each.

If 4 are playing they take 8 shapes each.

The game starts by the teacher (or a child not playing) calling out the name of a shape. For example : large red circle. The player having this shape, lays it down in the middle. The player on his left then tries to follow on, by joining to the first shape, either a shape of the same colour,
     or
one of the same shape.

The game will look something like this :

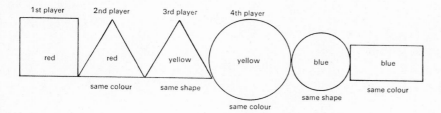

The first child to put down all his pieces correctly, is the winner.

---

note to teacher

This game is to train the children to keep 2 attributes in mind. Variations in the game can be made by using any other two attributes or even 3.

Setsplay card reprinted by permission of SEE, Inc., © 1967 by James Galt and Company Ltd. (England).

---

exploring symmetry

Symmetry is everywhere in the natural world and the man-made.

Mirror Cards and Triangle Cards (see reviews on page 188) are good materials for making some investigations, but there are many other ways to discover the nature of symmetry without buying expensive stuff.

One of the easiest is paper folding. Make a game of folding and cutting one piece of paper in various ways so that resultant shapes are always symmetrical. Ask kids to try to predict how a shape will appear before they open or unfold it in a new way.

There are two basic kinds of symmetry:
Mirror symmetry: the object has at least one line (axis) of symmetry,
Rotational symmetry: turning the shape less than one full turn, it will look the same. Or you can talk about a *point of symmetry*, which means that you can turn the shape about a point, which may not be in its center, and it will look the same.

Investigate symmetry in natural objects:

Cut fruits and vegetables to exhibit planes of symmetry.

Study photographs of people, animals, and trees. Use mirror or drawn lines to demonstrate where axis lines would appear.

Notice how what we *take* as symmetry in natural objects or people only appears that way. Small differences between one side and another give things in the natural environment their individual characters. (See Body Symmetry, page 159.)

Investigate symmetry in the man-made world.

Look at buildings and houses and find examples of symmetrical construction.

Look at constructions like roads, bridges, and telephone poles. Make simplified schematic drawings of them that can be folded to reveal the symmetries.

You can find some ideas for working with symmetry in *The I Hate Mathematics! Book,* and in the Nuffield Mathematics guides, especially in *Shape and Size* (△2 and △3).

Mirror Cards
Elementary Science Study

McGraw-Hill Book Company
1221 Avenue of the Americas
New York, New York 10020
teacher's guide, $3.87
box of cards and mirrors, $14.91

The object of activity with these cards is to discover mirror-image relations of simple patterns and shapes. Kids use a mirror to make matches between images on one card with those on "pattern cards" so that they can discover some basic principles of symmetry and geometrical relationships.

The kit materials are a set of four mirrors and a box containing twenty-one different card sets, arranged by increasing difficulty. The easiest ones call for making whole shapes out of partial ones. Harder ones play with different positionings and alterations of recognizable shapes, and the hardest ones work with more abstract geometrical shapes and groupings.

If you had a chance to look through one of these kits you could easily devise your own version with some felt-tip markers and durable card stock. Plenty of variations are possible, including some that children might create.

Triangle Cards

SEE, $27.50

It's hard to pin down just what these are, because they involve a broad range of mathematical thinking and activity. Also, selected parts of the set can be used with any age beyond three. Some of the "ways of knowing" they will allow you to play with are: attributes, sets, logic, symmetry, perception, classification, and comparison. Since they adapt to so many different ages and have a "game-y" nature, they would make an intriguing contribution to your "rainy-day" closet at home. They were intended for classroom use, however, and as such are beautifully designed for durability and convenience. The set includes small Triangle Cards, large activity cards, teacher's guide, and accessories.

logic and probability

Will it rain today?

How many times will we have mashed potatoes this month?

How late can I sleep if I need to be at school by 8:00?

All of these questions involve an understanding of and ability to make use of the laws of probability. Giving children experiences with probability and chance will help them solve problems and make decisions in a wide variety of areas.

Throw a pair of dice a hundred times and make a graph that shows your results. Do you see a pattern? Which was the most frequently thrown number? Why?

Why is tossing a coin a good way of deciding which team will bat first? What other choice-making technique will give an even, fifty-fifty chance (probability of one-half) to both sides?

resources

Probability Kit

Creative Teaching Associates
P.O. Box 293
Fresno, California 93708
$6.95

Materials and instructions for forty experiments in probability are included in this package. The contents are ten colorful spinners on sturdy cardboard, a set of thirty reproducible data-recording sheets, and a teacher's manual of activities for children aged eight to twelve (approximately). Although most of the activities involve using the spinners, questions such as these will be answered in the process:

When tossing a coin, what is the probability of getting four heads in a row?

How does the number of trials affect the accuracy of probability predictions?

In throwing a die, what is the probability of getting an even number?

Minnesota Environmental Sciences Foundation

Sampling Button Populations, $1.00
Genetics Variation, $1.50
Transect Studies, $1.50

The National Wildlife Federation
Educational Servicing
1412 16th Street, NW
Washington, D.C. 20036

These are a sampling of the Environmental Discovery Units put out by the National Wildlife Federation, all of which are excellent. These three are especially useful for learning how to sample populations, collect statistics, and form conclusions based on the assembled data. They are written for teachers, but the specific activities are clear and would appeal to kids.

The first one focuses on taking samples of button or bean "populations" and deducing the character of the complete population, with a few suggestions for adapting the procedure to organic sample studies. The second concentrates on collecting statistics and discovering patterns in human variation, and the third applies many of the same procedures to the study of organic populations in outdoor environments.

Together these represent a practical, interesting way of learning about statistics and probability.

Experiments in Probability and Statistics
Donald Buckeye

Midwest Publications Company
P.O. Box 129
Troy, Michigan 48084
$1.50

This book presents eighty experiments in probability. Although many of the activities would be difficult for elementary age children, they are adaptable and there are enough simple experiments to make this a very handy reference. Common household or classroom items — such as thumbtacks, coins, dice, marbles, newspapers — are the only materials needed to do these experiments.

Reprinted from *Experiments in Probability and Statistics,* pp. 1, 23, by permission of Midwest Publications Company, Inc., © 1970.

Experiment No. 3   ARRANGEMENT   Apparatus: coins

1. Arrange 3 coins (nickel, dime and penny) in as many different ways as possible.

2. Arrange 4 coins in as many different ways as possible.

3. Guess how many different ways you can arrange 5 coins and then try it.

4. Is there a pattern here? Look up the word permutations in the dictionary.

Experiment No. 64   TO BE SURE   Apparatus: box, green and red marbles

1. In a box put 10 green and 10 red marbles.

2. Guess how many marbles you will have to pick (without replacing) before you are sure that you have 2 red marbles. Now try it.

3. Would the results change if you have to have 2 marbles of the same color? Why or why not?

strategy games

There is a very particular kind of skill involved in strategy games. Chess and checkers are old standbys — and we think they're almost essential in any home or classroom where logical thinking is encouraged. In addition to the standard games, children can invent a whole bunch of variations to suit their own interests.

There are many, many others — some ancient (Mancala goes back several thousand years!), some relatively modern. It would be impossible to describe them all; here is a sampling of our favorites.

3-D Tic-Tac-Toe

This is a popular game with all ages. It can involve sophisticated strategy, but is basically simple to play. It is also an excellent way to familiarize kids with three-dimensional space relationships. The object of the game is to get four chips (or pegs or balls) in a straight line vertically, horizontally, or diagonally. 3-D Tic-Tac-Toe can be found in many local stores (sometimes under the trade names Qubic or Score Four); if you're stuck, Creative Publications has the version illustrated for $4.50.

Pictured here are just a few of the classic puzzle games that can be found in most local stores. Each game necessitates logical thinking and/or strategy, and all but Nine Men Morris (lower right) are solitaire games.

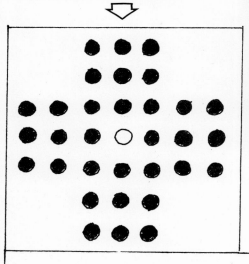

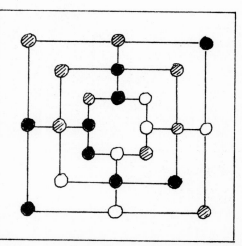

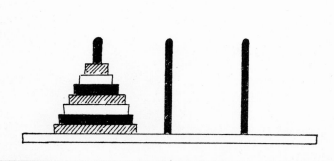

Mancala

Also known as Kalah, Ohwari, Mbala, Omweso . . . this game (and its endless variations) involves counting strategies and logic. It originated in Africa, where it was probably played with stones in hollowed-out holes in the ground. You can use pebbles, beans, marbles, beads, seeds — whatever is most handy. Egg cartons or cups make perfectly adequate "playing fields," although there are several commercial boards available. The basic game objective is to capture your opponent's pieces — removing them from one hole and distributing them around the board. Let your kids invent their own rules!

Master Mind

This is a new and exciting strategy game for two people that involves logical thinking and deductive ability. The "challenger" sets up a line of four colored pegs behind a shield; the opponent has up to ten moves to figure out the color and exact position of the hidden pegs. The strategy is similar to Jotto (see page 287) and a math game in which an opponent has to figure out a two- or three-digit number (response indicates number of correct numerals and/or positions). Master Mind utilizes manipulative materials (pegs) rather than words or numbers; SEE sells the game for $4.

Mudcrack Y
Craige Schensted and Charles Titus

NEO Press
Box 32
Peaks Island, Maine 04108
$1.50

The name derives from the appearance of the game board, which resembles the pattern made by cracked, dry mud. It is played by two people, who try to make a continuous line of colored spaces reaching to the border. It does not have to be merely competitive; players may try to find mutual strategies to arrive at a "perfect" game. The book includes a thorough explanation and sheets for over a thousand games. Creative Publications also distributes it.

arts and crafts

arts and crafts

"Art is found wherever man is or has been."* It is as natural to humankind as speaking — and a form of communication older than writing. We need to make an appreciation of beauty and an ability to express oneself through arts and crafts as important to our children as reading or writing.

That doesn't mean you need to know all about great artists, or push your child to become another Rembrandt! Try looking at the colors of a rainbow, feeling the veins of a leaf, becoming aware of the point where railroad tracks "meet," admiring the graceful structure of a bridge. In addition to appreciating the natural "art" of their environment, children also need to learn how to express their own feelings and unique perspectives through making pictures and designs, creating a form, or rearranging found materials into a pleasing pattern.

As Ann Wiseman so nicely expresses it in her introduction to *Making Things* (page 9): "We hope to excite new ways of seeing, feeling, and being, in order to preserve the innate creative potential in every one of us." The emphasis in this section is on activities, sources, and materials that we've found exciting to kids — and that require little or no "art budget," but lots of experimentation and imagination!

Experiments in Art, page 3; see review on page 196.

general resources

art supplies

"Art supplies" are numberless. There are all those things you can buy in an art supply store (many of which can be found in a "five and ten" or discount store) — construction paper, crayons, tempera paints, poster board, scissors, glue, and so on. But the materials needed to encourage imaginative expression with line, form, and color are everywhere.

Stopping to look at patterns in tree bark or a seashell or city streets, building a sand castle, making a collection of autumn leaves — all these experiences utilize only the natural environment. Making a gravestone rubbing requires nothing more than a piece of soft paper and a pencil or crayon (and a gravestone, of course!). And some of the most valuable "art supplies" are those that can be saved or scrounged.

The following list is only a starting point; it would be literally impossible to make it comprehensive! If you have a large selection of diverse materials available, your kids will invent their own ways to use them, combine them, create with them.

things to draw with

crayons, pencils, chalk, charcoal, pens, inks, watercolors, tempera paint + brushes, felt-tip pens

all kinds of paper

newsprint, construction paper, tissue, cellophane, oaktag + poster board, cardboard, aluminum foil, waxed paper, shelf paper, wallpaper samples, wrapping paper, scraps from printers, contact paper

scraps and leftovers from home or factories or trash cans

all kinds of material, yarn, string, ribbons, burlap, felt, rugs, fur, telephone wire, leather, wood, old stockings + socks, rubber, inner tubes, old sheets, wire mesh, emptied paper bags + boxes of all sizes and shapes, old picture magazines, newspaper, Styrofoam meat trays, wire hangers, mailing/paper towel/toilet paper tubes, window shades, candle stubs, Popsicle sticks, cans + jars + plastic tubs, soap, spools, egg cartons

books

Making Things, $3.95

Making Things, Book 2, $4.95
Ann Wiseman

Little, Brown and Company
34 Beacon Street
Boston, Massachusetts 02106

Subtitled *A Hand Book of Creative Discovery, Making Things* is one of the nicest, most comprehensive collections of craft activities for kids that we've seen. Each book is chock-full of activity ideas — each sure to delight your kids. Some of the directions are a bit too brief, and therefore hard to follow, but on the whole they are clearly illustrated and the ideas excellent.

Ann Wiseman is especially fond of weaving, printmaking, puppets, hammocks, and mobiles — but *Making Things* contains much more: how to turn chocolate pudding into finger paintings, fish into fossil prints, string and soapy water into gigantic bubbles; how to make paper, books, natural dyes, and thumb pianos!

With a Free Hand

Teaching Art: Sources and Resources
Adelaide Sproul

Van Nostrand Reinhold Company
450 West 33rd Street
New York, New York 10001

As different as these books are in some respects, they are united by the vision of the artist and teacher who is their author. Having had the good fortune to teach with her for a time, I watched how she put that vision to work. Her key word is "sources."

Primary sources for the arts include earth, air, water, and the qualities of light, dark, hot, and cold — the elements of the world we sense. Raw materials are primary sources, too, and are "earth (clay), wood, stone, color (which is pigment made from earth), and plants, and now various chemical colors" (*With a Free Hand,* page 16).

We've just discovered this is out of print, which makes us sad. Hopefully you can find a library copy.

Art from Scrap
Carl Reed and Joseph Orze

Davis Publications
50 Portland Street
Worcester, Massachusetts 01608
$5.95

This is an outstanding book — simply written and profusely illustrated with kids' artwork. In fact, the authors' use of illustrations makes this a unique craft guide — proving that a picture is indeed worth a thousand words! Each photograph is accompanied by a brief explanation of materials and/or technique used, which is enough to give the reader a very clear idea of the process without a lot of verbiage.

The ideas are exciting and unusual — taking common activities that "one step further" to spark your imagination. Throughout the book the authors recommend the use of common, everyday materials for printmaking, sculpture, collage, masks, jewelry, puppets, weaving, and stitchery.

Experiments in Art
Donald L. Stacy

Four Winds Press
Scholastic Magazines
904 Sylvan Avenue
Englewood Cliffs, New Jersey 07632
$6.95

"Art is an experiment in surprising one's self."

With this basic premise, the author proceeds to give detailed examples of ways to explore a variety of materials — through collage, printmaking, drawing, and three-dimensional forms. Experimentation is stressed throughout the book, and the illustrations are simple, imaginative, and fun!

Arts and Crafts You Can Eat
Vicky Cobb

J. B. Lippincott Company
East Washington Square
Philadelphia, Pennsylvania 19105
$4.95

If you think that art must be something permanent — think again! Art is much more than something to see; it's something people do. And you can transform ordinary foods into works of art that are as good to eat as they are to look at!

Make a mosaic salad, stained-glass cookies, a kohlrabi monster and other vegetable beasts, pancakes with inlaid designs! This inviting book takes full advantage of the kitchen as art studio, and packs a lot of learning into each creation. The directions and illustrations are easy to follow, but don't worry about making mistakes — you can always eat them!

See also Vicky Cobb's *Science Experiments You Can Eat,* reviewed on page 103.

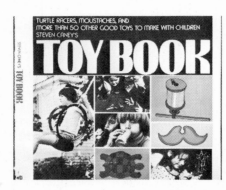

Toy Book, $3.95

Play Book, $4.95
Steven Caney

Workman Publishing Company
231 East 51st Street
New York, New York 10022

I wish I could save you a little money and recommend just one of these, but if you got one you would always be stealing it from your kids anyway, so you might as well get both volumes and have twice as many ideas to play with in the bargain.

These are collections of wonderful do-it-yourself toys, games, and other things to make for the youngest and oldest among us. None of those pretty things to give to your mommy; anything a kid would find in these books is worth doing for its own sake. The illustrations and directions are clear enough for kids to follow on their own. If you haven't buried your childlike instincts you'll end up making some of these things, too.

Creative Play Series

Van Nostrand Reinhold Company
450 West 33rd Street
New York, New York 10001

This series is distinguished for its extensive use of actual artwork by students to illustrate techniques and possibilities of form. Each of the volumes has been put together by experienced artists who have worked intimately with the medium and have a clear sense of order about the sequence of the exercises. They encourage you to teach artistic skills as seriously as you would techniques of writing or computation.

While the books are useful no matter what age child you're working with, their orientation is more heavily toward older kids and many of the examples were produced by high school students and adults.

publishers

The following publishers have a wide variety of arts and crafts books. If you are looking for guides to a specific craft, or want to have a well-stocked personal library of art books, we would strongly suggest that you write to them for catalogs.

Sterling Publishing Company
419 Park Avenue South
New York, New York 10016

Sterling has a large selection of all kinds of crafts books, most notably their Little Craft Book series. These are written for adults but are relatively inexpensive ($3.75 each), well illustrated with color photographs and diagrams, and clearly written. There are over sixty titles, covering a broad range of craft activities (string designs, mosaics, weaving, nail sculpture, photography without a camera, scrimshaw, masks, jewelry making . . .). Here are a few of Sterling's other books that sound particularly interesting to us:

Make Your Own Mobiles
Create Your Own Natural Dyes
Mosaics with Natural Stones
Creative Paper Crafts in Color

Van Nostrand Reinhold Company
450 West 33rd Street
New York, New York 10001

Every one of the Van Nostrand Reinhold books we've seen has superlative photography and nice, clear design. Their catalog has a huge listing of practical guides and other art books with enticing titles; you might want to get the catalog. The selections that especially appealed to us are listed below.

Using Natural Materials
Using Construction Materials
Teaching Film Animation to Children
Creative Play Series (see above, right)
Creating with Clay, Found Objects, Metal, Puppets (a whole series of 12 titles)

Davis Publications
50 Portland Street
Worcester, Massachusetts 01608

Davis Publications has a wide range of visually exciting arts and crafts books. They use examples of children's artwork extensively, and the directions are clearly written. Although most of the books we've seen are classroom oriented, the wealth of stimulating activities and the simplicity of their presentation would make them ideal for home use as well. The titles we've especially liked are:

Art from Recycled Materials
Art from Scrap (see p. 195 for review)
The Crayon
Creative Use of Stitches (see p. 216 for review)
Puppet Making through the Grades (see p. 276 for review)
Wall Hangings
Weaving without a Loom (see p. 212 for review)
Visual Communication

pictorial art

There are literally hundreds of ways to create interesting pictures and designs on a flat surface. Just give a kid a handful of crayons or markers and a piece of paper — I used to spend my ten-cent allowance on a new box of crayons for weeks on end! Add a pair of scissors, some glue, an assortment of colored papers, scraps of yarn or felt or magazines or cloth or anything you have around and the possibilities for creative expression are already endless!

We had a great deal of difficulty deciding what to include in this section. Our list of ideas seemed overwhelming — and worthy of a book all by itself! Anyway . . . we chose three of our favorite kinds of art activity — printing, collage-ing, and just "making pictures." Each is a "natural" with kids of all ages, and we hope they will spark your own imagination. Encourage your kids to "mess around," experiment with whatever materials they have handy, and just take pleasure in the whole wonderful *process* of drawing and painting and sketching and doodling and coloring and . . .

One more word about two-dimensional creations: encourage your children to draw stuff by valuing their efforts. Put as many of their creations up on your walls as possible — art projects done on a flat surface are easy to display. Our dear friend and invaluable assistant, Jan, has a whole wall of her home covered with her daughters' drawings; they used acrylic paints. It's colorful, beautiful, and inspiring to see!

Altair Design

More Altair Design
Ensor Holiday

Pantheon Books
Random House
400 Hahn Road
Westminster, Maryland 21157
$1.95 each

Coloring books with a difference, these are filled with geometric line patterns that will challenge your imagination! There are literally hundreds of ways in which to color in any one pattern — each creating a completely different design, simple or intricate. Thin colored markers are ideal for use with *Altair Design* books, and the results are strikingly beautiful and unique!

bottlecaps, screws, wood scraps, sponges, leaves, gears, cloth scraps, cans, tubes, string, paper clips, leather scraps, buttons, feathers, fish, tennis balls, golf balls, dominoes, puzzle pieces, keys, potatoes, onions, carrots, pebbles, beans, Styrofoam, rice, noodles, aluminum foil, shoes, spools, corn, cabbage, apples, seeds, glue, snaps, inner tubes, toothbrushes, aluminum foil, Elmer's glue, Popsicle sticks, yarn, heavy twine, washers, screw eyes, wrenches, bones, nuts and bolts, safety pins, potato peelers, cheese cutters, clothespins, bark, flowers, brushes, rubber bands, corrugated cardboard, matches, turnips, pencils, erasers, comb, shells, fingers, scissors, forks, knives, spoons

printmaking

Making a print requires three basic elements: 1) a shape, or character, with which to make a mark, 2) a medium (such as ink or paint) with which the mark is printed, and 3) a surface on which to print. An unlimited supply of objects . . . either scrap or still-in-use objects . . . are available for use as printing forms, and any one object may be used in repetition or combined with several other objects to make a composition. The printing medium may be regular printing ink, tempera paint, acrylics, or a stamp pad. The painting surface may be a fabric, wood, cardboard, or any paper, including printed newspaper. Try tissue papers, wrapping paper and paper towels.

— from *Art from Scrap*, page 11
(reviewed on page 195)

Paper, Ink and Roller
Harvey Weiss

Young Scott Books
Addison-Wesley Publishing Company
2725 Sand Hill Road
Menlo Park, California 94025

This is a well-illustrated, easy-to-read guide to basic techniques of printing. Step-by-step directions for press, transfer, potato, stencil, cardboard, and linoleum prints are clearly given. It was written quite a while ago and may be out of print, in which case check your local library for a copy.

Printmaking is easy for young children and yet can challenge adults. The variety of materials that can be used and their combinations are as limitless as the imagination. In addition to creating interesting designs or pictures for display, the ability to repeat a pattern can lead to the creation of original greeting cards, notepaper, and much more. Even background textures can be printed — using burlap, netting, or any other rough-surfaced material. Printmaking invites exploration and experimentation — play around with it, print, and enjoy!

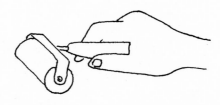

A *brayer* is an extremely useful (and sometimes necessary) piece of equipment for printing. Brayers can be found in any art supply store; you should be able to find one for under $5.00 with little trouble. J. L. Hammett (Hammett Place, Braintree, MA 02184) has one for $2.45.

press prints

"Press prints" are probably the simplest kind to do. Use a single object at a time; press it into a stamp pad or brush thick tempera paint on its surface. Then press it (ink or paint side down) onto a clean sheet of paper. Press firmly and don't let it slip around — use a finger, spoon, piece of cardboard, or brayer to press evenly.

A variation on this is to place the object on newspaper, ink it with brush or brayer, then place it on a clean sheet and press the paper onto the object.

Place the object on a clean piece of paper and then roll over it with an inked brayer. Object will appear white on ink-colored background.

Printing with parts of the body (fingers, hands, feet . . .) can serve as a nice lead-in to other activities (see pages 252–253).

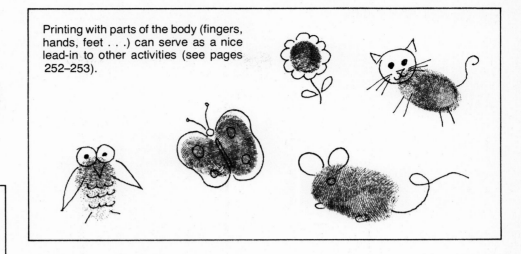

relief prints

Printing from a raised surface is called "relief printing." It is one of the most common and effective ways of producing original, handmade designs and pictures. One of the simplest ways to create a relief print with young children is to use cut cardboard shapes, glued onto a block of wood or another piece of cardboard. Ink or paint the raised surface and print!

Try string designs — or spread Elmer's glue on a piece of cardboard and let it dry before inking. Try gluing string or flexible shapes onto a cylindrical object (can, jar, spool, pencil, etc.) — then rolling your print!

You can buy linoleum blocks and special cutting tools for relief printing, or experiment with handy scraps. Cut and mount designs from inner tubing, felt, Styrofoam, wood, and so on, on any sturdy backing.

Cut a potato smoothly in half. Paint a simple block design on the face of one potato half. Then, using a small knife, cut away all the potato around the design (a depth of ¼" is plenty). Paint the raised design and print!

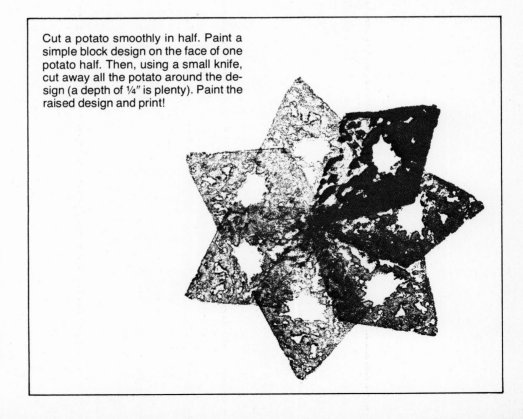

stencil prints

Stencil prints are the exact reverse of relief prints. Use an X-Acto knife to cut out a design from a piece of heavy paper or cardboard. (Keep in mind that you can't leave any paper inside a cutout shape unless it's supported.) Place your stencil on a clean piece of paper, window, or whatever. Roll ink over it with a brayer, dab paint on with a brush, or "spatter" it.

Draw a design with felt-tip marker on a Styrofoam meat tray or cup. Lines made with the marker dissolve the foam and leave a design ready for printing without needing sharp cutting tools.

collage making

Bringing together fragments of objects, paper, line, or color and attaching them to a flat surface in some designed way is the art of collage. Though it can be easy to do, some very sophisticated compositions can be worked out as well. This is basically a two-dimensional medium, and yet some of the most interesting collages are made by giving three-dimensional objects a prominent place in the design. It's a natural way to make some use of recycle scraps, too.

working materials

white glue
paper for background (something fairly stiff)
scissors
paints and brushes

newspaper
wallpaper samples
contact paper, scraps
magazine ads and photos
colored paper
cut-up boxes
colored tissue paper
aluminum foil
gift-wrapping paper
linoleum scraps
place mats

recycle items (metal, wood, leather, plastic, cardboard)
playing cards
match boxes
buttons
bottle caps, lids
blocks
nails and hardware
personal stuff
photos

seeds, beans, leaves
twigs, dried flowers
grasses
bark fragments
pebbles
bones

Some basic types of collage are described on these pages, but they are really just convenient categories by which to collect materials and see the possibilities. Any of these types could be combined with any of the others.

Paper Scraps

Here's a good place to start, since paper scraps are easy to come by.

Try random arrangements of torn scraps of colored paper, magazine photos, etc., until you get a design that satisfies you. Look for interesting contrasts of color, textures, and so on.

Collect four or more whole sheets of different-colored paper. Starting with one color as a base, cut a design from another sheet and place that design on the base. Cut a smaller and slightly altered version of the same design and place that on top of the previous one, and so on. When finished, you will have a multilayered collage. You can increase the three-dimensional effect by using layers of cardboard in between the colored sheets.

All by itself, scrap-paper collage has endless possibilities. Look at the variety of types of paper on the list and find your own ways of putting them together.

Cloth Scraps

scraps from home sewing box
lace
samples
rickrack
discarded clothes
yarn and thread
netting
burlap
felt

You can do many of the same things with cloth that you do with paper scraps.

Make composite human figures from contrasting colors and textures of material, letting design be as important as portrayal of an actual figure.

Cut cloth into squares, rectangles, and other geometric shapes to represent buildings, and make a collage view of a "soft" city.

Try ways of depicting a large-scale human face with cloth and other scraps.

Found Objects

If you're an expert scrounger of industrial scraps, here's a good place to use them. The only important criterion is that they be "gluable" — a ten-pound steel gear just won't do. But discarded clock gears might be lovely and easy to attach.

Make a collection of the types of things you carry around in your pocket, or of the stuff that ends up in "put-away-later" junk piles at home. A collage design made from these will be a direct statement about you and the things you do. (See Time Capsule, page 173.)

Collage a set of flat recycle scraps that have interesting shapes, patterns, or textures.

Make a picture from just wood scraps, or Styrofoam, or metal, or leather, or . . .

Natural Objects

Nature collages can double as interesting ways to display classifications of seeds and plants for study.

Collect seeds in quantities that represent the number produced by the mature flower or fruit of a given plant. Group each set of seeds on the collage according to some overall design.

Make a collage that shows all the different stages of growth in a single plant.

Show contrast in leaf styles, or put together a set of leaves with common attributes.

Wood Scraps

I would rather handle wood than any other material, except maybe good food. Scraps are easy to find, since most carpentry projects create a sizable pile of odds and ends.

Little ends and chunks lend themselves to complicated three-dimensionals that can be suggestive of towns, castles, animals, and airplanes.

mosaics

A mosaic is distinguished from a collage mainly by its use of many small pieces with similar characteristics glued side by side to build up a design. Try using:

    seeds
    macaroni, spaghetti, noodles

stones or pebbles
hardware (washers, nuts, nails)
cereal (Wheat Chex, Cheerios)
squares cut from paper
thumbtacks
tiles
eggshells

On a strong backing, sketch out a simple pattern in keeping with the sort of materials you plan to use.

As you construct the design, be sensitive to working out the best arrangements of the individual pieces to take advantage of their varying colors or textures.

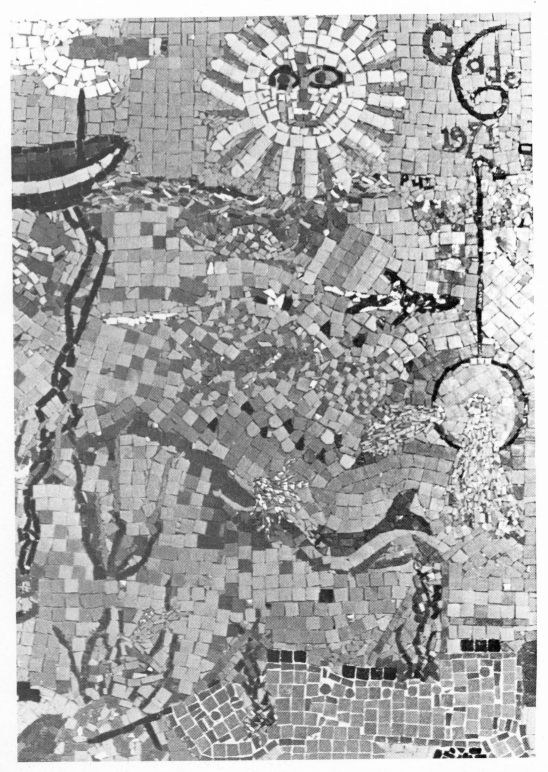

making pictures

Making pictures is a naturally fun activity for children of all ages. Kids will often select one object they feel comfortable drawing and do it over and over again. Keeping samples of these can be really interesting; I have a collection of my own drawings between ages eight and seventeen, and it's fascinating to trace their development. Houses, cars, people, airplanes, animals, flowers — all are popular subjects.

While it's important to help children feel comfortable drawing a variety of things, our emphasis here is to encourage them to use a variety of ways and materials to represent any object pictorially. Different materials necessitate seeing an object from a new perspective; cut-paper pictures, for example, show planes and shapes of an object, while line drawings can emphasize texture.

These clown drawings show the variety produced by utilizing different materials — as well as the strikingly diverse interpretations produced by individual children.

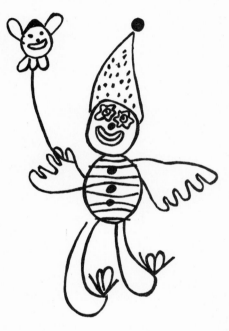

Magic Marker drawing, Amanda, age seven

Pastels, Paulo, age eight

Yarn and felt glued onto construction paper

sculpture and modeling

It seems to us that sculpture is a touchstone of our age. Maybe it's because we're manipulating so much junk all the time; maybe it's wanting to create our own handmade things in place of machine-made ones, or maybe it's a kind of nostalgic yearning for more primitive and tangible forms of expression.

In any case, it's a load of fun. And kids we know who aren't so eager to draw or paint pictures get into making sculptures from anything that's handy with very little provocation.

recycle sculpture

box sculpture

Cardboard boxes provide a basic set of forms for a fascinating array of sculpture.

> Collect some store boxes in a variety of shapes and colored patterns. Arrange them in a stack until you find a setup that is pleasing for the kind of spaces, texture, and colors it creates. Then glue them to one another to make a composite whole.
>
> ———————
>
> If you take one large box, cut it down so that it is fairly shallow, and divide up its interior into interesting spaces with smaller boxes, you have a wonderful "foundation" for a sculpture made from found objects of all kinds: tin cans, photographs, colored designs, masks, recycle scraps . . . anything. Work as you would with collage. Some of the interior boxes can be put in bottom-side up to make bold-relief surfaces for photographs or other graphics.
>
> If several people are doing one of these, put completed boxes together in a group assemblage, gluing them onto a large piece of triple-layer cardboard or thin plywood that can be fastened to a wall.

assemblage from packing materials

A large assortment of packing materials and containers, including egg cartons, dividers, grids, plastic "bubble" sheets, fruit separators, berry baskets, Styrofoam trays or packing shapes, salt boxes, box tops, paper pizza plates and boxes, and other molded paper containers, are ideal for large-scale assemblages.

Work for interesting contrasts of shape, size, depth, and types of shadows cast. What makes assemblage sculpture especially interesting is the play of light and shadow.

Paint the completed assemblage a solid color and then, if you want, accent certain parts of it with other colors.

Sculpture from Found Objects
Carl Reed and Burt Towne

Davis Publications
50 Portland Street
Worcester, Massachusetts 01608
$8.95

Junk sculpture does not need to look junky, as the projects in this book beautifully demonstrate. Bleach bottles, hubcaps, parts of old machines, string, paper cups, and egg cartons have all been skillfully transformed into works of art that would be the pride of any museum. Many were made by young artists, and the book's numerous and excellent photographs of their creations will provide inspiration to anyone who wants to make sculpture from our abundant trash heaps. The chapters are organized by specific scrap materials, in case you are especially well supplied with one material.

Junk Sculpture
Gregg LeFevre

Sterling Publishing Company
419 Park Avenue South
New York, New York 10016
$3.75

This sculpture-from-scraps book is explicitly a how-to manual, one of Sterling's Little Craft Book series (see page 196 for general review). As described in the introduction, "This book is designed to show you all the essentials you'll need to create your own junk sculpture, starting you off with simple projects using cardboard and other light materials, and moving you on to more complicated works in wood or metal." Like the others in the series, it includes provocative samples of work done by young artists.

sand-cast sculpture

You need:

   sand
   plaster of Paris
   frame or square of plywood
   tools to make impressions (tableware,
      pencils, kitchen implements, scraps of
      wood, short sections of tubing, shells)
   containers for mixing plaster
   small water sprinkler

Make an even slab of damp sand on your working base, smooth the surface.

and hollow out a depression appropriate to the kind of sculpture you're going to make. Sprinkle the surface lightly with water to make a more interesting texture.

With whatever tools you have on hand gently shape the surface of the depression according to your design.

Mix the plaster so that it becomes the consistency of very thick cream, and pour it into the mold, taking care not to break down parts of the design.

After about ten minutes, insert the ends of a bent paper clip into the top of the mold for a hanger.

After about half an hour the plaster should be hard enough. Remove the sculpture and wash it off under an outside faucet (plaster clogs drains).

paper sculpture

Everything I know and love about making things out of paper was introduced to me by Jim Bottomley, who besides having invented ''Spaceforms'' (see Paper Plate Polyshapes, page 181) runs a little teaching workshop in Watertown, Massachusetts. Ain't nothin' he can't do with paper. Out of this world of sculptured fantasy emerges everything from curly trinkets to superbly crafted reproductions of Castles-on-the-Rhine.

basic bending and building

Paper has grain; it will roll or bend smoothly with it, but not against it. Working with strips that are rolled either loosely or tightly is a good way to start.

By making a few fairly tight rolls and then letting them spring open where they want to, you can create wrought-iron-type forms for ornaments, interesting shapes.

Rolling the paper tightly around a pencil or thin dowel and gluing down the last lap gives you a solid stick to build with. Make lots and see what you can put together.

paper folding and cutting

Somebody should start a museum (a large one) for all the wild, wonderful paper-sculpture creations people make. On the other hand, most of the fun is in the doing.

One simple thing is a paper-bag puppet. Use small lunch bags; attach cut-out strips and flaps in whatever colors you want. One of the bottom folds serves as a mouth, open and shut by your hand.

Another is a mask made from a single sheet of folded paper. Draw half the face on one fold and cut it out.

Even large sculptures can be made by constructing with long strips of heavy paper or cardboard (especially the strip remnants from print shops). Build from the base up, gluing on supporting members as necessary. The final shape can be overlaid with mâché strips.

Building with Cardboard
Jon Lidstone

Van Nostrand Reinhold Company
450 West 33rd Street
New York, New York 10001
$4.95

In this era of packaging, scrap cardboard has become a commonplace material on trash heaps. The many forms in which it comes adapt to all sorts of uses for artistic and craftsmanlike creations, yet it is often overlooked as a raw material. This book can remedy that. The activities presented range from miniature models to impressive buildings, and from colorfully decorated masks to intriguing sculptures. Many projects start from just packing boxes and tubes. A simple format, including photographs arranged to show a sequence of construction steps, makes this an extremely useful craft book.

◁ Evie and Greg are experimenting with some origami paper folding

papier-mâchéing

You need:

    brown paper bags, torn up into narrow
        strips
    cellulose wallpaper paste, mixed with
        water into a jelly
    shallow container to dip strips in
    large surface covered with plastic to
        work on

Brown paper is strong and makes nice textures. The big trick is to do one layer at a time, letting each dry before the next. One of Jim Bottomley's instructors taught me how to make a terrific hollow-stump playhouse using a large single roll of cardboard with cutouts. The final layer of papier-mâché is wrinkled here and there for bark effect.

masks

Mask making is almost a whole field rather than a medium, since it draws on a huge assortment of materials, put together under innumerable and bewitching guises.

I always get a tingly feeling about masks, no matter how real or abstract, crude or elaborate; inevitably they become faces of the spirit world, full of mysterious, otherworldly expression.

Masks

Monster Masks
Chester Jay Alkema

Sterling Publishing Company
419 Park Avenue South
New York, New York 10016
$3.95 each

These are both from the Little Craft series (see general review, page 196) and very similar to each other in scope and format. *Masks* has somewhat more traditional techniques: applying papier-mâché, clay modeling, making paper cone or cube bases, using paper bags, and making use of some scrap materials. *Monster Masks* gets into a bigger variety of techniques for using unusual materials such as drinking straws, plastic foam, aluminum trays, or even seeds and gravel. Lots of masks tend to come out monsterish, so you really can't distinguish the two by their titles. Like the others in the series, they are good buys and immensely useful.

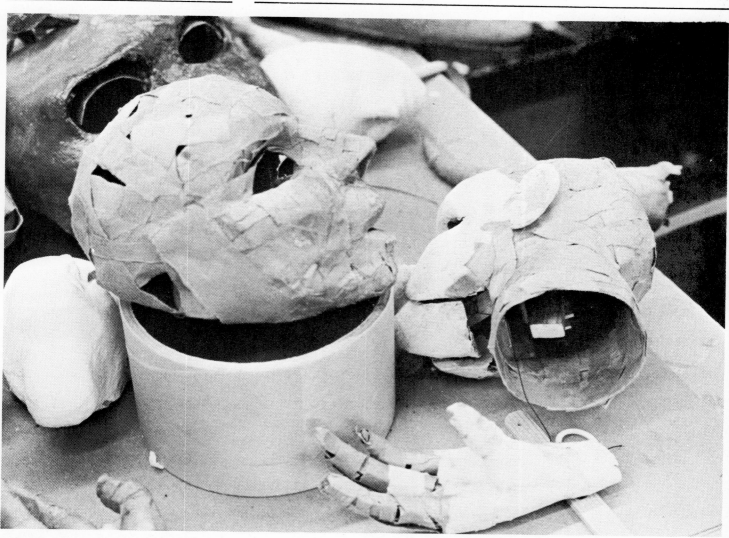

These papier-mâché heads show one way you could make masks; they were shaped around real faces at Jim Bottomley's workshop

clay

Some people feel that unless you go the whole route of modeling and then firing you haven't really made a bona-fide clay sculpture. The trouble with this attitude is that it nips experimentation in the bud. There is no question that kids eventually need to produce a permanent object, but it's even more important to let them play with the stuff long enough to discover a full scope of possible forms.

So, the first exercises can be just free experimentation to get a feel for the material.

Then pull in the horns and set some very limiting rules for the next stages, since clay is not a material in which structural principles reveal themselves very easily.

Possibly the closest thing to working with the earth itself, clay is an essential material for children. It is rich, real substance, satisfying to hold and to mold. Even more than with other art forms, the real meaning of clay activity lies in the forming process and not in the finished product. A child rolls, beats, pushes, and pinches, discovering new possibilities with each movement. What he finishes with is just one of those possibilities, which may itself be pounded down and molded into something new.

We advocate potter's clay because it is a natural substance, is cheap enough to have available in large quantities, and gives you all the options: drying unfired, firing, or reusing.

tools

your own hands
piece of wire and kitchen knife for cutting
short length of wood for beating
rolling pin
sponge for smoothing off
homemade punch for impressing pattern

finger textures

Roll or pound out a flat slab (extra damp clay) and imprint a series of designs, using fingers only. You might set these exercises:

sequences of fingertip forms in opposite directions
patterns of varying sizes, other regular textures of finger, or finger- and thumbprints
patterns of ridges: straight, curved, or boxlike. Press these out, using thumb and index finger together. (If a lot of kids are making these you can place the finished slabs together for an impressive group relief.)

After this, kids can branch out into more figurative slab designs made with finger pressure.

sculpture in clay

Try stamping designs, using bits of wood or pieces of cardboard at first and then other handy objects such as keys, nails, screws, and buttons. Usually, better results can be obtained by sticking with just one or two tools at a time.

For more three-dimensional sculptures from slabs of clay, cut and roll a rectangular slab into simple free-standing shapes. The key is simplicity; even one twist may create a beautiful and unique form.

Creative Clay Design
Ernest Röttger

*Van Nostrand Reinhold Company
450 West 33rd Street
New York, New York 10001*

The special quality of this book (as with the others in Röttger's series on children's art mediums) is its full presentation of actual work by children (and adults). In fact, most of the book is just that, accompanied by a brief commentary that identifies techniques, tools, and the development of a set of forms within one basic exercise. There is a nice clear order here, which proceeds from simple exercises that reveal fundamentals of shape and manipulation to more sophisticated projects by practiced amateurs of all ages. The author does not believe in what he calls "disorderly and slap-dash modelling," an attitude reflected in the impressively controlled, thoughtful sculptures by his students.

weaving and cloth

all kinds of yarn
material scraps
burlap
crochet hooks
leather scraps
dowels
grasses and weeds
spools
leather punch
screw eyes
nails
cardboard
oatmeal boxes
knitting needles
yarn needles
ribbons
twigs
sewing needles
embroidery thread
felt
twine
hardware cloth
straws
scrim
rug yarn

I know of no more naturally stimulating way of exploring texture, line, color, and design than working with yarn and cloth scraps with children. Whether weaving a belt, crocheting or knitting a scarf or book bag, sewing a caftan, or just creating a beautiful wall hanging, kids will take pleasure and pride in whatever they make.

These next few pages contain some "starting points" — let your kids experiment with as rich a variety of fabric and yarn scraps as you can find, and they'll create their own methods of expressing themselves! Look for earth colors, bright colors, rough, smooth, shiny, silky, fluffy, bumpy, thick, and thin pieces — *always* save scraps!

weaving

Weaving without a Loom
Sarita R. Rainey

*Sterling Publishing Company
419 Park Avenue South
New York, New York 10016*
$9.95

This is a beautiful book for beginning weaving, and is profusely illustrated with examples of children's weaving projects. The contents include weaving with paper, burlap, wire and cloth mesh (quarter-inch hardware cloth and scrim yield particularly pleasing results), cardboard, reed, pencils, and straws. A chart of design ideas for particular materials and a list of materials suppliers are handy supplements.

Although fairly expensive, *Weaving without a Loom* is one of the nicest, most visually attractive collections of weaving ideas for children that we've seen.

Simple Weaving, $6.95

Weaving on Cardboard, $5.95
Marthann Alexander

*Taplinger Publishing Company
200 Park Avenue South
New York, New York 10003*

Both of these books are excellent guides to a wide variety of simple weaving techniques. They are written in a clear, uncomplicated style for adults working with children. The ideas presented here are specifically geared to kids' weaving projects.

Weaving on Cardboard is particularly well illustrated, and the accessibility of cardboard makes it especially valuable for home and classroom use. The author shows how to make specific items, such as belts and handbags, as well as wall hangings.

Popsicle-stick loom

A Popsicle-stick "loom" is easy to make and use. It is basically a heddle, which creates a space between alternate warp threads when raised and lowered.

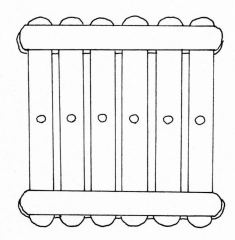

1. Drill holes in 6 Popsicle sticks (band together for drilling). Glue 4 sticks as shown, leaving at least ⅛" spaces.

2. Cut 11 lengths of yarn (about twice around waist for belt). Thread 6 lengths through holes (hole-yarn) and 5 through spaces (slot-yarn). Make ends even and tie into a large knot at each end — heddle will be in the center.

3. Tie one end to sturdy object and other end to waist with a belt or piece of extra yarn.

4. Make a shuttle with an extra Popsicle stick, wrapping yarn around it. Tie end of shuttle-yarn to knot at waist.

5. When heddle is raised or lowered, slot-yarn will move up and down, creating a space between it and the hole-yarn. Alternate raising and lowering heddle, sliding shuttle-yarn through in alternating directions.

To finish: untie original knots and retie them at the edges of weaving. Trim leftover yarn to create a fringe.

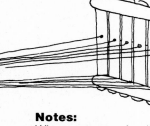

Notes:
When your weaving "gets away from you," retie it nearer your waist so you don't have to reach so far.

Use the heddle or your hand to push the shuttle-yarn back (toward you). Try varying tightness in several ways to create interesting patterns in your weaving.

other weaving ideas

Weave a wall hanging using natural materials and odd strips of cloth

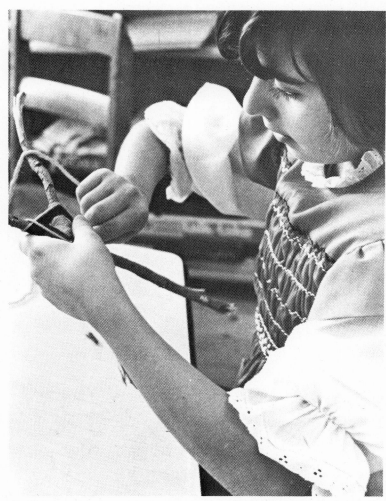

God's eyes are always a popular yarn project

Try weaving on a straw "loom"

Cardboard weaving is easy and fun

spinning and dyeing yarn

Spinning your own wool by hand is exciting for kids, and usually produces an interesting bumpy texture to the yarn. It's hard work and your kids may never get very far — but the results are super and sure to give them a greater appreciation of the craft.

You can usually purchase raw wool at a farm, or any well-stocked yarn shop can order it for you. I've gotten it from local farms and have never really bothered with cleaning and carding it; the natural oils keep fibers together. If you want to do a lot with this, get a copy of Elsie Davenport's *Your Hand Spinning* (Select Books, Box 626, Pacific Grove, CA 93950).

Pull wool to let a few fibers stretch; then spin them with your fingers until you have about twelve inches of spun yarn. Tie and wrap it around a dowel (use a potato or apple as a weight) as shown. Then spin the weight and pull the yarn gently as you do so. Stop periodically and wrap the spun wool directly onto the dowel — then transfer it to a spool.

Earth Guild / Grateful Union

15 Tudor Street
Cambridge, Massachusetts 02139

Regardless of what you're doing with yarn — spinning, dyeing, weaving, macrame-ing, etc. — this is the place to go! They have books, looms, materials, imported and hand-spun yarns, raw wool, and much more (pottery tools, candlemaking stuff . . .). Their catalog costs two dollars, but is well worth the price, since they also include lots of "how to" information. The Earth Guild Store (149 Putnam Avenue) is a delight to browse through, and the people there are not only knowledgeable about crafts of all kinds, but are also more than willing to share what they know.

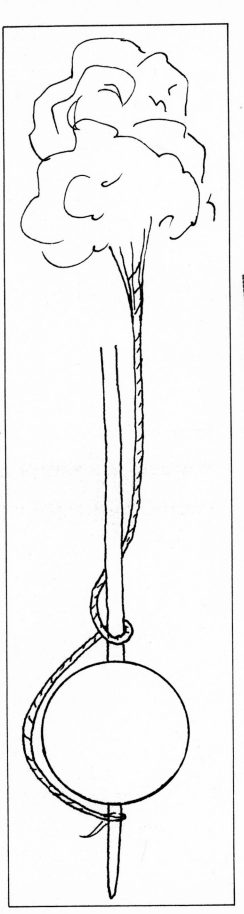

A natural follow-up activity to spinning your own yarn is making dyes from natural sources or dyeing the yarn with store-bought dyes. The earthy colors obtained from natural dyes look especially soft and beautiful in a weaving done with hand-spun yarn. Here are two books with detailed information on making dyes from natural sources:

Natural Dyes and Home Dyeing
Rita J. Adrosko

Dover Publications
180 Varick Street
New York, New York 10014
$2.00

The Complete Book of Dyes from Natural Sources
Arnold and Connie Krochmal

Doubleday and Company
501 Franklin Avenue
Garden City, New York 11530
$9.95

more activities with cloth

There are lots of interesting ways to use cloth "artistically." Two of the more popular techniques — batik and tie-dyeing — are described on these pages. There are several good books available on each one, but we've used Ann Wiseman's ideas in *Making Things* (see page 195 for review) quite successfully. Several different approaches to weaving, macrame, making simple clothes, and rya tufting are also included in this excellent crafts guide.

Packaged dyes are easiest to use for both batik and tie-dyeing. Follow directions on the packages — liquid dyes are best (use less water for stronger colors).

QUICK BATIK wax resist

can be done on paper or cloth with wax crayons melted candle stubs, paraffin or bees wax

Paper method crayon resist:

1. Draw a picture or design with crayons. press hard and cover all the paper.
2. Now scrumple it up.
3. now smooth it out and paint over it with ebony stain, ink or thin poster black. The cracking gives it a nice antique look.

Cloth and hot wax resist

1. Paint designs on almost any white or light-colored fabric. Bed sheets torn small are perfect.

a word of CAUTION: Heating wax can be very DANGEROUS. use a double boiler. Don't let it boil or smoke or leave it unwatched.

you need: cheap brushes, a box of paraffin. Double boiler Hot plate. pot holder. Iron. old coffee can. DYES, SALT Lots of news paper and pans.

1. Draw on cloth with hot wax (it should penetrate the cloth and look transparent in order to resist the dye later on).
2. Paint on colored dyes. use 5 and 10 cold water dyes and add a big spoon of salt to each color.
3. Iron cloth between newspapers. to remove wax and dry it quickly.

tie-dyeing

Tie or bunch your cloth in one of the illustrated ways (from *Making Things,* page 112). Then dip all or part of it into the dye; the longer it stays in the dye, the stronger the color. Retie it for dipping into different colors (you don't need to let the first color dry).

Many ways to Tie and Dye: with thread or rubber bands, and natural or commercial dyes.

twist   knot   tie

pleat   roll

puff   stitch   pinch

Making Things: The Hand Book of Creative Discovery by Ann Wiseman. Copyright © 1973 by Ann Wiseman. By permission of Little, Brown and Company.

Peter Learns to Crochet
Irene Levinson

*New Seed Press
P.O. Box 3016
Stanford, California 94305
$1.25*

This is a lovely, sensitive story of a boy who wants to crochet "all the warm things he would need for winter." With help and encouragement from his teacher, he learns how and makes a colorful book bag as his first project.

Creative Use of Stitches
Vera P. Guild

*Davis Publications
50 Portland Street
Worcester, Massachusetts 01608
$8.95*

*A needle can act like a brush.
A piece of brightly colored yarn like paint.
A square of burlap can be a canvas.
"Painting" with needle and thread can be fun!* (page 9)

This lovely book is well illustrated with examples of stitchery designs by children and craftspeople. It clearly describes several basic embroidery stitches — most simple enough for young children using blunt tapestry needles. The designs and pictures that can be created are colorful as well as easy and fun to do! *Creative Use of Stitches* is being revised and enlarged, and the price above is an estimated one.

carpentry and construction

Watching a child grab hold of a saw or a hammer for the first time usually gives the adult who's watching a powerful urge to take over and do it "right." Yet there is no greater satisfaction than watching that same child slowly develop the skills these oversized, clumsy instruments demand, and by their patient use, fashion a bench or a birdhouse or a model car with wheels that turn. Even if the efforts have been full of frustrations, the creator wins that special thrill of knowing that the result is uniquely her or his own. It is one of the best ways we know of building a lasting sense of self-worth.

a basic tool kit

- crosscut saw
- hammer
- eggbeater drill and bits
- plane
- try square
- C-clamps or vise

As a lover of tools, I have a grudging feeling about recommending only six tools to anybody, but the truth is that these really are sufficient for a huge number of simple, kid-style projects. If you're working with a large group of kids, or with a small group of very inexperienced kids, a greater variety of tools multiplies the dangers, anyway. Better to master the most common ones first. There's about thirty-five to fifty dollars' worth in this set, but hopefully you can borrow some.

On the other hand, if you've got kids who have pretty well mastered basic things and you're going to be able to supervise what they do, you could start expanding the kit toward this terrific set of twenty-two tools for making, taking apart, fixing, and constructing practically anything.

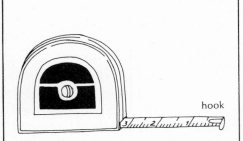

hook

Tape Measure
Most versatile measuring device, which you should get twelve feet long. It retracts.

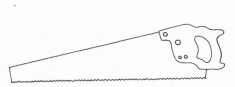

Crosscut Saw
Basic carpenter's saw, but cumbersome for kids until they get experience. Made to cut best across wood grain, it has a brother called the *ripsaw,* which works better cutting with the grain.

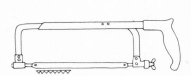

Hacksaw
For cutting metal, although kids sometimes use it like a backsaw for cutting wood, because it doesn't bind easily.

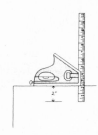

Combination Square
Most versatile squaring tool, for getting corners that way, measuring depths, scoring parallel lines, marking forty-five-degree angles, and leveling.

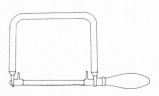

Coping Saw
A hand jigsaw for cutting shapes and curved lines in wood that isn't too thick. Breaks easily.

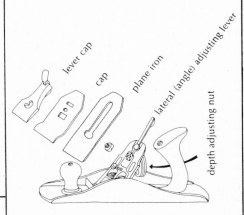

Plane
For smoothing edges and surfaces. You can get either a *block plane* (only six inches long) or a bigger carpenter's plane, or both, but it takes quite a bit of experience to operate planes effectively.

Fixed Square
More accurate, and easier to handle for kids who just want to come up with straight edges and square corners.

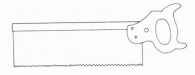

Backsaw
A crosscut saw with a stiff back, which makes it a good tool for accurate cuts no deeper than the width of the blade.

Surform
A recent invention that makes the kind of planing where you just need to smooth up a rough edge a lot easier. However, it's especially good for shaping soft materials, and is somewhere between a plane and a rough file.

Know-How: A Fix-It Book for the Clumsy But Pure of Heart by Guy Alland, Miron Waskiw, and Tony Hiss. Illustrated by Etti de Laczay. Copyright © 1975 by Guy Alland, Miron Waskiw, and Tony Hiss. By permission of Little, Brown and Company.

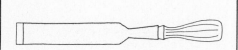

Chisel
Your basic wedge with a sharp edge, for cutting square holes or slots in wood or removing wood from places no other cutting tool will remove it from. One three-quarters of an inch wide will do for most things.

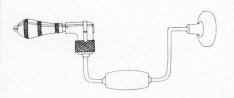

Brace and Bits
Old and satisfying tool for drilling fairly large holes (bigger than one-eighth inch). Needs about five sizes of bits.

Hand-push Drill
One of my most favorite tools, because it *feels* good and it drills small holes (pilot holes for screws, for instance) even more easily than a power drill or eggbeater drill does.

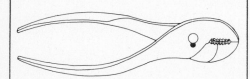

Slip-Joint Pliers
Not for nuts, but for all other grabbing, holding, and twisting needs.

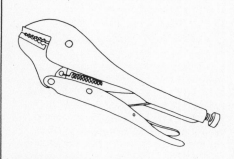

Vise Grips
Pliers with a built-in lockable vise. Invaluable.

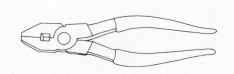

Side Cutters
For cutting coat hangers or other kinds of wire, or can double as pliers.

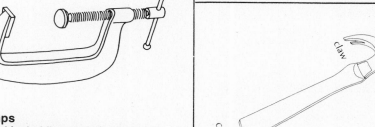

C-Clamps
Essential for holding work if you don't have a vise, but also for clamping together things you have glued.

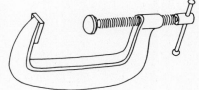

Utility Knife
Good for all thin-material cutting (except metals), but certainly the best all-around tool for cardboard. One of the most dangerous tools, no matter how you slice it.

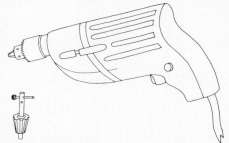

Power Drill
One of the first (and safest) power tools to put in kids' hands. Makes it possible to put holes accurately and quickly into just about anything.

Saber Saw
Especially good for cutting shapes, but if perfectly straight edges are not necessary, then it's a versatile saw for all purposes. It's possible for older kids to learn how to handle it with safety, as long as you're there.

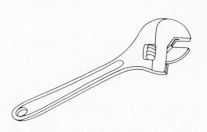

Hammer
For nails and chisels (unless you want to get a proper mallet for the chisels).

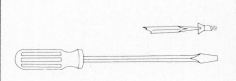

Screwdrivers
At least two sizes needed, and don't hammer on them!

Adjustable Open-End Wrench
For nuts of all shapes and sizes. Get a fairly hefty one.

books

If I Had a Hammer
Robert Lasson

E. P. Dutton and Company
201 Park Avenue South
New York, New York 10003
$7.95

A nice clean guide subtitled *Woodworking with Seven Basic Tools,* this has a deliberately limited scope but is generously illustrated with clear photographs. Except for a tape measure (an addition we won't argue with), the tools are the same as those we recommend in our basic list. Half the book is devoted to introducing the tools and essential skills; the other half details steps for building a half-dozen projects with beginners. Our only quibble is that boys predominate in the photos.

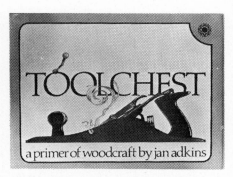

Toolchest: A Primer of Woodcraft
Jan Adkins

Walker and Company
720 Fifth Avenue
New York, New York 10019
$5.95

Jan Adkins books are worth collecting just because they're by Jan Adkins (see *The Art and Industry of Sand Castles,* page 74); it's an extra stroke of luck that he has done this woodcraft and tool primer. Curls of plane shavings and the fragrance of new-cut wood fill the cracks and folds of this book. It is written as a master carpenter builds: simple and strong. No matter what stage of interest and skill you've reached, you'll want to see it.

Know-How: A Fix-it Book for the Clumsy But Pure of Heart
Guy Alland, Miron Waskiw, and Tony Hiss

Little, Brown and Company
34 Beacon Street
Boston, Massachusetts 02106
$6.95

This too is a primer, for adults. More than a fix-it book, it's a lighthearted but informative guide to the inner workings of a house. Their approach is: if you understand how things are put together, you can be a lot more than a first-aider when it comes to fixing a switch, replacing broken windows, or painting a wall. The authors' unique sense of humor blends nicely with thorough explanations of how to use tools and make things right. "You have to drill very slowly through metal (the drill going 'gragglegragglegraggle' or 'whurrr') or you'll kill the drill. You can use a medium speed going through masonry ('warrrrrrrrrr') and a high speed on wood ('WREEEEEEEEEEEEEE')."

We think you should have it because it will help you and your kids become experts together and have fun doing it.

Recipe for Fixing a Lamp

Ingredients: 1 new lamp socket*
1 pair pliers — if necessary
1 screwdriver

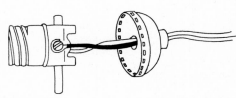

1. Lamp sockets say Press. They usually say it somewhere near the switch. Pressing here separates the old socket from the plate beneath it. If you're strong enough, press. If you're not strong enough, use pliers — but be careful not to be too strong with the pliers. Pull the plate with your other hand. It slides down and then one can remove the whole assembly.

2. We see a brass connection and a chrome connection. Unscrew the two wires, and throw away the old socket, connections, plate, and switch. It's tired. It's done its duty, and it deserves a rest. It can't be repaired — either the switch has gone bad, or the cardboard insulation in the socket has gotten tired of being cooked. The cost of a new lamp socket is nominal.

3. Slide the base plate of the new lamp socket over the wires, and attach the two wires to the two screws of the new lamp socket. Lamp cord insulation is all the same color so it'll look purty, and the only way you can tell the hot line is that the insulation around it is marked with a ridge or a series of ridges.

4. Press again, and squeeze the new lamp socket together with the base plate. You've got it.

* There are three different kinds of lamp sockets. One has a slide switch (*slide-click*), another has a turn switch (*snap-snap*), and the third has a chain switch (*zit-zit-zit-zit*). Fortunately, they are all essentially the same.

Know-How: A Fix-It Book for the Clumsy But Pure of Heart by Guy Alland, Miron Waskiw, and Tony Hiss. Illustrated by Etti de Laczay. Copyright © 1975 by Guy Alland, Miron Waskiw, and Tony Hiss. By permission of Little, Brown and Company.

Ray Brock

You Can Build a Table, and a Chair, Too!
Now You Need a Toolbox
Scooters Are Groovy, and You Can Build Your Own
If You're Ready, Here's the Car

The Dial Press
1 Dag Hammarskjold Plaza
245 East 47th Street
New York, New York 10017
$1.50 each

A unique little set designed for kids to use by themselves, these books form a pretty good primer for someone who has never even hammered a thumb black-and-blue. I think Ray Brock gets a little overcute in his attempt to appeal to the kids, but he is accurate about techniques and does an excellent job of breaking down each of the tasks into sensible and simple steps. The tools are few and basic and his projects are well chosen (at least I *think* kids still like to build wooden box scooters).

make your own jigsaw puzzles

If you have access to a power jigsaw (one superior — and safe — version of which is the Dremel saw, shown in photo at right), you can easily make your own jigsaw puzzles. Kids' drawings or paintings make ideal designs. Unless you're going to coat it with plastic spray, however, choose something that won't rub off in handling.

Carefully paste or dry mount the design on a thin piece of sturdy corrugated cardboard, Masonite, or hardwood-veneered plywood. Limit the overall size to 12″ × 9″. If the edges of the design and the piece it's mounted on don't line up exactly, make straight cuts with a regular crosscut saw to produce clean edges. (An alternative is to ask someone with a power table saw to do it for you.)

It can be cut freehand on a jigsaw, but first make a series of cuts in one direction across the width of the board, putting in whatever interesting curlicues can be managed on the saw. Then work crosswise on each of the strips to finish producing individual pieces.

Note: These make nice presents!

photography

Kids are naturally fascinated with photography, and the magic of developing and printing their own film makes the experience an even more meaningful one. In addition to the skill development and pure fun inherent in the process, there are hundreds of practical and educationally valuable uses for photography in home or classroom — projects, trip records, personal diaries, storytelling, just to name a few.

without a darkroom

The Workshop for Learning Things developed a classroom unit several years ago called "Kids, Cameras, and Communities" — utilizing a simple, inexpensive camera and requiring no darkroom for developing. With the back off the camera, you and your kids can actually see the aperture and find out how the various switches affect the amount of light entering it. The following two pages give simplified directions for using this camera, developing the negatives, and printing. *The Camera Cookbook,* a teacher's guide accompanying the unit, gives much more detailed information on the entire process, and would be a worthwhile purchase if you plan to do a lot with kids and cameras.

Both Workshop for Learning Things and SEE have all the materials necessary — in kit form as well as individually. Write for their catalogs for current prices and information on supplementary materials:

Workshop for Learning Things
5 Bridge Street
Watertown, Massachusetts 02172

SEE
3 Bridge Street
Newton, Massachusetts 02195

materials

These are the basic materials you'll need for taking, developing, and printing your own pictures. They are available in most photography stores (with the exception of the starred items, which can be purchased only from Workshop for Learning Things or SEE as far as we know); prices are approximate.

inexpensive camera	$2.60
120 film	$ .75/roll
*lightproof black bag	$5.00
developing tank	$8.00
Dektol developer	$1.80
fixer	$1.80
*glass sandwich	$1.00/3
studio proof paper	$5.00/pkg.

explore the camera

Take off the back, and look through the lens. Find the Ⓑ Ⓘ switch and notice what happens when you press the clicker for each setting. This switch determines how *long* the shutter stays open. Now put the switch on Ⓑ , and try the

switch in each position.

You will notice that the *size* of the aperture changes to let more or less light in. The last switch is for focus — you'll need to practice estimating distances unless you want to carry a yardstick around with you!

Load the camera and take some pictures! There are sixteen photos on the kind of film these small cameras usually take. You might have your kids choose a theme or story to tell (see *Painting with the Sun,* review page 226, for some good ideas).

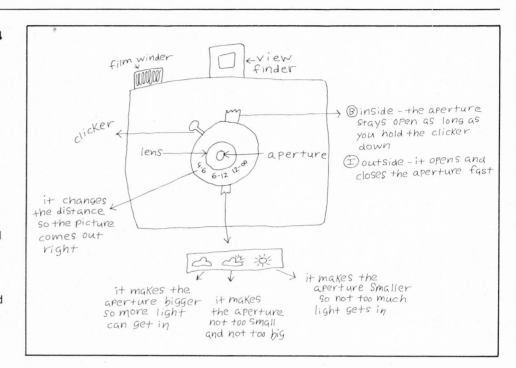

loading the developing tank

Materials:

black, lightproof bag (+ string)
developing tank (which includes metal weight and "lasagna")
film to be developed

"LaSaGNa"

PRACTICE THIS WITH SOME EXPOSED FILM 2 OR 3 TIMES!!!

Place developing tank and roll of film in black bag. Put an arm in each end of the bag and have someone tie it on so no light gets in. Unroll film and separate it from paper covering. Insert one end of the film

into the curled end of the "lasagna" — then roll them both together so the film is sandwiched between rolls of lasagna.

Place entire roll (film + lasagna) in tank, place the metal weight on top, and fit the lid on the tank securely. When you're untied, check the black bag to make sure only the paper from the roll of film is left (the film feels smooth and shiny). Now you're ready to develop!

developing

Materials:

Dektol developer
Kodak fixer

instructions for making a "working solution" on package

water
5 buckets
timer (clock or watch with second hand will do)
lots of old newspapers
clothespins (2 per roll of film) and clothesline
clean sponge

Set up buckets in a row with lots of newspaper underneath. It helps to label each bucket clearly as shown below. Dip developing tank into first bucket (water) until it's full; you can also use a paper cup to fill tank, but you'll need a separate cup for each bucket. Then shake tank gently for one minute. Empty water back into same bucket and proceed to the next. Repeat process with each bucket.

When you've completed the water-developer-water-fixer-water process, take negatives out of the developing tank. Hang them up with a clothespin at each end of the strip of negatives. Wipe on both sides of the negatives with a clean sponge — let them dry *completely* before printing.

1.   water 1 min.

2.   developer 5 min.

3.   water 1 min.

4.   fixer 5 min.

5.   water 1 min.

printing with the sun

Materials:

glass sandwich
studio proof paper
a sunny day!

Make a glass sandwich by taping a piece of glass to a piece of sturdy cardboard. Cut a piece of studio proof paper just a bit larger than the negative you want to print. Place the studio proof paper, shiny side up, with the negative on top inside the glass sandwich. Take it out-side and expose it to bright sunlight. When the outside edges of the studio proof paper turn dark purple, bring it inside and remove the negative — you have just made a positive print! Negatives can be used over and over again, so you can make as many prints as you like.

resource books

Writing with Light
Paul Clement Czaja

The Chatham Press
15 Wilmot Lane
Riverside, Connecticut 06878
$5.95

This is a lovely guide to seeing and capturing images with light — which is what photography is all about! Getting a suntan after taping designs on your back, making a pinhole camera with a rubber ball, learning how to use a darkroom — all these experiences and more are described in a clear, conversational style. *Writing with Light* suggests several simple experiments for young children, gives you a good understanding of basic photography, and helps you feel the delight of perceiving the world afresh.

Painting with the Sun
Murray Suid

Murray Suid
716 Garland Avenue
Palo Alto, California 94303

This is a delightful and invaluable "first book of photography" for kids. It's a collection of information, hints for taking interesting pictures, and lots of super project ideas — all written expressly for children. The photo illustrations are captivating (my favorites are from the "living comic"), and we consider this book a must for anyone doing photography with children!

If you have trouble finding *Painting with the Sun* locally, write to Murray and he will either fill your order himself or send it on to the current publisher.

How to Photograph Your World
Viki Holland

Charles Scribner's Sons
597 Fifth Avenue
New York, New York 10017
$5.95

Have you noticed the new tree on your block? Have you ever really looked at your family, or friends, or pets? This excellent book will help kids discover new ways to look and to see and to understand the world around them — and will show them (and you!) how to take photographs that will reflect their own personal view of it.

In addition to tips on how to use a camera, it suggests ways to take photos that tell a story or capture a mood. It's full of engaging photographs by the author that fully illustrate the various techniques and activities with humor and clarity.

movies

"Moving pictures" are an integral part of children's lives these days — cartoons, TV, and movies are all popular forms of entertainment. Making a moving picture is an exciting process for children and adults alike, though in most cases it does require some special equipment. For animated movies, probably the most important item (except the movie camera, of course) will be a single-framing device — which can be purchased separately and attached to your movie camera; it's not expensive. Here are a few good books that will get you started on making films with kids, along with some preliminary activities.

books

Children as Film Makers
John Lidstone and Don McIntosh

Van Nostrand Reinhold Company
450 West 33rd Street
New York, New York 10001
$7.95

The authors of this book believe firmly that children can make films — good films — on their own, from beginning to end. *Children as Film Makers* is a guide for adults who'd like to help their kids express themselves creatively through film, and it's the only book we've found that directs itself to working with elementary age children. In addition to technical information, it includes examples of children's projects and suggests that kids really are "natural film-makers"!

Film Making in Schools
Douglas Lowndes

Watson-Guptill Publications
165 West 46th Street
New York, New York 10036
$8.95

Although this book was really written for people working with high school students, it has a lot of excellent project ideas that could be adapted for use with younger children. It also contains several specific ways in which film-making projects could relate to other academic subjects; try "Drama Is Energy," "Who Are You," "Soap Powder Survey," "Superheroes," "Dance and Music," "An Evening at Home." Experiment with expressing emotions on film, taping weird sounds and filming something to match them!

Make Your Own Animated Movies
Yvonne Andersen

Little, Brown and Company
34 Beacon Street
Boston, Massachusetts 02106
$6.95

The Yellow Ball Workshop in Lexington, Massachusetts, is a place where children and adults make animated films. The students in our classes do their own art, story, animation, camera work, editing and sound. Film animation . . . combines the graphic arts of painting, drawing and sculpture with the art and techniques of theatre and film (Introduction, page 2).

In this excellent book Yvonne Andersen, director of the Yellow Ball Workshop, gives detailed information on the techniques she has developed for film animation by children — equipment needed, how to set up and use camera and lights, how to make cutouts, clay figures, sound effects, and much more. The illustrations are from Yellow Ball Workshop films, which have won many international awards, and the text is easy to read and to understand.

Paper Movie Machines
Budd Wentz

Troubador Press
126 Folsom Street
San Francisco, California 94105
$2

Making homemade cartoon movies is a fun hobby. But not many of us can afford all the equipment and film needed to get started. That's why this book was created. With these simple cutouts and a few odds and ends from around your home, you can actually construct all sorts of crazy gadgets for producing motion pictures without needing to buy anything else.

Some of the contraptions in this book are the forgotten works of mad scientists who gave them ridiculous names like "zoetrope" or "phenakistoscope." The names sound complicated, but the gadgets are simple!

Try your hand at drawing wheels turning, people walking, smoke rising or frogs jumping. Then use your talents to put together a story told in motion. Tinker with the devices a bit. Who knows, maybe you'll invent a movie machine of your own (page 2).

Films Kids Like
Susan Rice, editor
Center for Understanding Media

American Library Association
50 East Huron Street
Chicago, Illinois 60611
$4.95

Films are almost always a fascinating medium for children, and especially useful in classrooms when correlated with ongoing activities or concerns. *Films Kids Like* is a selective, annotated list of 220 "child-tested" short films (five to twenty minutes in length). The illustrations include stills from several films, reproductions of kids' artistic responses to them, and photos of children involved in follow-up activities.

The films were viewed by four-to-nine-year-olds — here are some discoveries made by the people who showed them:

We confirmed our belief that young children like films about other children and animals and monsters. They like funny films, especially slapstick. They like familiar fairy tales, no matter how colorless or uninventive the film, simply because they have so much fun anticipating the unfolding of stories they know by heart. We learned that there aren't many films that provide girls as central characters for the little girl viewers to identify with; those we did show were long remembered by the girls – and the boys (page 14).

activities

Paleidodromes

This is a very simple form of animation. You'll need two index cards, a piece of string, and some glue. Draw a picture on one card, and a related figure on the other.

Place the string crosswise between the cards (pictures facing out and one of them upside down), then glue them together. When you wind the glued-together cards on the string and then let go, the two pictures will appear simultaneously — creating a single image!

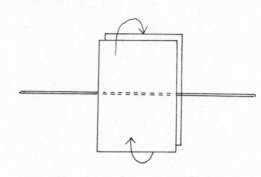

A Photo Story

Take an entire roll of black and white print film of just one directed activity — a ball game, dinnertime, building something with blocks or tools, or whatever. Then have it developed and printed on a contact sheet (which is a single sheet of photos exactly the same size as the negatives). A contact sheet is cheaper, and gives you an entire series of pictures in miniature. Cut them up, then sort and rearrange them to create a story of the activity.

"Candid Camera"

Use an 8 mm. camera to make a "candid camera" film. This is a particularly good activity for an entire family or a small group of children. Have each person take turns in front of the camera, looking into the camera as if it were a mirror — pantomime brushing your teeth, trying to get something out of your eye, shaving, combing or arranging your hair.

Flip Books

Making a flip book is a familiar, simple approach to animation. All you really need is a small scratch pad (3″ × 5″ or 4″ × 6″) and a thin marker or pencil. A simple drawing is made on the bottom page of the pad. On each successive page, the drawing is repeated but altered slightly. When the pages are flipped through your fingers, the drawing "comes to life." Drawings should be simple, since they need to be repeated over and over. Three kinds of movement are particularly suited to flip books: movement across a page, from side to side, and forward (toward you) and back.

music and movement

music and movement

making musical instruments

Music and movement play a lively role in every child's life and should be encouraged. Singing old songs on car trips with my family is a fond memory — everything from "I've Been Working on the Railroad" to "There's a Tavern in the Town"! *Song Fest** contains a collection of more than three hundred songs of all kinds that are great to sing with kids. The paperback edition, about $2.95, is readily available in bookstores around the country.

Whether or not you enjoy singing, making musical instruments is a great way to explore music with kids. We've started this section with some excellent resource books and a few ideas for instrument making.

*Edited by Dick and Beth Best, and published by California Music Press.

Musical Instrument Recipe Book

Whistles and Strings
Elementary Science Study

McGraw-Hill Book Company
Webster Division
1221 Avenue of the Americas
New York, New York 10020

These complementary units encourage kids' open-ended exploration of sounds, music, and making their own instruments. *Whistles and Strings* is a regular ESS unit with a teacher's guide and kit of materials. It contains lots of specific classroom activities and an organized procedure for introducing them. The *Musical Instrument Recipe Book* is simply an excellent collection of homemade instruments and directions on how to make them. (See pages 34–39 for a listing of other ESS units.)

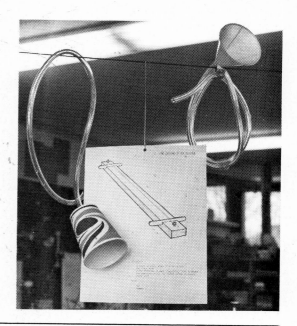

Kazoo

Before being sent off to the local music teacher to learn to play some instrument, a kid must first have the incentive to learn, and a comfortable feeling about his musical abilities. The KAZOO is a good instrument to begin experimenting with musical sounds because it can be played instantly, without musical instruction. Singing a tune in "do-do-do-do-do's" is the only talent needed, and that seems to come quite naturally. Even kids who are not musically inclined get excited with the high-pitched raspy sounds they're suddenly able to produce. The KAZOO is a real honest-to-goodness musical instrument—there are even KAZOO bands—and it can be made small enough to fit in your pocket.

tube. Make sure it's smooth and tight across the opening. Stretch a rubber band around the tube end to hold the wax paper in place. At the same end of the tube, about 1 inch from the end, punch a hole about as round as a pencil. In fact, a pencil is a good thing to punch it with. Now try to play. Hold the open end of the KAZOO around the outside of your mouth. Pucker your lips and begin singing or humming a song in "do's"—"do-do-doodle-oodle, do-do-doodle-oodle, do-do-doodle-oodle-do." Just keep it going with all the songs you know. Try "kazooing" to the music of a record or the radio. Jam with a KAZOO friend.

MATERIALS   TOOLS

paper tube   pencil
wax paper
rubber band

CONSTRUCTION

Hunt around for a paper tube—any size. Most common are the paper tube centers of paper towels and toilet paper rolls. Tear a piece of wax paper a few inches larger than the tube opening. Aluminum foil will also work fine, but the sound will be higher pitched and not quite as loud. Wrap the wax paper around one open end of the

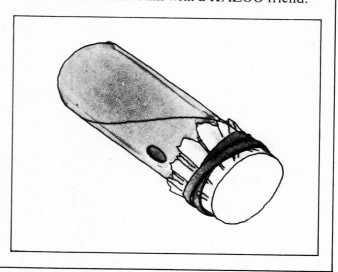

Make Your Own Musical Instruments
Muriel Mandell and Robert E. Wood

Sterling Publishing Company
419 Park Avenue South
New York, New York 10016
$4.95

Here is a handy book that gives simple directions for making instruments from household, natural, and inexpensive materials. Flowerpot bells, spoon syncopators, walnut castanets, a rattle made of lamb-chop bones, a rubber hose recorder, and wire hanger harps are among the more than one hundred ingenious instruments described. The text is concise, the drawings clear, and both are easily understood.

Instrument Making Handbook

Cooperative Artists Institute
7 Marion Street
Boston, Massachusetts 02130
$1

This is a series of single-sheet instructions for making traditional tribal instruments — shakers, tack-head drums, a tin-can kalimba, and a bamboo flute are a few examples. All are made with simple, easy-to-find materials and the directions are quite detailed.

How many different ways can you produce a sound from a string ("squidding line" works well)? Try plucking, rubbing, snapping — what happens when you attach it to something else?

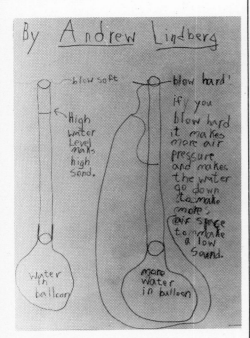

A self-designed experiment using clear plastic tubes to make sounds

Making a musical instrument often involves taking careful measurements. Is this math? Science? Woodworking? Music?

Any container that can be sealed and easily shaken will make a rattle, and any material that will move freely inside the container completes the job. Since there are so many possibilities, experiment with several combinations of materials. Make a variety of rattles and shakers to create a variety of sounds. Decorate each one with paint, contact paper, streamers, and such.

Rattles and shakers have been common all over the world since ancient times. Research the materials used in other cultures, past and present — can you make an African calabash or South American maracas?

Here are some suggested materials — try the same material in several different containers, and different materials in the same kind of container:

Containers:
  cups with lids
  1-serving cereal boxes
  wooden match boxes
  coffee cans, other small cans
  gourds
  large seashells
  ice cream containers
  cigar and shoe boxes
  milk jugs or cartons

Contents:
  dried beans, peas, seeds
  rice
  salt or sugar, rock salt
  marbles
  nuts
  sand, pebbles
  tiny shells
  beads
  tacks, paper clips

some experiments with sound

Sound
Science Teachers' Association of Ontario

Donco Quality Printers
212 Division Street
Kingston, Ontario K7K 3Z1, CANADA

Can you make a xylophone out of broom handles? Construct a simple working model of your voice box? Determine how far away a thunderstorm is by its sound? This teacher's guide encompasses a broad range of ideas for exploring sound vibrations in both musical and scientific ways. Unlike other books that offer sound experiments, this one steers away from advanced, overtechnical investigations of these phenomena.

some basic sounds

Cut the bottom out of a paper cup. Fasten a piece of waxed paper across the top with a rubber band. Hold the waxed paper part against your lips and either sing or hum into it.

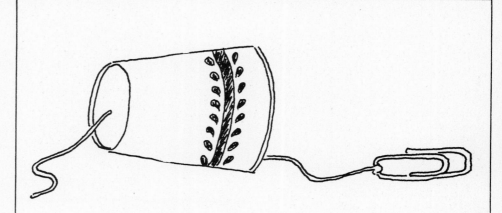

Tie a paper clip on a string, and poke the free end of the string through a hole in the bottom of a cup. Hold the cup in the air with one hand and pull downward on the string with the other, scraping it with your thumbnail as you do so. Can you predict what sound you'll produce?

Put a rubber band around a book and slide a paper cup under the band near one end of the book. Pluck the rubber band like a guitar string. How many different notes can you get?

tubes, tops, and blowing air

Partly fill a soda bottle with water. Blow across the top until you get a nice sound. Try changing the level of the water.

Cut a straw most of the way through and bend it 90°. Place it in a glass three-quarters filled with water. Use the horizontal section of the straw as a mouthpiece, blowing a stream of air across the end of the vertical tube. Try raising and lowering the straw in the water to change the sound.

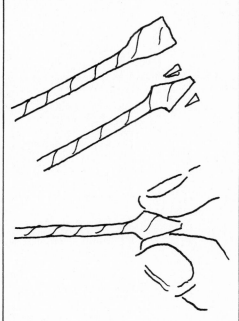

Flatten one end of a straw and then snip off the corners to make a diamond-shaped head. Squeeze the sides of the tip to barely separate the ends. Place the top well inside your mouth, but so that it does not touch anything, and blow hard.

sound vibrations to feel inside you

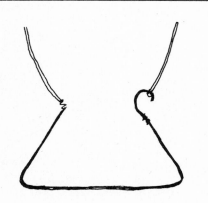

Twist open a wire coat hanger and tie two strings to the ends of the wire. Hold these strings to your ears and swing the hanger against a hard surface. Try bending the wire into different shapes. Tie on a fork or spoon in place of the hanger.

Hold one end of a yardstick or section of bamboo to your ear. Bend down (unless you're short enough already!) so that you can drag the stick along the floor as you listen. Do different surfaces change the sound?

Find a hardwood table with a fairly large surface. Have one person produce scraping, thumping, rattling sounds with a variety of materials while you put your ear against the surface.

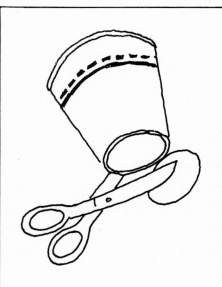

Cut the bottom from a paper cup. Hold the large end over a friend's heart and the smaller end to your ear.

resonating chambers

Most any kind of a can will do, although it is easier to work with something at least as big as a coffee can. Make a hole in the bottom and insert a wire that has been knotted or fastened to a washer, button, or whatever, so that it will *not* pull out. Attach the other end of the wire to the upper end of a stick that you stand upright on the can.

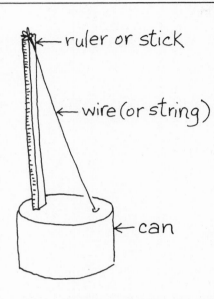

ruler or stick

wire (or string)

can

To play, pluck the wire with one hand and adjust the tension with the other by changing the angle of the stick. For a really big sound, use a metal washtub for your chamber.

Can you invent a guitar-style instrument with a resonating chamber?

resonating strings

This is a nice apparatus for experimenting with sounds that taut strings make.

Fasten a half-round stick to each end of a flat board on a table. Attach strings (or wires) to one end and let them hang down below the edge of the table so that they can suspend a pair of weights. (Cans filled with sand allow you to vary the tension.) Use a third, unattached stick as a movable bridge. (It needs to be thicker than the others.)

You now have three variables to play with so that sounds can be changed:

tension on the whole string

length of string between bridges

size or quality of string

Change the variables separately on the two strings for comparisons.

If you have trouble hearing fine tones, put your ear to the tabletop.

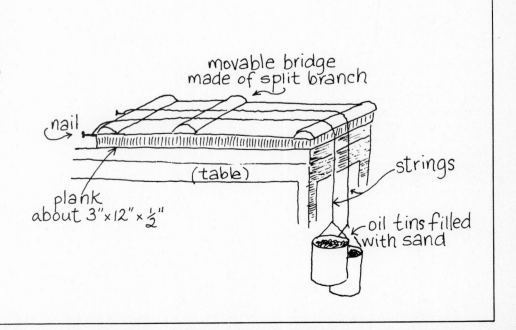

movable bridge made of split branch

nail

(table)

plank about 3"×12"×½"

strings

oil tins filled with sand

Doppler effect

Use a section of plastic or rubber tubing about four feet long and a half-inch in diameter. Find a whistle the mouth of which will fit tightly into the end of the tube. A tube-style whistle without a warbler is best. Practice blowing through the tube to produce an even, distinct note.

Now begin whirling the tube in a horizontal circle around your head while blowing the whistle steadily. A person standing several feet away, acting as listener, can try to detect changes in pitch as the whistle either approaches or recedes from him during its orbit.

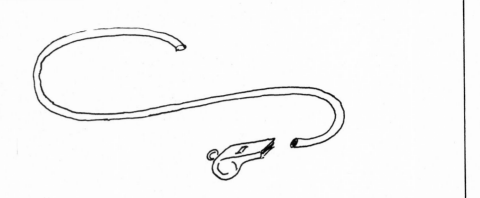

making vibrations visible

This might be a primitive version of a seismograph. Anyway, it offers a simple way to "write down" vibrations that you can hear at the same time.

Tape a hacksaw blade to a brick or block of wood and glue or tape a felt-tip pen to the free end so that the tip just touches a piece of bristol board. Set the blade vibrating, slowly drawing the cardboard beneath the pen. You should be able to produce a clear pattern of the vibrations.

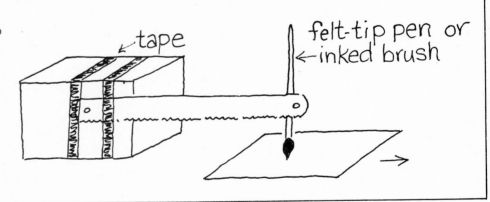

composing and recording your own music

Don't let that title scare you off — it can be easy to do, and it may just be the best possible way to introduce children to the whole world of music. I am definitely not a musician, but I learned how to do all this in one easy lesson from our good friend Diane, who teaches music in England.

You can *compose* by ear, and without using scales or any systems of notation — in fact, a large portion of the world's music is created that way, passed down by oral tradition alone. But *recording* the music demands a recognizable set of written symbols. As with written language, the number of possible systems is endless. The one traditionally used in the western world is the diatonic scale (do, re, mi, fa, sol, la, ti, do'), a reduced version of which is the pentatonic scale (do, re, mi, —, sol, la, —, do').

You can do your composing and recording in either scale, but Diane says that it is a lot simpler to stick with the pentatonic, especially for those of us who don't know much about music theory, formal rules of harmony, and so forth. It so happens that many international folk songs are pentatonic, even if they have never been recorded. Obviously, the composers weren't concerned about written symbol systems.

With the pentatonic scale you can:

compose simple tunes
harmonize tunes
compose two-part songs (two instruments; two voices; one instrument, one voice)
arrange a score for a combination of more than two instruments

Since there are fewer notes to work with, it is easier to use the pentatonic scale when composing on homemade instruments. Children will particularly enjoy and learn a great deal from recording their compositions *and* listening back to what they've invented (a tape recorder would be ideal for this purpose).

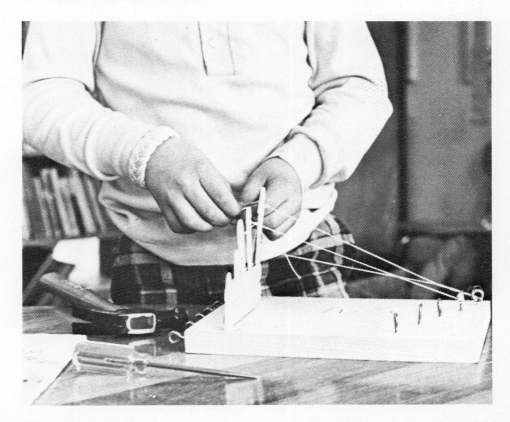

composing on a grid-score

One method of composing and recording that does not require previous knowledge of formal composition techniques is the "composing on a grid-score" system.

The "score" can combine *any* variety of instruments -— tuned or otherwise. In fact, any random sound-producing items that can be scrounged from kitchen, playroom, street, or classroom can be made use of. The notation system used is self-explanatory -— children will most likely devise fresh symbols to suit their own needs to add to those already used in our example.

The "grid-score" should be posted, or each child should have a copy. The numerals at the top of the score indicate the duration of the performance. They should be spaced at regular intervals and be determined by a "conductor" (perhaps with the aid of a preset metronome). Diane recommends that children should *always* conduct their own music, which seems an excellent idea to us.

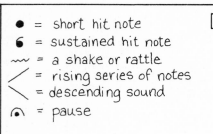

● = short hit note
♪ = sustained hit note
〰 = a shake or rattle
╱ = rising series of notes
╲ = descending sound
⌒. = pause

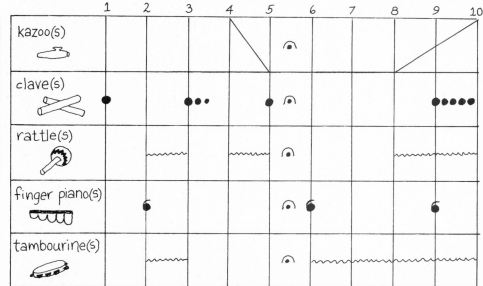

	1	2	3	4	5	6	7	8	9	10
kazoo(s)					⌒.					
clave(s)	●		●●●	●	⌒.				●●●●●	
rattle(s)		〰		〰	⌒.				〰	
finger piano(s)		♪			⌒.♪				♪	
tambourine(s)		〰			⌒.	〰				

Diane's color system for making music

Things you need:

a pack of sticky paper sheets in a variety
of colors (adhesive colored sheets are
a regular art supply item, but you can
also use contact paper)
a set of manila or bristol board cards in
long rectangular shape
scissors

The system works with any scale, and
kids can use it without any knowledge of
musical notation. In fact, you don't have to
explain anything about scales or formal
rules — they can just start right off making
music!

1. Decide on five colors to represent the
five notes in the scale, for example, red =
do, blue = re, and so on. (For simplicity,
we're using the pentatonic scale here.)

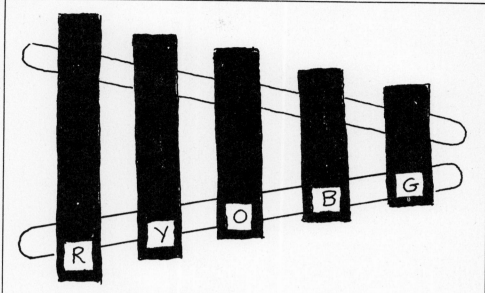

2. Cut a square piece or strip of each
color to stick on the notes of the instruments
you're working with. We suggest using
tuned percussion, such as one of those in
the *Musical Instrument Recipe Book* (see
page 232 for review).

3. Cut up the remainder of the sheets
into small squares (maybe one centimeter
or a quarter inch). These will become the
notes for recording a composition.

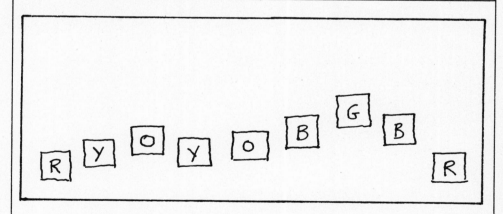

4. Now, by sticking a series of colored
squares onto a card, you can begin to compose. If you want to keep things as simple
as possible at first, don't worry about showing rhythms, how long a note should be
held, volume, or tempo. The colored
squares can be laid out in a straight line. As
soon as they get the feel of it, kids may
discover on their own how to indicate the
other features of a score; for instance, a
longer gap between two notes would
suggest holding the first one longer. One of
the things they may discover right away is
that placing the squares up and down on
the card helps in seeing the rise and fall of
tones.

There are two basic ways to go about composing with this system:

1. Put down a row of colored squares in random order. Play the sequence on your instrument and discover the tune you've just invented! Do you like the sound? If you're not satisfied, rearrange the colored pieces on the same or a different card until you like what you hear.

2. Play a tune on your instrument, just a few notes long. Anything that sounds right to you is a tune! Can you repeat it? Can you record it? You can, of course, write down the composition as you invent it, one note at a time; but it is hard to keep the whole tune in mind that way. For that reason, first tunes should be short enough so the whole thing can be recalled before writing. After it's down on the card in colored squares, ask a friend to play it for you. Does it sound the same as what you invented? If not, why not?

———————

Once you understand how easy it is to compose and record your own music with colored squares, try these activities:

Compose a tune from your own name, assigning colors to each of the letters in it.

Compose a song, either notes first or words first, but recording the two together on your card.

Find a poem (perhaps one you've written yourself), and compose a tune for it.

Figure out some ways to put in rhythm, show parts for several instruments playing at once, indicate tempo. What methods can you devise for writing these down?

Take one of these pentatonic songs and see if you can play it on your own instrument by ear; or make up an instrumental accompaniment to the song, using just two or three of the notes; or write down the whole song, words and music, with the color system and perform it!

"Shortenin' Bread"
"One More River to Cross"
"Camptown Races"
"Liza Jane"

movement

Children seem to be almost the embodiment of movement. They *use* their bodies constantly — jumping, skipping, running, crouching, dancing, tiptoeing, leaning. . . . Even when kids are engrossed in books their body postures express potential motion — a leg swung over the arm of a chair, toes wiggling with excitement, brow furrowed in concentration or a spontaneous laugh in response to a secret joke!

   Music has a wonderful way of stimulating all kinds of particularly imaginative movement. Here are some resources and activities to get your kids involved in the joy of movement at a conscious level — with or without music!

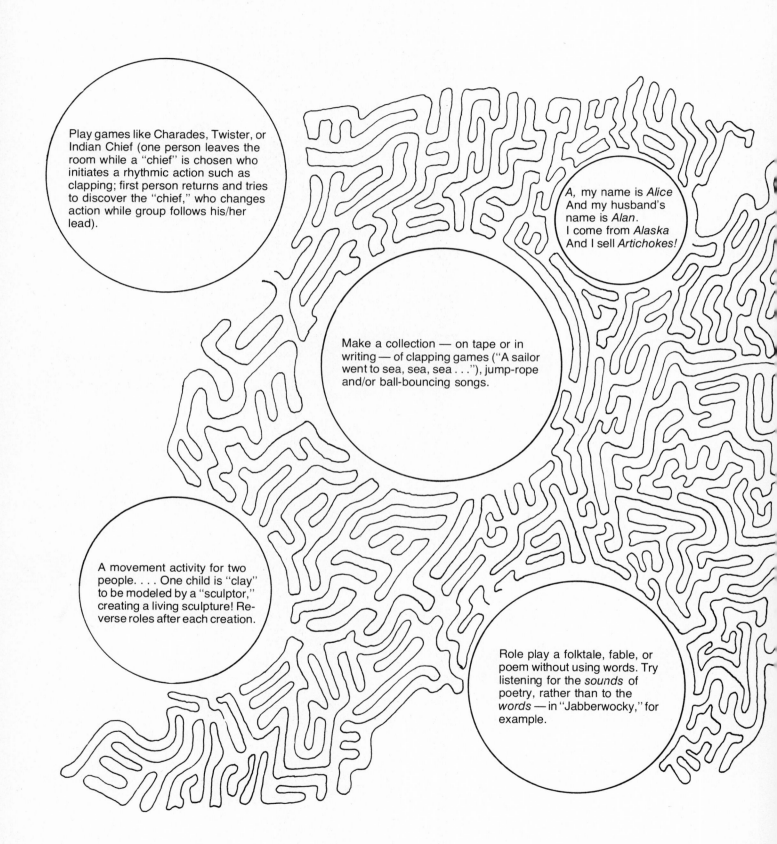

Play games like Charades, Twister, or Indian Chief (one person leaves the room while a "chief" is chosen who initiates a rhythmic action such as clapping; first person returns and tries to discover the "chief," who changes action while group follows his/her lead).

A, my name is *Alice* And my husband's name is *Alan*. I come from *Alaska* And I sell *Artichokes!*

Make a collection — on tape or in writing — of clapping games ("A sailor went to sea, sea, sea . . ."), jump-rope and/or ball-bouncing songs.

A movement activity for two people. . . . One child is "clay" to be modeled by a "sculptor," creating a living sculpture! Reverse roles after each creation.

Role play a folktale, fable, or poem without using words. Try listening for the *sounds* of poetry, rather than to the *words* — in "Jabberwocky," for example.

Be the thing!
Here are some favorites for indoors and out, with or without music — robots, circus performers, athletes, animals, kites, birds, a rock rolling downhill, marionettes . . .

Explore and learn some traditional folk dances from a variety of cultures.

Try drawing or painting to music too!

Choose a piece of music and have the child(ren) move with it, creating a dance or series of body images that reflect the mood of the music.
  Try *Carnival of the Animals* (Saint-Saëns), *The Planets* (Gustav Holst), or *Mass for the End of Time* (Pierre Henri). The latter is highly rhythmic, unpredictable, with a variety of weird sounds — perfect for imagining creatures from other worlds.

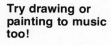

Play "catch" without a ball!

Weather is a good starting point for movement activity. Try expressing the effect of snow, ice, sun, rain → thunderstorms, a heat wave on people, animals, or growing things.

Creative Movement for Children
Jack Wiener and John Lidstone

Van Nostrand Reinhold Company
450 West 33rd Street
New York, New York 10001

Although written for the classroom teacher, this lovely book contains some excellent "starting points" for creative movement in any context. It's profusely illustrated with rather "arty" photographs, but the text is straightforward and easily understandable. It suggests using the basic movements of walking, sliding, jumping, and turning to express all kinds of creative activity and emotions.

Each locomotion has a distinctive character. . . . Thus walking shapes remind the child of inanimate moving things like puppets or robots, while sliding shapes might suggest snakes or gliding birds. But such imagery should not be forced on the child; it should grow out of the exploration of shapes rather than be the motivating idea for movement, so that the child can make free associations (page 37).

Movement Games for Children of All Ages
Esther L. Nelson

Sterling Publishing Company
419 Park Avenue South
New York, New York 10016
$4.95

Take off your shoes and socks before you start using this fun book of movement games! Begin by taking your pulse (in your neck), try Tag with a twist, or a "pizzazz" version of Musical Chairs (without the chairs).
All the action games in this treasury inspire imagination, freedom of movement, creativity, and confidence. They are all challenging and easy to adapt to any age level, although most are group activities.

Try making a Marvelous Machine where kids are the parts! Each part (child) repeats the same movement and sound over and over again, and must be connected in some way to another part. Choose one child to turn the machine on and off, speed it up or slow it down — even throw a wrench in to create havoc!

Reprinted by permission from the book *Movement Games for Children of All Ages,* © 1975 by Esther L. Nelson. Drawing by Shizu Matsuda.

Jump Rope!
Peter L. Skolnik

Workman Publishing Company
231 East 51st Street
New York, New York 10022
$2.95

Five, ten, fifteen, twenty,
Nobody leaves the jump-rope empty.
If they do, they shall suffer:
Take an end and be a duffer!

This simply delightful book contains everything from tidbits of jump-rope history to over 250 jumping rhymes. The engaging illustrations, unpretentious writing style, and fascinating contents make this a book to remember. The rhymes are old and new, international and regional, and altogether a great deal of fun for children and adults of all ages.

ourselves

ourselves

bodies

These days we're all looking a little more closely at ourselves: who we are, how we're made, how we feel, and what we value. It becomes more obvious all the time that math, writing, and reading are not enough; growing up means learning how to cope with conflicting feelings or with difficult choices like "Who is going to be my friend?" This kind of learning depends more on the inner resources of sensitive adults than it does on hard materials, but in this section we have put together a range of activities and books that may give you a place to start.

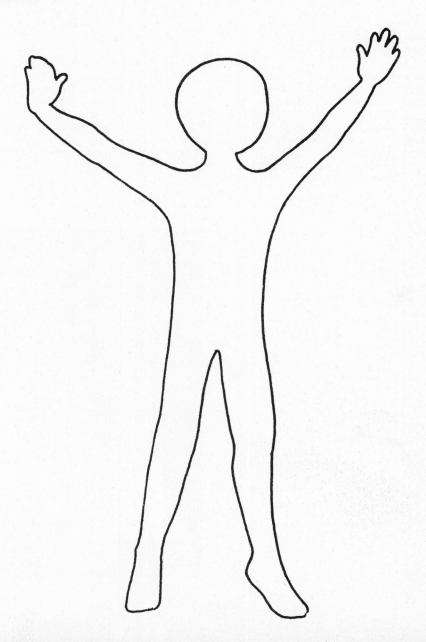

sexual growth

Sex, reproduction, and birth are natural processes with which children are often fascinated and with which we think they should feel comfortable. According to SIECUS (Sex Information and Education Council of the United States), "Parents, teachers and concerned community cannot choose whether or not they will give sex education — they can only choose whether they will do something positive or negative about it."

Watching the mating and birth of animals in home or classroom is a familiar yet altogether intriguing experience that helps kids gain an understanding and acceptance of reproduction as a natural process. It's not usually a good idea to bombard kids with detailed medical information in response to a simple question; but it is important to have ways of answering those questions honestly and without embarrassment to you or the child.

Familiarity with nudity can be a great help in making kids feel comfortable with their own bodies, particularly in regard to their genitalia. We feel frustrated that so few materials are available that give kids realistic images. Dolls are traditionally sexless, which seems ridiculous and can only foster embarrassment (in the manufacturers' attempt to avoid embarrassment!) about our

own very real "private parts." We are still awaiting an American source for sexually realistic dolls, but hopefully *One Big Family* indicates the beginning of a trend in the right direction.

Where Do Babies Come From?
Margaret Sheffield

Random House
201 East 50th Street
New York, New York 10022
$4.95

Never before in a book have the questions young children ask about birth been answered so gently, so lovingly, and so directly. Here, beautifully adapted to the printed page — for the adult to read and look at along with the child — is the famous award-winning BBC program "Where Do Babies Come From?," which has been used in primary schools throughout England and is regarded as one of the finest attempts ever made to deal with a child's dawning curiosity about the beginnings of life.

On one side of each double-page spread, a simple text explains one stage in the process of conceiving and giving birth to a baby and tells the child about the parts of the body involved. Facing it: a beautiful, softly colorful painting, honestly explicit without being stark or frightening.

Of the various books currently available that deal with the process of reproduction and birth, this is definitely our favorite. It is both tactful and honest, and we cannot think of a more acceptable way of presenting this information to young children in book form.

One Big Family

Sales Distribution Center
Unitarian Universalist Association
25 Beacon Street
Boston, Massachusetts 02108
$4/set

This unusual set of fourteen paper dolls not only is sexually realistic but also shows people at different stages of growth. Young children, a chubby woman, a black couple, and an old man are among the cutout figures.

Kids will enjoy coloring in and designing clothes for all of these paper dolls, perhaps imagining a group of them as a family, but their primary value lies in their realistic portrayal of children and adults. They are a part of a multimedia unit on feelings written by Barbara Hollerorth and entitled *The Haunting House* (see page 263 for review).

How Babies Are Made
Andrew C. Andry and Steven Schapp

Time-Life Books
Little, Brown and Company
34 Beacon Street
Boston, Massachusetts 02106
$5.95

This is a simple, direct introduction to the process of reproduction for young children. It is beautifully illustrated with colorful, cut-paper figures. *How Babies Are Made* has a particularly nice way of explaining this natural process, relating the pollination of flowers and the development of seeds to the fertilization of an egg and the growth and birth of animal babies.

Although it is easy to read, it's the kind of book that parents or teachers and children will want to read together, sharing the wonder of it all!

Show Me!
Will McBride

St. Martin's Press
175 Fifth Avenue
New York, New York 10010
$12.95

Here is an incredibly beautiful "picture book of sex for children and parents" originally published in Germany. Its striking, explicit photographs could evoke hours of informative and intimate conversation with your kids about human sexual development. The captions are children's spontaneous responses to the pictures, and an explanatory text for adults is included at the back.

A word of warning — you are more likely than your kids to be taken aback by this book's frank presentation of all kinds of sexual relationships. Although the photographs emphasize the warmth, tenderness, and humor of sex, many people will not feel comfortable showing them to their children. *Show Me!* is a unique, remarkable book, but one to look through carefully before purchasing.

body fun!

Go outside on a sunny day and have a friend (perhaps your child!) trace your shadow — then swap. Can you fit into each other's shapes? If you draw with chalk right on the ground, go back an hour or two later — can you still fit into your shadow? Why not? If you make your shadow shape on paper, cut it out — a group of shadow shapes would make a fantastic wall design! (Or just use a bright light indoors to create shadow shapes — try positioning the light at different angles and heights relative to your body.)

Get a large piece of mural paper and lie on it — have a friend trace your body. Then paint in your hair, face, clothes, and so forth. How many wacky positions can you invent? Try several before you decide how you want to be traced.

Are you a square or a rectangle? Lie down on the floor (you could even do this standing) with your feet together and your arms stretched out at both sides. Have a friend take two measurements — one from fingertip to fingertip, the other from head to toe. How do the measurements compare? What shape are you?

Bodies
Barbara Brenner

E. P. Dutton and Company
201 Park Avenue South
New York, New York 10003
$5.95

Everyone has one. With it, you can stand on your head, play in the mud, hold a frog, blow up a balloon, laugh, sweat, breathe, swing, or splash!

This beautiful, *alive* book, with its captivating black and white photographs of kids doing all those things and more, explores the fascinating subject of bodies and shows what fun it is to have one — one that's uniquely yours. It's a book that's sure to delight both you and your children.

me, myself, and I

Kids seem naturally turned on by making a book about themselves. After all, it's the subject they know most about! And the possibilities for contents, as shown on these pages, are endless.

A really nice related activity is to make a "me poster" — a collage of drawn or cutout pictures and words that show your "favorite things." It's a great way to get kids sharing and communicating at the beginning of a school year; or it could be an annual family activity with lots of comparisons from year to year!

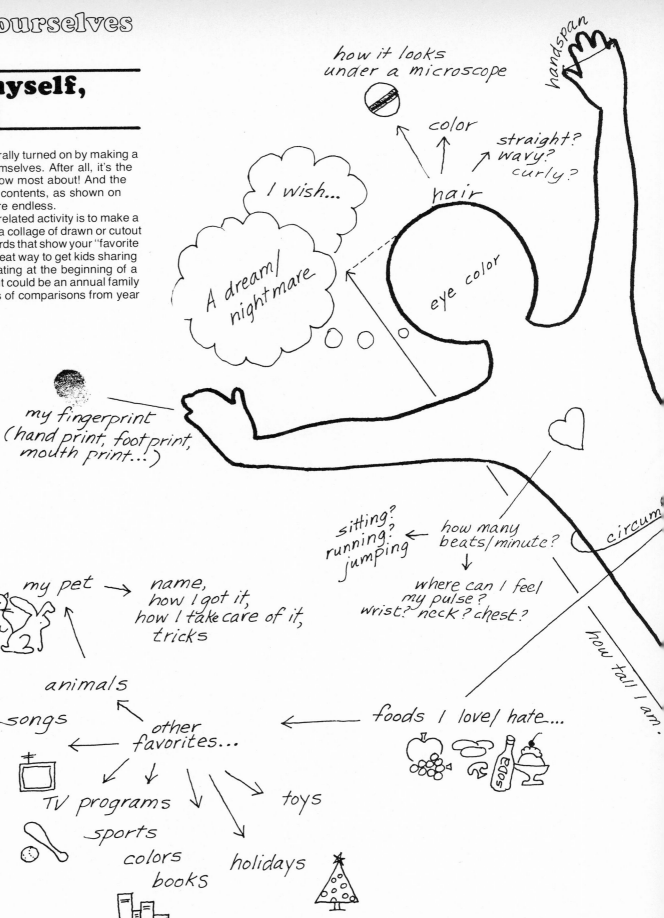

how it looks under a microscope

handspan

color

straight? wavy? curly?

hair

I wish...

A dream/ nightmare

eye color

my fingerprint (hand print, foot print, mouth print...)

circum

sitting? running? jumping

how many beats/minute?

where can I feel my pulse? wrist? neck? chest?

how tall I am

my pet → name, how I got it, how I take care of it, tricks

animals

songs

other favorites...

foods I love/hate....

TV programs

toys

sports

colors

holidays

books

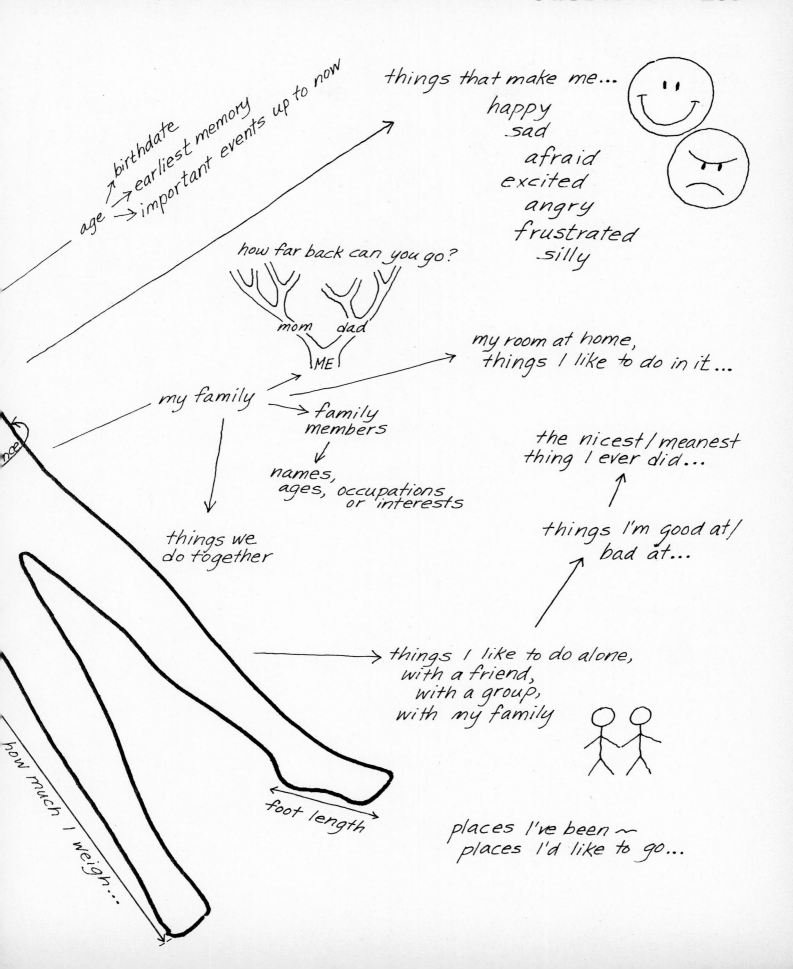

birthdate
earliest memory
age important events up to now

how far back can you go?

mom   dad

ME

my family

family members

names, ages, occupations or interests

things we do together

how much I weigh...

foot length

things that make me...
happy
sad
afraid
excited
angry
frustrated
silly

my room at home, things I like to do in it...

the nicest/meanest thing I ever did...

things I'm good at/ bad at...

things I like to do alone, with a friend, with a group, with my family

places I've been ~ places I'd like to go...

from egg to chick

Even though it requires a great deal of patience, hatching chicks or ducklings in home or classroom is an unforgettable experience. You can usually obtain fertilized eggs from a local hatchery or poultry farm. Try opening and examining an unfertilized egg first to get a clear view of the contents. Can you find the tiny white spot where life would begin if the egg had been fertilized?

Then, place about a dozen eggs in your incubator and carefully follow the procedures for hatching. As the embryos start to grow, you can take out single eggs periodically and break them open into a shallow dish to observe stages of development. Have a copy of *Window into an Egg* (reviewed on page 255) handy to clarify what you see in each stage, and perhaps also photos of the human embryo for some interesting comparisons. After three days a chick embryo will usually show the heart beating, which may continue for half an hour.

You may not want to sacrifice any of these precious eggs, of course, and there are some ways of observing changes without breaking them open. If you have a stethoscope, listen every day to see when

you can pick up the heartbeat from a whole egg. Hold up an egg to a strong light source to see the shadowy outline of the embryo.

The most exciting stage occurs on the twenty-first (or sometimes the twenty-second) day, when the chick pecks a window in the shell and begins to enter the world. It will take several hours of exhausting work for the little critter before it emerges all the way out of the shell and squats there, looking helpless.

cardboard incubator

You can buy an incubator, but they're expensive enough to make it worthwhile manufacturing your own. Here's the simplest plan we've found:

1. Find two cardboard boxes, one of which can fit inside the other with space left over for insulation between them. Cut the top off the small box but leave the flaps on the other.

2. Before fitting them together, cut a window in the bottom of the large box about six inches square and tape a piece of glass or Plexiglas into it. This will be the observation window after you turn the box on its side.

3. Cut a slit in the top of the small box to receive and hold in place the cord of a single light bulb fixture. Put the light in place. Also put in a thermometer and a small dish of water. The eggs will be placed on the floor of this box.

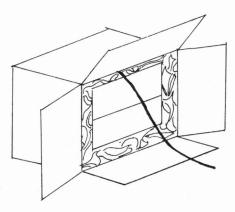

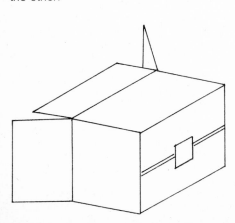

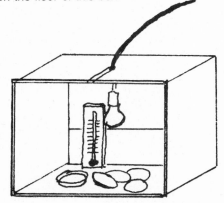

4. Now slide the smaller box into the larger, open face toward the observation window, and pack crumpled newspapers into the spaces between them.

Temperature inside the incubator must be maintained at 103° F (40° C) night and day for twenty-one days. Before you put in the eggs, experiment with the size of the bulb and the amount of newspaper insulation until you arrive at the right temperature.

The water dish keeps moisture in the atmosphere of the box. The eggs have to be turned three times a day, mainly to ensure even heating.

seeing life begin

Window into an Egg:
Seeing Life Begin
Geraldine Lux Flanagan

Young Scott Books
Addison-Wesley Publishing Company
2725 Sand Hill Road
Menlo Park, California 94025

There are not so many fundamental differences among eggs of living things. Whether life begins inside a mother's body, within the petals of a flower, or among the rocks at the bottom of a stream, it begins with an egg.

You can think of an egg as a package. It is nature's neat and handy package that holds a new life from a mother and father. The mother and father may be people, or they may be a hen and rooster, or a male and female elephant, or goldfish, or grasshoppers. Trees, flowers, vegetables, all have eggs and their eggs turn into seeds that grow into new plants (page 9).

Because most of these eggs are both small and fragile, it's not easy to get a close-up look at the whole miraculous process as it unfolds. But chicken eggs are among the largest in nature, and scientists have been able to seal a miniature window into a fertilized specimen so they can photograph in detail each stage of its growth into a chick.

This book is a photo essay for children of one such process, showing every observable change from Day 0 to Day 23. The narrative is fluent, possibly readable for even a nine-to-ten-year-old with ordinary skills, though most appropriate for an adult and child reading together. It would be helpful to supplement this with a color photo series or a film, however, because small black and white stills do not capture movement or delineate fine differences.

bones

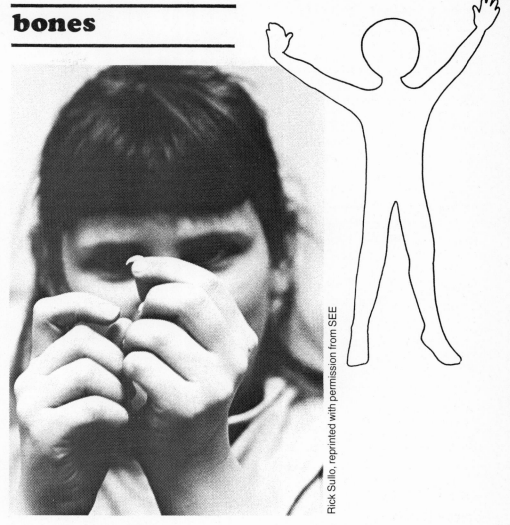

Rick Sullo, reprinted with permission from SEE

Bones Teacher's Guide

Bone Picture Book
Elementary Science Study

McGraw-Hill Book Company
Webster Division
1221 Avenue of the Americas
New York, New York 10020

Studying bones with kids means sampling bits of the work that archaeologists, zoologists, ecologists, natural historians, and even behavioral psychologists commonly perform. As these guides demonstrate, that does not mean that you and your kids have to turn into specialists in order to have fun learning about bones together. Here is a surprisingly large variety of activities with which to explore the manifold structures and functions of living creatures. You can do any of these investigations without previous training, as long as you have a reasonable amount of patience and are willing to let discoveries come gradually. You can adapt them for home or for school, use them as an extended single unit or as individual sets of activities.

The photographs, particularly those in the *Bone Picture Book,* are superb. You could go a long way with just these photos, which are arranged for provocative comparisons and accompanied by teasing questions. However, the richest experience would result from handling, classifying, charting, or putting together some real bones; and for that kind of work (play?) it is worth having the beautifully executed *Bones Teacher's Guide* (which in fact has reproduced photos from the *Picture Book* in reduced size, along with descriptions and additional observations).

Many of the specific activities explained in the teacher's guide are offered in summary form (on the next page). We have omitted information about other parts of the unit available from ESS distributors (see page 34), including disarticulated skeletons of mink, rabbits, and cats, as these are expensive and require extreme patience for a lengthy, exacting process. There is so much you can do with bones from the butcher, your kitchen, the fields, and personal collections — not to mention the bones in your own body — that it seems unnecessary to use purchased kits.

using real bones

One good way to get an inside look (literally) at how animals, including humans, are designed is to examine their skeletal structures. A surprising number of mysteries about function and behavior can be solved by deduction when you study these bones, especially if you can work with the real thing.

Dem Bones

Materials / Activities	Set of odd, found bones	Chicken skeleton (disarticulated)	Kids' own bodies	Pictures of bones, skeletons (X-rays?)	Skulls, found or pictured
Determining location of bone in a skeleton or body and guessing at function.	Allow for inaccurate conclusions based on sound guesswork.	Work without model of complete animal.	Discover by feeling and probing; name functions.	Reverse perspective from whole to part.	
Comparing like and unlike bones of separate animals or of same animal at different stages of growth.	Classify similar-looking bones first, then think in terms of function.	Compare chicken bones	and contrast people bones.	Use photos or X-rays of individual bones and whole skeletons.	Look especially at teeth and jaws.
Assembling all or part of a skeleton.	Find a few bones that fit together.	Much patience is needed for complete skeleton.	Construct model from scrounged materials.		
Deducing specific functions of parts, or behavior of whole animal.	Ask how size, strength, structure, shape indicate function or behavior.	Emphasize function of parts in relation to known behavior.	Look at how variation in skeletons affects functioning.	Study adaptations of specific bone structure for special functions.	Examine skull size in relation to whole animal.
Measuring, counting, feeling, charting bones.	Make comparative charts.	Use variety of activities.	Let kids work with each other's bodies.		Determine skull capacity with sand; compare quantities.
Drawing imaginary version of whole animal.	Wild approximations possible.	Work without actual picture.	Draw imagined skeleton of own body.	Try for accurate representation.	See if head helps guessing at whole.
Comparing to nonliving "skeletons."	Wonder about structural design of building materials.	Bird bone structure compares with aircraft design.	Find machines with same strength and maneuverability.	Compare buildings to fixed skeletons.	Compare containers for protective design.

skeletons from scraps

If you've shopped for a human skeleton lately you'll realize that even a partial model costs $150 or more. It's a lot more satisfying to construct your own version out of scrounged materials, anyhow. In fact, there is no better way for kids to become familiar with what is inside their bodies. Making a skeleton may lead to investigating muscles, organs, or circulatory systems ("Why does this rib cage have to bulge out?" "What holds the bones together in a real body?").

Supplies for Scrap Skeletons

branches and twigs
aluminum foil
papier-mâché materials
chicken wire
thin uncovered wire
Styrofoam pieces
Elmer's glue
small handsaw
whittling knife
surform
rasp
sandpaper
hand drill

The Process

Kids use their own bodies as sources. (If five or six are working together, then choose one to be the consistent model during construction. It has to be somebody willing to be touched a lot!) Start with limbs, as it is relatively easy to locate these and feel their general outlines; making them is just a matter of finding branches of approximately the right diameter and cutting them to length. (Have kids make measurements throughout, using a cloth tape measure.) As a rule, any elongated bone can be made from a branch. Short ones, such as finger sections, can also be made from twigs. You'll need a six-foot table space to lay out each model as it is being constructed. Drill holes in the ends of bones so that they can be wired together.

By the time they get beyond the limb stage, if not before, kids will discover that there are many bones for which they cannot get an accurate conception by touch alone. The ESS *Bones* guides will help, but you may want to search out additional charts, X-rays, or reference books for other views. Don't let these become your major sources, though, as they will bog down the whole project in needless details.

Large shapes like the pelvis can be first molded in aluminum foil (mold it around the subject's head for that part) and then copied in chicken wire, to be laid over with papier-mâché.

Experiment with Styrofoam for making certain parts, especially ones that do not have to take any stress. This material is easily shaped with a surform tool, rasp, or rough sandpaper.

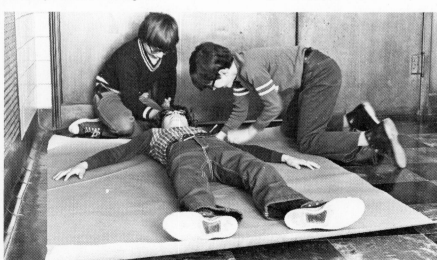

Another way to begin is to first trace body shapes and then sketch in bones

general resource books

Ourselves
Macdonald Educational

Purnell Educational
850 Seventh Avenue
New York, New York 10019
$4.99

One of a series of British teacher's guides (see page 91 for review), this book contains a wealth of concrete activities designed to help kids learn about their own bodies.

. . . The whole emphasis of this Unit is on aspects of ourselves that can be discovered at first hand. Children are always interested in themselves. In their weight, height, eye colour. In whether someone has his first toe longer than his big toe, in who has the longest legs, in who can do something more quickly, more skillfully than others.

In order to satisfy this interest they will have to question one another, take measurements, get one another to perform certain tasks, carry out tests, record information and make their findings intelligible to others (Introduction, page 1).

You . . . and Me
Richard L. Kimball

Educational Science Consultants
P.O. Box 1674
San Leandro, California 94577

Although this workbook is decidedly classroom oriented, it has some valuable ideas on ways to explore your own body that would be applicable in any situation. Its emphasis is physical — including investigations of senses, measuring with parts of the body, directions for making a chicken skeleton (see pages 255–257 for related activities with bones), and much more! The activities are interesting and the accompanying directions and questions are explicit, though almost too "programmed."

Your Senses
Examining Your Environment

Winston Press
25 Groveland Terrace
Minneapolis, Minnesota 55403
$3

This book takes a very scientific approach to exploring the five senses. It contains detailed information on the way in which you sense something (how your eyes and ears work, for example), as well as a wide variety of experiments for comparing your sense perception with those of friends or classmates. It is directed at upper elementary age children, and is lavishly illustrated. (See page 28 for other titles in this series.)

Investigation 29   Hair

Some hair is long; some is short. Some hair is thick; some is thin. There are many kinds of hair. Write all the words you can think of that tell about your hair. My hair is:

_____   _____
_____   _____
_____   _____
_____   _____

Look at one hair with a magnifying glass or microscope. Draw what you see.

Tape hair here.   Draw here.

Choose a piece of someone's hair that is very different from yours. Look at this hair closely. Draw what you see.

Tape hair here.   Draw here.

Here are some ways this hair is different from mine.
_____
_____
_____
_____

How many hairs do I have on my head? _____
Numbers of hairs I guess. _____   Number of hairs counted. _____

Here are some reasons I think I have hair in my nose and ears _____
_____

Does anyone in your class have the same numbers of hairs that you do? _____
Do girls have more hair than boys? _____
Do you get more hair as you grow older? _____

sensory activities

Take a twenty-minute walk outdoors. Bring a tape recorder with you and leave it on. When you return, make a list of all the sounds you heard; then play back the tape and listen for those you missed!

Have a "mystery sounds" contest. Tape a whole variety of sounds (water dripping, a sneeze, door opening, breathing, person walking . . .). Then have a friend try to identify the sounds from your tape recording.

Blindfold yourself and take a walk with a friend guiding you. Try doing this without any conversation or verbal directions. Eat a meal, walk up stairs, enter a building, cross a busy intersection. How do you feel? Compare impressions with your friend.

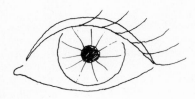

Read a book about Helen Keller or Louis Braille. Learn the symbols in the Braille alphabet; try writing a sentence, poem, or story by punching dots in paper with a pin.

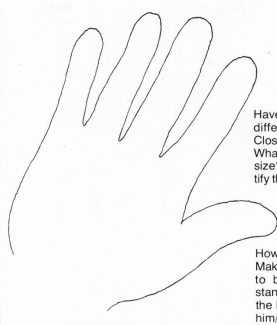

Have a friend put an object (or several different objects) in a closed box. Close your eyes and feel the object(s). What words express how it feels — size? Shape? Texture? Can you identify the object?

How well do you know your friends? Make a circle and choose one person to be blindfolded. Another person stands in the center of the circle, while the blindfolded person tries to identify him/her by touch alone.

Cut small cubes of carrot, onion, apple, and potato to the same size. Close your eyes and hold your nose, then have a friend place each piece of food in your mouth. Can you tell the difference in taste? What happens if you keep your eyes closed, but don't hold your nose?

Put a variety of liquids (ketchup, syrup, vinegar, salt water, perfume, turpentine . . .) in closed, opaque bottles or jars. See if you can identify them by smell.

Remove all the 2s, 3s, 4s, 5s, and 6s from a deck of playing cards, so that you have a total of twenty cards. Blindfold yourself and have a friend shuffle the cards and turn over one at a time — thinking hard about each number as it's turned over. Try to identify the card as your friend concentrates. Your friend should keep track of your correct answers. Just by luck, chance, or guessing, a person can probably identify five cards out of twenty — if you can name ten or more correctly, you just might have ESP! What further tests could you devise?

outdoor play

When most of the children in the nation lived on the land or at least had access to big, open spaces, special playgrounds were hardly needed. Urbanization has changed all that; children tend to get confined indoors in a way they never used to be because there has been no good place for them to go and maybe nothing to do, either. At the same time, people who study children's physical, social, and emotional development have made us newly aware of just how important outdoor play is during kids' growing up. Kids need to discover and test their physical powers, learn how

to interact with others, and practice solving many kinds of problems. Well-equipped playgrounds can provide at least some of these opportunities. Also, this is a territory where children, parents, and schools can work together. Here are a few references and specific suggestions for constructing your own outdoor play spaces.

Build Your Own Playground
Jay Beckwith

Houghton Mifflin Company
2 Park Street
Boston, Massachusetts 02107
$7.95

Subtitled *A Sourcebook of Play Sculptures, Designs, and Concepts,* this is a full explanation of the kinds of processes amateur planners and builders might go through in order to create their own playgrounds. As such, it contrasts with *Handcrafted Playgrounds,* which contains mostly visual plans. This book does have a large number of photographs (and a few sketched details) showing intriguing designs for play structures, many of which utilize concepts markedly different from Friedberg's. Both books assume the use of found materials and homegrown labor in construction.

Handcrafted Playgrounds
M. Paul Friedberg

Random House
201 East 50th Street
New York, New York 10022
$12.95

The best description of this book is one contained in the author's foreword, from which we quote:

Handcrafted Playgrounds is a sketchbook of designs based on two very simple premises: Anyone can build a playground and the actual process of building it can be as important as the finished product. It gives the builders (who should certainly include the children for whom it is planned) a chance to shape their environment, to create something to answer their specific needs.

I have tried to provide as wide a range of designs as possible. From the simplest, like the tire swing, which requires only the knot tying the ropes or cables, to fairly complex wood structures, which call for power tools such as drills, saber saws, etc. And I have included enough technical information so that the sketches can be followed literally or can serve as points of departure for the reader's own skills and preferences. Whatever your expertise with tools, there are playground designs to match it.

Friedberg's sketches are beautifully clear and detailed and he's a renowned architect who's won many awards for playgrounds — a fact that may help justify the big price tag on this book. It's definitely worth having if you're going to be tempted into building your own.

feelings

There are lots of interesting, fun ways to get kids involved in exploring and understanding their own feelings. Recognizing, accepting, and learning to express emotions is an important skill that will help kids deal with themselves and others in a healthy, positive way. The following activities are just a few of the possibilities, and are ones with which we've had particular success.

All About Me

I am a girl who gets mad when someone is fresh to me. I like to carve in wood and to draw pictures. I am good in math, and I like math, too. I like to eat spaghetti. My favorite friend is Fredda. I can speak two languages. I am white. I have brown hair, and brown eyes. I like animals, but I don't have one. I am Israelian and I came to United State 6 months ago.

Make several posters that stimulate written responses (graffiti-style) of situations and things that elicit a particular emotion. The posters might be entitled "These things make me feel *bored* . . ." or "Happiness is. . . ."

Choose a Snoopy picture that you like. Think of a time when you felt the way Snoopy feels in your picture. Describe that feeling *without* saying what the mood is. You may also describe your facial expressions or how you move your body, hands, and so on, when you're feeling that way. This can be done either orally or in writing. If the description is written, read it to another person or to your classmates and see if they can identify the mood or feeling from your description.

Choose a feeling (it might help to think of a situation in which you felt that way) and act it out in front of your family or friends. Use exaggerated facial and body expressions — but no talking allowed! See if your audience can identify the feeling you're trying to express.

An activity to really put you in touch with your feelings: wear a sign that expresses your feelings of the day, hour, or moment! For example: "I'm feeling cuddly — HUG ME!" or "I'm feeling grouchy — DON'T BUG ME!"

Establish a "Leave Me Alone" chair or corner for those times when you or your kids just really need to be left alone!

resource and activity books

Here are several books (along with a sampling of their suggested activities) that are excellent resources if you're doing anything with your kids about feelings, values, and decision making. All adults who work with children play many roles, and counseling — helping kids understand themselves and get along with others — is a major one. Neither of us is an expert in this field, but we've found all of these books very helpful.

Anger and the Rocking Chair: Gestalt Awareness with Children
Janet Lederman

The Viking Press
625 Madison Avenue
New York, New York 10022

Frederick Perls, the father of Gestalt awareness, described Janet Lederman as a person "who is in touch with herself and the world and thus can teach children in despair how to get in touch with themselves and their world." Her book is, at once, poetry and guidance and hope. Of her approach, she can say:

We deal with images . . .
with imagination
with imaginary problems.
We need to enter into the real "other" human being . . .
NOT an image of
the teacher
the poverty child
the Spanish-speaking parent
the administrator
the black parent
the white parent
We need to open ourselves . . . to open our vision, to open our senses. We need to be aware of what IS and to relate with what IS (page 17).

This is not so much a contradiction of *Put Your Mother on the Ceiling* (see page 263) as it seems; it is simply the other side of the same concern for helping children make a clear distinction between reality and fantasy. Children imagine. In that mind they invent and dream; in that mind they can also distort their world into a frightening, confusing place. Ms. Lederman shows how adults can help them grow out of confusion.

"What did you do, Mark?"
"I bit you."
"What did I do when you bit me?"
"You spanked me."
I take your hand. You let me. You do not pull away. Together we walk over to the rocking chair. You sit on my lap. We talk. We hug. I pet you. You feel good to me. You are a child. I am an adult. I give you a cloth to wipe the perspiration from your face.
"What do you want to do now, Mark?"
"I don't know" (pages 20 and 21).

The Haunting House
Barbara Hollerorth

Sales Distribution Center
Unitarian Universalist Association
25 Beacon Street
Boston, Massachusetts 02108

This is a multimedia curriculum unit for young children that contains a lot of excellent and unique materials for dealing with feelings. In *The Haunting House* curriculum, children find and remember places that are haunting houses for them, and delight in perceiving what makes a home for others — people, animals, and special things. They create places of "at homeness" — places for solitude and dreaming and intimacy with others — places to go out from and return to in their daily living.

The "leader's guide" to this unit is wordy and unwieldy; but the ideas, activities, and supplementary materials are very special.

Pause now.
Look back on your years of living in homes.
Unlock your memory and imagination.
Close your eyes . . . remember . . .

Remember a hiding place, a crying place, a place with friendly people.
How did you feel there?
What did you do?

Imagination
Zephyros Staff

Zephyros Educational Exchange
1201 Stanyan Street
San Francisco, California 94117

Created by Zephyros as one of their unique publications for adults teaching kids to become liberated, expressive individuals (see general review on page 14), *Imagination* comes on bold.

The authors say it is a guide that "provides a means to stimulate some of the processes by which imagination can be used as a learning tool." It lives up to that claim, but with such an abiding sense of fun and free play that it would be hard to imagine anyone turning it into just another lesson plan. The book features a well-known mime team (Robert Shields and Lorene Yarnell) who on various pages become everything from movie actors to dream figures. With their bodies all the basic emotions are expressed, acted out in a variety of dramatic modes, and at the same time presented as concrete activities. Interestingly enough, there is no heavy stress on dramatic play itself as a form of imaginative expression for kids. Instead, things like poster drawing and dream recording predominate.

Imagination Cards

Included in the book are two pages of ingenious card faces that can be cut out (they should also be mounted on heavier stock) and dealt to players, who arrange them in visual "sentences." They suggest assigning roles for cards such as noun, adjective, verb, and so on, but that is not essential.

It's O.K. to "stretch" the meanings of the various cards . . . for instance, the card with the horn could represent a horn, a jubilant feeling, or even the horns of a mountain goat! The cards with people might represent yourself, or others, or maybe emotions or actions or whatever else they suggest to you. . . .
Use your imagination. . . .

Put Your Mother on the Ceiling: Children's Imagination Games
Richard DeMille

The Viking Press
625 Madison Avenue
New York, New York 10022

DeMille's book presents a series of games from which an adult and a child or an adult and a group of children can take a brief, deliberate plunge into fantasy. Each game is a set of short prescriptions to be read aloud ("Put a girl in one corner of the room / Give her a red hat"). After each slash the reader pauses to allow a child to picture that thing, add a special feature, or tell about something else the image conjures up. These are role-playing activities confined to the theater of the mind, allowing for a spacier kind of imagining than one might elicit from active role playing in a real setting. They help children become quick-change artists, able to switch easily from reality to fantasy, from down here to up there, from one role to another, and back to reality again.

The games deal with feelings almost incidentally, since they are mainly directed toward developing respect for the power of the imagination to play freely with reality and even to create a new, expanded awareness of the dimensions of one's own reality. The applications for such imagining skills are boundless; a scientist's hypothesis, a poet's language, and an artist's new images all emerge from this facility. Yet the book also presents a tool for helping a child recognize a wider spectrum of feelings and find positive acceptance for them.

DEVELOPING INDIVIDUAL VALUES IN THE CLASSROOM

practical activities, teaching ideas, approaches to help students clarify their values

Developing Individual Values in the Classroom
Richard L. Curwin and Geri Curwin

Learning Handbooks
530 University Avenue
Palo Alto, California 94301
$2.50

"Value clarification teaches students a process which they can use to examine their own lives, to take responsibility for their behavior, to articulate clear values and to act in congruence with their values" (page 7).

It sounds like a tall order, but this small book is packed with concrete starting points specially designed for use with elementary age children. The activities include ways of exploring and expressing feelings, making group decisions, comparing values or opinions with others, and integrating values into regular curriculum areas. Each activity is clearly explained, easy to do, and fun for kids! One chapter even contains a series of valuable guidelines for creating your own value clarification activities.

A familiar way of getting to know your values is to make a list of the things you can do *without!* Try making such a list for yourself, your family (maybe you can do without arguments about which TV program to watch — or without any TV at all!), your classroom, your school, or your community.

— adapted from *Happy Birthday to U.S.,*
page 39 (reviewed on page 15)

Make a list of things you and your family or friends get angry about. Then rate each item on the list with numbers from 1 to 5 (a "1" indicating a situation in which you get extremely angry; a "5" for a situation that doesn't anger you at all). As an extension of this activity, role play the situations with a friend and discuss your different responses to the "boiling point" situations.

— adapted from *Developing Individual Values in the Classroom,* page 35

Activity #3: People I Admire
FOCUS:
Most people admire others and emulate qualities they observe in others. Usually the people we most admire are those who are successful at something we would like to do well. Here students will examine qualities they admire in others to identify personal goals for themselves.
MATERIALS:
Paper and pencils.

PROCEDURE:
The students will list admirable qualities they observe in other people. They will then take steps to apply these same qualities to their own goals and behavior.
DIRECTIONS:
1. Have the students list five people they admire. Those listed must be real people, but they can be known personally or be famous people that the student has never met.
2. Next to each person's name, have the students list at least five things that make the person admirable. For example: "My Father: (1) He is considerate; (2) He is brave; (3) He buys me presents; (4) He is responsible; (5) He can be trusted."
3. The students now have created a list of qualities that they admire. Have them circle each quality that they think also applies to themselves. Have them put a star by each quality they would like to incorporate in their own lives.
4. Finally, have them list at least two things they can do to incorporate the starred items, and write a self-contract for each. Example: "Be brave: (1) Tell my mother right away when I break something. (2) Tell my friends I don't want to play when I really don't want to."
5. Later, have the students record their progress and report on their success or failure with self-contracts.
FOOTNOTE:
This activity can be done by first listing various qualities and then asking students to list people who demonstrate each quality. For example: "List three people who are creative, who are brave, who are honest or who are successful."

Activity #5: In My House We . . . .
FOCUS:
A child's definition of himself is derived in large part from the structure and patterns of his family. In this activity the students examine and share with others the rituals that exist in their homes. Differences in ethnic and religious backgrounds will expose the students to the variety of ways their classmates and their families observe certain events.
MATERIALS:
Large sheets of construction paper or newsprint, crayons, paints.
PROCEDURE:
There will be a general discussion of an event all students have experienced with their families, followed by individual students recalling what connotation the situation holds for them. Students will communicate their family patterns through pictures which may be shared with the class.
DIRECTIONS:
1. Ask the students to choose an event (suppertime, bedtime, first snowfall, chores, shopping, etc.) that will be familiar and interesting to the whole class.
2. Have the students consider the family rituals which are part of that specific event for them.
3. On a large piece of paper, perhaps 3' to 5' in length, ask each student to create a picture strip showing his or her family on that occasion.
4. The students are to include the people who would be present and the actions which would probably take place. Each picture need not be precise, but the natural sequence of the event is to be reflected in the placement of the pictures in the strip.
5. Once the picture strips are completed, set up a gallery where the students can tour and discover how their family's rituals are like or unlike their classmates.
QUESTIONS FOR DISCUSSION:
1. What is a ritual?
2. How important are rituals in people's lives? What function do they serve?
3. How important are rituals in your family's life?
4. How different was your family's observance from most of the other students?
5. What can you do to change your family's ritual to make it more fun or interesting?
6. What makes your family's ritual special to you? What changes would you never want made?

Tensions Our Children Live With
Dorothy T. Spoerl, editor

Beacon Press
25 Beacon Street
Boston, Massachusetts 02108

This excellent collection of over fifty open-ended short stories is designed to help parents and teachers comfortably deal with a wide variety of conflict situations that often arise at home or in classrooms. The stories are intended to encourage discussion and/or role playing — helping kids understand their own conflicting feelings, make difficult decisions, accept differences in others, and much more.

This book was written in 1959 and it does not include situations dealing with sex-role stereotyping, nor do the stories do much to counteract such stereotyping. This seems a minor limitation, however, when you realize its unique character — it *does* present a simple, positive way of involving kids in a consideration of the problems they face in their daily social relationships.

Values Clarification: A Handbook of Practical Strategies for Teachers and Students
Sidney B. Simon et al.

Hart Publishing Company
15 West Fourth Street
New York, New York 10012

To fill that gaping hole in school curriculums and perhaps home living rooms where clarification of personal values ought to be experienced, the authors present a collection of concise, practical strategies. Games, discussion, formats, and unique exercises are presented for "making [children] aware of *their own* feelings, *their own* ideas, *their own* beliefs, so that choices and decisions they make are conscious and deliberate, based on *their own* value systems."

One major qualification: you will need to select carefully and make adaptations for working with younger children, since many of the exercises are designed for adolescents.

"I learned . . ." Statements

The teacher (or parent) prepares a chart with the following (or similar) sentence stems. The chart may be posted permanently, or it may be posted just when it is to be used.

I learned that I . . .
I realized that I . . .
I remembered that I . . .
I noticed that I . . .
I discovered that I . . .
I was surprised that I . . .
I was pleased that I . . .
I was not pleased that I . . .

Kids might complete these sentences right after some other values/feelings activity or work with them at the end of a day filled with many activities. They might share their most meaningful statements with others in a group. There is no need for them to explain or defend: emphasis is on the "I."

— adapted from *Values Clarification,* page 163

-ing Name Tags

Each member of a group of kids is given a large index card and a felt-tip marker. On the cards they are asked to write their first name in large letters along with six words ending in "-ing" that tell something about who they are — for example, piano-playing, reading, fun-loving, fighting, baseball-ing, hard-thinking. On the other side they repeat their name and list six words that report specific facts or statistics about themselves — such as neighborhood, height, weight, last name, brothers and sisters, age.

When the cards are complete, kids choose the side they will expose to the group and fasten the tags to their clothes.

Now they are asked to roam around the room reading one another's tags; looking at clothes, eyes, and faces; and asking questions if they feel like it. The leader also participates.

Of course, categories for the descriptive information could be different, or "-ing" words could be replaced by other stems such as *-able, -ful, -ist,* or *-less.*

— adapted from *Values Clarification,* page 174

Value Exploration through Role Playing
Robert C. Hawley

Hart Publishing Company
15 West Fourth Street
New York, New York 10012

The most encouraging statement in the author's foreword is that he avoided role playing for the first fourteen years of his teaching — encouraging, because he follows that with 165 pages of explicit, easy-to-duplicate ideas for role-playing activities that he has worked out with kids.

It is only a partial limitation that his book is geared for older kids, since the lion's share of ideas are easily adaptable for younger ones. Dramatic play comes naturally to the young anyway, as witness cops and robbers.

Hawley takes care of some of the threats in the introduction, noting that people who fear a lack of control over whatever emotional forces get unleashed in role-playing situations are forgetting how much more dangerous playgrounds can be in that regard. He thinks the biggest deterrent is really that people just haven't known the techniques for utilizing role playing as a classroom tool. If so, his book is a full-scale attempt to overcome that ignorance.

Impromptu Role Plays

What's impromptu is the role playing; your knowledge of how to structure it and the kids' sense of how to do it are not. I do not mean that it is hard to get into. The following method is simple and adaptable to innumerable situations.

The situation is that Sam has been trying to get permission from his parents to play outside after dinner. He asks, "What should I do when my mom and dad start bringing up other things and don't answer my question?"

The leader says, "You be your mother, and I'll be you. Show us what you mean."

During the role playing that follows, the leader might expand participation by saying, "Anyone want to help Sam speak for his mother?" or "I need some help. How would one of you answer if you were Sam?"

Generally, these impromptus should be brief and informal. The purpose is not necessarily to solve problems within the role play, but rather to make the situation concrete so that the discussion that follows will be more directly helpful.

— adapted from *Value Exploration through Role Playing,* pages 60–61

breaking down stereotypes

Talking with kids about feelings and values will help them appreciate human similarities and differences. They will learn, for example, that all people feel angry but express anger in different ways. They should begin to appreciate the importance to their own values and choices of their differing cultural, racial, and/or religious backgrounds. It is impossible to overemphasize the necessity for kids to have experiences that can lead to a feeling of self-worth, as well as to an acceptance of others.

Many people have put a lot of thought and effort into ways to make such experiences accessible to children. There are a growing number of books being written for children that attempt to portray traditionally stereotyped peoples in realistic ways. Even TV programs and commercials have begun to take into account that not all of us are from upper-middle-class, white suburban families with a standardized life-style.

It would be beyond the scope of our book to direct your attention to all the resources that might deal with one or more of our cultural, racial, or religious minorities. Check to see if there is an agency in your area that might have information pertinent to your particular concerns (such as a federal Office of Economic Opportunity or a commission against discrimination at the state level). The most important thing is to help your kids understand and break down their own stereotyped attitudes while developing a healthy, positive view of the rich variety of human experience.

On the next page are some resources and activities related to sex-role stereotyping, a special concern of ours and one that affects boys and girls of all racial, economic, and ethnic backgrounds.

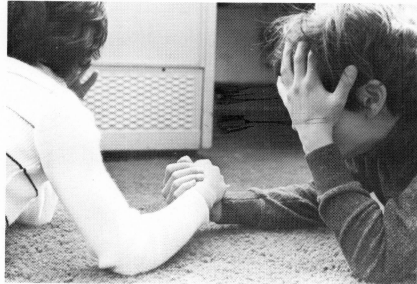

One of many bouts in which Jenny and Andrew tested their arm-wrestling strength — they discovered that Jenny invariably won right-handed matches, while Andrew won left-handed ones!

Mommies at Work
Eve Merriam

Scholastic Book Services
904 Sylvan Avenue
Englewood Cliffs, New Jersey 07632
75¢

Women at Work
Betty Medsger

Sheed and Ward
475 Fifth Avenue
New York, New York 10017
$7.95

Kids respond enthusiastically and wholeheartedly to visual stimuli. These are just two of the many books about women; their similarity and special advantage for kids lie in their extensive use of pictures to show the many kinds of jobs that women do. *Mommies at Work* is written for young children; its simple text and engaging pic-tures show women in a dozen or more occupations. *Women at Work* is "a photo-graphic documentary" directed at people of all ages. It contains commentaries about their work by the women pictured (well over a hundred) — doing everything from dancing to catching lobsters! Both books are available in paperback.

Nonsexist Curricular Materials for Elementary Schools
Laurie Olsen Johnson, editor

The Feminist Press
Box 334
Old Westbury, New York 11568
$5

This is a package of printed materials gathered by the Clearinghouse on Wom-en's Studies, an educational project of the Feminist Press. About one-third of it is de-voted to general information for teachers — "consciousness razors," checklists for evaluating standard curriculum materials, statistical information on the status of women in the United States, and more. The remainder of the packet details spe-cific activities and projects for classroom use, including a student workbook for upper elementary grades and a "student bibliography" of children's books with strong female leads.

Sex Role Stereotypes
Sandy Daitch, Louise Lansberry, Linda Stern, and Jean Williams

Teacher's Guide
c/o Louise Lansberry
49 Parker Street
Watertown, Massachusetts 02172
$3

Here is an extremely valuable resource for teachers who would like some concrete ideas on how to combat sex-role stereotyp-ing in their classrooms. The guide was de-veloped by a group of women in the Bos-ton area who have been and/or are teachers. It includes a few articles on sex-role stereotyping, a checklist of "sexist at-titudes and expectations of teachers," a handy list of teacher resources, and de-tailed lesson plans. The suggested activi-ties are geared to elementary age children — here are a few (from pages 26–31):

Have kids talk about their own families' expectations of them as a boy or girl; do their parents expect different things of them as a boy/girl than they do of their sister/brother?

Examine magazine ads; what are men and women doing? What would a Martian, for example, conclude about the abilities, interests, roles, etc., for us male and female earthlings if this were all the infor-mation they had to go on?

Ask a girl what she wants to be when she grows up. Then ask what she would want to be if she were a boy. Do the same with a boy. Ask why there is a difference in expectations or desires if the difference exists.

Give each child a news story from the newspaper. Have each child write down the descriptions used for men and those used for women. Compare the descrip-tions.

Have kids make up their own non-sexist commercials for household products, toys or games.

Read and discuss nursery rhymes and fairy tales. Have children consider alterna-tive endings to "they lived happily ever after." Have children re-write and act out de-stereotyped versions of the stories. (E.g., portray Cinderella as responding in anger to an unreasonable demand, danc-ing with many men at the ball, and not marrying the prince.)

Make up [math] problems that provide alternative roles for both boys and girls, e.g., girls building something, boys going shopping or cooking.

Have kids talk about their toys, starting with toys they played with at an earlier age; discuss what these toys were/are teaching them to do, to be interested in, to see about themselves.

beginnings

*"When you think how things are —
and you don't know how they began —
and how they will go on —
and you don't know whether they
    will end —
then you can go on thinking and
    thinking —
and never stop."*

*Perhaps as long as there have been
stars in the sky and people who could look
up and see them, men have been wondering. As long as there have been sunrises
and sunsets, . . . seeds growing into flowers and trees. . . . As long as babies have
been born and old people have died, and
there have been people who loved them.*

*Some of these stories about beginnings
were told again and again for years before
anyone was able to write them down.
Some were lettered on clay or chiseled
into stone. Some were written with pens
on long rolls of sheepskin or papyrus.
Some were told by people who never
learned to write at all. They were told by
the grandfathers and grandmothers. Children, when they grew up, told the same
stories to their children.*

*Sometimes they sang the stories.
Sometimes they danced them in pantomime. Sometimes they painted pictures
of the stories on the walls of their caves or
temples.*

*All the stories in this book, except the
ones from the scientists of today, were
told before telescopes and microscopes
had been invented. No people had
explored the earth far from its own shores.
The ancient people of Iceland knew nothing of the sunny plains of Africa or Australia. The Japanese thought their eight
small islands surrounded by an ocean
were the whole earth. . . .*

*In order to appreciate these stories, one
needs to try to put himself imaginatively
into these different small worlds. In what
kind of country and climate did the people
live? How did they keep alive? What dangers did they have to face? What sort of
picture had they made in their minds of the
shape of the earth and sky?*

*Each story is different from any of the
others, yet there are some important ways
in which they are alike. Why is this? What
are the questions which are not yet fully
answered?* [They may never be answered
at all, but] *we must "go on thinking and
thinking and never stop"* (Introduction).*

*Sophia Lyon Fahs and Dorothy T. Spoerl,
Beginnings: Earth, Sky, Life, Death. Copyright ©
1958 Starr King Press; copyright © 1937, 1938
Beacon Press. Used by permission of Unitarian
Universalist Association.

BEGINNINGS:
Earth, Sky, Life, Death

By SOPHIA LYON FAHS & DOROTHY T. SPOERL

ILLUSTRATED WITH PHOTOGRAPHS AND DRAWINGS

Myths, legends, and scientific narratives of how things began —
from a score of ancient and modern cultures, races, and religions.

*Beacon Press
25 Beacon Street
Boston, Massachusetts 02108*

I was first introduced to this very special
book more than ten years ago, and am so
pleased to be able now to share it. *Beginnings* is a collection of stories — fifteen
myths from all over the world, plus three
"stories from the scientists." Each of the
myths is preceded by a short introduction
to the people and land from which the story
came.

Reading these stories aloud with your
children is a beautiful way of sharing an
understanding and appreciation of the variety of ways in which people have tried to
answer the eternal question of "how it all
began."

language

language

general resources

There are lots of whole "language arts programs" around, in an attempt to package the acquisition of reading and writing skills. No kit of materials can do more than extend a teacher's resources, however, and only a few are recommendable — all of them relatively expensive and school oriented.

The following are kits and materials that at least encourage a broad, often interdisciplinary, view of language arts. They include a wide variety of concrete ways to involve kids in working and playing with language, are visually appealing, and are not confined to dealing with skills as ends in themselves.

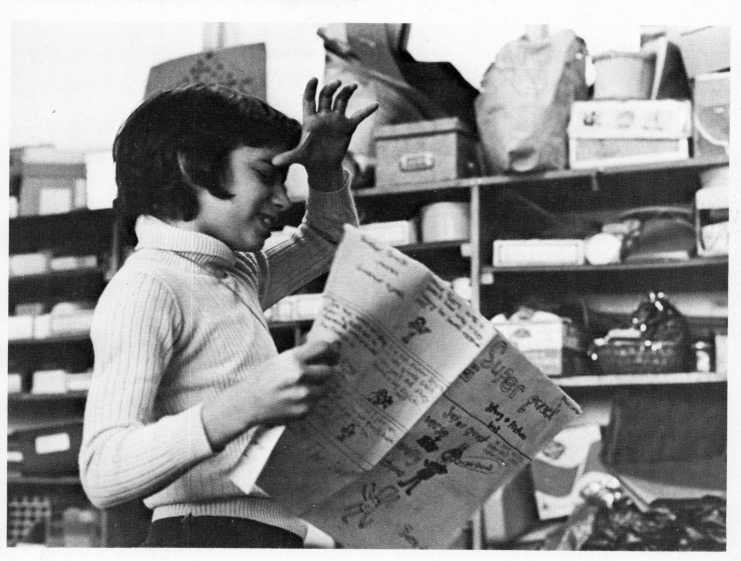

People Projects

Addison-Wesley Publishing Company
2725 Sand Hill Road
Menlo Park, California 94025

These are 120 colorful activity cards, divided into three sets according to age levels. The ideas are exciting, although the cards are an awkward size (approximately 10" × 13") for classroom use.

The Amazing Life Games Theater

Houghton Mifflin Company
1 Beacon Street
Boston, Massachusetts 02107

This is a kit of activity cards, short films, and miscellaneous materials geared to very young children — preschool through first grade.

Interaction

Houghton Mifflin Company
1 Beacon Street
Boston, Massachusetts 02107

Colorful activity cards, books, films, cassettes, and games are the major components of this series of kits for grades kindergarten through twelve. The program and materials were developed as an extension of Moffett's *A Student-Centered Language Arts Curriculum* (see review at right).

A Student-Centered
Language Arts Curriculum
Grades K-6:
A Handbook for Teachers

James Moffett

A Student-Centered Language Arts Curriculum
James Moffett

Houghton Mifflin Company
1 Beacon Street
Boston, Massachusetts 02107
$5.20

This is a handbook for teachers — a curriculum guide that integrates speaking, listening, reading, writing, and acting out. It is an excellent resource and has become almost a classic in its field, well worth careful reading. It was perhaps the first book to deal with communication skills and language development as a whole process — a process that should *actively* involve children in a wide variety of language experiences.

The multimedia kit *Interaction* was developed on the basis of the principles and guidelines described in this book.

drama

We have traditionally put so much stress on teaching children how to write that we have tended to ignore the oral side of children's early language development. Yet by that neglect we often reap poor writing. Teaching writing as a set of skills all by itself doesn't work, because writing is just a code form of the language that kids have been hearing and speaking in many different ways for years before they put a pencil to paper. Teaching language skills, including written expression, has to start from this oral experience if it is to be effective.

We have also come to recognize that young children find *acting out* as natural a form of expression as speaking. So, oral and dramatic communication go together as the place to start from.

with puppets

Puppetry combines oral and dramatic expression in a way that is ideally suited to children. Whether they are making puppets, improvising with them, or producing whole plays, kids are controlling a powerful medium literally at their fingertips.

The big key is *movable* puppets. A construction-paper face on the end of a stick is a puppet, but it is not a very effective actor.

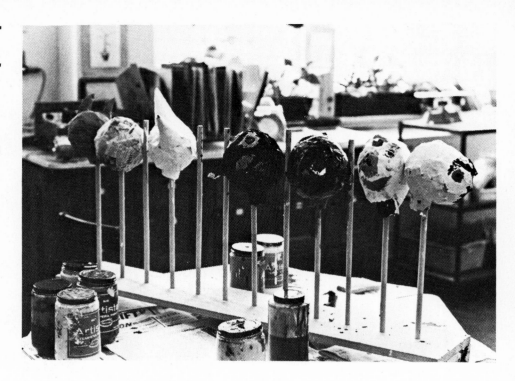

making them

You might start with *paper-bag puppets,* because they are easy to make and they have a built-in movable mouth. (See page 208.)

Really big-mouthed but nevertheless appealing puppets can be made from paper plates folded in half.

1. By stapling half of a second plate to the top of the upper jaw but leaving it free at the back you can make a convenient pocket for the operator's four fingers. (The thumb goes underneath.)

2. Add things to the mouth first, stand-up or bulging eyes, ear extensions, nose, teeth, etc. Paper plates are also easy to color with crayons, paint, or felt-tip markers.

3. Then attach a cloth sleeve to the lower jaw to provide a body-costume for the puppet and a means of hiding the operator's arm. This can be sewn or stapled in place.

There is a nice similarity between children and *sock puppets:* they can both use whole bodies to express themselves.

1. Find a loosely knit sock roomy enough to fit the operator's arm and hand easily, and cut a slit across the foot where the mouth should be.

2. Cut a piece of felt to fit inside the mouth, folding it at the midpoint first. Stitch it inside. The four fingers will slide into the upper jaw, and you can glue a piece of cardboard under the lower jaw to make a firm surface for the thumb.

3. Add the trimmings to give it character: buttons for eyes; various yarns stitched in for hair, eyebrows, mustaches, and ears; colored felts, sequins, lace, and dress accessories for other special features.

More sophisticated puppets are created by turning a sock inside out and stuffing the toe (head) with cotton wool.

I. Make a tube of heavy rolled paper about five inches long and wide enough to fit the first and second fingers. Place the tube so about half of it will be inside the head and the rest will be sticking down into the body. Tie the sock closely around the midpoint of the tube.

2. Cut two slits for armholes where arms should be and sew on small cloth tubes. (The puppet is manipulated by placing first and second fingers inside the head, thumb in one arm, and the other two fingers in the second arm.)

3. Add trimmings and costume.

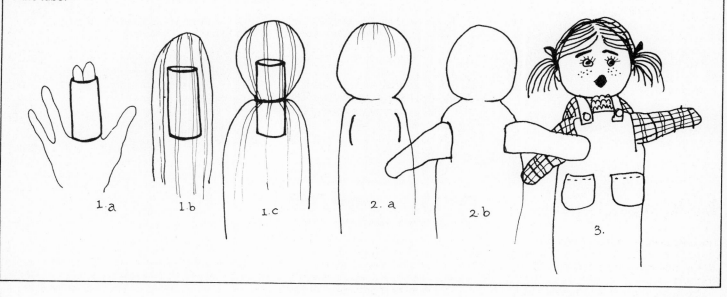

puppet plays

The next big key to puppeteering is to really *do* something with it! Too often, kids have a ball making them, clown around with them a little bit, and then the puppets end up in Mom's bottom drawer. Make sure your kids have a stage set up and learn some of the basic conventions so they can get past the giggling and really let their characters speak for them. There are three main ways to perform:

Conversational dialogues or skits by puppets representing friends, members of the family, or combinations of stock characters are an invaluable way for kids to express hidden feelings and work out resolutions to everyday human hassles.

The rich fantasy world in which most kids spend a lot of time can come to life in *puppet-show stories* they create for themselves. Fully developed plays call for learning characterization, scriptwriting, and production techniques, and draw out a wide range of talents or skills.

The small scale of a puppet theater makes the business of producing *sophisticated plays* much easier to handle than doing them on a regular stage with human actors. Here is certainly one of the finest ways to foster oral language skills, teach dramatic form, or make history come alive. The Greek myths became unforgettable delights to my son's fourth grade class as a result of their puppet dramatizations.

resources

Making Puppets Come Alive
Larry Engler and Carol Fijan

Taplinger Publishing Company
200 Park Avenue South
New York, New York 10003
$9.95

This is one of those lucid, beautifully wrought books that can be authored only by people thoroughly grounded in their art. It is not written for children's work and it is not an introductory manual; yet it is certainly a book to use if you're going beyond one puppet show. All the basic movements and techniques are simply explained and clearly illustrated. Well recommended by professional puppeteers.

The Puppetry Journal
Puppeteers of America

The Puppetry Journal
2015 Novem Drive
Fenton, Missouri 63026
$1.25 each
$12.00 adult subscription
and membership in
Puppeteers of America

This bimonthly put out by the major U.S. puppeteering organization is a useful aid if you're going whole hog on puppets. Besides reporting all the workshops, exhibitions, education programs, and events in the world of puppetry, it publishes an annotated book list (including compilations of plays) available from the Puppetry Store.

The Puppetry Store
Director: Marie Samanisky

3500 Tyler, NE
Minneapolis, Minnesota 55418

A national source for books and other items of interest to the puppeteer.

Puppet Making through the Grades
Grizella H. Hopper

Sterling Publishing Company
419 Park Avenue South
New York, New York 10016
$5.75

This may not be the best available for sheer techniques of making puppets, but it is good. The many excellent photos showing examples of each type of puppet made by children are its most recommendable

feature. The directions are cumbersome; I'd like to have something with steps laid out in simple, diagrammatic form. Sterling has another called *Puppet-Making* for $3.50 that might be worth trying.

How to Be a Puppeteer
Eleanor Boylan

E. P. Dutton and Company
201 Park Avenue South
New York, New York 10003
$4.95

Written so that older children can read it, this book is an excellent introduction to the art of puppeteering (though not to puppet making). The author talks a lot about how to choose plays or design your own and includes half a dozen actual scripts. Write to her, 142 Pine Grove Avenue, Newton, MA 02162, for other collections she has printed herself.

---

with people

When you mention drama, some people immediately envision an entire production replete with stage, costumes, memorized lines, and harried directors. I've tried it a few times, and now I would rather not do it.

That's all right, because it turns out that what is really valuable for kids can be done in a much simpler way. Improvisations, games, role playing, awareness exercises, and the like can be fitted into any context and designed to foster many different skills. If you understand language skills as broadly including perception, self-awareness, thinking, and expression, then it should be clear how it is that kids can utilize dramatic techniques to increase their language powers. In fact, if all of us learned enough about acting things out, we would be much better communicators. (See also the movement activities on pages 244–245.)

Found Theatre
Carolyn R. Fellman

Children's Museum
The Jamaicaway
Boston, Massachusetts 02130
$4

Here is the right book for learning how to do kids' plays that won't leave you feeling used. Thank you, Carolyn Fellman. It is not yet beautifully put together (the author says it is "still in its formative stages"), but

we urge you to locate a copy. The book is full of ideas for creating theater out of what's available, and that covers children's own unique imaginings as well as props and costumes scrounged from trash bins or grandmothers' attics. She believes in devoting plenty of time to improvisational games and movement activities before attempting bigger productions and the book offers some good suggestions for working those out. If you can't find a copy, write the author at 313 South Aurora Street, Ithaca, NY 14850.

Smiles, Nods, and Pauses
Dorothy Grant Hennings

Citation Press
Library and Trade Division
Scholastic Magazines
50 West 44th Street
New York, New York 10036
$3.95

Subtitled *Activities to Enrich Children's Communication Skills,* Hennings's book is based firmly on the point of view that nonverbal communication is as important as the verbal kind. She has obviously had enough experience to make a careful selection of exercises that work well with all the elementary ages.

From what we have seen, it is certainly the most comprehensive and aptly written handbook available for "acting out" ideas. There are tons of suggestions for doing pantomime and predramatic exercises; acting out stories, songs, book episodes; telling original stories or structuring improvisations; role playing; working with sounds, records, films, and TV commercials; investigating features of body language; and developing other powerful means of telling by showing. A most valuable book to own and use.

Improvisation for the Theater
Viola Spolin

Northwestern University Press
1735 Benson Avenue
Evanston, Illinois 60201

Until recently, this book has been the best known and most widely used guide to dramatic improvisation. Now that the field has blossomed there are others to choose from, including several more appropriate for younger children or for the classroom specifically (see *Smiles, Nods, and Pauses,* above). Spolin's is an intense, professional approach to acting techniques leading up to full-scale productions, yet because she is devoted to teaching amateurs how to loosen up and discover themselves, her exercises have wide usefulness beyond training for the theater alone.

If you are doing more than tentative experimentation you will find the book a gold mine of intriguing games, role-playing exercises, and other improvisational techniques adaptable to your own group of kids and their needs.

Make a flow chart of things your hand usually does. It might look like this.

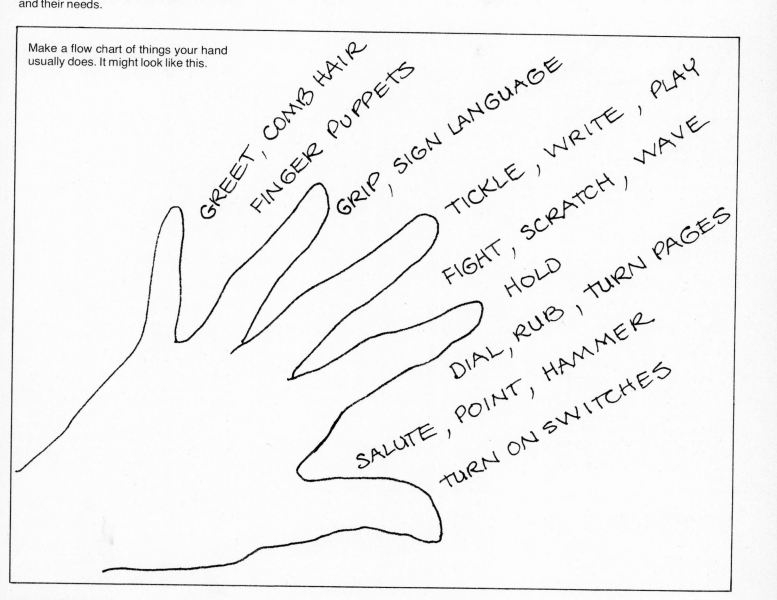

GREET, COMB HAIR

FINGER PUPPETS

GRIP, SIGN LANGUAGE

TICKLE, WRITE, PLAY

FIGHT, SCRATCH, WAVE

HOLD

DIAL, RUB, TURN PAGES

SALUTE, POINT, HAMMER

TURN ON SWITCHES

one hand

As a way of exploring the body's potential for expressing things, find out what your hand alone can do.

Make picture books about one-handed and two-handed activities.

Take one hand gesture and enlarge it into a whole-body dance movement.

Then try new ways of looking at and doing things with your hands:

Make up a play for two hands, using them as you would puppets.

Observe the various hand gestures people use for nonverbal messages and make a pictorial record of these.

Invent a sign language.

Collect a series of photographs of people's hands from magazines, your own camera, or sources like the *Family of Man*. Think about and describe their differences. Do the same for animal "hands."

expressive movement

Expressive movement is dance and drama at the same time. It is a way of teaching kids that the kind of body language that comes naturally to them can become a very explicit form of communication. Do it in short stints only and don't make a big production out of it, as a general rule. Some simple movements are suggested on this page; use them for themselves or as preliminaries to other kinds of drama.

Lying on the floor, how many ways can you move your legs?

How can you express "something that smells rotten" with movement?

If a tree could walk, what would its movement look like?

How do people who think they are perfect move?

How does a machine that presses juice out of apples move?

How does a baby move? How does the same person move when he or she has become very old?

How does a loud sound move? A quiet sound?

What is a movement that shows how thunder sounds?

Role-Playing Situations

Done with sensitivity, role playing is a powerful tool for revealing (among other things) the tension between what people feel and what they convey on the surface. Invent a conflict situation and print opposing roles on separate cards. For instance:

Card A, Giver: You are giving a birthday gift to a very good friend. You picked it feeling it would very much please him or her. Present your gift expressing your eagerness.

Card B, Receiver: Your best friend is giving you a birthday gift. Express your immediate appreciation. But when you open it, you find you don't like it. Your friend is looking at you, waiting to see how you like it. You try to give your reaction in a way that does not hurt the friend's feelings.

The players should start acting without any preliminary consultation or knowledge of the opposing role. Words are allowed.

— adapted from *Smiles, Nods, and Pauses,* page 111

Face Plays

It is surprising how much can be conveyed by the face alone. Try using eyes, nose, and mouth to mimic a pot of oatmeal cooking, taffy being pulled, or a sponge filling with water. Actors will have to stretch more than their imaginations.

Single-Prop Solutions

Build a series of scenes of simple stories around the use of a single object, for instance, a tin can. You are all on a bus trip but run out of gas in the middle of nowhere. Use the can to remedy the situation. This activity also makes a good story-starter for creative writing.

Scene Shift

Act out a story, a poem, or episode, but keep changing the setting and make the action correspond. For instance, Hansel and Gretel in a city, in the jungle, on a small island.

Charades

The audience tries to guess the exact phrase, title, or simple word from the pantomimed clues of an actor. The whole group should first agree on some common signals to communicate the category of the words, number of words, number of syllables, and so on.

Action Words

Write a sentence where everyone can see it; for instance, "The poor man _____ into the room." Distribute cards on which various words that would fill the blank are written (*crept, hobbled, dashed, marched, crawled, sneaked, fell*). Actors take turns performing the action while others try to guess at the word. Adjust the language to fit the age you're working with.

Portraying Feelings

Make feeling-word cards printed with such words as *confused, excited, tired, bored, anxious, angry,* or *dreamy*. Members of the group watch the actor's portrayal of the feeling and try to guess what it is. Play it a second time through with the rule that actors may use only facial expressions to convey the feeling.

Pantomiming Simple Actions

Any of these actions can be pantomimed directly, but the actors can refine their non-verbal skills by first performing the actual motions with the props and carefully observing their actions. Examples:

peeling a banana and eating it
taking off tight-fitting boots
threading a needle
throwing and catching a ball
playing jacks
cracking and eating a nut

Comedy Skits

Put together a grab bag of comic situations printed on slips of paper. Examples:

someone trying to drive away a
    bothersome mosquito
someone trying to walk on slippery ice
someone trying not to sneeze while
    threading a needle
someone trying to open a locked door
    when both arms are loaded with
    packages

Volunteers take a slip from the bag and pantomime it with exaggerated motions.

poetry

Poetry writing with kids presents an ideal challenge to adults who believe that children's learning involves a lot more than basic skills. Here's a door into the richly imaginative world that schools often shut out of childhood, or so the argument goes. In recent years the challenge has been met repeatedly. Highly creative teachers' published accounts of techniques they used and the poems that resulted have increased the confidence of believers.

Patience, freedom from narrow conventions, and willingness to take down a lot of dictation in the early stages are principles universally advocated.

Some of the books and a smattering of especially useful techniques are noted on page 282.

Playing with my friends
Ball, tag and hide-and-go-seek
It's sneaky and fun!

Timmy

Wishes, Lies, and Dreams

Rose, Where Did You Get That Red?
Kenneth Koch

Vintage Books
Random House
201 East 50th Street
New York, New York 10022
$2.45 each

As a member of the Teachers and Writers Collaborative, Kenneth Koch taught poetry writing to elementary school kids in New York City. Both these books come out of that experience. They are largely collections of poems the kids wrote after Koch showed them how to find ways of putting what they cared about into their own fresh metaphors and rhythms. The results are proof of the techniques: these poems are never frivolous or stale.

In the first book the poems came from a series of assignments that played on simple themes and set a few easy rules, like using a color in every line or beginning every line with "I wish." Clearly, it would be tempting to adopt these formulas in a mechanical way and to ignore the sensitive teaching that must go with them.

The author's lengthy introduction provides some more clues about how he elicited these high-quality poems. For *Rose, Where Did You Get That Red?* he tried a different approach: reading selected works from great poets and helping children respond to them in a way that suggested new forms, styles, and language for their own imaginings. The results are no less successful, and in fact even more impressive since they demonstrate that young kids have a surprising ability to identify with and enjoy adult poetry.

Children Write Poetry: A Creative Approach
Flora J. Arnstein

Dover Publications
180 Varick Street
New York, New York 10014
$2.50

This was actually written before the current enthusiasm for children's poetry had surfaced, but it is based on the same assumptions and contains a lot of very solid advice from a teacher who knew what she was doing. She is especially clear about the need for patient use of many different techniques to foster children's confidence in their poetic "voices." As with acting out, no one should expect to see innermost fears and private fantasies in the first few attempts. In the same way, inhibitions about the mere act of writing down have to be overcome by sensitive maneuvering. Ms. Arnstein's book helps to show the way.

These exercises were designed by those clever souls in the Teachers and Writers Collaborative while working in New York schools. (See page 288 for review.)

List of Words
Write a list of words on the board; try to make an interesting and colorful combination. One writer chose: bulldog, headache, lamp shade, pole-vault, concept, baloney, Alabama, planet, wiggle, and, running, however, angel, iceberg, filing cabinet. Lists may be longer or shorter. Have the kids weave as many of these words as possible into a poem or story.

Mistranslations
Offer a poem in a foreign language (say, German) to be "translated" according to whatever the sounds and rhythms suggest. It may be best to have the child do this orally, with you as a scribe, so as to make the act of playing with associations that much easier. You can get interesting results, partly because the child is working with a rigid structure and yet is tantalized into playing wildly with language.

HÄLFTE DES LEBENS

Mit gelben Birnen hänget
Und voll mit wilden Rosen
Das Land in den See,
Ihr holden Schwäne,
Und trunken von Küssen
Tunkt ihr das Haupt
Ins heilignüchterne Wasser.

Weh mir, wo nehm' ich, wenn
Es Winter ist, die Blumen, und wo
Den Sonnenschein
Und Schatten der Erde?
Die Mauern stehn
Sprachlos und kalt, im Winde
Klirren die Fahnen.

(Original German, by Hölderlin)

HALF DAY LEAVE
(Mistranslation)

The General burned his hand,
And all the windmills roared.
The land was called Dense.
He had been helping Haup Schwane,
And a trunk fell on General Kussen's head.
The trunk hit Haup Schevane, too,
They fell in Heilgnuchterne Lake.

We admire General Kussen they would say,
When winter came he died, and all the people cried.
He had been shot by Captain Pot.
The day of his funeral the people all cried,
They had been sad because he had died.

Joey Perkins
Grade 5

Reprinted from *The Whole Word Catalogue*, p. 43, by permission of Teachers and Writers Collaborative, © 1972.

Here are a bunch of formula-style approaches that are good icebreakers but should be used as sparingly as you would any other neat gimmicks. Belabor them, and you end up right back with the dead poetry kids write when they think it consists of nothing more than rhyming words and doggerel.

Color: Write a poem using a different color in every line.

I seem to be: Has the form "I seem to be (a) _____, but I'm really (a) _____."

Lies: Write a poem with a lie in every line. Write a poem with a whopping lie in every line!

I remember: Write a poem in which every line begins "I remember. . . ."

Dreams of the future: Write a poem in which every line begins with "I am going to. . . ."

I wish: Write a poem in which every line begins with "I wish. . . ."

Comparison poems: "_____ is like _____." E.g., Thunder is like bowling. Clouds are like a feather.

I used to be: Has the form "I used to be (a) _____ but now I'm (a) _____."

Kids you suspect of having poetry in them may be inspired by hearing the published work of other young poets. Here are two popular books.

The Me Nobody Knows, edited by Steven Joseph, 1969
Prose is included too, but everything in it has the poignant impact of "Children's Voices from the Ghetto" (subtitle). Material is by high school age kids.

Miracles, edited by Richard Lewis
This is a book of poems written by English-speaking children of all ages in countries around the world. The selections are short but beautifully expressive; the imagery is often striking.

writing

Both my parents have a love of words that they've successfully communicated to me. I vividly remember playing all kinds of word games, telling "round-the-table stories" after supper, and listening to shaggy-dog stories; even now I enjoy doing crossword puzzles with my mother and engaging my father in semantic "discussions"!

Young children have a natural fascination for letters and the written word that should be encouraged throughout their growing years. Writing is one of the primary forms of communication and a rich, enjoyable involvement with words is a key to its development. We hope the activities and resources in these pages will help you to stimulate your children's love of language, enrich their vocabularies, and unleash their creative use of words through written as well as oral expression.

alphabets and letterforms

Here are a few interesting ways to play with letters. There are numerous alphabet collections in book form (ask for a Letraset catalog at your local stationery or art supply store) — use them to explore the art of lettering. You and your children might like to start a notebook in which to copy down your favorite alphabets or create your own.

Make a rubbing of letters (or words) found on buildings, gravestones, manhole covers, or wherever. Collect a whole alphabet of rubbings.

Make a geometric design by repeating one letter over and over again — rubber stamps work well for this activity. (See page 289 for source of alphabet stamps.)

Look for letterforms in the environment — how many can you find? Take photos of all the O-shapes in your house, classroom, or neighborhood.

Choose a letter and cut out as many forms of it as you can find in magazines or newspapers; make a collage.

Choose a word and write or draw its initial letter in a way that expresses the word's meaning.

Choose any letter and make it become a part of something that begins with that letter. Can you make a whole alphabet this way?

BBBBBBBBB
BBBBBBBBB
BBBBBBBBB
BBBBBBBBB

boring

electric

Choose a word and write it so that you show its meaning by the style or form in which it is written.

CLOUDY

spidery

FAT

LOOK

Take a Handful of Letters
Tammy Orvell

Education Development Center
55 Chapel Street
Newton, Massachusetts 02160
$2.50

This book is about printing with homemade letters. It tells how to make four different kinds of printing sets and includes suggestions for their use.

There is a tradition that when a Jewish child was introduced to study, he was given a slate covered with honey. As he licked the honey, the alphabet appeared. So the child learned to associate learning with sweetness. This book is intended to be in that tradition (Introduction, page 3).

Take a Handful of Letters contains a delightful assortment of activities for children's exploration of letters and words through printing, mostly with rubber stamps. They are sure to spark your own imagination as well as your child's!

From *Take a Handful of Letters*, p. 16, reprinted by permission of Education Development Center, © 1974.

Alphabets and Images
Maggie Gordon

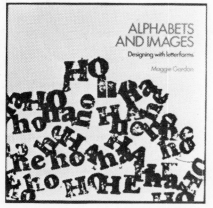

Charles Scribner's Sons
597 Fifth Avenue
New York, New York 10017
$7.95

Here is an exciting and fresh approach to a few of the many interesting and varied ways of looking at letterforms. Although geared to adults with a special interest in graphic art, its very special blend of activity ideas and visual impact makes it ideal for encouraging children to experiment with letter and word forms.

playing with words

Word games can be played anywhere, indoors or out, at any time or season, with any number of people, by young and old alike, and with no special equipment! They are fun to play around the dinner table, en route to anywhere, at parties, in lieu of TV watching, in the classroom.

Games to Improve Your Child's English
Abraham Hurwitz and Arthur Goddard

Simon and Schuster
630 Fifth Avenue
New York, New York 10020
$7.95

For parents as well as teachers, *Games to Improve Your Child's English* is the best collection of language activities we've seen. It contains over two hundred carefully selected word games — puns, conundrums, rhymes, puzzles — reflecting the endless variety of language. The fun of playing these games with your children will awaken their eagerness to learn, to think, to imagine, to listen, and to express their ideas. An additional incentive to add this excellent reference book to your personal library is that it is newly available in paperback.

talking games

There are numerous paperback word game and puzzle books available — look for those that suit your own needs and/or interests. Here are a few of my favorite word games, which don't even require paper and pencil!

Hink-Pinks are two rhyming words, usually in adjective-noun combination (e.g., "fat cat"), which players have to guess when given either synonyms, such as "obese feline," or a general meaning clue: "What you'll get if you feed your kitten too much." A two-syllable rhymed pair is a Hinky-Pinky; here's a Hinkety-Pinkety — "an evil preacher."

"I Spy with My Little Eye . . . something beginning with *S.*" This is a simple game for any number of people. The group needs to look for things in view that begin with the given letter — narrowing down until the exact item is discovered.

Pig Latin is a kind of code language that is fun to use and decipher. Remove the initial letter or sound of each word and add it with "ay" at the end of the word (use *y* with initial vowels). Ityay illway oundsay ikelay isthay! Try creating other code languages with your kids.

Riddles are always a favorite with children — those that involve puns are some of the best word puzzles around, especially when they're invented spontaneously. Whenever, as children, we asked to be excused (from the dinner table), my father invariably wanted to know, "What did you do wrong?" Groan! Here's a more typical riddle-pun: "What has four wheels and flies?" Answer — a garbage truck, of course!

Willie Words are particularly good for largish groups. "Willie likes pillows but not beds, grass but not flowers, tennis but not golf. . . ." Give a series of Willie's likes (double-letter words) and dislikes until someone discovers the pattern; rather than give it away, that person should join in giving the clues. Try making up other letter-clue likes and dislikes.

Ghost is a game for two or more players — especially fun on long car trips. First player says a letter; other players add to it, one letter at a time, in turn — having an unfinished word in mind, but trying *not* to make a word! When forced to end a word (e.g., S-T-O-R-), you get a "G" but may continue playing, starting another word, until you become a full "GHOST." If you can't think of a word with the combination of letters already given, you may challenge the previous player — if he/she *does* have a legitimate word in mind, you get a GHOST letter; if not, he/she gets one.

commercial games

There are a whole bunch of commercial word games on the market these days. The following are a few "old standbys" that would enhance any home or classroom games shelf; all are available in toy and department stores throughout the country.

Anagrams
These are an assortment of wooden letter squares for making words; I use them mostly for helping kids create their own crossword puzzles.

Probe
The object is to guess opponents' words, letter by letter, accumulating points as you go along — small letter cards are laid out face down on a plastic grid.

Scrabble
Players create their own words with wooden letter squares in a crossword fashion on a special playing board — many children like the standard version better than Scrabble for Juniors.

Spill and Spell
Perquackey
Crossword Cubes
All three of these use letter dice that are thrown and then arranged to make words, usually within a certain limited time.

two favorite word games

Here are two of my favorite paper-and-pencil word games. They are really only suitable for children aged nine and up, although younger children with rich vocabularies and a love of words would also enjoy them.

Dictionary
— a game for a group of five to eight people

Materials:
dictionary, paper, and pencils

Directions:
1. Pass out paper and pencil to each player.
2. One person looks through dictionary until he/she finds a word that no one in the group knows.
3. Dictionary-person then says and spells chosen word. Each person in group writes it down with a made-up definition; dictionary-person writes down actual definition.
4. All papers are passed to dictionary-person, who reads all definitions aloud (with as straight a face as possible!).

EXAMPLE: "muliebrity"

of or pertaining to mules
a disease of the pancreas characterized by inflammation and discoloration
state of being muliebrious
womanly nature or quality
the quality of extreme stubbornness

5. Each person in group votes on which definition he or she thinks is correct.

6. SCORING: 1 point for correct guess; 1 point for each time your definition is chosen as correct by another player.

Notes:
Dictionary-person keeps score for one round, then dictionary is passed to next player. Game continues, and points are accumulated, until each player has had a turn as dictionary-person (who scores no points).

This is a very funny game even when played for no points at all! Scoring can be a time-consuming nuisance in very large groups.

Jotto

— a word game for two players, each with a secret five-letter word that his/her opponent tries to figure out

Materials:
paper and pencils

Directions:
1. Each player chooses a secret five-letter word and writes it down.
2. Each player writes an alphabet on his/her paper, to cross off letters as they are eliminated.

3. TO PLAY: Players take turns calling out five-letter words, and writing them down as they are called. Opponent must tell *how many* (not which) letters in called word are identical to those in secret word.

EXAMPLE (see below): If my word is *speed,* and my opponent calls "ghost," I would tell my opponent that there is only one letter common to both words. I do *not* tell which letter *(s)*.

4. OBJECT: By eliminating and discovering letters, to be first to figure out your opponent's secret five-letter word.

Sample Game

A B Ç D Ⓔ F Ǵ Ⓗ Ⱦ J K Ӿ L M N Ⓞ Ᵽ Q Ɽ Ⓢ Ⱦ U V W X Y Z

my word: SPEED
opponent's guesses:

G	H	O	Ⓢ	T	1
F	L	A	M	Ⓔ	1
H	O	M	Ⓔ	Ⓢ	2
T	R	I	C	K	0
Ⓟ	R	I	C	Ⓔ	2
T	R	Ⓔ	Ⓔ	Ⓢ	3

opponent's letters: S O H E
my guesses:

G	Ⓗ	O	Ⓢ	T	3
P	R	I	C	K	0
Ⓢ	T	Ӿ	Ç	Ӄ	1
Ⱦ	Ɽ	Ӿ	Ç	Ӄ	0
Ᵽ	Ⓞ	Ⓢ	Ⱦ	S	2
Ⱦ	Ⓗ	Ⓞ	Ⓢ	Ⓔ	4

Notes:
   Double letters — each counts as a single letter.
   It is helpful to ask three words at the beginning that do not repeat any letters.

   A response of "none" is helpful, since you can eliminate those letters and use them to figure out other letters.

more games and activities

The following assortment of language activities has delighted kids of all ages. See page 20 for sources of game materials, such as blank playing cards.

Crazy Context
   Rewrite a paragraph from a favorite book and delete all the adjectives, nouns, and/or verbs. Have a friend give you an appropriate word for each blank (say, "Give me a verb, a number, a plural noun . . .") — then read the paragraph aloud. The results are sure to be hilarious!

Anagrams
   Think of a word, then scramble the letters or make a different word with the same letters (earth/heart). Write the scrambled word down or make it out of cardboard letter-squares; have a friend try to unscramble it.

Palindromes
   Make a collection of words (and sentences?) that read the same whether written forward or backward. Here are some examples: wow; noon; A man, a plan, a canal — Panama!

Order
   Make a set of cards (at least thirty) with a word on each. Deal five cards to each player; first person to put them in alphabetical order is the winner. You can also establish a scoring system and accumulate points, playing several rounds.

Crossword Puzzles
   Kids really enjoy making up their own crossword puzzles, and take great pride in having their friends solve them. Here's an easy way to do it! Use anagram or Scrabble squares, or make your own out of sturdy cardboard. Arrange them into words in a crossword fashion — it helps to have a theme (animals, foods, flowers, etc.). Then transfer to ½" graph paper, draw lines, insert numbers, and make up clues. To make multiple ditto copies, staple the graph paper directly onto a ditto master — then draw lines and insert numbers (do the same with clues).

Fishy Contractions
Make a set of paired cards (e.g., cannot/can't) with which to play Go Fish. Players are dealt five to seven cards, with the remainder scattered face down in center. Each player in turn asks for a match to card in hand, drawing from center if opponent has no match. Player with most matches wins game.

Magic Squares
Make a three-by-three-box square and insert letters and/or blends in each box. Start in any box and move from one to another to make as many words as possible — do not jump over any box. You can order a *Magic Squares Game Book* (a collection of ninety magic squares designed for student use by Sally and Ralph Childs) from Educator's Publishing Service, 75 Moulton Street, Cambridge, MA 02138.

l	*t*	*r*
i	*e*	*u*
d	*o*	*p*

Word Bingo
Make up a Bingo game that matches synonyms, antonyms, rhymes, scrambled words, compound words. You'll need playing cards (nine or twelve words per card), calling cards, and covering pieces.

Feely Box
Cut a hole in a largish box and cover it with cloth so you can't see inside. Put a variety of things in it (one at a time!). Reach in and feel the object — write an adjective or phrase describing its size, shape, and texture.

sentences and beyond

Teachers and Writers Collaborative

186 West Fourth Street
New York, New York 10014

Teachers and Writers Collaborative brings together writers, teachers, and students for the purpose of creating new ways of using language. Their approach encourages children to create their own literature from their own language, experience, and imagination. The collaborative places professional writers in classrooms, conducts training workshops for teachers, and maintains detailed diaries of its work.

These diaries, along with the writing of students, are the raw materials for Teachers and Writers publications — newsletters, curriculum materials, anthologies. We have found these publications invaluable for helping children express themselves in writing; two of our favorites are *The Whole Word Catalogue* and *Imaginary Worlds*.

The Whole Word Catalogue ($4) is a wonderful collection of activity ideas for stimulating children's writing — personal writing, collective novels, diagram stories, fables, spoofs and parodies, and language games. It also contains a valuable list of materials, resource books, information on printing, and examples of children's written responses to the "assignments."

Imaginary Worlds ($3) is Richard Murphy's personal account of a curriculum he designed to allow sustained independent writing by students. Children invented their own Utopias of time and place, invented their own religions, new ways of fighting wars and making peace, different schools. They produced a great deal of extraordinary writing, much of it reprinted in this book. One of the most exciting aspects of this project is its tremendous scope — the possibilities for interdisciplinary activities are endless!

Making It Strange
Synectics, Inc.

Harper and Row Publishers
2500 Crawford Avenue
Evanston, Illinois 60201

Which takes up more space — a PICKLE or
a PAIN?
How is a GIRAFFE like a RUBBER BAND?
When would the SEA look like CHOCO-
LATE PUDDING?

What COLOR is SURPRISE?
Is MUD sneakier than MIDNIGHT?

Making It Strange is a series of four workbooks ($1.65 each) designed to help children learn the art of inventive description by the conscious use of analogy and metaphor. The exercises stretch kids' imaginations and help them develop new ways of perceiving and vividly describing the world around them. They are fun as well as funny! One of the most frequent activities is "Be the Thing!" — the tail of a kite, a piece of bubble gum, a burning candle, a teabag, zero, a spider trying to spin a web in a storm. *Making It Strange* is a unique and refreshing approach to creative writing.

A Day Dream I Had at Night
Roger Landram

Virgil Books
Teachers and Writers Collaborative
186 West Fourth Street
New York, New York 10014
$3

The author and two other teachers from New York elementary schools organized a project that would get the kids in their classes interested in writing and reading their own literature. The results were published in this inspiring and useful book. Their method consisted of encouraging kids to tell stories orally so that these admirably patient teachers could take it all down and give it back to them in printed form (and sometimes also on tape). What came out this way was a fantastically rich collection of fantasy, folktale, poetry, dream record, clear exposition, and original myth. They even had them "rewrite" some curriculum materials in language more understandable to kids. The final result was that kids in these classes not only began to take themselves seriously as writers but found a whole new incentive for reading, as well.

In Other Words
W. Cabell Greet et al.

Scott, Foresman and Company
1900 East Lake Avenue
Glenview, Illinois 60025

A thesaurus is a "treasury of words" — *In Other Words*, a unique writing resource for children, is available in two volumes. The Beginning Thesaurus is well illustrated and contains example sentences that clearly show shades of meaning among synonyms and antonyms. The Junior Thesaurus includes more than three thousand words — most of which are precise and vivid synonyms or antonyms for overused "entry words." Both are handy references for children, useful at home as well as in the classroom.

writing without handwriting

A *typewriter* is a wonderful tool for encouraging children's writing — especially for kids who have a hard time with handwriting. In fact, we think typing skills should be taught along with handwriting, since so much of our written communication as adults is done on a typewriter (even though beautiful handwritten work has a unique, personal appeal).

Taking *dictation* for children is another way of stimulating creative writing. Kids have much larger vocabularies — even at a very young age — than they can use when concerned with spelling, grammar, punctuation, and such. Children's dictated stories will be richer and more imaginative, and the stimulus to read their own work will be considerably enhanced.

Roger Landrum, in *A Day Dream I Had at Night* (see page 288 for review), describes a special "oral literature" project that heavily utilized dictation and produced some beautiful, original stories by kids who were unsuccessful at reading and writing. He cautions:

Copying the stories down is slow work. Not all of them are interesting. Only a few are truly exciting. You can get sleepy — with or without coffee — or bored or nervous. But copying the dictations down is crucial work. The way you listen affects the children. It can inspire a child if you respond — laughing, groaning, nodding, exclaiming. If you lose your concentration the kid will drift too (page 13).

Printing is a naturally exciting activity for kids of all ages. A set of alphabet stamps and a stamp pad can be bought at local five-and-tens, and will foster a wide variety of printing projects (see our review of *Take a Handful of Letters,* page 285, for activity ideas). Many print shops have old presses and wooden type that they no longer can use, and that can be purchased at reasonable prices.

The Workshop for Learning Things

5 Bridge Street
Watertown, Massachusetts 02172

The Workshop for Learning Things has the most comprehensive set of printing materials for kids that we've seen, including a complete printing press kit (components available separately). All the items on the facing page are reprinted from their 1974 catalog, pages 14–15.

PRINT✳NG

Things printed speak, even the simplest. The child's hand, painted with poster paint and pressed to the paper, bespeaks self and person. We are moved by the printer's hand, his self and person stencilled on the cave wall in France, across twenty thousand years.

And printing, both object & word, is the essence of abstraction, that great first step that leads to writing and reading.

We see printing used by many teachers in many classrooms-- young kids and older, long projects and single words, or pictures. Threading through all the activity is an involvement in communication--in reading & writing--that underlines why most teachers brought it there.

JTLTLTLTLT

Printing need not be elaborate. It can be the dirty fingertip smudging the paper, the car-track on snow. It goes from there towards the typewriter and the printing press.

BOOKS
LABEL PRESS   BA007-4 $1.00
This booklet suggests a lot of ways kids have used those plastic label makers--the machines that extrude a strip of colored plastic with raised white letters--to print with. It's very simple, a casual way of getting many copies from one start.

CHILDREN WRITE   BA005-4 $3.00
A folder of pieces of children's writing, reproduced by adult's methods, but certainly of special interest to children who are making their own books. Some of these pieces are illustrated by drawings, some by photographs the kids made. Included also is a thoughtful essay on children's writing by Edith Baxter.

ERASER STAMP MAKING KIT
GA300-4   3 lb. $13.00

Erasers can be cut in much the same way as a linoleum block print, but the eraser is smaller & softer, so it's much less of a deal. They can be printed by using an office stamp pad: thump, thump--no tubes of ink, rolling out or cleaning up. This casualness has led quite a few teachers and their kids into simple, strong results with a myriad of uses. Here are gathered together all the tools and materials you need to get going and a booklet of beginning instruction and ideas to borrow.

LARGE RUBBER ERASERS
                 GA030-4   1 lb.   1 dozen $4.20
SMALL RUBBER ERASERS
                 GA031-4   1 lb.   1 dozen $3.60

ALPHABET STAMP KIT
GA200-4   2 lb. $8.25

ALPHABET STAMPS

All the materials you need to use these rubber alphabet stamps-- an idea sheet, wooden blocks to mount the letters, stamp pad & re-inker, a storage tray--are here. These letters have many uses, both playful and formal, and are always conveniently ready for instant printing.

Our printing press kit is deceptively simple--plenty of real metal type, stored in a many-compartmented box, a lucid way of building lines of writing, ink to roll on, a plain pressure plate to get the inked words onto the paper. This simplicity and the concomitant understanding of what they're about, allows children a great versatility in how they use these materials-- from printing their name on paper to a class book of poems. We've seen exciting work from 1st to 7th graders, and adults, using these tools.

PRINTING PRESS KIT
GA100-4   25 lb. $130.00

story ideas

There are hundreds of ways to get kids involved in telling or writing stories — and any one "theme" or "story starter" will produce as many different stories as there are children! Here is a list of our most frequently used and/or popular story provokers.

wishes
dreams/nightmares
spooky stories
silly sentences ➤
picture file
letters
advertisements
TV commercials
scripts
newspapers/magazines
made-up songs
collections ➤
diaries
"just so" stories
fables
myths/legends
"be the thing"
round-the-table stories
captions
directions/how-to
interviews
sensory writing
grab-bag stories ➤
science fiction
time travel
imaginary creatures/places

Bewitched bumblebee Beethoven bought blue brandy at a Brazilian bar, but Batman's blind buddy Bill bought Budweiser beer. (4th grade)

Willie the wacky walrus washed white wormy wigs with water in wild wonderful Washington on a winter Wednesday. (3rd grade)

Make up long sentences for each letter of the alphabet (a particularly good activity for small groups or families). It's okay to use a dictionary, as long as at least one member of the group knows the word. Here are a couple of examples:

Kids might enjoy making collections of songs, rhymes, riddles, jokes, recipes, superstitions, idioms — these make terrific books (see pages 292–294).

Put three odd items (or a larger selection from which to choose) in a paper bag. Have your kids write a story incorporating the miscellaneous objects in some way (even transforming them into something else — e.g., a comb might represent a monster's teeth).

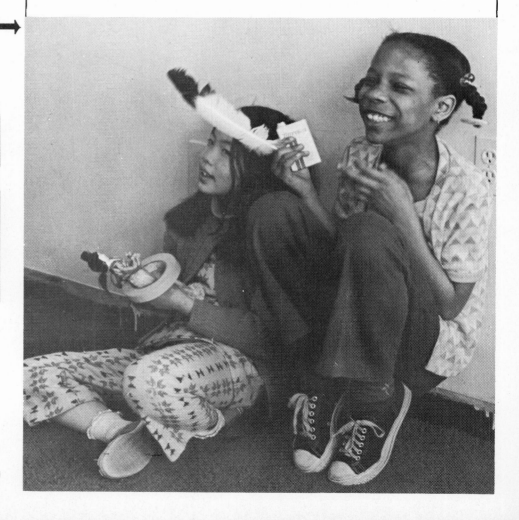

Title Twisters

*Teacher's Exchange of San Francisco
600 35th Avenue
San Francisco, California 94121*

Each of these two 9″ × 9″ cardboard spinners contains four hundred possible titles for creative writing! Kids enjoy the crazy combinations they can get — a great imagination stimulator for children who "don't know what to write about." Have you ever heard of "The Purple Tingle-Tangle"?

lost my money

a movie theater

meeting Sam

getting lost

fire station

watched a robbery

department store

I take a walk

Make up a story using a flow chart to keep track of sequence, add details, and so on.

have a big sundae

my mother is mad

my house

Sam's House

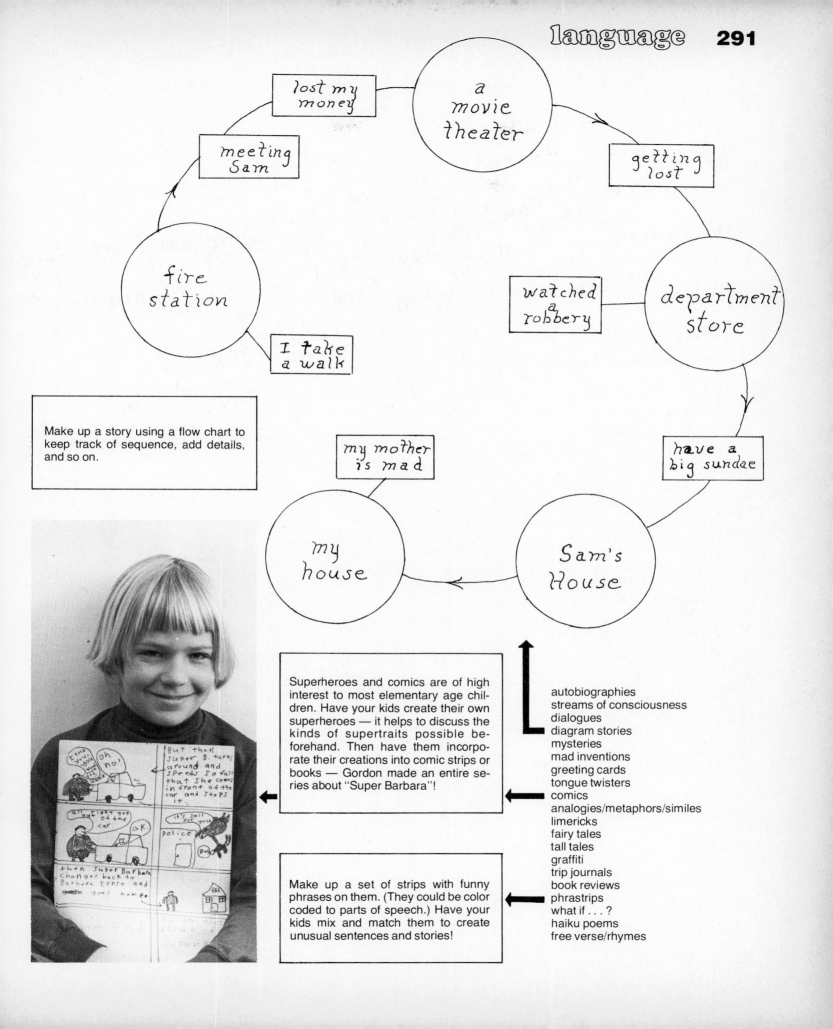

Superheroes and comics are of high interest to most elementary age children. Have your kids create their own superheroes — it helps to discuss the kinds of supertraits possible beforehand. Then have them incorporate their creations into comic strips or books — Gordon made an entire series about "Super Barbara"!

autobiographies
streams of consciousness
dialogues
diagram stories
mysteries
mad inventions
greeting cards
tongue twisters
comics
analogies/metaphors/similes
limericks
fairy tales
tall tales
graffiti
trip journals
book reviews
phrastrips
what if . . . ?
haiku poems
free verse/rhymes

Make up a set of strips with funny phrases on them. (They could be color coded to parts of speech.) Have your kids mix and match them to create unusual sentences and stories!

bookmaking

Making books is exciting and fun for adults as well as kids, and an ideal project for doing together! Whether it's a blank book for notes or a story already written and illustrated, there's a special pride in binding it yourself that can never be obtained otherwise. Here are a few bookmaking activities you and your kids might enjoy:

Write and illustrate a story, make it into a book, and then read it aloud for others to enjoy — younger siblings make a super audience!

Try making a collection of songs or recipes or poems or riddles and binding it into a book as a gift.

Personal diaries or "me books" (see page 252) are ideal for books created wholly by yourself.

Make a "trip book" for recording notes and pictures of special trip experiences. Use maps on a hard cover.

signature binding

This sewn binding is one of the simplest and most common forms of bookbinding. It usually works best for making "blank" books — for addresses, notes, personal dictionaries, diaries, etc. — since the pages need to be folded. Simply cut a cover the same size as your paper, then fold both in half. Sew along fold in at least three places; tie a knot inside book unless you want it to show.

Sewing pages together in this way creates a "signature," which can be used with other signatures to make a larger bound book — see directions for hardcover books on the next page.

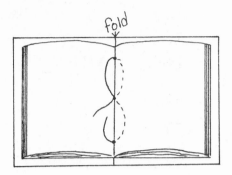
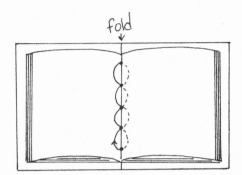

Japanese bookbinding

This is a very simple technique that can be used by very young children with little assistance (age five and up). It is especially useful for binding loose sheets of paper — stories, pictures, song or recipe collections, and so on.

1. Cut covers out of poster board, oaktag, or even construction paper to size of paper to be bound.

2. Draw a straight line along edge to be bound, about ½" from edge. Put paper and covers together.

3. Make evenly spaced dots along line (½" to 1" apart); then punch holes at dots with an awl or other poking tool. Holes should go through covers and paper — it helps to use clothespins or clamps to hold it all together.

4. Thread yarn or embroidery thread and put it through first hole; wrap it over top edge and thread it back through same hole. Pull it from back through second hole, wrap around edge and return through same hole. Continue in this way until you reach the end of the line.

5. Wrap yarn/thread around end and do a simple running stitch (in one hole and out the next) back along line, so that all spaces are filled. Wrap around end and tie in a knot.

6. Crease cover at seam so pages will lie flat when book is open.

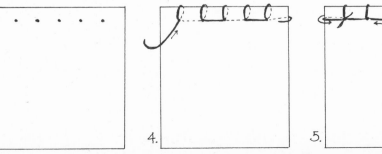

hardcover books

Children take great pride and delight in making a really professional-looking, hardcover book. It takes more time than the simple bookbindings on the previous page, but is well worth the effort.

Make a Cover

1. Cut two pieces of cardboard to overlap paper size by about ¼".

2. Cut two pieces of fabric, wallpaper, wrapping paper (any attractive paper or material — try designing some yourself) about 1" bigger all around than the cardboard.

3. "Wrap" and glue paper or fabric onto cardboard as shown (you can either cut off or fold corners). Glue sticks, which cost about eighty cents in stationery stores, work really well with paper coverings — they're less messy too!

Binding the Pages

There are two basic methods of binding the pages of a book together . . .
1. Make several *signatures* with folded paper (see directions on page 292) — use more than three holes for a smoother binding. Sew or tape signatures together as shown, slipping thread or tape underneath loops from signature binding.

2. Stack loose sheets of paper neatly and press between two flat sticks (rulers work nicely) with spring clamps. Support the paper, binding edge up, by resting it on the clamps. Brush binding side with *padding compound* (available at printers or printers' supply houses). Let dry and give it a second coat. Padding compound is a glue that remains flexible when it dries, so the pages of your book will turn smoothly.

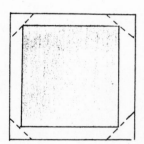

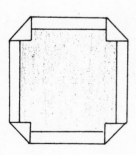

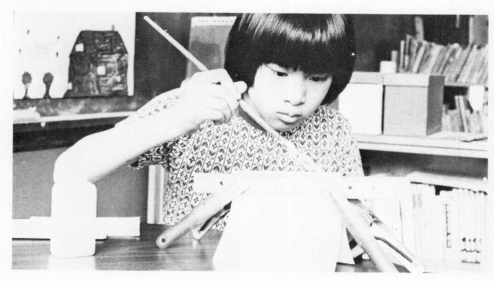

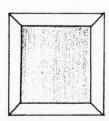  

Putting It All Together

1. Cut a piece of 1″ cloth tape the length of covers (along edge to be bound) and lay it, sticky side up, on a flat surface.

2. Place bound pages between covers, bound edge flush with cover edges. Press together and set bound edges lengthwise onto center of tape. Tap down a few times to secure tape, then wrap tape smoothly around and onto front and back covers.

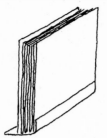

3. Holding book at right angles to each cover in turn, glue first and last pages to covers.

4. When glue is dry (no waiting if you use a glue stick), glue endpapers to inside of covers. Endpapers are made from any pretty paper cut to cover size to give book its "finishing touch."

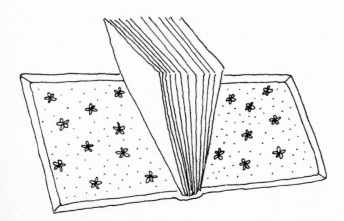

How to Make Your Own Books
Harvey Weiss

Thomas Y. Crowell Company
666 Fifth Avenue
New York, New York 10019
$5.50

This is an easy-to-read, well-illustrated guide to making personal, one-of-a-kind books — diaries, stamp albums, travel journals, flip books, comic books, and more. In addition to clear directions on how to make a variety of simple bindings, *How to Make Your Own Books* includes a good selection of ideas for the kinds of books you might want to make.

Creative Bookbinding
Pauline Johnson

University of Washington Press
Seattle, Washington 98105

If you decide to get deeply involved in the art of bookbinding, this book is for you — it is far too technical for the casual bookmaker! It contains a wealth of information on the history of books, detailed directions for a variety of sophisticated as well as simple bindings, suggestions for making unique and beautiful covers, and a handy list of suppliers.

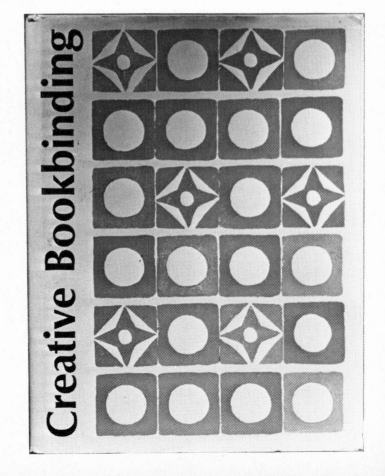

reading

Reading is fun — and an important skill with which kids should feel comfortable. Just think about the many times your child couldn't hear you because his or her nose was buried in a comic book! Whether read for pure pleasure (escape? fantasy? adventure?) or for information (how to build something, care for a pet, make a cake . . .), books have a special appeal to kids of all ages. Read to your children, have them join a public library as soon as they're old enough, and take them with you to browse through bookstores. Here are some resources we've used to help foster a love of books and reading in our kids.

Reading, How To
Herbert Kohl

*Bantam Books
666 Fifth Avenue
New York, New York 10019
$1.95*

"Anyone who reads with a certain degree of competency can help others who read less well. All of us, from the very youngest children to the oldest members of our cultures, should come to realize our own potential as teachers." Based on this premise, *Reading, How To* is a remarkable book.

It gives legitimacy to our long-held, intuitive belief that children learn to read naturally, much as they learn to walk or talk — with encouragement, guidance, and patience from anyone who already knows how, rather than from programmed instruction of any kind. It contains specific information and activities that will make children feel comfortable and enthusiastic about learning to read, and give any adult confidence in "teaching" (i.e., helping kids learn) reading.

Let's Read Together

*American Library Association
50 East Huron Street
Chicago, Illinois 60611*

There are hundreds of books that delight children — and more being published every day! For those of you who are confused by the sheer quantity of children's books, *Let's Read Together* will be a welcome guide. It is an excellent annotated and selected list of "books for family enjoyment," organized by special interest as well as by age level (preschool through teenage). The descriptions are brief and include specific recommendations, mention of awards, other titles by same author or in series, and publication data.

Picnic of Sounds: A Playful Approach to Reading
Lillian A. Buckley and Albert Cullum

*Citation Press
50 West 44th Street
New York, New York 10036
$3.50*

*Lamb chops, pork chops, and chocolate chips.
Step right up and wet your lips.
Chew! Chomp! Chew and Chomp!
Chew! Chomp! Chew and Chomp!*

The fifty-seven "playlets" in this book give young children valuable practice in hearing and saying specific sounds — consonants, vowels, blends, or digraphs. Many of them are humorous; some are happy, some sad, some scary or mysterious — and some are just plain silly. Children will quickly respond to the mood, and they will enjoy acting out the incidents and shouting or whispering the lines over and over again. *Picnic of Sounds* also contains imaginative ideas for follow-up activities — art projects, discussions, vocabulary building, stories to write or tell, and much more.

some favorite books

Here is a list of some of our own favorite books for children. They appeal to a wide range of ages and interests, and most are available in paperback. Starred (*) titles are those we've found especially good for reading aloud.

The Adventures of Tintin, Hergé
In this series of unique comic books originating in France, a boy adventurer in company with a daffy sea captain roams the world and even the moon sleuthing out wonderfully complex mysteries.

*Amelia Bedelia, Peggy Parrish
A maid causes incredible havoc in the household by following the literal meaning of every instruction given to her. Imagine what happens when she is told to "dust the furniture," or "dress the chicken." At least five books.

*A Bear Called Paddington, Michael Bond
One in a series about an endearing, bumbling bear, whose best intentions nearly always turn to disaster (and occasionally into unexpected triumphs). *Cricket in Times Square* lovers will fall for these, too.

The Borrowers, Mary Norton
A series of four about the doings of a miniature family living beneath the kitchen floor of an ordinary family in an English country house from whom they "borrow" various things to fill their needs.

Charlie Brown, Charles Schultz
Inhabiting a world devoid of adults, Charlie and his friends Snoopy, Lucy, Schroeder, et al., bumble through all the embarrassments, mishaps, and pleasures that ordinary kids recognize as a mirror of their own. Several different books in comic-strip format.

*Charlotte's Web, E. B. White
The most popular of White's tales, this delightful account of a barnyard spider who brings a pig named Wilbur to uncommon glory never fails to move its readers, mainly because of the author's superb artistry.

*The Cricket in Times Square, George Selden
One small cricket from Connecticut arrives in a Times Square newsstand and becomes an interesting new friend to Tucker Mouse and Harry Cat as well as a special pet to Mario, the son of the newsstand keeper.

Encyclopedia Brown, Donald J. Sobol
Very popular series (at least half a dozen); each book is made up of ten short mysteries solved by a boy supersleuth. Readers are meant to try solving the crime themselves, checking the answers in the back.

Henry Huggins, Beverly Cleary
At least eight different books about a true-to-life kid with a talent for getting into funny escapades.

*Island of the Blue Dolphins, Scott O'Dell
An inspiring tale, based on a fragment of historical lore, about an Indian girl who with great resourcefulness learns to survive for eighteen years alone on an island off California.

*James and the Giant Peach, Roald Dahl
A marvelously wild fantasy about a boy who by crawling inside a magic peach escapes his evil aunts and enjoys a long adventure with its other inhabitants. Delightful songs and rich wordplay spice the tale.

*J.T., James Wagner
A bedraggled cat befriended and lovingly cared for by a young boy in the ghetto helps teach him how to cope with loneliness, loss, and the need for possession. A warmly human tale enhanced by sensitive photography.

Little Bear, Else H. Minarik
This book and its five successors are among the biggest charmers in the flood of easy-to-read publications. The stories center on Little Bear's play, but always the theme of Mother's understanding and love comes through with enough humor to prevent oversweetness. Illustrated in Maurice Sendak's inimitable style.

The Littles, John Peterson
Similar to *The Borrowers,* but for younger readers, this series of six follows the adventures of little people with tails who live inside the walls of an ordinary house.

*Mike Mulligan and His Steam Shovel, Virginia Lee Burton
Young kids are always enthralled by the story of how Mike and his outmoded steam shovel win their way to a new but unexpected existence in the little town of Popperville.

*Pippi Longstocking, Astrid Lindgren
Pippi is a remarkable nine-year-old Swedish girl with incredible strength who lives alone, except for a monkey and a horse. Her fantastic stories and escapades are shared with the two children next door. There are two other books in the series.

Rabbit Hill, Robert Lawson
Little Georgie the rabbit, his family, and friends live in a lively and amusing fantasy world that they learn to share with a human family who come to live on their hill. *The Tough Winter* is a sequel.

*The Trumpet of the Swan, E. B. White
A boy befriends a trumpeter swan family, one of whose cygnets is born mute. The story revolves around giving the swan voice through a toy trumpet, giving rise to some amusing but poignant complications.

What Do People Do All Day?, Richard Scarry
Richard Scarry's books depict the everyday world in a way that both delights and informs young kids and beginning readers. This one is a fanciful but fundamentally accurate version of *How Things Work* (and what people do), geared to the very young.

*Winnie-the-Pooh, A. A. Milne
This classic and its companion *The House at Pooh Corner* are combined in the *World of Pooh,* about a captivating place where Christopher Robin and his unforgettable friends encounter many absurd adventures.

*The Little House, Virginia Lee Burton
Part of the magic in this enduring but simple story lies in the pictures, which relate the fortunes of a little house as it changes from a well-loved country home to an abandoned house in the city and back to new distinction in the country. A glimpse at a miniature cycle of history.

Little House in the Big Woods, Laura Ingalls Wilder
The beginning of a series of eight about a pioneer family enduring the everyday pleasures and hardships of life on a Wisconsin homestead as experienced by Laura Ingalls.

sources

Just browsing through your local bookstore should turn up a multitude of children's books — I find it very hard to tear myself away! Paperbacks have become increasingly popular for good reason: their illustrations are beautifully reproduced from the original publications and they are considerably cheaper. These are a few sources of paperback books well worth knowing about.

Scholastic Book Services

904 Sylvan Avenue
Englewood Cliffs, New Jersey 07632

Here is a superb source for children's paperbacks — possibly the largest selection in the country. They have an excellent selection of biographies, record-book combinations, Charlie Brown stories, activity books, discovery science books, and award-winning "classics." Send for their *Reader's Choice Paperback Catalog* (K–12) for a complete, descriptive listing of titles.
Scholastic also has two book clubs specially geared to elementary students. A monthly selection of books can be ordered at reduced rates through classroom teachers — write for bulk order forms of Lucky Book Club (K–3) or Arrow Book Club (4–6).

Dell Publishing Company

1 Dag Hammarskjold Plaza
245 East 47th Street
New York, New York 10017

Dell's Yearling Books are designed for children in grades two to eight. Although the selection is smaller than Scholastic's and includes fewer books for primary children, these paperbacks are among the best around. *Charlotte's Web*, the *Paddington* series, *Island of the Blue Dolphins, J.T., Pooh* books, *The Secret Garden,* and Lloyd Alexander's *Book of Three* series are only a few of their award-winning titles. Send for their free catalog, *Dell Paperbacks for Elementary Schools,* for a complete listing.

The Feminist Press

Box 334
Old Westbury, New York 11568

Lollipop Power

P.O. Box 1171
Chapel Hill, North Carolina 27514

Most of the children's books published today reinforce sex-role stereotyping and socially acceptable family situations. These organizations publish several paperbacks for children that offer a wide variety of role-model and life-style choices for children to identify with. Other feminist groups across the country — All of Us (Oregon), New Seed Press (California) — are also starting to publish nonsexist books for children; there is certainly a need for them!

kids' magazines

It's surprisingly difficult, in this media-rich age, to find a kids' magazine that really captivates the audience it was intended for. We thought we'd seen the answer a few years ago with the appearance of *Kids,* a colorful magazine exclusively devoted to original artwork, writing, and activities by kids. Alas, it seems to have vanished altogether. Here are the few remaining choices that we think are worthwhile.

Cricket

Open Court Publishing Company
1058 Eighth Street
La Salle, Illinois 61301
$1.25 each; $10.00 / 9-month subscription

Expensive, but a good literary periodical with plenty of stories, poems, a few informational articles, and a scattering of activities in black and white.

World

National Geographic Society
Washington, D.C. 20036
$4.85 / 12-month subscription

A new publication by National Geographic that seems to include the things they do best in a format well designed for kids, including those who don't read much. Lots of real-life adventure, world history, games or crafts based on international themes, and, of course, excellent photos — all for a good price.

Ebony Jr!

Johnson Publishing Company
820 South Michigan Avenue
Chicago, Illinois 60605
$.75 each; $7.00 / 10-month subscription

Stories, plays, letters, plenty of crafts and other activities are colorfully illustrated in this publication about black culture. They often do features on popular show personalities, and there's a lot of material about Africa.

Ranger Rick

Mostly a nature magazine; see page 55 for review.

index

index

a

abacuses, 143
ABC's of the Ocean, 74
Abrams Planetarium, 80, 81
Absolutely Mad Inventions, 128
Action Words, 279
activities
 animals, 43–51, 54–55
 astronomy, 79–80, 81, 82, 85
 bodies, 199, 249–260 *passim,* 277, 278
 carpentry and construction, 219, 220, 221
 cloth, 214, 215–216
 composing and recording music, 239–242 *passim*
 computation, 141–149 *passim,* 152, 153, 154
 cooking and chemistry, 101–105 *passim*
 dinosaurs, 75–77
 dirt, 72
 drama, 274–275, 277–279
 electricity, 114, 115–117
 feelings, 261, 262, 264, 266, 267, 279
 fossils, 78
 heat, 107–112 *passim*
 logic and probability, 189, 190
 magnetism, 118, 119–120
 math, general, 131–140 *passim*
 measurement, 155–176 *passim*
 mechanics, 122–123, 124–127
 movement, 243–245, 246, 278
 musical instruments, 232–238 *passim*
 nature, general, 25–26, 27
 photography, 223, 224, 225, 228
 pictorial art, 197–203 *passim*
 plants, 58–62, 65, 67–68
 poetry, 282
 rocks, 71
 sculpture and modeling, 206–210 *passim*
 shapes, 177–187 *passim*
 water, 93, 96–97, 98
 weather, 73
 weaving, 211, 212–213
 writing, 283–284, 288, 290–294
 see also games; puzzles
activity cards
 Color Cubes, 186
 computation, 145, 146, 150
 geoboards, 183
 language arts, 272
 math, 136–137
 Pattern Blocks, 182
 People Pieces, 185
 tangrams, 179
 Triangle Cards, 188
Activity Resources Company, 149, 182
 math source, 135, 138
adjustable open-end wrench, 219
Adkins, Jan, 74, 220
Adventures of Tintin, The, 296
Aesop's Fables, 50
Aftermath, 132–134
Alphabets and Images, 285
alphabets and letterforms, 284–285

alphabet stamps, 289
Altair Design, 197
Amazing Life Games Theater, The, 272
Amelia Bedelia, 296
American Science and Engineering
 ESS developed units, 34–39
 and scientific supplies, 90
 and pendulum supplies, 122
Anagrams, 286, 287
Anger and the Rocking Chair: Gestalt Awareness with Children, 262
angle-Master, 168
animal cages, 44, 46–48
animal care, 42, 44–45
animal hospital, 55
animals
 activities, 43–51, 54–55
 books, 42, 49, 54
 developed units, 54
 magazines, 55
 organizations, 55
 study materials, 41
Animals Are Like This, 54
anoles, 45
ant farms, 50
aquarium, 47
area measurement, 162–168, 170
art, pictorial, 197–203 *passim*
Art and Industry of Sand Castles, 74, 220
art display, 7
Art from Scrap, 195, 198
arts and crafts, general
 books, 195–196
 materials, 195
 sources, 196
Arts and Crafts You Can Eat, 196
Asimov, Isaac, 74, 85
astronomy
 activities, 79–80, 81, 82, 85
 books, 81, 83, 84, 85
 materials, 81
Astronomy, 81
Attribute Blocks (A Blocks), 184
attribute games and problems, 184, 185, 186, 187

b

backsaw, 218
batik, 215
batteries, experiments with, 115, 117, 119
Batteries and Bulbs, 117
Beachcomber's Book, The, 74
Bear Called Paddington, A, 296
bedding, for small pets, 44–45
Beginnings, 170, 171
Beginnings: Earth, Sky, Life, Death, 78, 268
Bicycle, The, 126
bike mechanics, 126–127
bird feeders, 52–53
birds, 45, 52–53
blocks, measuring, 168

Blotner's (Lawrence, Mass.), 21
bodies
 activities, 199, 249–260 *passim,* 277, 278
 books, 250, 251, 257, 258, 260
 measurement using, 159–161, 164
 for scrap skeletons, 257
Bodies, 251
body clock, 172
body graphs, 155
Bone Picture Book, 255
bones, 255–257
Bones Teacher's Guide, 255
bookmaking, 292–294
Book of Flying Saucers for You, A, 85
books
 activities, general, 14–16
 animals, 42, 49, 54
 arts and crafts, 195–196
 astronomy, 81, 83, 84–85
 bodies, 250, 251, 255, 257, 258, 260
 carpentry and construction, 220
 cloth, 214, 216
 computation, 142
 cooking and chemistry, 102–104
 dirt, 72
 drama, 276
 electricity, 114, 115
 evolution, 78
 feelings, 262–268 *passim*
 on games, 18
 heat, 108–111 *passim*
 language arts, 272
 logic and probability, 190
 magnetism, 118
 math, 132, 135
 measurement, 170, 171, 174
 mechanics, 122, 123, 128
 movement, 246
 musical instruments, 231, 232, 233, 235
 nature study, general, 27–28, 30, 32
 ocean, the, 74
 organization of space, 4, 5, 8
 photography, 226–227
 pictorial art, 197, 198
 plants, 63–64, 66–68
 poetry, 282
 quiet corner, 7
 reading, 295–297
 rocks, 70
 science, general, 91–92
 sculpture and modeling, 206, 208, 209, 210
 shapes, 179, 182, 183, 185
 water, 94, 95, 97–98
 weather, 72–73
 weaving, 212
 writing, 285, 288, 294
Borrowers, The, 296
bottles, 95
Bottomley, Jim, 207, 208, 209
box sculpture, 206
brace and bits, 219
Branley, Franklyn M., 85
brayer, 198, 199, 200
Brock, Ray, 220
Brown Paper School series, 14, 132, 174
Buck, Margaret Waring, 32
Building with Cardboard, 208